Zwickau in Transition, 1500–1547

Susan C. Karant-Nunn

Zwickau

in Transition, 1500–1547: The Reformation as an Agent of Change

Ohio State University Press
Columbus

Library of Congress Cataloging-in-Publication Data

Karant-Nunn, Susan C.
Zwickau in transition, 1500–1547.

Bibliography: p.
Includes index.
1. Zwickau (Germany)—History. 2. Reformation—
Germany (East)—Zwickau. 3. Social change. I. Title.
DD901.Z9K37 1987   943'.21   86–31267
ISBN 0–8142–0421–X

To
FREDERICK McKINLEY NUNN

Contents

Acknowledgments

I wish to thank Helmut Bräuer, James Kittelson, Robert Scribner, and Gerald Strauss for taking the trouble to read the entire manuscript of this book and to give me their excellent advice. This book is better than it would have been without their participation, and through their comments I have learned a great deal. I am indebted as well to the staffs of the library of Karl Marx University, the Stadtarchiv and the Ratsschulbibliothek of Zwickau, and the Weimar Staatsarchiv.

On occasions too numerous to recall, I have availed myself of the professional expertise of my husband, Frederick M. Nunn, an experienced historian and author. The wisdom of his judgment has shown itself over and over.

The research for this book was financed in part by grants from The American Philosophical Society, the International Research and Exchanges Board, and the Portland State University Foundation.

Zwickau in Transition, 1500–1547

Introduction

A dialectical tension exists between historians who are inclined to synthesize, to stress the features that institutions of the past have shared, and historians who, content to focus on individual examples of those institutions, emphasize the characteristics that make each unique. It is the perennial question of the forest and the trees, the figure and the ground; in the end both must be seen. This is a book about one of the trees; yet it would not have been written without the stimulus of one of the observers of the forest, Bernd Moeller. The present era of research on German cities during the Reformation got under way in 1962 with the publication of Moeller's essay *Reichstadt und Reformation*.[1] In this seminal work Moeller made a number of generalizations concerning the relationship between society and religion in the imperial free cities, and a number of his assertions will be treated here as they relate, or fail to relate, to Zwickau. He said, for instance, quoting Franz Lau, " 'The Reformation was never the work of a town council.' "[2] In Zwickau, admittedly a territorial rather than an imperial city, the Reformation was just exactly that: the work of the town council. Others of Moeller's statements do ring true for Zwickau. Moeller probably did not suspect that his brief treatment would go on inciting tree-gazers for a full quarter-century and beyond.

Another of Moeller's essays, "Probleme der Reformationsgeschichtsforschung," published in 1965, at the time probably affected young historians even more deeply than the earlier one.[3] Moeller called for historians trained as historians, not as theologians, to take up the subject of the Reformation in all its facets, not just its intellectual content. He declared, "In the last decades our research has been concentrated almost exclusively on Reformation *theology*. . . . Consequently, we

3

have frequently lost sight of the Reformation as history, as an event of the distant past, and as a complex network of historical relationships."[4] A. G. Dickens sounded the same clarion in an address in London in 1978, by which time, he was aware, some progress in the desired direction had been made. "My present purpose," he said, "is to urge that the German Reformation should be subjected to genuinely historical analysis. . . . We should apply to this highly complicated series of changes the same multilateral techniques as those we apply to any other major historical movement."[5] Not only should *historians* study the Reformation, but they should be prepared to find concrete reasons—social, economic, and political as well as religious reasons—for its appeal. Moeller's and Dickens's caveats have inspired this study.

Anyone visiting the book exhibits at meetings of the American Historical Association nowadays will perceive another marked influence upon the present generation of historians: the growth of interest, and the improvement of methods, in investigating social history. We in the historical profession today are more determined than our predecessors to recover all aspects of the life of the common man. How this bent evolved is a subject of its own. However, it would be wrong to attribute it entirely to the rather belated success of *Annales*-school French historians in attracting Americans' and Germans' attention. Of earlier and greater effect in the United States were the longstanding, if sometimes antiquarian, efforts of the English to know how average people had existed before them. What American graduate student of history prior to World War II had not heard of and admired G. G. Coulton and Eileen Power? Their narrative, descriptive approach—in short, their sensitivity to the content of their sources—is once again eliciting approving comment as the preoccupation of the sixties with numbers and graphs abates and practitioners of our trade employ a range of means of examining ages past.

By far the most potent shaper of the questions we ask as we look backward today is Marxist ideology. It has been difficult for some of us who find that ideology distasteful, particularly in its frequently encountered dogmatic and humorless forms, and who have ourselves witnessed the intellectual coercion of students and faculty alike in East German universities, to arrive at the point of acknowledging our debt. Although it is true that Marxist historiography has failed to appreciate the power of religion *qua* religion—no negligible shortcoming in Reformation studies—it is hard to imagine what this field would presently be like if no one had put forward the thesis of the Reformation as "early bourgeois revolution" (*frühbürgerliche Revolution*).[6] However dubious a concept this may appear to most Western scholars, they have had to accept the challenge thrown over to them and prove the ideologues wrong; and the ideologues in turn have increasingly felt impelled to legitimize their assertions in foreign eyes through documentation. The exchange has been constructive for all parties involved. Most new scholarship on the German Peasants' War has been a response to East German historians' assertions.[7] Marxist historiography has had a tremendous heuristic impact upon Western research, and obviously not just upon Reformation research.

The fruits in Reformation studies of all these and other germinal trends have been, first, a push to reexamine urban history from a new perspective, using social-scientific methodology; second, the creation of research groups, so far all in Germany, specializing in late medieval and early modern cities: at Tübingen, at Münster, at Greifswald; and third, the appearance of a swelling stream of articles and books that promises to keep us happily supplied with professional reading matter for some time to come. Among the authors of masterful recent books are Thomas A. Brady, Jr., Ingrid Batori, Erdmann Weyrauch, and Olaf Mörke.[8] The informed reader will know that there are many other scholars producing admirable books and articles in this category and how very long a list of the pertinent literature now would have to be.

In his textbook *Die Reformation im Reich*, Peter Blickle presents a tidy, perceptive summary of the conclusions arrived at by researchers up to 1982.[9] He uses Nuremberg as the leading example of a city—a large city, an imperial city—in which the adoption and course of the Reformation were determined by the ruling patriciate.[10] This pattern of reform is the *Ratsreformation*. Memmingen, a middle-sized imperial city of southern Germany, represents that type of Reformation which is the product of pressure applied by a majority of craftsmen to those in authority—the *Gemeindereformation*, or communal Reformation.[11] Kitzingen, a small city that formed part of the domains of Markgraf Kasimir von Brandenburg-Ansbach, is the epitome of the third type, the *Fürstenreformation* or princes' Reformation. Here what began with small steps toward reform by the town council changed its character during the Peasants' War as citizens sympathetic to the peasants joined the uprising. With the defeat of the rebels, the prince took over and directed the subsequent course of religious reform.[12] Blickle clearly sees the complicated interaction and overlapping of motives for taking up reform.[13]

5

New literature is appearing at a rapid pace. Kaspar von Greyerz's recent article, "Stadt und Reformation: Stand und Aufgaben der Forschung," summarizes the publications of the decade from 1975 to 1985 and includes a valuable bibliography of the works cited.[14] It should be read by everyone who wishes to know more about German cities and the Reformation. Von Greyerz rightly sees the difficulty inherent in constructing typologies of the urban Reformation. I quite agree with his recommendation that, in the future, historians pay more attention than they have to sixteenth-century mentalities and that they employ socioanthropological concepts in regard to the early modern period.

The obvious next question is why Zwickau? Steven Ozment remarked more than a decade ago that social historians of the German urban reform lacked understanding of the intellectual dimensions of the early modern religious movement and tended "rather to be homesteaders, squatting within limited geographical regions and historical periods and cultivating them."[15] As to the first accusation, since he wrote, several historians of the Reformation and society, such as Brady and David Warren Sabean, have clearly demonstrated their familiarity with both social scientific methods and theology.[16] Others of us acknowledge our ongoing struggle to grasp late medieval nominalism. As to the second, that we are homesteaders, I confess it. I confess to homesteading in a region that, owing to modern political circumstances, has been little cultivated by the new generation of historians. I set up camp, as it were, in Zwickau because no other Western scholar was working on it and because I gained access to the city archives. For the latter I am grateful to the pertinent authorities in the German Democratic Republic.

Yet there are more substantial answers to the question, Why Zwickau? It could be maintained that Zwickau was the second city in Europe, after Wittenberg, to become Protestant. Although there is no identifiable date of conversion, leading city councillors attracted to Martin Luther invited his close friend Nicolaus Hausmann, the outspokenly Lutheran preacher in Schneeberg, to be their *pastor* early in 1521. Many German cities had felt the homiletic effects of reform-minded *preachers* by February 1521, when the invitation went out, but the decision to make a confessed Lutheran spiritual head of all Christian souls in Zwickau reveals a level of governmental commitment not evident elsewhere at so early a date.[17] The magistrates knew what they were getting in Hausmann, and they were getting what they wanted.

6

With the arrival of the new pastor in May 1521, Luther's became the officially condoned creed. *Alea jacta est.*

Manifestations of popular discontent with the Catholic hierarchy in Zwickau were similar to those in other German cities. A number of artisans, not only the most numerous woolweavers, desired to overthrow certain old religious institutions and directed much energy toward that end. In 1520, 1521, and 1522, artisans' and councillors' goals, at the elementary level of terminating the sway of priests and friars in urban affairs, coincided. Nevertheless, as elsewhere, much remained to be done to create by mid-1525 a thoroughly ordered and triumphant Lutheran polity.

Because of the division of Germany after World War II, no recent detailed study of the history of this town by a Western scholar had been possible. Both world wars had a dramatically curtailing effect upon German research in humanistic disciplines, and after 1945 West German's and non-Germans' access to surviving archives in the eastern zone was extremely limited. Of twentieth-century monographic studies, we have on the Reformation only Anne-Rose Fröhlich's seventy-four page "Die Einführung der Reformation in Zwickau," which appeared in 1919 and is far more narrative than analytical.[18] Of surveys in the form of long articles, we have Helmut Bräuer's "Zwickau zur Zeit Thomas Müntzers und des Bauernkrieges," published in 1974 and factually accurate but colored by Marxist ideology.[19] Of Western social historians, Robert Scribner has provided us a brief but high-caliber treatment of Zwickau in "The Reformation as a Social Movement."[20] Scribner, who has been one of the most tireless callers for, and practitioners of, analyzing the links between Reformation and society, would agree that a closer scrutiny of Zwickau needed to be undertaken.[21]

Despite the gaps in our knowledge of Zwickau at a time when research on cities was flourishing in West Germany, the difficulty in gaining access to the archives might have been dissuasive had it not been for the magnetic attraction of the mysterious radical outbursts accompanying Zwickau's move to the Reformation. Zwickau's uprisings in 1520 and 1521 featured the mystic Thomas Müntzer and the self-proclaimed "Zwickau Prophets." Beginning with Friedrich Engels, Marxist historians had cast Müntzer as a major early modern visionary, as a paragon of pre-socialist virtues, to be contrasted to the allegedly anti-popular, pro-capitalist, pro-prince Martin Luther.[22] Here is a conspicuous example of our Eastern colleagues, through their own assertions, setting a research theme for us as well as for themselves. On both sides of the Berlin Wall, all things associated with the career of Müntzer took on new hues. Because Müntzer had preached in Zwickau from May 1520 until his dismissal in April 1521, Zwickau itself had to be reassessed. During his eleven-month sojourn in Zwickau, Müntzer appeared to have begun to formulate his social revolutionary teachings. Although the extent of their development in Zwickau still cannot be demonstrated, the process undoubtedly owed something to the turmoil that marked the Reformation era there. In sum, as a result of East German historiography, further study of Zwickau during the early sixteenth century became urgent.

And what about the Zwickau Prophets? What can be gleaned from extant documents about the formative years of the two who were Zwickau natives? What experiences shaped their religious convictions and pushed them into the limelight? What part in their engendering did circumstances in this small city play? The fundamental insight of modern social historians into the interaction of society and religion had yet to be applied to one of the most obvious candidates available. Until a closer analysis was attempted, it was possible to go on viewing the craftsmen's strike of 1516–17 on the one hand and the popularity of Thomas Müntzer and Niclas Storch on the other as wholly separate phenomena. This myopia demanded to be corrected.

Is this, then, a book about the Reformation in Zwickau? However uncertain about that I may have been when I first entered the city archives, I quickly found that it could not be. It had to be a book about the *effects* of the Reformation in Zwickau. While I began looking at the background to and the course of the reform, I quickly found that the Reformation was an intruder that produced a catalytic upheaval in society. Its very interruption of the usual patterns of life in Zwickau made changes possible in nearly every sphere. It focused existing antagonisms on religious issues even though those antagonisms had been far more complex in their origin, and it drove the three principal points of view on religion—the Catholic, the Lutheran, and the radical—into open conflict. When that conflict had been resolved, Zwickau was socially, economically, politically, and culturally of a different nature than before. Although I have paid close attention to the course of events, it is my intent that this should be a book about the manner in which crisis facilitates change. In early sixteenth-century Zwickau, the crisis was the Reformation; the change was multidimensional.

The Venice of Saxony

*I*n the late Middle Ages, the elector of Saxony did not know with precision where his own lands ended and those of his rivals began. These political boundaries were not, as they are today, fenced, mined, and guarded by grim-visaged, uniformed men and their dogs. Maps were crude and approximate. The first Lutheran visitation committees, sent out to eliminate lingering papism, had to ask local nobles and border villagers whether such and such a hamlet belonged to His Electoral Grace. On the edges of their domains, the princes zealously watched chiefly the highways over which toll-paying merchants and invading armies were likely to come. Away from these few arteries, peasants and petty nobles were dominant. They held sway respectively in their rustic villages and in their castles and manor houses.

Zwickau lay in such a border region. Of course, the elector was in no doubt about Zwickau being his. Frederick the Wise, elector during those years of flux when the Reformation got under way, called Zwickau his "pearl," and because of its river, moat, and great lake, his "little Venice." Modest as Zwickau was with its approximately seven and a half thousand residents, it was the largest city in all his principalities.

Still, Zwickau was something of a border town. It lay just on the northern edge of a relatively underdeveloped, ill-accessible, sparsely populated, stunningly beautiful hill country called the Erzgebirge (German for Ore Mountains), which we in the West know mainly for its peasant handicrafts, the charming products of which bedeck our Christmas trees. Around 1500, however, most people in the forested Erzgebirge worked at mining the recently discovered veins of silver, or they handled provisions for the miners.

Zwickau catered to, and looked to, the south. It is indisputable that

9

the best cloths its woolweavers produced went into international trade, making their way as far as Poland;[1] woolweaving was Zwickau's only major industry. Nevertheless, its populace and its everyday traditions derived from its own hinterland and from the south. It fed and clothed the miners, and its better-off citizens and the city council invested in the mines. Between 1531 and 1552, its immigrants came overwhelmingly from the surrounding area and from the south including Austria.[2] It was only natural that when in January 1547 the new elector Moritz of Saxony drove the Zwickauers out of their homes in the dead of winter as a punishment for their loyalty to the displaced Johann Friedrich, most took refuge in the south, in Schneeberg. Schneeberg was its "especially friendly neighbor."[3]

Boundaries then being as they were, news and rumor as well as a range of peasant and artisan opinion permeated the hills and made their way to Zwickau. Governments, however much they saw themselves as the guardians of orthodoxy and propriety, could not stop them.

The name Zwickau, Wendish in origin, first appears in 1118 in a deed of endowment of the Church of Saint Mary by Countess Bertha of the Wiprecht von Groitzsch family. Zwickau refers here to a region and not a town. Along the river that is now called the Zwickauer Mulde, a tributary of the Elbe, there were initially a number of Slavic settlements. Germans gained the upper hand throughout "middle Germany" during the eleventh and twelfth centuries, and as they spread, so did Christianity. Towns multiplied during the ensuing generations— not because the Germans were inclined toward an urban existence and the Slavs not, but as one consequence of the rapid population growth that all Europe was experiencing. During these years a number of towns were born in the so-called Vogtland, an early administrative territory encompassing some of the Erzgebirge. Zwickau, just beyond the northern edge of the Vogtland, came under the same influences as they and regarded them as her brethren. Like Zwickau perhaps half these neighbors were accorded full legal status as cities; that is, they received from their overlord formal charters of liberties.

Countess Bertha owned the site of the future city of Zwickau. When she married Count Dedo von Wettin, she made a present of this land to her nephew Dedo von Rochlitz, who, however, was the son of Konrad von Wettin. By 1212 Zwickau was referred to as a town (*oppidum*) and was clearly the property of the Wettin family, the ancestors of Frederick the Wise.

The area underwent many vicissitudes before coming down to Frederick the Wise.[4] Though it was relieved of the obligation to collect and pay the count market tolls, probably in the early thirteenth century, by 1289 or 1290 King Rudolf governed it and turned it into an imperial city. It was now called a part of the Pleissner land even though its special status set it apart from the country around it. Theoretically it was to be governed directly by the emperor. Zwickau formally retained the status of imperial city at least until 1307. After that it reverted, in practice anyway, to the condition of a town owned by the Wettins, whose star in the meantime had waxed again.

Zwickau's internal development throughout followed the pattern of cities under Wettin dominion. The counts oversaw the lives of their urban subjects by means of a *Vogt* (hence Vogtland) or a judge (*Richter*), later a *Schösser* or *Schulze*, who initially were in charge of justice as well as administration. They had the advice of a select group of citizens (*Schöppen* or *Geschworenen*). Eventually these citizens, whose advice-giving origins are revealed in their collective name *Rat*, took over internal governance, and from 1444 even the dispensing of all high and low justice.[5] The prince's representative was not eliminated but retained the right of oversight. This evolution was complete as long as three generations before the Reformation. The city's organs of self-rule were thus fully formed a good twenty-five years before the discovery of silver in immediately neighboring lands, an event that ushered in Zwickau's period of flourishing, its "blossom time" (*Blütezeit*).

On the brink of a new chapter in its history—for our mental convenience let us say around 1500—Zwickau could look back on a stable and quite typical past. By our lights it was a humble town, lacking anything like the luster of its southwest German counterparts such as Augsburg or Nuremberg, or of Prague in Bohemia. It was modest in size, attainments, and influence. Its years as an imperial city had been too few to permit the accumulation of much glory. Or it may be more accurate to say that Zwickau's geographic and demographic circumstances militated against the rise of a glorious city. In any event, Zwickau's citizenry in 1500 did not share our advantage of hindsight, and they took great pride in their town.

Zwickau's metabolism quickened after the 1460s, when rich silver ore was discovered on the Schneeberg, about twelve miles to the southwest. Silver had been detected in the Erzgebirge (which obviously took its name from these events) before 1170, but the original sites had

11

quickly been exhausted.[6] Treasure-seekers had had to make do with modest yields of iron and copper ore and with coal. The Schneeberg lay closer to Zwickau than did Freiberg or the later mining towns of Marienberg and Annaberg and so had greater consequences for our city.

Although no detailed record now exists, few of Zwickau's sons and daughters enriched themselves through private speculation in mines that subsequently "paid off." A number of Zwickauers did join the ranks of people, including princes, buying mining shares (*Kuxe* or *Berganteile*), but very likely these investors incurred as many losses as they reaped profits. Such speculation was a risky business indeed. Nonetheless, one or two men's spectacular gains produced some obvious advances for Zwickau. Above all others, Martin Römer "the Rich," a long-distance wool merchant with depots in Nuremberg and Venice, endowed his city with treasure estimated at anywhere from 15,000 to 101,000 Rhenish gulden.[7] Either amount was vast enough. Römer's gifts benefited Zwickau's churches and its famous Latin school as well as its hospitals and other civic institutions. Martin Römer died in 1483, the year of Martin Luther's birth.

Given the very few phenomenal fortunes made gambling with mining shares, the mines' chief effects upon Zwickau were of two sorts. In the first place, all ore from the Schneeberg initially went through Zwickau. According to the chronicler Petrus Albinus, a Zwickau spice dealer was the employer of those who first found silver. This shopkeeper took samples home and had them assayed by a local goldsmith, who confirmed their value. The spice dealer and some other Zwickauers now formed an association for exploiting the wilderness of the Schneeberg. Their hopeful prince placed the association under the ultimate supervision of his military official (*Amtshauptmann*) in Zwickau.[8] Through these early years, all ore had to be taken to Zwickau for processing, weighing, recording, and disbursal. The Saxon princes —the Albertine duke and the Ernestine elector—jointly governed all the Saxon silver mines and together claimed a tenth of the silver produced. They also enforced their right to buy at an artificially low price the rest of the silver and thus enjoyed a true profit of nearer a quarter than a tenth. They paid the salaries of the Zwickauers and others who helped administer the mines.

Second and more important, all the activity on the Schneeberg relied upon Zwickau's food and clothing market. Schneeberg, after all, was simply a mountain before a town of the same name arose in 1479. The people who went there hoped for silver in their pockets, not sustenance won through the craftsmanly arts of cloth production and food processing. These came along near the mines quickly enough, but not before their absence and then their modest scale had helped swell Zwickau's coffers. Far more Zwickauers made money through providing miners than through the purchase of *Kuxe*. Zwickau was something of a boomtown. Its physical development during the late fifteenth and early sixteenth centuries bore witness to the growth of its population and the swelling of its purses (see table 1). The town had already been fortified to some extent in the thirteenth century, and by the fourteenth century there were walls and gates. Erecting more towers can be a response to military threat; it can also be a means of expressing civic pride and displaying wealth. In 1473 a tower was added to the Frauenthor (Our Lady's Gate), and between 1486 and 1545 the wall encircling Zwickau was almost entirely renovated. At one time the city could boast of forty towers and bastions flanking the walls.[9] Al-

TABLE 1

SOME URBAN IMPROVEMENTS, 1453–1543

1453–70	Choir and apse of St. Mary's Church enlarged
1461	St. John's Hospital and chapel endowed
1465	Choir added to St. Katherine's Church
1473	Tower added to Frauenthor
1479	Martin Römer gives Zwickau new school building
1506–36	Nave of St. Mary's Church extended, enlarged
1507	Chapel to St. Mary built outside Frauenthor
1507	Chapel to St. Margaret built in Töpfergasse
1508	Chapel to the Holy Cross built outside Frauenthor
1508	Foundation stone laid for new Franciscan friary
1511	Two mills (Obermühle and Mittelmühle) improved
1511	Smaller lake dug next to the large lake
1512	Council builds first mangle house, oil press
1518	Enclosed stairwell added to front of city hall
1520	Hospital for syphilitics built across Mulde
1522–25	Drapers' hall (*Gewandhaus*) built on market
1523–24	Paper mill built
1530	Two new ponds dug, one near Schedewitz, one by St. Moritz's Church
1538	New pulpit and baptismal font installed at St. Katherine's Church[a]
1543	New organ in St. Mary's Church played for first time
Throughout	Paving of marketplaces, streets, churchyards

[a]The pulpit bore the coat of arms of recently deceased Burgomaster Hermann Mühlpfort, of whom most of the common people attending this church had not been fond. This decoration may have been a deliberate affront to them.

13

though the Turkish threat did loom, as crusade taxes and special prayers for victory against the encroaching Moslem attest, and though wars with one's neighbors were always a possibility, military readiness was surely not the only ambition of those who directed public works.

There were other signs of expansion. From at least the mid-fourteenth century, Zwickau had the right to have a special annual market (*jahrmarkt*). This is first mentioned in 1348. A jahrmarkt was distinct from a market that merely served the inhabitants and the local peasants; it was a fair to which merchants from outside the neighborhood came, wholesalers dealing in large quantities of goods. Zwickau's lasted for eight days. This came to be called the Trinity Fair, since it opened on Trinity Sunday in June, shortly after Whitsun. Later on—we do not know when—Zwickau was permitted to add a fair at Advent, four weeks before Christmas. Then in 1491 Emperor Frederick III granted the city a third trade fair, which in 1500 took place six weeks before Easter.[10] At the end of the fifteenth century, Zwickau was an important site for the exchange of goods.

The city faced demographic pressure in these years. Land in and adjacent to the town was practically unavailable by 1493, when the pastor, Stephan Gülden, by arrangement with the city council and diocesan authorities, traded his glebe land for a salary. The land was immediately divided into thirty-three plots for the use of as many burghers.[11] The mid-century chronicler Peter Schumann reports that on 25 August 1530 every human being in and just outside town was counted, even a baby one-hour-old.[12] Although documentation of this census has apparently been lost, Karl Hahn saw it as recently as 1925. According to Hahn the tally included "young and old, citizens, new arrivals, and all occupants, even the journeymen and servants." There were 7,677 persons.[13] Using the 1531 register of the tax for the war against the Turks (*Türkensteuerregister*), Helmut Bräuer has independently estimated a population of 7,365, the closeness of which to the census result bespeaks the wisdom of his approach.[14]

Zwickau could not easily accommodate a population of this size. At the end of 1529, Pastor Nicolaus Hausmann described the city's overcrowding in a letter to the council: "Everyone complains that the city is completely full and the young people exceedingly many; the people suffocate one another in the little houses, like the spawn of toads."[15] During the ensuing decade, things may even have gotten worse. If Fernand Braudel is correct about a general European birthrate in the early modern period of forty per thousand people, then using Emil

Herzog's table of births in Zwickau for the period 1537 to 1546, we arrive at a population of slightly under nine thousand, declining after the War of the League of Schmalkald to seven thousand.[16] However, these numbers lie more in the realm of speculation than does the outcome of Mühlpfort's census.

Zwickau's appearance on the eve of the Reformation was that of a flourishing late medieval German town. Visitors from the south German cities would not have compared it favorably to the places in which they resided; despite the elector's wishful appellation, seasoned travelers would have detected no resemblance between Zwickau and Venice. Nevertheless, they might have felt some admiration for people in one of the empire's less advanced regions for not living at the profoundly rustic level that their prejudices had led them to expect. Here were to be seen some of the features of civilized life: several attractive buildings, a modicum of polite society, even a few intellectuals with whom one could discuss what in Zwickau was still the new learning—humanism. Zwickau was impressive because of the contrast between it and the rough land and people beyond it. There have ever been differences between eastern and western Germany, as Norman Pounds has pointed out.[17]

Zwickau was a four-gated city (see the groundplan, p. 16). The Nuremberger arriving from the west entered through the Frauenthor, as its name suggests, the portal nearest Saint Mary's Church. Visitors may have tried to time their journey so that the gates were open when they got there. If a guest appeared between dusk and dawn, he had to wait outside until the morning light, when the gates were unlocked. Many people dwelled outside the wall by 1520, so travelers did not have to wait in a deserted landscape. True suburbs had grown up on all sides of Zwickau and afforded lodging and sustenance to the sojourner. The traveler still would have noticed many barns outside the walls.

When the portals opened, the people inside had been up for hours. The bakers had long since baked their bread for the day, and the woolweavers had been at their labor for about three hours. City folk's work was hardly governed by the sun.

Within the walls not all the curving, irregular lanes were yet paved, a noticeable difference between the true metropolises of southwest Germany and our town. Probably only the principal market square and the grain market had undergone this improvement by 1500, but other main roads were soon to follow. Until then, in inclement weather the newcomer had to pick his way through the sloppy, unhygienic streets,

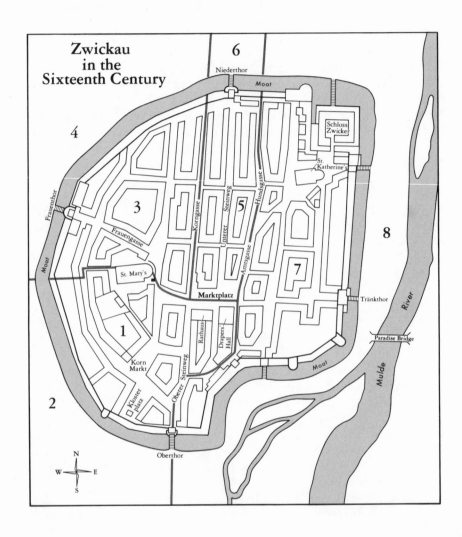

Zwickau
in the
Sixteenth Century

4

6

Niederthor

Moat

Schloss
Zwicker

St.
Katherine's

Frauenthor

3

Frauengasse

Korngasse

Unterer Steinweg

5

Hundgasse

8

Moat

St. Mary's

Amtsgasse

7

Marktplatz

Tränkthor

River

1

Rathaus

Drapers
Hall

Paradise Bridge

Korn
Markt

Oberer Steinweg

Moat

2

Kloster
platz

Mulde

Oberthor

N
W E
S

into which citizens persisted in emptying their chamber pots. Around barbers' shops blood ran in the gutters, and the neighbors complained. Unreliable sanitary facilities plus the presence of many unrestrained dogs and soon-to-be-barred livestock such as pigs, goats, and chickens forced inhabitants and visitors alike to watch where they were going. It was better, then, not to study the design of Saint Mary's Church too intently. Yet it would have been hard not to admire it as one proceeded along the Frauengasse and into the shadow of Zwickau's largest, most imposing church. During the fourteenth and fifteenth centuries, fire had severely damaged the edifice three times. Newly prosperous city fathers showed off their wealth and refinement in the rebuilding. They enlarged it. To a previously simply Gothic structure, they added an impressive four-sided belfrey to house a new, large bell. After the discovery of silver, as more and more money entered the economy, the city was able to afford a great dome for the belfrey and gables on either side. The visitor, if sensitive to such things, might have noticed a similarity between the church's newly extended choir and the choir of Nuremberg's own Saint Lawrence's Church.[18] Even at first glance, without inspecting the recent interior vaulting or the stunning altar with its gilded saints by Veit Stoss and its paintings by Michael Wolgemut, Albrecht Dürer's teacher, the traveler would not have thought this a negligible building.

The more modest structures around Saint Mary's housed the numerous priests who recited masses at the church's twenty-four side altars. There was an ossuary in the churchyard. Along the dark, narrow side lanes were crowded together the weathered wood and plaster houses of Zwickau's citizens, broken by gardens and the sometimes unshuttered entryways into urban interior courtyards. The more imposing homes of the rich, with stone foundations and decorative features, dominated the main thoroughfares and part of the marketplace. With these exceptions the abodes of rich and poor shared all quarters of the city, though there was greater prestige in living on the west side than on the east. Strict residential segregation applied now, with the Jews all but totally banned, to craftsmen such as the smiths, whose particular trades rendered their dispersal throughout the city undesirable, at least in the eyes of their fellow citizens. In 1534, at the council's request, Elector Johann Friedrich ordered all the smiths to live in the Frauenviertel inside or outside the walls, ostensibly so that their coal fires would not endanger the whole city.[19]

Proceeding to the southeast, Zwickau's guest soon emerged into the expanse of the marketplace, dominated on its southern edge by the town hall. This center of city government was an ordinary edifice even after the addition of an enclosed stairwell to the front in 1518. It consisted of three stories plus the usual fenestrated attics. Arms, money, and records were stored in it. It contained two council chambers, conference and court rooms, and the famous Saint Jacob's Chapel, which was converted into a patrician saloon in 1537.

The marketplace was an open expanse only on those days when no market was held. When business was being transacted, the great irregular square was jammed with artisans' stalls, with hawkers, with peasant and merchant visitors, with magistrates watchful for infractions and opportunities for gain, with ordinary shoppers, and with dogs. At Zwickau's three annual trade fairs, a person could scarcely move about. At the usual semiweekly markets, the crowding was less acute. These latter catered mainly to local needs for food and clothing and were attended by few wholesale merchants.

Any reasonably hale individual could have walked across Zwickau in fifteen minutes. The intramural portion was about a kilometer in length, slightly less in width. Almost any route would have taken one through the marketplace, past the figurative eye of the city councillors ensconced in their Rathaus. Yet although so modest in size, the town did not reveal its entirety to the casual traverser. The main streets ran along the north-south and east-west axes, and one needed not penetrate the quarters themselves. Most permeable of the quadrants, however, was the southwest, in the midst of which stood the Franciscan friary and the grain market, bread for the soul and bread for the body. To know the northern half of Zwickau, the stranger had to depart from the main artery, the Unterer Steinweg, and walk into the alleyways among the cottages and sheds. In the northeast he inevitably oriented himself by the towers of the elector's castle, Schloss Zwicker (only its replacement in 1590 was called Osterstein),[20] and by the belfrey of Saint Katherine's Church, which had originally served the spiritual needs of the castle's inhabitants. Schloss Zwicker was new by medieval standards, having been torn down and wholly rebuilt a century before. As one might expect, it had a life and an outlook independent of Zwickau's. Most citizens had only heard tell of the Hussite attacks on their hometown two-and-a-half generations earlier, but life was never without threat of war. Just now the Turks were on the move. The common people paid taxes periodically to impede the infidel's progress into Europe. The danger from the west resulted from the French king's invasion of Italy in 1494 and the consequent war between France and the Holy Roman Empire. If the French were victorious, who could say how far into Germany they might pursue their imperial foe. And then there were the lesser wars among nobles. Frederick the Wise and his cousin George the Bearded did not waste much love on each other, and Zwickau was ever at odds with the petty nobles in its environs. The ramparts of this fortress afforded Zwickauers a somewhat greater sense of security than their walls alone.

Saint Katherine's Church had gradually detached itself from service to the castle. By the sixteenth century, this simple Gothic structure was associated with the craft guilds, particularly with the woolweavers, who constituted Zwickau's largest, economically most important guild. Before the Reformation this church was staffed by a preacher and eleven altarists. On Saint Katherine's neighbors, especially the house-holders of the Hundsgasse (Dog Lane), historians would blame much of the unrest that attended the early years of the Reformation era.

No stranger went unnoticed in Zwickau. The city councillors on Sundays and holy days scrutinized unfamiliar faces from their special pews and made inquiry after services. Members of the town's growing bureaucracy informally kept tabs on people. In part they and all their neighbors did this without reflecting, without malice aforethought, in the spirit of small-town dwellers who are moved by a desire to know who is doing what around them. In part officials wished not to overlook any eligible taxpayers. And in part Zwickauers were suspicious of out-siders and sought by alertness to protect themselves. Personal acquaintance made possible a degree of social control without laws and court procedures that is not practicable in a very much larger group. In Zwickau no one could remain anonymous. People would have known when our hypothetical Nuremberger went on his way, out the Nieder-thor (Lower Gate) toward Leipzig, or out the Tränkthor (Drink Gate) and over the Paradise Bridge toward Dresden.

The End of Communal Ideals: City Government

Throughout northern Europe, in cities that remained Catholic as in those that decided for the Reformation, the sixteenth century was a time of division of offices, specialization of bureaucratic function, and in general of government rationalization. One sees this same process at work in princely and royal administrations; it is a salient feature of the so-called early modern monarchy. Be this as it may, in each territory, town, and village specific circumstances attendant upon, impeding, or facilitating change were unique. In Zwickau the Reformation enabled the oligarchs to realize their dream of nearly total control without a coup d'état—without openly rejecting traditional political forms and imposing alien ones. The forms remained the same, or nearly so, but they were increasingly devoid of their earlier content. The communal government of 1500 still seemed to stand in 1530, but in reality it no longer existed.

Something Old, Something New: Structure and Function

As the sixteenth century opened, Zwickau had twenty-four city councillors, twelve making up the new, or ruling, council and twelve the old. Each September the twelve outgoing councilmen elected their successors and submitted their list of nominees to the elector. On Saint Moritz's Day (28 September) or Saint Michael's Day (29 September), the old council relinquished the meeting chamber in city hall to the newcomers. What now became the "old council" joined the new only to consider matters of extraordinary import and urgency. From 1520 such matters arose with increasing frequency, keeping the old council active much of the time.

A man was admitted to the rank of councillor for life. Even in years when he was not reelected, he was to be addressed as *Herr* and could legally wear as fancy clothes as those in office. Only the elector had the power to remove formally the honors and the burdens of membership.

The council traditionally met three mornings a week, on Monday, Wednesday, and Saturday. Gentlemen admitted to the ruling body for the first time were obliged to deposit twenty florins as *neuherrengeld* with the treasurer, a loan fund for other men of the council. They also hosted a meal (*collatio*) at the Rathaus for the experienced councillors, at which the drinking sometimes got out of hand. Most ungentlemanly behavior could be seen on these occasions. In an effort to improve the council's image, the elector abolished this collation in 1524.[1]

In no sense were the newcomers truly new. Since Zwickau's citizenry at large played no part in the selection of their governors, the city councils were in fact a self-perpetuating oligarchy based on personal relations more than on wealth. They were not a plutocracy in the strict meaning of the term: the city's wealthiest men sometimes did not sit on the council. Some of the councillors were men of only medium-sized fortune. Great gaps in extant documentation make a prosopographical study of the councillors' blood, marital, and business ties impossible, but available examples are almost unanimous in their testimony. New names appear on the lists of Ratsherren, but the scents of blood and money are strong in each case.

In the sixteenth century, self-perpetuating oligarchies were not thought by nature corrupt. Hardly anyone believed in democracy. Virtually across Europe people believed that prosperity qualified one to take part in government whereas, conversely, impoverishment disqualified one. Even so the people had customary rights, and we shall see a growing resentment within the citizenry of the patriciate's intrusion into aspects of popular existence hitherto unregulated.

There were practical reasons why those who ruled had to be better off than average. The demands of public office, great enough at the beginning of the century, became enormous by the mid-1530s,[2] so burdensome, indeed, that Johann Friedrich personally expanded conciliar membership to twenty-eight for three years, from 1534 to 1537.[3] It was the council's own fault that its work increased. During the first four decades of the sixteenth century, the councillors unremittingly strove to bring every phase of public life under their control. Such an endeavor, and even more its success, required each councillor to devote nearly all his working hours to the city. Men whose families or businesses could not carry on independently would have been ruined by inclusion in the council. Some councillors claimed to face such ruin and begged the prince to release them from civic office. Frederick the Wise and his brother Johann the Constant were inclined toward leniency and sometimes allowed a candidate to demur.[4] Johann's son and successor, Johann Friedrich, hardly ever did. Johann Friedrich instructed the council to elect men of means so that they could survive their incumbency financially.[5]

Electors had been known to force their own nominees upon the council. The councillors were greatly annoyed in 1501 when Frederick the Wise insisted that they add Erasmus Studeler, Stuler, or Stella to their incoming council. He unseated Lorenz Steudener to make room; he was unmoved by the other councillors' entreaties.[6] Studeler had migrated to Zwickau and become a citizen in 1498. He was a medical doctor, something of an intellectual, and a most contentious personality. He served the city in part by inventing its early history.[7] Except when very ill, he remained among the privileged gentlemen until his death on 2 April 1521.[8]

The council's official assignment was "to promote the common good, to satisfy the poor and the rich, to appoint honest, upright, pious, and trustworthy men to offices as necessary."[9] In reality the councillors' traditional tasks were to keep order, to oversee the administration of justice, and to regulate all those activities that made up Zwickau's economic sphere. Just about anything could fall under the rubric of keeping order, and the council realized this. Like all city councils, it saw to the construction and upkeep of walls and public buildings. It hired messengers, watchmen, gatekeepers, jailers, an executioner, and other ever more numerous servants of the state. It issued sumptuary rules and set regulations for weddings and other entertainments. Just leave a young woman standing in the middle of the dance floor and see what happens, it admonished the city's escorts and swains![10] Any efforts to see that the populace at large was provided with potable water were presumably countermanded by the absence of a citywide sewage system and the fact that butchers and tanners were allowed to work upstream from town. Nevertheless, fishermen could catch salmon in the Zwickauer Mulde—not very likely today. The council had excess dogs put to death, the markets and then the main streets paved, and strangers watched. It approved or disapproved additions to houses. It kept the prostitutes in line before it declared this profession illegal in 1526.

One of the ways by which the councillors tried to improve public order was through a system, long familiar elsewhere, of wards or quarters (see the city's groundplan, p. 16). In 1500 the citizens already recognized four geographic quarters—the southwest quarter, or Oberviertel, named for the city gate called the Oberthor to the south; the northwest quarter with the Frauenthor and hence called the Frauenviertel; the slender northern quarter, the Niederviertel, with its Niederthor looking toward Glauchau and Altenburg; and the fat eastern quarter, the Tränkviertel, with its Tränkthor overlooking the Mulde and the Paradise Bridge. During the fifteenth century, these divisions had been assigned quartermasters (*Viertelmeister*), whose functions were few, unremunerated, and concerned with public safety. During the expansive early sixteenth century, the council found it expedient to have not only Viertelmeister but to assign them helpers, and even to appoint "streetmasters" (*Gassenmeister*) and assistants. Their duties are not defined in the records, but so numerous personnel surely had to watch for lawbreaking and unrest as well as for fire. The councillors tried to select men whom they considered reliable for these purposes.

All the council's duties were originally privileges conceded to Zwickauers over centuries by Wettin princes. The right of the magistrates to perform these tasks set the city apart from both countryside and towns of lesser stature, which the elector ruled through his officials or through nobles of lower rank. Collectively, Zwickau's patricians desired to increase their magisterial purview. Individual complaints were never about the burden of ruling itself but about the personal hardship caused by helping to bear that burden. The patricians of Zwickau were proud of their accumulated prerogatives.

The city council had legal jurisdiction within the walls and among the outside villages that pertained to Zwickau. A Vogt, sometimes nicknamed Richter, presided over the city court, which after 1500 progressively sat for longer and longer hours each week. This reflects the magistrates' growing interest in control of the citizenry rather than a marked rise in either lawlessness or litigiousness. In this period the Vogt was invariably on the city council—an experienced, trusted member at that, since the powers of his office were second only to those of the ruling burgomaster.

The Vogt's court met in a chamber of city hall. His staff consisted of four jurymen (*Schöppen*) who were also *Ratsherren*; legal advisers;

23

and a number of lesser employees needed to apprehend transgressors and carry out sentences. By the sixteenth century, the city fathers had worked out a system whereby the Vogt of the old council was chief among the jurymen, and the Vogt of the new council presided. Thus there was no shift in judicial personnel, and members of the old council enjoyed no real relief from civic service in alternate years. Furthermore, this intimate connection between court and council meant that the council was apprised of every legal case and could exert its influence at will. Any uncooperative judge or juryman could easily find himself unappointed the next time around.

The common man came to resent the thoroughness and partiality that characterized the council's use of court authority; yet its ideals of the application of justice were lofty. A wooden panel over the entrance to the courtroom bore the motto "One person's story is but half a story; both parties' account is the whole story."[11] In the statute book for 1507 stands the following prescription of the council for the Vogt:

> The judge shall say no word to anyone [before him], either to improve, approve, or reprove; but [he shall] hear each person diligently and in an orderly manner decide what is good. He shall use his authority on no one out of favor, love, friendship, hate, or envy, or because a gift or present [has been made]. [He shall] follow up without timidity what his jurymen [recommend] after a grievance [has been heard] and judgment pronounced; and he shall help each person to obtain justice.[12]

The council held the external court as tightly in its grip. Outside the walls—that is, in the villages under city rule (Marienthal, Planitz, Wolfsgrün, Altmannsgrün, Niederhohndorf, Reinsdorf, Stangengrün, and Weissenborn), in the immediate suburbs, and on rural estates belonging to Zwickau or the council—the so-called Osterweihe Court held judicial sway. It had been founded in 1350 when the village of Osterweihe, destroyed a century later by the Hussites, had become the property of the council.[13] The name remained even though the hamlet was gone.

Here the judge was called *Schultheiss*. The Schultheiss's court met inside Zwickau in the city hall. The Schultheiss too was a powerful member of the council, third after reigning burgomaster and Vogt. He too had four Schöppen, who were the previous year's Schultheiss as leader, one other member of the old council, and two gentlemen of the new council. Resident in the villages were helpers of the court called "village judges" (*Dorfrichter*). Chiefly by means of the Osterweihe court, the council dominated the countryside and intruded in peasant life. Zwickau regarded control of its hinterland as crucial to its well-being. The elector agreed. In 1511, however, when the Rat proposed to integrate the Schultheiss's and the Vogt's courts, both under the Vogt, in effect eliminating the distinction between rural and urban jurisdictions, the prince did not consent.[14]

The Schultheiss's record books show more clearly than other sources the council's efforts over the decades to impose Roman law on its rustic neighbors, at the expense of customary and Germanic law. Close scrutiny of the hundreds of individual cases is still needed. Saxon law had never been adequate to the task of regulating the multifaceted and commercial life of cities, and so the urban gentlemen of the empire found Roman law appealing. The cities were the points of entry of this "foreign" law into the countryside, a development the rural folk could not fail to note in spite of their lack of sophistication. Their traditional *"gehegte Dingbank"*—as its name reveals, some sort of railed judicial bench—together with the rural autonomy and age-old practice that it represented rapidly gave way to the city court, within which urban ways and urban interests were advanced. In a moment of unusual candor in about 1490, the city fathers pronounced their dissatisfaction with Saxon law. They had, they said, obtained the consent of artisans and community in bringing cases of slandor not before the *gehegte Dingbank* but before the entire city council. They had done this, they continued, because penalties for such offenses under Saxon law were too light. Saxon law thus had only a slight deterrent effect.[15]

Having introduced Roman law in practice, the council needed only to give the new principles formal status in a law code. Such a task required trained lawyers, which the gentlemen were not, and attempts in 1514 and 1526 came to naught. Finally, in early 1536 the patricians prevailed on their new city lawyer Mag. Antonius Beuther and another legal expert Dr. Konrad Lagus to undertake this labor. They evidently did not finish the job, and part of what Beuther did was controversial; but their effort served as the basis of a successful endeavor in 1569. Zwickau's law was now officially romanized although it built on, and retained many elements of, Saxon law, especially as preserved in Zwickau's law code of 1348.[16]

There is hardly any aspect of the city council's assigned responsibilities that may not be regarded as intertwined with regulation of the economy. The councillors had long since divided up among themselves supervision of all notable public activities in Zwickau. As the council brought new areas under its dominion and as it expanded its involvement in old ones, councillors had to take on more than one supervisory office.

From 1510 on Zwickau could no longer make do with just one city treasurer (*Kämmerer*).[17] During the teens it tried but failed, and after 1517 but before 1542, two Kämmerer are invariably listed in the annual lists of public officials (*amtsbücher*).[18] The treasurers had possession of council and court seals. They were in charge of disbursing all city revenues including property tax (*geschoss*) and of keeping accurate records of every transaction. When authorized by the council, they loaned sums from civic coffers to members of the council and their relatives, to the elector, to members of the nobility, and to other approved citizens. They had to collect the interest owed by all of the above. Occasionally, with conciliar assent, they accepted investments on which they paid out an annual interest of five percent (four percent to women and other persons of low status).[19] They gathered the cash and produce owed Zwickau by peasant tenant farmers and other obligees. They kept track of sums taken in, and expended by, holders of the council's many offices in carrying out their assignments.

Each September the treasurers leaving office had to render a complete account to the incoming council. They also helped the new treasurers during the period of transition. Frequently, however, at least one of the new treasurers was already familiar with his duties, having served in the capacity before. From 1530−31 through 1544−45 Georg Hechelmoller held the position eight times, but this is the most extreme example available. Several names do appear just once. The average number of times that an individual served as treasurer between 1503 and 1545—ignoring eleven scattered years for which data are missing—was 2.17. From at least 1526 the treasurers were also *furmunde*; that is, they acted on behalf and in the stead of women and children in inheritance and other legal cases.

Another of the posts that the Rat retained for itself was that of construction supervisor (*Bauherr*). Two councillors took on this office in most years, though from 1534 only one did. Was the reason for this decrease the fact, indisputable, that fewer buildings were being erected? May we take this as a sign of Zwickau's economic slowing? The Bauherr had to have expertise in building and in judging the quality of materials. This position, then, could not circulate throughout the council.

The construction supervisor saw to it that the council's wishes were fulfilled in the putting up or augmentation of public edifices such as, respectively, the new drapers' hall and Saint Mary's Church. They bought and sold lumber. They were charged to watch for violation of the council's regulations for new houses and for additions to existing structures. Above all, fire hazard was to be avoided. As the population grew and swelled far beyond the walls' capacity, the council limited the keeping of livestock within the town and then banned it altogether. Thus, it wanted to be informed about barns and sheds, too.

A councillor well trained in the martial arts occupied the post of armor master (*Harnischherr*). In 1522 the council named two men to this job, and after the Peasants' War of 1525, the number temporarily rose to three. In that year of danger, the council had to reprimand Herr Blasius Schrott for doing a very bad job.[20] The armor master was actually in charge of all the city's defenses, from watchmen and weapons to leading off to battle the town's human contribution to the elector's army against the rebellious peasants in 1525.[21] Arming the city took money; this office was consequently closely tied to Zwickau's public economy. Money to field a city militia came from the public treasury. Whenever the elector needed troops, he ordered the council to impose a special tax (*heerfahrtgeld*) on the populace.

The councillor or councillors who oversaw the procurement of wine for the council's own consumption sometimes traveled as far as the Rhineland in search of the best. The *Weinherr* purchased most of the supply closer to home, in the vicinity of the Saale River and from western Bohemia. Indeed, some wine was produced in Zwickau's immediate neighborhood, but in most years it was not of high quality. The council set prices for the sale of wine and beer in taverns. The Weinherr helped collect the electoral tax (*tranksteuer*) of ten percent on wine and beer. It is not clear whether the wine procurer also played a role within the city in the brewing of beer. It appears that the council held this directly in its collective grasp, since restrictions on brewing were a major bone of contention between the gentlemen and the artisan population. The wine master did, however, convey communion wine to Saint Mary's Church from the council's own stores. The council had engaged in this philanthropy since 1467.

The fish master (*Fischherr*) oversaw fishing on the city's several lakes and the Mulde River. City employees hauled the catch to the marketplace and offered it for sale. Revenues from this enterprise belonged to the city and were sizable. In 1525 the treasurer recorded a profit of "95 schock, 42½ groschen" (273½ florins) from the sale of fish

27

from the large lake alone.[22] After each fishing, each councillor received some fish free of charge, which the common people intensely resented. In 1518, in the face of renewed complaints, the council reaffirmed its right: "Since formerly whenever the great lake was fished the councillors were all given an honorarium or gift of fish, this shall continue to be done."[23]

The Fischherr also saw that the smaller lakes and ponds on properties of the council outside the city were properly farmed and that peasants did not poach. At the beginning of the century, if ordinary folk wanted to eat fish, they had to buy it from the council. By 1544 citizens were allowed to hunt and fish under some circumstances.[24]

The council likewise monopolized the milling of grain. At the start of the sixteenth century, two councillors oversaw the operation of the mills. In 1513–14, 1515–16, and 1517–18, only one gentleman's name appears on the list of officeholders, but in 1518–19 there are two again. After about 1526 there were three *Mühlherren*, the result of Zwickau having built a new mill (the "new" or "meadow" mill) to meet the needs of a growing population. The millers themselves, one plus a helper for each mill, were employees of the council. Both populace and councillors mistrusted them. The former feared that the millers might not return to them all the flour that their grain had yielded, and the latter suspected that the millers, as commoners, might try to cheat the council of some of its profits. The Mühlherren were supposed to see that Zwickau had enough grain on hand to see it through a famine year. The craftsmen revealed in their annual petitions to the council that they did not think adequate stores were kept. If they were, they seemed to think, why would the price of grain be rising?

The council set the price of milling grain. Each customer paid with a percentage of his flour. The peasants around Zwickau had to market their produce there and not out in the country where they lived. After an abnormal growing season, one in which flood or drought had reduced the harvest, buyers from well outside the area competed with council and average citizens for available grain and drove the prices up. Though statistics are lacking, councillors and some other entrepreneurs strove to manipulate grain prices to their advantage. Some apparently connived with the growers in the countryside to buy up supplies. Luther himself believed that this was occurring, and he may have known.[25] Perhaps his were not mere paranoid utterances.

The council's foddermaster (*Futterherr*) looked after meadows and other lands owned by the city. With the aid of a stableman, he saw to the care of the council's horses and conveyances. Zwickau's public cowherd and swineherd (the latter also herded goats) were the charges of the foddermaster. Each user paid a nominal fee to have these men and women watch their livestock by day. The council kept these fees low as part of its plan to discourage the people from letting animals run loose in the city. It eventually outlawed the keeping of animals in town, a move that enraged many guildsmen, above all the bakers, who fed their unsold wares to pigs that in turn provided shortening for their baked goods. Bakers wanted swine conveniently near their ovens. The city bleaching house also fell within the foddermaster's purview.

In 1538 the council joined the responsibilities of this office to those of the *Baumeister*. The Baumeister may have found this load too heavy even though the duties of the foddermaster were manifestly light. In 1540, therefore, the gentlemen separated the offices again and placed the foddermaster in charge of grain for humans as well as beasts. He was now to ensure that the city had adequate stocks on hand of rye and wheat.

The position of *Holzherr* (master of wood) is first mentioned in the *Amtsbuch* for 1527. Two men were assigned it until 1534. Since lumber pertained to the Baumeister, the Holzherren were to obtain wood for heating and cooking. The smiths may have used coal for their special purposes, but wood was the common householder's only fuel.

Procuring wood had long been a preoccupation of the council. The nobles were staunchly of the opinion that the forests were theirs and theirs alone. They saw Zwickau's search for wood as a dire encroachment upon their ancient terrain and did their utmost to hinder the floating of tree trunks through their waterways. In the prolonged altercations between city and knights, the electors decreed repeatedly in Zwickau's favor. This hardly damped the fires of controversy. Both because of civic need for fuel and because of the politically ticklish nature of his job, the Holzherr held an important position. Also, the area around Zwickau was rapidly being deforested. By the late 1530s, the council regarded as something of a blessing a flood that washed sizable tree trunks and limbs from distant hills down the Mulde and onto the city *rechen*, a great wooden rake-like structure whose "tines" entrapped large objects in the water and prevented them getting mixed up with mill wheels and other processes carried on farther downstream. The burgomaster himself went out to inspect the resultant logjam and urged the collection of the lumber since wood by then was very scarce in the vicinity.[26]

The council monopolized the sale of wood and set prices for it. It used wood in place of monetary compensation to the lowly of the city, such as midwives and jailers, who intermittently performed services for it. This precious commodity was not made equitably available to all. The people repeatedly alleged to the council the illicit behavior of the Holzherren. They claimed that these men did not permit many citizens to buy any wood at all and obliged them to freeze.[27]

A listing of the traditional duties divided by the city councillors among themselves only partially reveals the extent to which the economy rested in these patricians' hands. And, of course, in reality the economy was never as fully under their direction as they imagined, a fact that rising inflation brought to their attention.

Originally the councillors had received no remuneration for their labors other than expense money if they made a trip to the ducal court in Weimar or to the Saale to procure wine. For this very reason, several dispensations and small honoraria had been conferred on them. They were traditionally free of the obligation to pay a number of small, specific taxes such as *wachgeld* (for guarding the city, especially at night), *grabengeld* (for maintaining the water-filled moat outside the wall), *hirtengeld* (for paying the public swineherd and cowherd), *marktgeld* (for buying or selling goods in the market), and *heerfahrtgeld* (for arming and fielding a militia if the need arose or the prince demanded). As we have seen, the gentlemen got free fish whenever the lakes were fished, and each received two pieces of woolen cloth a year.[28] They did have to put up twenty florins on being elected to the council for the first time, but they were able to borrow from the fund so produced; and at the end of each conciliar year, the interest on all these outstanding loans was divided among them.[29] All of these exemptions and gifts taken together did not constitute a lordly salary; they were nominal compensation only.

At some time during the late fifteenth or early sixteenth centuries, a rate of monetary compensation for the official activities of the burgomasters and councillors had been arrived at, to be paid out each year:[30]

Burgomasters	14.29 florins each
Vogt	20.00 florins
Schultheiss	17.14 florins
Kammerer	5.71 florins
2 Weinherren	14.29 florins each

2 Fischherren	8.57 florins each
Bauherr	14.29 florins
Harnischherr	5.71 florins
3 Mühlherren	2 pigs fattened at the mills
Futterherr	Use of council's meadow, second cutting of hay (*grummet*), manure from city stables
4 Schöppen	8.57 florins each
6 other members old council	2.86 florins each

These amounts were not to be considered salaries, but rather remuneration for expenses incurred in performing their duties. Then in 1524 Frederick the Wise and Johann the Constant decreed that the ruling burgomaster should receive in addition an actual salary of fifty florins while in office and the non-ruling burgomaster twenty florins.[31] This was satisfactory until inflation had taken its toll. In 1539 the council proposed some substantial raises for its membership and also some marked changes in the manner of computing compensation that would have had the same effect.[32] Johann Friedrich did not approve. Except for the burgomasters, he did not favor the gentlemen being salaried at all. The men had to be content with their established perquisites.

Conflict: The People versus the High and the Mighty

Starting early in the sixteenth century, relations between the governing circle and the populace at large deteriorated markedly. Politics in Zwickau had never been characterized by sweetness and light. It is in the nature of men that those who have little will resent those who have much. The haves ever appear to look down on the have-nots even when they are not really doing so. Frequently, of course, they *are* doing so. Charity, however desperately needed and eagerly accepted, may be resented and the giver esteemed less than ever before. Prior to the discovery of silver on the Schneeberg, fortunes in Zwickau had ranged from poor to moderate. Before the mid-fifteenth century, Zwickau was nothing but a small town sitting astride a couple of trade routes. It did not offer a substantial market for goods produced outside its hinterland. The only item it contributed to regional commerce was woolen cloth of respectable but not luxurious quality. Apart from cloth it made

31

its living as a local market and in providing merchants with food and overnight accommodation. Not the seat of a bishopric, not an administrative center, Zwickau attracted few pilgrims to view its unspectacular relics. However modest it was, its inhabitants appear to have been reasonably content and to have identified with one another.

The opening of the mines nearby changed everything. Zwickau's raison d'être expanded almost overnight. The town now dealt in provisions for the fortune-seekers on the Schneeberg. Some native sons made a great deal of money and in so doing set themselves apart from the many who either did not or who made and lost it. This new elite looked outside the locale and aped the styles and manners of their counterparts in Nuremberg and Augsburg. Social and cultural as well as economic differentiation took place. The traditional outline of government was not transformed: the two councils and their basic auxiliary posts remained; but wealth, attitudes of superiority and contempt, and a burgeoning population modified the councillors' conception of their role.

As the century opened, the citizenry were accustomed to gather in September to witness the entry into office of each new council. There were several parts to this ceremony. The new councillors were introduced; the old council, in the presence of all the burghers, rendered financial account to the new; the people swore to obey the new magistrates for the good of their community, the city; and then representatives of each guild and of non-guild craftsmen orally recited not only their grievances but matters that they thought, for the well-being of all, the councillors ought to know about. This whole process was referred to as *huldung* or *holdung* (*Huldigung* in modern German), the swearing of allegiance. Its name aside, it constituted a display on either side, the governors and the governed, of concern for the other. Underlying the public rendering of accounts was a sense that those in charge were answerable to their subjects for what they had done. Huldung symbolized the complementary nature of the parts of the body politic.

Within little more than a decade, all this changed. In 1524 the council announced that it would not parade its account books before the masses but would permit only eight representatives of guilds and community to witness this transfer.[33] It had Duke Johann's prior approval for this, which it had labored since mid-1522 to obtain.[34] In unprecedented fashion these men were compelled to take a solemn oath not to reveal anything they had heard, and among themselves the city fathers fiercely insisted that none of their rank could discuss anything that went on at council meetings. Those who did would be censured or punished.

The metamorphosis of favorable or neutral attitudes into hostile ones on either side, and the actions that both reflected and heightened this feeling, predated the Reformation. Underlying all was the council's wish to make changes that seemed salubrious to it and a concomitant awareness and resistance of these alterations among the people. All the extant artisans' petitions to the council included the request that the guilds be allowed to follow their old customs and that no more innovations be made.[35] That wish, of course, the council did not grant.

One of the most objectionable of the conciliar changes is an elusive one. At the end of the magisterial year 1509–10, the council severely restricted and heavily taxed brewing rights.[36] Peter Schumann cryptically noted, "Around Michael's [Day, 29 September] the honorable council and all the authorities (*obersten*) in this city regulated (*geordnet*) the beer measure."[37] Up until then any householder who was willing to pay a slightly higher annual property tax could brew and had only to observe certain broad guidelines as to when brewing began, when it ended, and how much beer might be produced. In 1437 Dukes Friedrich and Wilhelm had confirmed that in Zwickau any homeowner paying a property tax of ten groschen a year might brew three times, using twenty-four scheffel of barley if he was a craftsman, sixteen or eighteen scheffel if he was a "common man"; a guildsman paying a tax of fifteen groschen might brew four times, five times [*sic*] if he was a common man; any man of whatever status who paid twenty groschen or more in *geschoss* could brew six times but no more.[38]

Beer was an integral part of both diet and recreation in Zwickau. Those who did not brew could easily buy their drink from a neighbor. Rules about serving beer by the drink were lax, and even clergymen sometimes turned their homes into public houses to augment their incomes. Why the council suddenly took it on itself to impose a heavy tax on brewers, to establish rigidly each season or year the volume of the beverage that could be produced, and apparently to enforce price levels more rigorously than before is something of a mystery. Professor Martha C. Howell has stated that during the late Middle Ages and early sixteenth century brewers discovered that hops preserved as well as flavored beer, and that this realization made brewing a potentially large-scale industry of interest to businessmen, who now took the job away from house- and alewives.[39] As for licensing itself, other cities had practiced this for generations, and Zwickau may have been late in coming to it because it remained for so long a small town with pronounced ties to the rustic life that surrounded it.

Zwickau had struggled at least from 1421 to limit the production of beer in the hamlets around it—above all to keep the peasants from drinking "foreign beer," beer brought into the area from outside. Only drink fermented in Zwickau was available for consumption within the walls, with very few exceptions. The people were used to that. But the new and severe regulation of 1509–10 maddened them. In September 1510, just after it had renewed the ordinance of the previous administration, the council discussed the fact that the copy of the law posted outside the Rathaus had been smeared with excrement. The councillors resolved to identify the person who had committed this offense.[40] So little responsive to popular sentiment were the gentlemen that in the early 1530s they extended their regulation even to the poor man's beverage, the weak and unmalted *kofent* beer. Interestingly enough, the artisans protested in 1534 that councillors' wives were selling kofent beer.[41] Whether related to this or not, the guildsmen repeatedly complained that the price of this small beer was rising dramatically.

Money was an important motive among the councillors. In 1509–10 the city collected 1,669 florins in "beer debts" alone, that is, money that citizens owed for the first time and had not immediately been able, or refused, to pay.[42] This is a huge sum, more than all the property tax paid in 1512–13, 1,258.66 florins.[43] I do not know whether the use of hops was now better understood and whether technological insight thus bore on the councillor's decisions. But the patricians did move at about the same time to govern and to draw revenue from those other precious commodities that every living soul had to have, salt and grain. If it wished to enhance civic income and to place the onus on every back, the items to tax were indeed beer, salt, and grain. Through the ages rulers have recognized this. The council in Zwickau controlled the mills and indirectly the price of grain. Every resident was obliged to take his grain—rye for the poor and wheat for the rich—to one of Zwickau's mills and pay with a portion of the flour produced for having it milled. Complaints were legion about the rich going out to the peasants and buying their year's harvest so that prices in the city would be high, non-negotiable, and beneficial to the responsible entrepreneurs. Or they met the peasants in town, before trading hours began, and bought all they had. In 1517 the smiths' guild accused the marketmasters themselves of this unconscionable practice. The other guilds were more tactful and did not identify the guilty parties.[44] Whether person-

34

ally engaged in this enterprise, the councillors responded with prohibitions. Complaints never diminished, suggesting that enforcement was lax.

Formerly salt had been just like any other item in the marketplace. However, on 25 September 1510, not long after the controversial move to restrict brewing, the council scribe wrote, "One is to think about and look for ways for the council to take over the sale of salt, in view of the certain benefit to the community that would result."[45] At some time during the 1510s, the council took the sale of this staple into its own hands. It set the price that it was willing to pay to an outsider bringing it in, and it determined the price per measure to citizens. All now had to purchase it from the council and the council alone, and it was obvious that a heavy tax had been appended. So assiduous were efforts to circumvent this monopoly that the council created a special office in 1522, sometimes held by two councillors, for supervising the sale of salt. During the 1530s the appointed salt seller was not even available on market days. Tradesmen's protests grew louder and louder. They demanded at least the regular sale of salt, saying they would not mind paying the tax on it.[46] At least through the thirties, they seem to have begged in vain; but by the early 1540s, *krämer* could again sell salt, a parallel to a late developing leniency on brewing.

As the council moved to curb what the people had always regarded as their rights, tempers flared. A major outburst occurred in the late summer and autumn of 1516. In late September all the guilds refused to pledge the usual allegiance to the new council. The council feared violence and won time by requesting a detailed list of grievances (*anträge*). This list is so revealing that it is worth including in its entirety.

GRIEVANCES PRESENTED TO THE COUNCIL BY THE CRAFTSMEN
22 September 1516

1) . . . We request [that you] graciously leave us by our old custom and usage and convention so that each citizen in guild and community may know how to behave to the council and his lords. We have often requested this and gained the council's consent, but it has not been kept by it [the council]. It often happens that we or our fellow citizens are punished with physical pain and fines and not according either to Saxon law or city customs.

2) We also request that no renter be allowed to brew unless he possesses deed and arms, as it has been for ages.

3) We also [request] that we be allowed to brew as in the past. It was not proper this past year [and] worked to the council's advantage and our

noticeable damage. Our [rural] neighbors benefited greatly from it. The princely order and decree by which the city was highly and graciously favored by Your [sic] Electoral and Princely Graces was not a little weakened. They clearly state that foreign beer may not be served within one mile all around the city of Zwickau. This princely order was violated this year because of a lack of beer; we were not able to provide the country people with beer. And foreign beer had to be imported into the city and into the countryside. A kanne was sold in the council's cellar for five pfennige that was worth only three.

4) On the matter of making malt, that we have been injured on every hand is clear to see. [We ask that] each person be allowed to malt as in ages past.

5) It has also been shown how home-owning citizens have been imprisoned on the council's instructions for slight infractions. And he [a home-owner] has been sat down in prison and fined two or three schock [5 2/3 to 8 1/2 florins] for misdeeds not worth five or eight groschen [1/4 to 2/5 florin]. By such means poor people come to impoverishment. Also, we have no idea where such fines and money go. Also, it has for some while been the council's practice to give the court's staff (gericht knechtten) more credence than a house-owning, truthful citizen, and on the say-so of the aide, burghers can be questioned closely, for no good reason. This happens often.

6) It has often troubled the poor people to be called before the council. First one day is named and then another, and then a decision is delivered without a hearing. This is injurious to the poor as we have often said.

7) Also, for ages it has been the custom of the city to allow a person to make beer and wine free for his household, and if someone let a neighbor have a kandel or so or gave some to sick people, this has always been without prejudice or punishment. Now this year if a person had bought Zwickauer beer and a neighbor or good friend had come to him and drunk with him, the council arrested him [the host] and imprisoned and punished him.

8) Also, this year the poor people have suffered great injury at the hands of the council's servants when they have brought in kandeln and other containers [of beer], and in addition to that they have had to pay a fine of a good schock [2.86 florins] and more. It was proper [for the people to bring in beer] because the city of Zwickau was not provided with beer this past year, as a consequence of which one had to listen to insulting talk from both nobles and non-nobles who had business in the city.

9) [This article is crossed out:] Also, the people whom the council sent out to inspect the meat and bread looked for their own advantage in the process, and when a poor person wanted to buy something with his

money, the inspectors bought that very item right out of his hands. [The following was inserted instead:] The sworn masters of the butchers' guild cause difficulty among the people, contrary to their oath.

10) New taxes were placed this year upon the craftsmen and the community by the council, to which the craftsmen and the community have not consented. In this past year they have suffered great injury [from the taxes].

11) It is also a custom of the city that the council always have two treasurers, which is not now being done, nor has it been done in the [immediate] past. Rather, the office is being filled by one person. We poor folk mislike this. It was also provided by Our Gracious Lord [the bishop] of Naumburg that two councillors and two men from the community should be made elders of the church (*kirchvettern*). The council has broken this rule too and entrusted the treasury of the city and also the church offices to one man [Hermann Mühlpfort] as everyone can see and which is dangerous to the whole community.

12) We request also from the council an account of what is on hand, whether money, debts, or other. Up to now this poor community has been satisfied in good faith to accept [the council's account]. This poor community is not inclined to do this any longer because [the council] has used up and done away with notable sums of money in matters that had no reason.

13) Also, we request that the council diligently oversee the mills so that the deception does not go too far, as it often has, by which the poor have been injured.

14) Also, poor and rich alike are burdened by the oath that they have to take every year, even though the confirmation letter given by Our Most Gracious and Our Gracious Lords [Frederick the Wise and his brother Duke Johann respectively] does not say anything about this. Each person knows how to keep his oath after he has taken it the first time.

15) Also, poor and rich are burdened by having to pay the property tax twofold. We request that you leave this in accordance with the old custom.

16) Also, the council, without the advice and consent of the guildsmen and community, has loaned money at interest now and again. We ask for an acounting.

17) We ask that the council's [beer and wine] cellar be stocked with good drink, which to now has not been the case. Poor and rich would like to be able to buy such at a fair price and in full measure.

18) Also, we are grieved that when the lakes have been fished, because of [illegal] advance selling, an inequitable distribution occurs.

19) We find ourselves also aggrieved that the Abbot of Grünhain in Zwickau [probably the administrator (*Hofmeister*) of the Cistercian

outpost in Zwickau, the Grünhainer Hof] brews [beer] in his courtyard and serves it and puts out a sign.

20) We wish to be informed of the reason and the circumstances surrounding the Abbot of Grünhain's investing money and accruing interest [in Zwickau] without our knowledge and consent.

21) Jorge Plancke left a testament which clearly said that he willed one thousand florins principal, from which his wife was to have fifty florins [in interest] a year as long as she lived. After her death the principal would belong to the whole community, poor and rich, so that the streets could be improved. We want to be informed how much the council received from him, in addition what other debts we hold from the nobility, and what community funds the council itself [has borrowed and] owes, to the best of its knowledge.[47]

Two more articles appear on one copy only, to which the council did not respond. Presumably these were not on the final list.

a) Also, it is desired especially by the woolweavers that the drapers' hall be built, in consideration that an honorable council will derive no small benefit from it.

b) With regard to wood, it is plain to all how the price has been raised. It is our opinion that if somebody is in need of it, he should be given it for four groschen.

The council's reply is long and verbose. Its points can best be summarized:

1) The council denies making any changes. A number of people are inclined to rebellion and quarreling day and night, and if they were to be punished in accordance with Saxon law, they would soon be poor. Besides, the council could not make innovations without the prince's permission.

2) The council has only made exceptions for widows with young children, strangers living here temporarily, etc. But since the citizens ask that this leniency be discontinued, it shall be.

3) Two years ago there was too much beer. Last year the council investigated and found that there were still 1,100 to 1,200 containers of old beer on hand, which was being sold for less than the normal price. The beer ordinance of last year that forbade people to brew more than half the normal amount was to take care of the old beer. In the beginning you praised that ordinance! We only brought in foreign beer when the supply began to give out. We are continuing to try to get brewing within a mile of the city eliminated.

4) We had already decided to let everybody malt at will.

5) The council has been too lenient and lets many infractions go lightly punished or not at all. If people were not punished for their insubordination, they would be all the more disobedient. We present our bill every year in the presence of the elders from every guild and the community. We do not believe the servants of the court without a thorough investigation.

6) We cannot tell how long a court case is going to take. We are as quick as possible.

7) Anyone is free to have beer or wine for his own household, but he may not sell it to others. Also, he may have only Zwickau beer. Otherwise people would sell it everywhere. We shall think further about this.

8) [This answer does not seem to jibe with article 8.] You all know how it damaged the city that the pastor could serve foreign beer and sell it to everyone. So the council had no choice but to punish this severely since the pastor would not let himself be dissuaded from the practice. The fine was one good schock and forfeiture of the keg. But no one was punished that severely last year.

9) [The council did not respond to this grievance.]

10) The council refers back to the answer it gave for article 3.

11) Two treasurers get the finances all tangled. It is no novelty to have fewer than four church elders. We know of no requirement that it be done this way. We always select pious, honest men such as the present treasurer, who is also the council's treasurer. You could not demonstrate that there is even one florin more or less than there is supposed to be.

12) We show our accounts to your representatives. All of you could not be present and give your opinions.

13) We will look into the mills.

14) A single oath might be sufficient.

15) No one on either council can remember the property tax doubling—unless it was when the sword groschen was current, and then the new coins were worth less. We too would like to be free of property tax as we have to pay it.

16) We show your guild elders the accounts every year.

17) We shall get good wine for the council's cellars.

18) Each councillor gets a couple of carp and a couple of pike as an honorarium each time the large lake is fished. Otherwise the fish should be fairly shared out and each person get his money's worth.

19) The council does not like what the abbot does either, but how can we stop it? The monks bought this freedom from the council for four hundred florins.

20) Your representatives see the accounts.

21) Regarding Georg Planck's will, only a couple of councillors re-member anything about this. The city probably did not receive money from his estate. There was the widow's third anyway, and then the case was probably sent to the *Oberhofgericht*.[48] But this was handled by our predecessors and not us.

The gentlemen concluded that they were always looking out for the interests of the whole city and the community.[49]

The future burgomaster Oswald Lasan wrote a brief summary of these events:

> Around the time of Michaelmas there arose such a great divison in Christian love between the council and the community that they [the community] refused to do homage to the Honorable Council at the cus-tomary time. So things stood for eight days, and soon a rumor and storm poured forth [that] conventicles [were being] held at the castle and else-where. These now were quieted by the Honorable Council [which] cau-tiously and wisely forestalled [them]. The worthy burgomaster Master [Laurentius] Bärensprung with clever wit brought the matter to My Gracious Lord [Duke Johann], who afterward commanded the commu-nity to stop [its misbehavior] and to be obedient, etc.[50]

On 2 October 1516 many men formally accepted the council's reply to the community's petition. On 5 October Duke Johann ordered all craftsmen to obey the council. One could hardly resist the instructions of this personage without dire consequences. Johann's support of the council was ultimately decisive, though the spirit of rebellion persisted into 1517 with decreasing popular participation in it.

What are we to make of this? Which of these claims and counter-claims are to be believed? It is unfortunate that detailed corroborating or discrediting data are not available. Even so, in a general way it is possible to evaluate the allegations. One remarkable aspect of the craftsmen's grievances is how many of them have to do with brewing: seven of the twenty-one. Brewing rights and the council's arbitrary alteration of them were a principal reason why the artisans rose up en masse against the magistrates. In no other period of unrest, not even during the Peasants' War, did this uniformity of opinion exist among the guildsmen. Furthermore, in their responses the councillors ac-knowledged their actions. They *had* been attempting to govern brew-ing, changing their rules from year to year depending on stocks of drink on hand. They admitted to punishing citizens harshly who purchased beer from the pastor or the Hofmeister. This, they said, was the only avenue available to them since they could not stop the clergy from serving beer. The council *had* resolved in September 1511, because it had found no way of forcing the absent pastor to stop his vicars' dispensing drink, "hereafter to put in prison those servants (*gsind*), male or female, who are caught with the parish beer" until they agreed with the council not to drink that beer again, "except pregnant women should be spared [imprisonment]." The scribe observed that, ironically, the craftsmen had just approved this policy in the huldung![51] Nevertheless, the revolt of September 1516 was in a real sense a beer rebellion.

At the same time, it was directed against the council's strongly suspected though unproven fiscal improprieties. Another seven of the articles have to do with the council's management of community finance. It may seem curious that the guildsmen raised such questions when every year their delegates received an accounting from the outgoing council. But that account rendering was always cursory. In an hour or so, who could help either to explain or to grasp the city's ledgers for a full year? The delegates, moreover, were chosen for their popularity and solidity within the guilds, not for their aptitude as inspectors of books. Very likely those who heard the financial reports of the about-to-be old councils heard a jumble of meaningless numbers. Simple men, mostly uneducated, the guild representatives were wholly unprepared to evaluate the byzantine and only partially recorded finances of the council. Their presence was politically but not fiduciarily significant to the artisan population. It was a symbol of an earlier concept of the responsibility of the parts of the body politic to each other. This symbolism was now outmoded: it had no anchor in the adversarial reality of politics by 1516. The common people were not yet prepared to admit that the old communal ideal was gone, and one sees their wish to adhere to the communal values in the language that is used in the grievances: "our old custom and usage and convention"; "new taxes . . . to which the craftsmen and the community have not consented"; "without the advice and consent of the guildsmen and community."

The council did its best to keep the craftsmen from knowing its monetary business. It asked Duke Johann to reduce to a total of eight the number of men allowed to examine the accounts, and the ruler complied in 1524.[52] The council carefully guarded the details of its financial affairs. Indeed, it found that slipshod bookkeeping may be an additional guarantee of confidentiality. This may be part of the reason why the accounts of the community chest were found by parish visitors and later by electoral inspectors to be in a most disorderly and incomplete state.[53] In 1523 the scribe actually recorded an order to falsify the books for purposes of deceiving the public. Fire had broken out on Vogt Conrad Reichenbach's property. Fines were regularly imposed on property owners in such cases, to keep all citizens watchful and cautious. "With regard to the punishment for the fire, because of his [Reichenbach's] urgent request, let one good schock suffice; but nevertheless, however one can do it, write down three schock in the ledger so that the community will have no cause to say that one punishes them [ordinary folk] but spares the members of the council, etc."[54]

There are abundant examples of councillors seeking personal economic advantage in the course of governing the city. These examples lend credence to the guildsmen's allegations in the original article 9 and in article 18. In the end, the council used as its retort to the fiscal grievances the guild deputies' annual "inspection" of the city books. This was no answer at all, as both sides well knew, but the guildsmen could hardly acknowledge their incapacity to assess the information given them.

Dissatisfaction over brewing and money led the craftsmen to collect their other smoldering resentments over other types of suspected conciliar misdeeds. Some of these had to do with current practices of the council, and others were dredged out of the collective memory and were barely recognized by the city fathers. A major and continuous annoyance to the populace had long been successive councils' blatant disregard of custom in all areas of life. Cities are, of course, ever the mortar and pestle within which traditions are ground to dust and mingled with other, often new, ingredients. The product is hardly recognizable to those social elements that see in innovation a dire threat to their way of existing. As said, virtually all extant lists of artisan grievances, the earliest dating from 1479, contain an entreaty to be left "by their old usages." In the *anträge* presented in 1516, there is an additional spirit of urgency, as though the council had finally crossed the threshold into the realm of unacceptable degrees of change. In particular, the people had become disoriented, not knowing any longer what infraction would incur what penalty. The councillors had moved away from small fines to steep ones, and from any fines at all to corporal punishment and imprisonment, the latter barely a part of Saxon law.

The council's reply contradicts itself. The councillors deny abusing the established Saxon law, stating that they could not do so even if they wished without princely authorization. But they also remark that lawlessness had taken on such proportions that, if the consequences were merely the fines prescribed by their Saxon forefathers, the populace would soon go broke in paying them. Hence, the governors say they have been compelled to find alternative punishment; they verify the people's accusation.

The council was bound to triumph, for the elector and his brother stood behind it. The princes' attitude was that governing was no prerogative of the masses, whom God had created to labor and obey. Conciliar misdeeds, whether individual or collective, were a matter for electoral reprobation. Nevertheless, the structure of government as much as the outlook of the magistrates hindered even the delivery of allegations from the lower echelons to the highest. Normally, channels were to be adhered to. The people must make complaints only to the level above them, that is, to the council, and the council would pass on only its version to the ducal court. Where popular and conciliar stories were incompatible, the elector decidedly favored the council. These are commonplaces. They nonetheless help explain why magisterial abuses seldom met with rectification or even modification and why under duress the people were tempted to revolt.

Was this bloodless rebellion of 1516 successful in achieving amelioration of objectionable conditions? It was not. The council shrewdly selected small, mainly inconsequential ways of calming the people, ways that were advantageous to it and in keeping with its larger objectives. Armed with Duke Johann's command to the citizenry to submit, the councillors set about demonstrating their magnanimity. They said that burghers could malt at will—they still could not brew. They agreed to watch the millers and their helpers, for the council's suspicions coincided with the people's. They allowed that a single oath of obedience to the magistrates might suffice for each person. They were only too glad to ensure that there was excellent wine and beer in the council's cellars. They commiserated genuinely with the commoners on the Grünhain abbot's right to brew and sell beer. They offered, then, four apparent concessions and one dose of sympathy. That was all. That they were a bit more moderate in their judicial dealings with the people is doubtful. Certainly complaints continued to arrive. The bladesmiths told the council in September 1520 that the servants of the city court "use great physical coercion on the citizens for the sake of a small debt. They bind his arms behind his back and want to put his thumbs in a stock."[55] In sum, there is no evidence that relations between council and artisans improved after 1516. Tensions lay just below the surface and periodically erupted, usually on a small scale. The people seem to have despised Councillor Studeler, for example. Franz Knobloch, whose wealth amounted to a tidy 1,200 florins in 1523, had to apologize publicly in 1518 for declaring, "The doctor [Studeler] punished me as if I were a *geheyndiger* rogue [some sort of slur involving one's mother; not even the Brothers Grimm are precise] and is a cause of the unrest between the council and the community; and if I knew that his house was unlocked, I would go in and stab him in his bed."[56] Sometimes the magnitude of popular hostility became fully apparent, as during and after the Peasants' War, when inhibitions on aggressive behavior shrunk like a delicate garment boiled in the laundry.

The Peasants' War and outbursts of opposition to the council accompanying it convinced the gentlemen that their anti-popular measures were proper. In September 1525 they were uncertain whether to have huldung at all. They finally called the guilds to their presence seriatim to avoid the riot that they feared would ensue if all their subjects were to gather in one place. With Elector Johann's approval, they forbade even guild masters to assemble without express permission from the council. From March 1528 two members of the council had to be present even at condoned congregations.[57] Journeymen could gather only with the permission of the Rat and in the presence of at least two of their governing Four Masters (*Viermeister*).[58] Finally, in about 1539, Johann Friedrich prohibited the masses in all his cities from coming together for any reason, "for seldom or hardly does any good come of it."[59]

On 28 October 1525, the council extended to noncitizens the oath of obedience. No one could take up residence in the city without first coming before the council itself and swearing to be loyal to the city and to abide by its laws. Even if they should not become citizens, they must renew their oath every year, "especially the men."[60] Those without ambition ever to dwell permanently in town must report annually to the Schultheiss.[61] Here we see that in the end the artisans' plea that one oath suffice for a lifetime came to naught.

The common people were not to know what their governors were doing. The city fathers increasingly treated everyone and everything as theirs to direct, and they strove to impede the flow of information around the city. This may have been wise since many of the councillors' discussions concerned strategies for expanding control and extracting greater revenues from the populace. Strong drink makes tongues wag no matter how stiff the drinker's prior resolve, and so the council finally ordered its members not to imbibe with non-councillors.[62] To make this separation practicable, the council, led by Burgomaster Oswald Lasan, transformed the Saint Jacob's Chapel in the city hall into its own exclusive tavern.[63] The townspeople naturally jeered this conversion of a place of worship into a saloon where they might not set foot unless invited and accompanied by a councillor. They believed that a chapel was consecrated ground and that to divert property from sacred to secular purposes, and particularly to such a profane purpose as this, was to cooperate with the devil.[64] In addition, in the public mind, this exclusive bar was a daily and tangible reminder of the councillors' efforts to make themselves a separate and superior caste. In 1535 the patricians were admonished further to keep a certain distance between themselves and employees of the council because fraternization diminished the councillors' stature.[65]

Attitudes of animosity showed themselves again and again. Those that are specifically connected to the Reformation we shall come to later. Wholly separate from the Reformation, one encounters a profound lack of sympathy on both the popular and the magisterial side for the other. Stephan Roth served the city council as scribe from 1528 until 1543, when he was elected to the council proper. During many of his years as scribe, he took minutes at the council meetings. He decorated the pages with editorial remarks, with his views of people and issues under discussion, with citations from the works of classical authors and from the Bible. He often expressed his disdain for the masses, their failure to be governed by reason, their materialism, and their lack of respect for their superiors. He called the populace "a many headed monster."[66] He opined that "nothing is more harmful a pestilence in a republic than a popular magistracy."[67] Despite his devotion to the Lutheran faith and to scripture, he remained generally anticlerical after the coming of the Reformation. He recorded his private scorn for Pastor Leonhard Beyer with unflattering comments about "priests" as a group. In all fairness it must be noted that he disapproved, too, of the corruption and quarrelsomeness of the city councillors. His harshest graffiti may be interpreted as directed against councillors and commoners alike. On one occasion he quoted Cicero:

"Oh, wretched state of our city and provincial administration, where devotion to duty breeds hatreds, carelessness breeds recriminations,

45

where firmness is dangerous, kindness begets thanklessness; where talk is full of treachery, affability with danger; where every man's appearance is friendly but the minds of many are full of anger; hatreds are concealed, flattery is open! They look with expectation for the judges when they are coming; they are deferential to them while they are present; they desert them when they are leaving."[68]

Roth was indeed, as Georg Müller has put it, a man of aristocratic tendencies.[69] At the same time, he was devoted to humanistic *and* Christian ideals. He believed in a life of reason and of righteousness, using the classics as his guide to the former and the Bible to the latter. He did not find the two incompatible. He did certainly come in conflict with people—Martin Luther was merely the most renowned—but the common people did not identify him as one of the avid self-aggrandizers. Roth himself, as is visible above, acknowledged that this type did exist within the conciliar ranks, and it never ceased to sadden him.

Hermann Mühlpfort is probably the best example—there are several available—of a man who successfully ingratiated himself with the powers that were, but who unrestrainedly used his office and his position in society to benefit himself. It was surely not incidental to the craftsmen's article 11 in 1516 that Mühlpfort was that single treasurer into whose hands both city and church finances had been placed. Frederick the Wise had appointed Mühlpfort to the city council in 1510; he had not been elected.[70] In 1517 the people were circulating a bitterly satirical poem about him, but the verses have not survived.[71] The burghers mistrusted him and no doubt would have found some irony, if they were aware of it, in Luther's dedicating his treatise "On the Freedom of a Christian Man" to him. That very dedication, written at a time when Luther was not acquainted with Mühlpfort, is responsible for all subsequent generations' favorable estimation of the man, a judgment that deserves revision. Mühlpfort has enjoyed for centuries the reputation of a Lutheran stalwart (which in his way he was) and the man who more than any other, more even than Pastor Nicolaus Hausmann, was responsible for establishing the new faith and for casting out both Catholicism and evangelical heresy by virture of his high civic office.[72] It is high time for the dark side of Mühlpfort's character to be acknowledged.

When the altar dedicated to Saint Helena, endowed by Hermann's uncle Heinrich in 1498, was taken over by the city, Hermann, who stood at the forefront of efforts to bring Catholic benefices with their properties and incomes intact into the Lutheran coffers, now strove just as hard to divert this altar's revenues to himself and his siblings.[73] His colleagues on the council refused to permit this. After no small altercation, and with Mühlpfort condemned to several days' comfortable incarceration in the Rathaus, Mühlpfort appealed to the elector and apparently had his way.[74] In 1529 he persuaded his fellows to let his sister have and sell a chalice belonging to that altar "on account of her poverty."[75] Electoral policy on endowments vacillated markedly during the 1520s and 1530s, the princes ever making exceptions to their general rule that urban endowments all should fall to community chests. The people must have known of, and mocked, Mühlpfort's hypocrisy.

Less well known, at least until after his death in 1533, was Mühlpfort's misuse of land and moneys belonging to his wife's family, the long since ennobled Römers. Mühlpfort served as *furmund*, that is, as trustee and legal representative, for some of his wife's nieces and nephews. The Römers vociferously alleged wrongdoing such as Mühlpfort's appropriation of a meadow, half of which has been given in testament to the city and the other half of which had been supposed to be guarded for the children.[76] In 1536 Burgomaster Oswald Lasan confronted Mühlpfort's son, beginning with these words: "In view of the fact that your father took over this meadow without any good title. . . . "[77] Mühlpfort had been obligated to distribute to the city and to the young Römers interest from investments, but he had kept it instead.[78] The council tried hard to keep this scandal strictly secret in order to save face.[79] Stephan Roth recorded and initialed his own conclusion in 1538. He said that Mühlpfort, as burgomaster,

> well knew and perhaps alone knew that the council and the administrator [of the Rich Alms fund endowed by the original wealthy Martin Römer in the fifteenth century] were themselves supposed to receive the interest. He collected the same interest as curator to his advantage, so that he could carry out the administration of the [Römer] trust in a statelier fashion. In his own account he shows that expenditures [from trust revenues] are greater than income. . . . Did it not befit the burgomaster, in consideration of his oath of office, to think more about the well-being of council and community property than about his own or his charges' use and advantage?[80]

It should be added that Mühlpfort was perpetually in debt. After his death some of his lands had to be sold off in order to satisfy his creditors.[81]

Just how much of all this came to the attention of the masses is unknown. Small towns being as rumor-permeable as they are, some of the secret must have leaked out. Whether the leaks were accurate is doubtful. It is also unimportant. However shy of the mark in content, they gave the people one further verification of councillors' self-serving behavior.

Extant records are full of allegations of official misconduct. It is certainly true that though service on the council threatened some men like Barthel Kühn and Hans Vilberer with economic ruin, others like Hans Schonborn and Dr. Stephan Wilde saw their fortunes multiply during their incumbency. (See tables 2–4 for the councillor's assessed wealth.) One of the historian's difficulties is in not knowing how much of a councillor's economic gain or declain while in office was actually related to his duties. Mühlpfort, despite his debts holding assets worth 9,550 florins in 1531, may have been wealthy because he had married a Römer or because he had inherited property. Nevertheless, it is fair to note that his holdings in 1523 had a much lower value, 2,400 florins, and that he had only one or two conciliar peers in the rate at which his wealth grew while he held public office. Whatever his assets, he had what economists refer to as a severe "cash flow problem." He was not able to pay his Türkensteuer in 1531, which may have been a factor in his illicit use of money belonging to the city and to his young relatives. Be that as it may, Mühlpfort was not popular among the masses, some of whom showed him their scorn and were punished for it.

Dr. Stephan Wilde increased his assets markedly between 1531 and 1542. He was taxed on 1,150 florins in 1531, three years before he joined the council, and on 4,259 florins in 1542. By the latter date, he had made himself a country squire, with a large acreage, buildings, and accoutrements near Weissenborn. Once again, one dare not attribute this to rascality or unbridled opportunism. For one thing, while on the council he continued to serve Zwickau's elite as a medical doctor, and he charged fees for his ministrations. For another, he invested in the silver mines.

The Role of the Reformation

The people of Zwickau knew who the corrupt, self-seeking, or lackadaisical members of the council were. Even though council meetings were closed and confidential, the citizenry soon saw in force decisions that had been made in city hall. They knew in general that councillors

48

TABLE 2
Assessed Wealth in 1523 of Councillors for 1522–23
(In Florins)

Laurentius Bärensprung (1504–33)[a]	1,030
Gotthard Büttner (1520–37)	800
Nickel Günther (1517–36)	800
Nickel Hennel (1515?–26?)	1,400
Wolff Jacof (1515–48)	2,150
Barthel Kühn (1517–31)	550
Christoff Kühn (1517–31)	470
Veit Lasan (1520–25)[b]	951
Hermann Mühlpfort (1510–34)	2,400
Nickel Mülich (1515–30)	680
Nickel Partt (1515–39)	970
Ludwig Preuss (1505–30)	809
Cunrad Reichenbach (early 16th–1530)	560
Michel Richter (1514–31)	1,156
Michel Sangner (1521–29)	1,090
Simon Sangner (late 15th–1523)	675
Philip Schaunfus (1520–36)	1,196
Wolff Schicker (1507–50)	570
Blasius Schrott (1515–34)	200
Ilg Schwemmel (early 16th–1525?)	1,325
Hans Vilberer (1520–after 1545)	500
Burkhard Waldauff[c] (1517–32)	740+
Hans Wildeck (1521–29)	700
Balthasar Zopf (1514–23)	425[d]
Caspar Zorn (1505–40)	1,203

Source: WSA, Reg. Pp 368[2–4]: "Vorzeichnus der ligenden grunden vnd gutter Im Weichbilde der Stadt Zwickau Wirderung etc."

[a] In parentheses are years of service on council; sometimes service was interrupted.

[b] Engaged in unidentified controversy with Rat, was imprisoned, moved away.

[c] The sixteenth-century spelling of this name is retained since Baldauff never occurred in the sources I consulted. He owned land elsewhere, too.

[d] Assessment of his widow after his death on 2 January 1523.

and their families and friends availed themselves of loans from public moneys that were not accessible to them. The main reason, however, that relations between councillors and populace deteriorated badly during the first half of the sixteenth century was that the councillors, as the people saw it, usurped authority that had never pertained to them before. They lorded it over ordinary folk in an unprecedented manner. They extended the magisterial arm into hitherto unpenetrated crannies of public and even private life. Most late fifteenth-century records

TABLE 3
ASSESSED WEALTH OF COUNCILLORS FOR 1530–1531
(In Florins)

	1523	1531	1542
Laurentius Bärensprung (1504–33)[a]	1,030	1,400	—
Gotthard Büttner (1520–37)	800	789	—
Nickel Günther (1517–36)	800	1,450	1,800[b]
Georg Hechelmoller (1526–63)	—	500	1,036
Wolff Jacof (1515–48)	2,150	700	1,000[c]
Barthel Kühn (1517–31)	550	900	550
Christoff Kühn (1517–31)	470	—	—
Ludwig Lindner (1528–34)[d]	570	560	—
Hermann Mühlpfort (1510–34)	2,400	9,550	—
Nickel Partt (1515–39)	970	1,040	—
Michel Richter (1514–31)	1,152	—	—
Peter Sangner (1530–after 1545)	865	965	1,325
Philip Schaunfus (1520–36)	1,196	945	—
Wolff Schicker (1507–50)	570	840	880
Sebastian Schnee (1530–57)	1,800	1,000	1,850
Blasius Schrott (1515–34)[d]	200	200	—
Barthel Tzscheppener (1527–31)	—	—	—
Hans Vilberer (1520–49)	550	990	600
Burkhard Waldauff[c] (1517–32)	740	895	—
Bonaventura Werner (1528–38)	525	2,700	1,000
Caspar Zorn (1505–40)[d]	1,203	1,195	—

SOURCE: WSA, Reg. Pp 368[2–4]: "Vorzeichnus der ligenden grunden vnd gutter Im Weichbilde der Stadt Zwickau Wirderung etc."; Türkensteuer, ZSA, Ax AII 17, Nr. 19a; ZSA, Ax AII 16, Nr. 12.

[a]In parentheses are years of service on council; sometimes service was interrupted.
[b]Assessment of his estate.
[c]Financially ruined in 1545. Council gave him 70 florins, free housing for "one year or two" (ZSA, *Ratsprotokolle*, 1544–45, *1545*, fol. 33).
[d]Excluded from council 1534; elector probably consented only in 1538.

of major conciliar action contain the phrase "with the complete knowl-edge and favor of the other council, of the guildmasters, and of the entire community." This language ceased to be used early in the six-teenth century. The comparatively docile shoemakers' guild declared in 1532 what had long been obvious to all: "It used to be that without the guilds' and the community's knowledge and consent, important deci-sions were not made. We request that this [consultation] continue. [Those instances] where this was not desirable would be apparent to all."[82] The shoemakers were trying to revive a dead horse.

The Reformation alone did not destroy the fabric of reciprocal rela-

TABLE 4
ASSESSED WEALTH OF COUNCILLORS FOR 1541–1542
(In Florins)

	1531	1542
Hans Andres[a] (1535–44)[b]	500	760
Georg Berreuter (1534–57)	500	710
Georg Blobitzsch (1531–47)	760	750
Simon Braun (1541–63)	—	3,060
Hiobst Göppfardt (1532–51)	14[c]	421
Georg Hechelmoller (1526–63)	500	1,036
Johannes Hoffman (1541–43; 1547–?)[d]	2,350	2,500
Wolff Jacof (1515–48)	700	1,000
Barthel Kühn (1515–43)	900	550
Oswald Lasan (1534–after 1546)	—	3,338
Michel von Mila (1526–46)	3,163	6,140
Dr. Leonhard Nather (1535–45)	600	1,000
Paul von Neuenmarkt (1539–after 1545)[e]	1,200	1,528
Peter Sangner (1530–after 1545)	965	1,325
Wolff Schicker (1507–50)	840	880
Erhard Schmidt (1532–after 1545)	583	754
Lorenz Schnabel (1533–after 1545)	480	600
Sebastian Schnee (1530–57)	1,000	1,850
Hans Schonborn (1536–46)[f]	1,000	3,050
Lucas Schutze (1540–46)	—	5,237
Hans Stublinger (1531–after 1545)	900	1,187
Hans Vilberer (1520–49)	990	600
Dr. Stephan Wilde (1534–after 1545)	1,150	4,259
Peter Zipser (1536–45)	—	2,500

SOURCE: Türkensteuer, ZSA, Ax AII 17, Nr. 19a; ZSA, Ax AII 16, Nr. 12.

[a]Committed adultery and fled city, dying in 1545.

[b]In parentheses are years of service on council; sometimes service was interrupted.

[c]If Göppfardt really had so little wealth on entering the council, there must have been compelling political reasons for admitting him.

[d]Johann Friedrich made him an official *Zehntner* in Schneeberg in 1543; after the prince's defeat in 1547, Hoffman returned to Zwickau.

[e]Von Neuenmarkt was a nobleman who had taken up residency and citizenship in Zwickau. No urban property was listed for him in either 1531 or 1542, though even as a noble he would have had to pay. The figures given are for a woman who I think is his mother and with whom he may have lived.

[f]Moved away in 1546 and returned in 1553.

tionships that clothed the body politic in Zwickau during the late Middle Ages. Under the influences of wealth and humanism, the conciliar class by 1510 had already come to regard itself as superior to, and responsible for, the "child-like" masses. It saw itself as obligated to promote and guarantee the smooth functioning of urban life. What occurred in evolutionary style was a shift in the ethics of those in positions of authority, which in turn elicited an outspoken ethical opposition from the common man. The magistrates in the fifteenth century, even while enjoying a technically higher status than those outside the governing circle—even while being addressed as *Herr* and being entitled to adorn their persons more showily—had acknowledged the organic wholeness of society. The craftsmen in their guilds were as legitimate if lesser participants in public life, and both privileged and ordinary men had to labor together if the community were to flourish. To submit to the city's duly chosen councillors was as dignified and necessary as for the councillors at the appointed hour to receive the people's homage. No one lost face, not the councillors in submitting their accounts for inspection, not the citizens in promising to obey the new council. Zwickauers altogether formed a whole that was rooted in, and perpetuated by, traditions understood by all.

The councillors were the first to become dissatisfied with the status quo. Their newly acquired affluence, which turned merely successful master craftsmen into merchants of diverse goods; their superior education in the classics and in contemporary humanist literature—in short, their greater worldly wisdom—revealed to them the incapacity, the baseness of their lowly fellows. The word *Ratherr* had a more potent, even glorious, sound than ever before.

From what seemed to them a loftier position than their predecessors had occupied, they examined Zwickau's condition with a critical and ambitious eye. They felt themselves exclusively appointed to govern, and their definition of that verb included far more than in the past. These were not necessarily corrupt and power-hungry men but men whose concept of their proper sphere had genuinely expanded. They were men, most of them, of ethical conviction who may not have noticed what is to us a marked, even if evolutionary, departure from the self-perception of an earlier generation of Herren. Laurentius Bärensprung and Hermann Mühlpfort entered the council in 1504 and 1510 respectively. They were imbued with the new spirit.

The artisans, spared the mental burden of sudden riches and the disorienting effects of humanist education, adhered to the ethical principles of their fathers. They were certainly not advocates of democracy. Who among them would have advocated an equal place in urban affairs for the numbers of day laborers or servants who made their mean livings among them? Nor were the guildsmen individualists. But as members of their respective corporations, the guilds, they revered the age-old pattern of politics, the familiar laws, the respectability that huldung and advising the council on knotty problems accorded them. This was the way things had been done; this was the way things were properly done for the good of all. They knew themselves to be part of the communal organism.

In response to blatant and frequent conciliar departures from the norm, the craftsmen became uneasy, then restive. A collision between the ethics of rulers and ruled was inevitable. It occurred in 1516 and resulted in the defeat of the guildsmen on the one hand and in the ducal legitimation of the new conciliar principles on the other. No longer could the oligarchs be accused, openly at least, of usurpation, for the elector's brother Duke Johann, in rejecting the artisans' grievances, implicitly confirmed to the council the right to govern in its new, exclusive, thorough style.

What effect on these developments did the Reformation have? As I shall shortly demonstrate in some detail, the city council perceived that a major obstacle to its expanded rule was the institutional Catholic church, numerous of whose representatives were to be found in Zwickau. One hardly needed to look for them, for they were ubiquitous. Especially the Franciscans and the Cistercians, but secondarily the Dominicans and the secular clergy, owned property and exercised jurisdictions in and around the city that the council coveted. At the same time, as throughout Europe, many people of every socioeconomic condition resented the greedy and exploitative deportment of the clerics. Average people and patricians in Zwickau could find common ground for complaint here, at a time when otherwise their paths diverged. As we shall see, theirs was a temporary alliance, the chief outcomes of which were two: the council succeeded by means of the Reformation in ejecting once and for all the Catholic powers from their midst and acquired thereby a significant material and jurisdictional windfall; the partisanship toward this preacher or that preacher that some burghers displayed, particularly between 1520 when Müntzer came to town and 1525 with the unrest of the Peasants' War, led the council to seek, and the elector to grant with his blessing, the nearly absolute dominion of the Herren over all other citizens. The Reformation brought the prior age of communal wholeness and advice and consent to an end—an end foreshadowed for over a decade, to be sure, but nevertheless only now to an end. Henceforward communal values were but a memory.

Technically, Zwickau was ruled before as after by an oligarchy, but the oligarchy after 1525 was significantly different. Bernd Moeller's assertions about German imperial cities hold true for Zwickau as well: the late medieval *corpus christianum* was dead; the relationship between the magistrates and members of the community changed; and "the old conception of the solidarity of the citizens before God was no longer deeply felt."[83]

The Reformation in Zwickau, however, did not produce "a new awareness of their original communal foundations."[84] On the contrary. The people had learned in 1516 that the prince backed the council and that humble folk had very little chance of attaining their political goals. They resorted to sass and evasion. They ridiculed the councillors' behavior as Peter Schumann recorded, referring to 1540: "A game is going around now that is called 'Assaulted': When a man from the community or another citizen in the course of presenting a matter happens to say a word or two too many, particularly touching on the gentlemen of the council, he is run off to jail. But the tower is *locked* behind *him*."[85] They made up poems of derision that no pronouncements seemed to inhibit.[86] They posted them where everyone would see them. On Palm Sunday, 30 March 1539, Burgomaster Oswald Lasan went down to the Mulde to view the wood that had washed down from the forests during torrential rains. A glover named Lorenz Teufel accidentally (or so the man maintained) poked out Lasan's right eye with a pole. Some creative citizen was not moved to compassion by the magistrate's misfortune but amused a number of his fellows with the following doggerel:

> When Oswald Lasan became head of this town
> He turned many things here upside down:
> He tore out the chapel in city hall
> And made a saloon for his councillors all.
> He built a tin shop in the common wood
> That the tinsmiths as quickly abandoned for good.
> He removed the iron work from Saint Mary's
> And made a cage for naughty kiddies.
> He went down to the river on Palm Sunday,
> Where the devil (*teufel*) struck his right eye away.[87]

Up until the crisis of the Schmalkaldic War, mutual antipathy characterized the relationship between the councillors and the city's ordinary citizens. Having abandoned the policy of the late fifteenth century, which urged leniency and a certain benevolence upon wielders of power, the council failed to understand, much less to find a remedy for, what they increasingly regarded as lower-class truculence. However, as we shall see, fomenting and leading this truculence were members of the councillors' own property-owning class. As a result it is hard to view the divisions in Zwickau strictly as "class conflict." This is too facile a description. Unquestionably the poor resented those who did not have to worry about where their next meal was coming from. Unquestionably the poor suffered more acutely than others as Zwickau's economy foundered. But any coalescence of malcontents depended entirely on leadership from home-owning guildmasters who seemed to be frustrated by their own failure to enter governing circles.

The Gleam of Silver,
The Shadow of Dearth:
Zwickau's Economy

*A*s recently as half a century ago, before Marxian schemes of history had to be taken into account even by "bourgeois" historians, some of the greatest scholars of their day, such as Johan Huizinga and C. H. Haskins, could write what have become their classic works with barely a reference to medieval economic life. Since the mid-thirties such enterprises have become all but unthinkable. Non-Marxists, people unconvinced that modes of production and material interests dictated the form and the content of all human affairs, nevertheless had at least to glance in the direction of the material component of life, acknowledging thereby the potentially great influence that the workaday world exerted upon such seemingly nonmaterial activities as prayer and the writing of poetry.

In the realm of German medieval and early modern studies, the mid-thirties marked the appearance of such pioneering works as Wilhelm Abel, *Geschichte der deutschen Landwirtschaft vom frühen Mittelalter bis zum 19. Jahrhundert,*[1] and M. J. Elsas, *Umriss einer Geschichte der Preise und Löhne in Deutschland vom ausgehenden Mittelalter bis zum Beginn des neunzehnten Jahrhunderts.*[2] Today we take it for granted that economy and Reformation interacted, in Zwickau and everywhere else, but that the nature and extent of the interaction varied from time to time and from place to place. A close look at Zwickau is warranted. In Zwickau a general economic decline exacerbated the tensions that were already mounting between patricians and craftsmen. Some of these tensions found release in the drama of religious change.

The Sources

The kinds of analyses, based on mountains of data from multitudes of sources, that economists are able to do of modern cities are not possible for sixteenth-century Zwickau. What remain for us to peruse are two types of documents: first, the Türkensteuer records of 1531 and 1542 and the general property assessment of 1523, and second, the intermittent council minutes (*Ratsprotokolle*) from 1510 to 1545. The tax for the war against the Turks was periodically levied on all property in Zwickau, real and moveable. Adult dependents in the household of another, who had no property but personal effects, paid a capitation, or poll. Therefore, all properties had to be assessed and the number of adults in each household, with the exception of master craftsmen's and merchants' wives, recorded. This was done by a small committee of councillors together with the council's scribe. They had, we presume, to go from house to house so that neither goods nor eligible persons could be concealed. For this reason the tax registers tell us in roughly what proximity individuals lived to one another. The tally was carried out quarter by quarter, beginning with the Oberviertel within the walls, to the southwest (I am calling it quarter 1), and the Oberviertel without the walls (quarter 2), and proceeding clockwise to the Frauenviertel within (quarter 3), the Frauenviertel without (quarter 4), the Unterviertel within (quarter 5), the Unterviertel without (quarter 6), and, finally, the Tränkviertel within (quarter 7) and the Tränkviertel without (quarter 8).

From the twentieth-century perspective these tax registers leave something to be desired. As said, wives of master craftsmen and merchants are not referred to. Still, because marriage was a prerequisite of guild membership, we can be fairly certain that most guildsmen had wives, except for those whose wives had died and who had not yet remarried. Minors, a definition of which is not provided, are never even alluded to unless they had inherited property.[3] The destitute did not have to pay even a head tax, and they do not appear, nor do residents of hospitals. Essentially, anyone gainfully employed, which most children were not, was liable for the poll, and some girls went out at a tender age to serve in a neighbor's home. This is not much help, however, since we cannot tell how old the city's 304 maids in 1531 or its 289 maids in 1542 were.[4] Above all, we are handicapped by the scribes' failure to be consistent in their record keeping. The scribe in 1531 put down many journeymen's names and provenance. The scribe in 1542, trying no doubt to lighten his task, often did not even note journeymen's names but just wrote *knapp* or *knecht*. Nor was either careful to record householders' professions. The result is that the Türkensteuerregister yield information chiefly about the wealth of property owners and only incidentally about the condition of any other residents.[5]

The council minutes provide a very different view of things, astatistical, biased, and impressionistic as they are. They show us the daily problems that the councillors had or chose to deal with, and they expose, albeit anecdotally, the position of certain guilds and of a number of individuals. They complement the Türkensteuer ledgers nicely, obliquely pointing out the danger in coming to conclusions on the basis of numerical evidence alone.

The Economic Relationships

As stated earlier, the gentlemen of the council throughout the late fifteenth and early sixteenth centuries considered that regulation of the economy was their bounden duty. They were the corporation above all other secular ones, and that meant above the craft guilds. No new guild could be founded without their say-so, no governing articles of a guild could be altered unless they approved, no innovation made unless they consented.

In 1503 Zwickau had nine formal guilds, here listed in the order of their perceived importance: woolweavers, bladesmiths, smiths, shoemakers, bakers, butchers, tailors, tanners, and linenweavers.[6] By 1505 furriers had been added. Coopers and joiners appear on the official roster for 1533 and hatters for the following year.[7] Crockers are added in 1538 and pursemakers in 1544.[8] The council also kept track of all other trades even if just one man of master's status practiced them in the city. In 1542 sixty-three other crafts were noted, added most recently a bookbinder (1536) and a papermaker (1539). Actually, there had been at least one bookbinder and a papermaker before this, suggesting that this list was simply more complete than previous ones.

All of these unincorporated crafts were accorded a collective status just below that of the largest guild, that of the woolweavers. These skilled non-guildsmen altogether constituted the "community" (*gemeyn*), which chose four representatives each year to relay their grievances to the council and to carry back instructions. One has to be careful

TABLE 5
Zwickau's Artisans

	Masters			Journeymen	
	1531	1542	1540[a]	1531	1542
Woolweavers	243	189	230	219	191
Bladesmiths	7	4	7	6	3
Smiths	53	53	45	47	55
Shoemakers	18	14	20	16	14
Bakers	34	14	44	17	8
Butchers	31	?[b]	31	14	?
Tailors	14	17	25	10	22
Tanners	11	3	25	4	?
Linenweavers[c]	9	1	14	3	?
Furriers	8	4	8	5	?
Coopers	12	8	12	13	18
Joiners	7	3	6	7	2
Hatters	4	1	0	1	2
Crockers	5	4	7	6	9
Pursemakers	7	4	3	5	5

SOURCE: Türkensteuer, ZSA, Ax AII 17, Nr. 19a; ZSA, Ax AII 16, Nr. 12; Paul Kummer, "Gewerbe und Zunftverfassung in Zwickau bis zum Jahre 1600" (Ph.D. diss., University of Leipzig, 1921), 27.

[a]Number of masters who owned a home; see note 8, below.

[b]Question marks indicate that the scribes identify no one in the category.

[c]Under pressure from the city council and guilds of Chemnitz, which had been given a monopoly on linen production, and despite Chemnitz's being Albertine, the elector revoked Zwickau's right to have a linenweavers' guild in 1541. Low numbers reflect this.

to discern when by *gemeyn* the council is referring to just this assembly of varied artisans and when it means the whole citizenry of Zwickau.

Compared with the woolweavers' guild, for which by hand tabulation I can verify the existence of 243 masters in 1531 and 189 in 1542, all the other guilds, with the exception of the smiths', were small (see table 5). In consideration of the scribes' negligence or inconsistency, one may be certain that membership in all the guilds was somewhat greater than recorded in the Türkensteuerregister. The poorer a man was, the less likely were the scribes to record his occupation.

Each guild in its assembly traditionally elected its heads, called "Four Masters" (*Viermeister*), each year. The smaller guilds chose only two leaders but still called them *Viermeister*. These leaders policed the guild and enforced its rules. They accepted apprentices, received credentials from foreign journeymen, inspected master works, and ensured the quality of the everday products turned out by the guildsmen. They handled minor infractions and turned major ones over to the city council. They administered guild finances and properties, if any. The woolweavers', the smiths', and the bakers' guilds each owned a house, though the weavers' is for some reason not listed in either Türken-steuerregister. It was indeed free of *Geschoss*, but that should not have exempted it from the tax for the war against the Turks. Perhaps this was among so-called public properties for which the council offered no tax until reprimanded by the elector.[9]

So large was the woolweavers' guild that no Viermeister could do all the necessary administering. The weavers had an intermediate council of twenty-four masters, called "the Twenty-four." As in the case of the Rat itself, during the Reformation era the number occasionally rose above the traditional twenty-four but soon subsided again.[10] The Twenty-four shared all the duties borne by the Viermeister alone in less numerous guilds.

In view of the nature and extent of the Viermeisters' responsibilities, it is no wonder that these guild leaders often came in conflict with rank-and-file members. There is, however, no clear pattern here. Some guilds repeatedly elected proved opponents of the city council, demonstrating thereby a certain solidarity. In those cases, at least, tension within the guilds was lower than between the guilds and the city council. In 1524, because, it said, of continual insubordination, the council assumed the right to approve or reject the woolweavers' new Viermeister.[11]

The Viermeister devised the petitions presented to the incoming council in late September each year. They received the councillors' replies and took these back to their constituents. The guild structure cannot be seen, therefore, as solely economic in function. It was ever highly political (and obviously social as well). Through their guilds all artisans made their concerns known to the magistrates. If public pressure was ever effective in altering a course of action decided upon by the ruling patricians, it was applied through the guilds.

Goods changed hands in Zwickau in three settings. There were first of all shops run by people in their domiciles. Many personal services were performed there, too. Apothecaries received customers there, as did tailors, who had to take measurements for bespoke apparel. Even bakers had traditionally sold bread through their own front windows, a practice that in our era the council attempted to discourage because, the gentlemen thought, if kept in the marketplace, the bakers could less easily practice deceptions such as foisting off on the public under-weight rolls or offering loaves that had not entirely cooled. Zwickauers disliked warm bread.[12]

Secondly, there were the regular markets, in the market square, at which inhabitants bought and sold much of what they needed for their everyday existence. They began early in the morning, as soon as the market master hoisted his signal flag. The biggest markets were on Wednesday and Saturday. Craftsmen moved their booths, called benches (*bengke*), into the marketplace and laid out their wares. It perpetually annoyed them that hawkers of anything not reserved to guildsmen crammed the interstices and hindered access to their own goods. The council scribe himself observed in 1536 that everyone who was unemployed took to hawking.[13] Housewives brought out their cheeses and their cooked fruits (*mus*). Enterprising hawkers even toured the villages, which they were quickly ordered to stop doing.[14]

The specially licensed, large trade fairs that Zwickau was entitled to host constituted the third forum of exchange within the walls. During the early sixteenth century, these fairs took place beginning on Invo-cavit, the sixth Sunday before Easter; on Trinity Sunday in June; and on Saint Katherine's Day, the fourth Sunday before Christmas. Each lasted for eight days, from one Sunday through the next. Some long-distance merchants visited these markets, particularly dealers in wool cloth, wool, and grain. Zwickau sat astride the trade route linking Nu-remberg with Leipzig and points farther north and northeast. The Reichenbacher and Leipziger Strassen are the modern remains of this commercial highway. Other and varied goods were to be found in the market, and many of them traveled into and out of Zwickau along other available paths. But almost the only items of greater than local or regional significance were those mentioned, and of these three only wool cloth was a recognized international commodity. Zwickau served otherwise as a place for the exchange of mundane provisions for the surrounding territory.

At both large and small fairs, the council's inspectors moved from bench to bench, examining the artisans' handiwork, testing weights and measures, watching for infractions. Were the rebellious butchers forcing people to buy inferior meat along with the good? Were they selling kinds of meat at the same bench that could not easily be distin-guished by the lay person, such as ox (more highly valued) and cow (less highly valued)? Were there dogs around the butchers' tables, which produced, the scribe noted, a most unappealing situation (*viel unlust*)? So disobedient were the butchers that the conciliar office of meat inspector was added by at least 1509 to keep the butchers in line.[15]

Certain goods were examined in advance of sale as well as at the markets. Wool cloth was one of these. Originally, maintaining the quality of its product had been the weavers' guild's own responsibility. Guild rules were specific about the size of finished cloths, the dyes to be used, and how the exportable lengths were to be marked. During our period the city fathers, most of them originally woolweavers, involved themselves in the inspection. At some time between 1522 and 1526, the council undertook this new role. By September 1526 the scribe could list a councillor as inspector of market-ready cloth and nine men, including one councillor, as examiners of raw wool. One could always defend the inspection of wool to guildsmen as insurance that they were not being cheated (fleeced?) by unscrupulous wool-producing outsiders. But very soon the emphasis came to be placed on the work of the artisans itself, and this could not be so justified.

By 1526 the council had added bread inspection to its rapidly expanding sphere, and shortly afterward also linen and leather. Just as suddenly, during the late thirties, the scribe dropped all these offices from his annual roster. At this time the council was attempting to reduce the onus of its duties as well as the size of the bureaucracy. Its policies stayed the same, and it imposed harsher and harsher penalties upon violators of every sort of regulation.[16] The patricians were keeping close track of the city's products whether or not their means is evident.

Obtaining the raw materials of its trades bound Zwickau tightly to the world outside its boundaries. It imported all its wool, wheat, livestock and leather, dyestuff, and wood, though not necessarily from great distances. Woad and other dye plants probably came from farthest away, indirectly from the woad dealers of Erfurt, but purchased mostly from middlesmen from around Weimar and elsewhere in Thuringia.[17] As the population grew, more and more rye and wheat were imported. There is evidence too of butchers having to go farther afield for beasts to slaughter. Not surprisingly, some local opportunists invested in acreages if they did not already own them and raised animals to sell as meat and wool to the butchers and weavers respectively. For both these reasons the butchers had to pay higher and higer prices for animals. And then there was inflation.

Zwickau had long possessed the right of economic control of its hinterland. The electors' successive confirmations of the city's liberties did not use this phrase, but whatever the words, economic control was meant. From at least the fourteenth century, the dukes drastically circumscribed the skilled trades and other commercial activities that were being carried on near Zwickau, within the so-called *Bannmeile*, not an English mile but a measure sufficiently commodious to include about thirty nearby villages, even some belonging to knights.[18] All of this was intended to guarantee the success of the urban market. The princes were specific. For their most urgent requirements, Wilhelm Landgraf zu Thüringen and Markgraf zu Meissen proclaimed in 1421, after the struggle had persisted for decades between the city and its peasant and noble neighbors, Planitz might have one smith and one taverner; Crossen the same; Lichtentanne, Umkan (?), Stein, and Steinpleis, one smith each; the Schonberger hamlets one smith and one taverner each; Riebensdorf, Saint Michael, Saint Jacob, Saint Nicol, one taverner each "as for ages past," but they might not brew or malt; Pölbitz, Eckersbach, Auerbach, Plan, Kulitzsch, Rutsmansdorf, Schneppendorf, Judenhain, Niederhohndorf, Helwigsdorf, Rothenbach, Marienthal, and Weissenborn could have not one craftsman of any type.[19]

Controversy and evasion never ceased; declarations of the above principle came forth repeatedly over the years. *Geleit* records show quantities of Schneeberger beer going to Reinsdorf, for instance.[20] In the early sixteenth century, the knight Rudolf von der Planitz deliberately disobeyed his prince's commands again and again.[21] Nevertheless, officially residents of the countryside, whatever their rank, were to give their business exclusively to Zwickau's craftsmen.

The peasants were not to sell their produce anywhere but in the urban market. It was equally forbidden for any person to go out to the land and deal there with the rustics. Complaints of noncompliance were numerous, many of them no doubt the result of actual circumvention of the law. The bladesmiths asserted in 1517 that certain (well-known) citizens right in the marketplace itself were buying up grain at one florin per *scheffel* and selling it for twenty-four groschen (1 1/7 florins).[22] The smiths were less discreet and accused the market masters themselves.[23] Other allegations may have been exaggerated as inflation made itself felt in the 1520s and sent people, including Martin Luther, in search of scapegoats.[24] Many residents, including councillors, were convinced that inflation was caused by unscrupulous men who toured the countryside buying up grain, which they then stored until the ensuing scarcity elevated prices. But as the gentlemen of the council specifically proclaimed against the buying up of any item from the peasants, they were probably not moved exclusively by popular paranoia. They were in a position to know what the city's moneyed class was doing. Some of them may have participated.

The State of the Economy

Historians have referred to the late fifteenth and early sixteenth centuries in Zwickau as the city's "blossom time" (*Blütezeit*). By this they have meant that the city expanded, paved its main streets, built imposing public and private edifices, promoted its school, saw a growth in the numbers of educated leaders, had a printer, and moved from Catholicism to Lutheranism. They have meant, too, that the city enjoyed a preeminence within Ernestine lands and an unprecedented princely esteem—we might add, because the land division (*Teilung*) of 1485 had happened to allot the larger Leipzig and the more pleasantly situated Dresden to the other (Albertine) branch of the Wettin family.

These physical and cultural developments were an accompaniment to economic growth. Money flowed into the town after 1470. Most benefited chiefly, as said, from the greater traffic through town, from the need to provision the miners in Schneeberg and weigh and vouch to the princes for the silver. Zwickauers dealt in goods and services on a new scale. Prior to this they had relied on the north-south trade route on which they lived to sustain them. Now they had a dual economic purpose.

Very few immense fortunes were made. The Römer, Federangel, and Tretwein families were among the exceptions. Particularly Martin Römer, who had trading ties to Nuremberg and even Venice, was of a generous nature. His personal philanthropy filled the "Rich Alms" (*Reiche Almosen*) fund, provided a three-story school building for the Gymnasium, and financed a number of other amenities such as the digging of the large lake. Römer had been ennobled in 1470, and his heirs did what they thought befitted the nobility and moved to the country near Marienthal. Here some of them still resided in the Re- formation era. As we have seen, Hermann Mühlpfort's wife was a Römer. By the sixteenth century the Federangels and the Tretweins had either moved away or died out, with the single exception that in 1531 an Urban Tretwein, otherwise not a property owner, held twenty florins' worth of *leibzins*, a tax of feudal origin that a few peasants still owed "on their bodies." By 1542 he was gone.

In the sixteenth century, Zwickau's new magnates made their money from land. The Türkensteuerregister do not reveal precisely what the richest man in 1542, Hans Unruh, or the richest woman, Magdalena Heynlin, were doing with their land. Unruh made his money in mining and moved to Zwickau from Annaberg in 1537; in 1542 he presided over assets valued at 18,690 florins. Heynlin, the widow of councillor Nickel Heinel (or Hennel), together with her children in 1531 operated a business worth four thousand florins and had 1,240 florins' worth of property besides. A number of adults, at least fourteen, lived on the Heynlin lands and paid rent. Others were on the woman's payroll. In either case Unruh was able to pay his tax for the war against the Turks, but Heynlin could afford not one heller of hers. Only a quarter or so of this fortune remained intact among her likely heirs in 1542.[25] Probably much had been used up paying her debts.

Unruh's accumulated possessions in 1542 were far and away the largest in the city.[26] Unruh was the brother-in-law of Burgomaster Oswald Lasan but did not sit on the council himself until 1545, a date of entry so late that Moritz of Saxony, the new elector, did not feel threatened by his presence in the council but confirmed him in 1547. Nearly all the councillors of the Reformation period were better off than average citizens, but other than Unruh only four had truly sizable fortunes: Mühlpfort (9,550 florins in 1531), Michel von Mila (6,140 florins in 1542), Lucas Schutze (5,237 florins in 1542), and Dr. Stephan Wilde (4,259 florins in 1542).

Others were striving to amass wealth, of course. Helmut Bräuer has alleged, for example, that the leaders of the woolweavers' guild used collective wool purchase as a means of enriching themselves at their humbler colleagues' expense.[27] The weavers told the council in 1532, "Some burghers here are said to make the price of [raw] wool in the countryside rise, which injures our guild."[28] They stated the next year that the wool merchants were exporting wool and mixing good wool with bad. If this did not stop, they added, the guild would decline.[29] Greedy, unscrupulous individuals can be found in every society in every age, and there is no evidence in Zwickau of successful efforts to accumulate large amounts of capital to the detriment of rank-and-file woolweavers or other artisans. The weavers' guild was suffering during much of the period that we are examining, but the reasons for this are more likely several and complex than single and simple.

Even during the time when Zwickau merchants and craftsmen were provisioning the mining settlements to the south, Zwickau's fiscal health depended too greatly on one product, wool cloth. This had ever been the case. The time of expansion offered a hope of diversification, but this hope was short-lived. Schneeberg especially, at first reliant on Zwickau, rapidly developed its own guilds and its own market. This was to be expected. In 1522 Zwickau's bakers revolted when journeymen came up from Schneeberg and tried to work there. The local journeymen and some masters, too, protested that since Schneeberg had no bakers' guild, it could not legally take on apprentices or produce journeymen. The Zwickau bakers wanted to throw out the Schneebergers. When the council did not cooperate, the bakers stopped baking and some departed for Kadan, in Bohemia, a destination not without significance.[30] Frederick the Wise and Johann supported the council. They decreed that Schneeberg did have a proper bakers' guild and that its journeymen were professionally legitimate. They were to be accorded all the usual privileges, and the rebels were to submit or forfeit their citizenship.[31]

This conflict is just one of the signs that Zwickau was having to adjust as Schneeberg matured. Another is the transfer of Zwickau's mint, opened in 1530, to Schneeberg at the end of 1534.[32] In 1541 Zwickau's monopoly on floating logs and cutting and selling lumber in the area was eliminated. The elector gave Schneeberg permission to perform these functions in the summertime. Zwickau retained the right in the autumn and during Lent.[33] In 1542 the council complained to Johann Friedrich about the damaging effect on Zwickau of Schneeberg's newly built mills.[34]

Zwickau never found a replacement for the commerce lost to Schneeberg and other towns in the Erzgebirge. On the other hand, Schneeberg did not have a location that enabled it to flourish from interregional trade. The hilly, rocky Ore Mountains permitted of no amber waves of grain. Many foodstuffs and other items still had to be imported. Some of the salutary burden of sustaining life in the undulant south thus continued to rest on Zwickau. Zwickau's market in the Erzgebirge contracted; it did not collapse.

Inflation posed unfamiliar problems all over Germany, not just in Ernestine lands.[35] Beginning in the 1520s, prices began to rise noticeably. Luther wrote to George Spalatin in April 1531 about the high cost of food in Wittenberg and the clamor of the populace.[36] In Zwickau the people begged the council for rectifying action. In 1534 the bladesmiths lamented to the council, "Poor people cannot afford even their daily food because of higher prices, especially of butter, cheese, milk, bread, meat, and grain. Please look into this."[37] Nicolaus Hausmann, seeking to have an old debt dismissed, drew the councillors' attention to the damage inflation had done to him.[38] In 1540, after he had left for Plauen, Paul Rebhun, who had taught in Zwickau from 1535 to 1537, wrote a piece with the title "Complaint of a Poor Man Burdened with the Cares of Inflation and Hunger."[39] (See table 6.)

Everyone sought to understand this perilous phenomenon. The council proclaimed, "Because many complaints come before the council about the peasants and transporters storing up barley and grain [on the property of] the innkeepers (*wirdten*) and [other] citizens and by this means waiting for higher prices, indeed in this way causing inflation, this practice is to be stopped and the innkeepers or burghers punished for it."[40] The elector himself believed that inflation was caused by the buying up and exportation of grain. He decreed in 1534 that "because it is common knowledge that for several years in our lands and those of the Highborn Prince George, Duke of Saxony, etc., our dear cousin, an unseemly and rapid increase in the cost of grain has occurred and it is hard to buy," no one could buy it and take it out of Wettin territories.[41] He repeated this prohibition in 1539 and 1540, and his successor Moritz did the same in 1551.[42]

Neither people nor magistrates seemed to think that anything other than human greed and betrayal might have produced these undesirable price elevations. As the setter of prices on goods in daily use, the council at first simply refused to permit the butchers to charge more for meat or the bakers to bake smaller loaves. For a least two decades, the practitioners of these two crafts were locked in a bitter dispute with successive councils, which consumed much time in council sessions.

In the years before the Schmalkaldic War, the butchers were repeatedly imprisoned and the bakers charged ruinous fines of up to one florin per violation.[43] In these contests, unlike some others, the populace sided with the council. They, indeed, were the victims if the butchers were allowed to charge more or the bakers to offer underweight loaves or no penny loaves for the poor, or if they cut down on the proportion of the more costly wheat in relation to the cheaper rye in their baking. City folk could not stomach the coarse, dark peasant bread, which was apparently all rye. The people had, in fact, been imploring the gentlemen of the council to let them bake at home if they had the means—many citizens had fire for cooking and heating

67

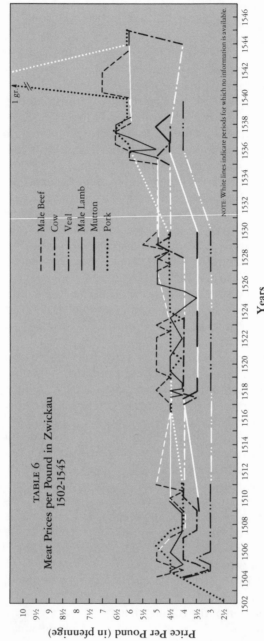

Years

TABLE 6

TABLE 6

Meat Prices per Pound in Zwickau
1502-1545

NOTE: White lines indicate periods for which no information is available.

Price Per Pound (in pfennige)

Male Beef
Cow
Veal
Male Lamb
Mutton
Pork

anyway. Both in an effort to prevent fires in this city of tinder and to promote the bakers' guild, the councils refused. But in October 1540, in a curious reversal, they relented, though all private ovens had to be inspected for safety. No doubt this was part of the council's revenge on the recalcitrant bakers. So far as can be detected, however, the established bakers stayed in business, still pressed hard by the higher prices they were forced to pay for flour.

The councillors absolutely refused to raise wages. Maids and the less numerous menservants earned besides their keep from nothing (especially maids worked without pay) to eleven florins per year, the latter being extraordinarily high, suggesting that the recipient was actually a finely skilled individual doing the work of a master craftsman. More typical was pay under two and up to five florins a year, probably doled out weekly as a few pennies or a groschen in pocket money (see tables 7 and 8).[44] There was no change in this between 1531 and 1542, and people in menial occupations were destined to remain dependent and propertyless unless inheritance or some other uncommon event altered the course of their lives.

Many men (and women, too) were day laborers. In the 1531 Türkensteuerregister, sixty-eight are identified, and in 1542 none. The figure for 1531 is far too low, and in 1542 the scribe simply regarded such people's employment as too lowly to note. Of the sixty-eight named day laborers of 1531, only three were owners of meager properties by 1542. In general these workers could never collect enough

TABLE 7
HIGHEST PERMISSIBLE DAILY WAGES, 1508

Barley, oats, and hay rakers	9 d.[a]
Grain cutters	16 d.
Day laborer (task unnamed), with meals	1 gr.
Day laborer, without meals	20 d.
Binder of sheaves	2 gr.
Grass cutter	2 gr.
Oats and barley reapers	3 gr.[b]

SOURCE: Otto Langer, "Zwickauer Lohntaxen aus dem 16. Jahrhundert," *MAZU*, 8 (1905): 26.

[a]Twelve pfennige (d.) equal one groschen.

[b]Herzog records that in 1482 stone cutters, masons, carpenters, and cabinetmakers, if masters, could be paid 18 d. per day with meals or 2 gr., 3 d. without. Journeymen got 15 d. with meals, 1 gr., 9 d. without (*Chronik*, 2: 127).

TABLE 8
Highest Permissible Wages, 1545

	With meals	Without meals
Common day laborers		
Carnival to Easter	10 d.[a]	
Easter to Michaelmas (29 Sept)	12 d.	
Michaelmas to Martinmas (11 Nov.)	10 d.	
Martinmas to Carnival	8 d.	
Carpenters and masons		
Easter to Michaelmas		
Master		3 gr.
Journeyman		2½ gr.
Michaelmas to Easter		
Master		2½ gr.
Journeyman		2 gr.
Half-timberers (wattle-and-daubers)		
1 May to Michaelmas	1½ gr.	2½ gr.
Garden workers		
Diggers (*grebern*)	1 gr.	1½ gr.
Hops stakers	15 d.	2 gr.
Hops pickers	6 d.	
"All other garden work such as weeding, trimming (*anlegen* [?]) hops, and all similar work that the women are accustomed to do"	8 d.	
Field workers		
Grass mowers	2 gr.	3 gr.
Oats and barley mowers	2½ gr.	3½ gr.
Sowers of oats		3 d.[b]
Sowers of other grains		4 d.[b]
Cutters	16 d.	
Seed gatherers (*ansammern* [?])	9 d.	
Binders	3 d.[c]	1½ gr.
Rakers of hay, barley, and oats	8 d.	15 d.
Grummet[d] rakers	6 d.	14 d.
Threshers		
St. Lawrence (10 Aug.) to Michaelmas	12 d.	
Michaelmas to Martinmas	9 d.	
Martinmas to Carnival	7 d.	
Carnival to Easter	9	

Source: Ordinance of 21 November 1545 (Otto Langer, "Zwickauer Lohntaxen aus dem 16. Jahrhundert," *MAZU*, 8 [1905]: 28–30).

[a]Wages listed are per day unless otherwise noted.
[b]Per scheffel sowed.
[c]Per *schock*, i.e., sixty sheaves.
[d]Second and third cuttings of hay.

money to purchase real estate. For all we know, the three in question may have inherited theirs or acquired it through marriage. Anyone paying more than the amounts in table 7 was to be fined "*1 ald schock*" (twenty groschen).[45] When the weaver Stephan Harreinweil, a leading and well-off follower of Thomas Müntzer, paid three groschen a day to a barley mower, the council punished him with the prescribed fine.[46]

Women are specifically mentioned only once in the wage tables. Women typically performed those jobs at the low end of the scale, such as weeding and hoeing. It is not clear whether they got as much money as men for doing, say, field work, or not. Very often women were not paid as much as men for the same work in the sixteenth century, but I have found instances in Thuringia where they were. If the work and income were not merely seasonal—most were confined to certain times of year—a laborer might have realized an income of twelve to thirty-six florins annually. In reality, laborers all by themselves rarely attained this level of revenue. Many families had more than one laborer, and these would have been that much more secure—certain, that is, of nourishment and shelter if not much else.

The urban journeyman, or even the non-agricultural unskilled laborer, probably had the advantage over agrarian workers of being more likely to labor gainfully in winter and inclement weather and thus to be that much more sure of material sufficiency. Journeymen were not always paid by the day but in many trades were maintained in a master's household. Some rented rooms in other houses and supported themselves and their families—journeymen increasingly had families—separately from master guildsmen. In that case they had to be given money as opposed to room and board. As advancing to master became less automatic, there was a tendency to put journeymen on a set wage. In either instance there was almost no prospect of setting money aside for investment in property. Journeymen and laborers had small chance of rising into the class of property owners and entrepreneurs, though for journeymen the hope at least existed that they would eventually attain master's status and improve their condition in life.

The frustrations of day laborers in the face of inflation became evident during the 1530s. It came to the council's attention in 1538 and again in 1540 that day laborers were refusing to work for the old wages. The gentlemen issued a new order and had it read out to the populace.[47] On 10 July 1542, the masons who were working on the city wall went on strike. They attracted some other workers to their cause, and all demanded pay of not less than fifteen groschen per week. The old rule for day laborers not receiving meals limited them to twenty pfennige per day or ten groschen for a six-day week. All the rebels were summarily imprisoned.[48]

Langer states that three years later, however, in November 1545, the council increased the masons' weekly compensation to take inflation into account. Between Easter and Michaelmas 1546, they were to have sixteen groschen.[49] If strikes were successful, it was only when war loomed and the diligence of the workers in question was of the essence. Other laborers were not so fortunate, as table 8 shows. Wages did not rise during the first half of the sixteenth century and hardly at all even in 1565.[50]

The tax records inform us that, in contrast to laborers, most property owners in Zwickau in 1531, if still present in 1542, were economically better off after the eleven-year interval. They appear to have benefited from expansion and inflation. It looks remarkably as if the city's poor were indeed growing poorer and the non-poor (rich would be the wrong term here) farther removed from the threat of poverty. One might question whether the assessors were not appraising the same properties higher in 1542 than in 1531, only making it seem as if people were prospering. The answer is no. Not only were the councillors determined to hold prices and values at their customary levels, but they did not stand to gain from wringing more money out of the populace for this tax against the Turks, all of which went to the elector. Furthermore, several buildings can be identified with certainty as the same ones for both the 1531 and the 1542 levies, and these are assessed at exactly the same rate. The houses owned by the bakers and the smiths are two of these.

A sample of seventy property owners present on both the 1531 and the 1542 tax rosters swelled their assets during the eleven-year interval by an average of 188.5 percent. Only six of the seventy incurred losses. This compares with an average gain among the councillors during the same period of just half a percent. Reliance upon the tax registers alone could lead one to suppose that Zwickauers were flourishing during these years. As observed, however, it was becoming more and more difficult for those not already economically established to gain that initial foothold. To see this we must look to other sorts of evidence, much of it from our other main source on Zwickau's economy, the council minutes.

The people in society who were surviving and even gaining from inflation were spending their discretionary income on land and on luxuries—or at any rate on what an earlier age would have designated

72

as wholly expendable goods and services. Owners of substantial houses were having water piped into their courtyards from springs in Reinsdorf and Pöhlau; a preserved *Rohrsteg* including a section of the ancient wooden water pipe may still be seen on the river southeast of town. The well-off were digging or procuring cellars in the side of the hill on the opposite bank of the Mulde. The new guilds specialized in the manufacture of such items as belts, purses, and gloves, the better to outfit an expanded polite society. Though not formed into a guild, goldsmiths thrived during the 1530s. Hawkers of every sort of ware became shopkeepers (*kramer*) between 1531 and 1542, and shopkeepers became merchants. Women wanted a more attractive dinnerware than the ordinary *töpffer* sold, and several individuals, among them women, came to deal exclusively in the new "white ware."[51] Wolff Meyerpeck started out as a room-renting bookseller with assets worth 28.6 florins in 1531, and by 1542, partly by virtue of a strategic marriage to printer Gabriel Kantz's widow, he was an independent printer owning property worth 550 florins.

It is an intriguing question whether journeymen in the various crafts were having a hard time gaining admittance to the ranks of the masters (see table 9). The elusiveness of the answer is exacerbated by the failure of most named journeymen of 1531 to reappear in 1542. Of 298 forty-nine were still listed in 1542. Why were they gone? Was it a

TABLE 9
JOURNEYMEN ATTAINING MASTER'S STATUS BY 1542

	Total Number[a]	Achieved Master's Status
Woolweavers	28	12
Smiths	9	6
Bakers	4	4
Goldsmiths	1	1
Carpenters	1	1
Warpers	1	0
Chandlers	1	1
Saddlers	1	1
Bladesmiths	1	1
Tanners	1	1
Potters	1	1

SOURCE: Türkensteuer, ZSA, Ax AII 16, Nr. 12.

[a]Of the 298 journeymen listed in the Türkensteuer records for 1531, only forty-nine remained in 1542.

consequence of the scribe's nonchalance about names? Partly, no doubt. But more decisive was that despite the true origin of their name (*journée*, because they were originally hired by the day), journeymen journeyed. They sojourned in a town other than that in which they had been apprenticed, and then most went home. Possibly they did not all wish to go home—we do not know. But nearly all of the forty-nine who were still present in 1542 were members of Zwickau families. Their guilds had not compelled them to travel—not all guilds did by the sixteenth century[52]—or they had gone away and returned. Of these just twenty-nine had succeeded in becoming master craftsmen after eleven years; twenty still had journeyman status and still lived as dependents in other men's homes. They had accumulated few worldly possessions.

Though the number of examples is not great, it suggests a pattern. Journeymen from local families could become masters, and if they stayed at home, in all trades except woolweaving and the closely associated warping, most eventually did. It is tempting to speculate about the seventeen men, sixteen weavers and one warper, who were still *knappen* in 1542, that they were pertinacious, unambitious, or home-loving bodies not to have given up and sought their fortunes elsewhere. Many of the Zwickau youths who appear in 1531 as *knappen* and disappear by 1542 must have departed after years of frustrated efforts to advance. One can imagine that the same sorts of conditions obtained in the cloth-producing industries of other regional towns and that only native sons had a serious chance of becoming masters. Marrying a master's daughter helped, but not everyone could manage that. We do not know the fate of the "leavers."

Prejudice against outsiders, especially in a time of decline, shows itself now and again. The bakers pressed the council in 1541 to allow them to promote only Zwickau journeymen to master. The council said no, that this would be strictly self-serving (*eigennutzig*). [53] Nevertheless, the few available statistics hint that what the bakers wished to legalize was already common practice.

The evidence mounts up that, regardless of their occupations, people incapable of buying their homes, that is, of breaking into the propertied class, were faring badly. Begging, which had been outlawed by a newly Protestant council, threatened to become commonplace again during the 1530s. "Foreign" beggars, too, beset the city beginning in the early 1530s. The council eventually ordered these and other troublemakers (*stertzer*) driven out of the area.[54] The council was told over and over again and could see for itself that poverty was raging in the

TABLE 10
WOOLWEAVERS' ECONOMIC STATUS

Wealth (in florins)	1496 Number	Percentage
0–10	1 ⎫	57.85
11–300	80 ⎭	
301–2,000	50	35.71
2,001–30,000	9	6.43

Wealth (in florins)	1542 Number	Percentage
0–100	91 ⎫	
101–200	45 ⎬	69.36
201–300	27 ⎭	
301–400	19 ⎫	
401–500	9	
501–600	9	
601–700	5	
701–800	8 ⎬	27.66
801–900	3	
901–1,000	5	
1,001–1,500	4	
1,501–2,000	3 ⎭	
2,001–2,500	3 ⎫	
2,501–3,000	2 ⎬	2.98
3,001–4,000	1	
4,001–6,000	1 ⎭	

SOURCE: Max Müller, *Das Tuchmacher-Handwerk*, pp. 45–46, 49–50.

community.[55] One of its reasons for disposing of more of the churches' papist treasures at this time was to make more money available to the overburdened and depleted community chest. Pastor Leonhard Beyer was correct in his allegations of misadministration of chest funds.[56]

Zwickau's economic foundation stone, the woolweavers' guild, was not thriving (see table 10). Council minutes suggest this as early as 1525, when the council forbade wool merchants to go out privately to the nobles and other sheep raisers and buy up wool. It took this action "so that the poor masters are not entirely crushed (*vndergedrugkt*)."[57] In 1526 the council limited each master to the production yearly of fifty finished cloths, apparently in an effort to enforce high quality. The weavers complained bitterly and said that this would ruin them. The governing gentlemen were adamant for more than a decade, raising the number to fifty-two only in 1536.[58]

The council's scribe noted during Lent 1535, "Woolweavers' guild. Since it has been noticed in the guild accounts that the guild is not doing well, and as there are several articles drawn up by [the guild's] committee, these should be discussed with [all] the masters of the guild and also with the Twenty-four, and should afterward be shown to the Four Masters so that the craft may come to good health and improvement."[59] In June of the same year, more information is provided.

> With regard to the woolweavers' debt to the guild. Because as a result of a lack of diligence (*unvleis*) the guild of woolweavers has incurred great debts and counter-debts, and as this council is obliged and willing to seek the guild's good health, it has been decided that in order to collect the debts two gentlemen of the council are to be appointed. In the little old room in city hall, these in conjunction with the Four Masters are first to set the dates by when the debts of the Four Masters [themselves] are to be paid and then to call in the debts of the others. . . .[60]

The next year the council insisted that dealers in raw wool must bring their wares into the drapers' hall and not to their homes so that they could not take the best for themselves and force the low quality (for the price of high) upon the poorer and vulnerable masters.[61] If Max Müller is correct in stating that the average price of a *stein* of raw wool remained in most places at thirty-five groschen from 1507 to 1564 while in Zwickau it rose to forty-eight groschen by 1529, then local conditions and not just regional ones must be examined for causes of the guild's deterioration.[62]

Early in 1537 the weavers were near revolt over the fulling mill. Some, the council learned, were meeting late at night to discuss the situation, and they cursed the councillors and called them babbling monkeys (*lollaffen*) for doing nothing about the problem[63] We hear no more about this.

In June 1537 the council accepted money from the weavers' guild as an investment. They needed the income, the scribe explained, because they had just bought a meadow.[64] Indeed, they bought another one from Stephan Roth in 1540 for seven hundred florins.[65] Why had the weavers, despite their manifest financial predicament, spent some of their dwindling guild funds on pieces of land? This purchase, however ill-advised, may reflect the tendency to regard real estate, especially rural tracts, as a guarantor of economic security and to invest in it whenever one had money available. Surely they did not think to produce wool themselves.

In February 1538 the secretary remarked summarily, "Betrayal [in the sale of raw wool] increases greatly just now."[66] And shortly after this, he observed that the guild's account for 1537 again showed "a somewhat sizable loss." He wrote down the councillors' opinion that this was caused by a lack of industry (*unvleis*).[67] Again in the summer, he noted that this guild was in marked decline. The purchase of the essential dye plant woad was being carelessly handled as was the provision of nearly every other raw material ("unordentlicher bestellung fast aller notwendiger sachen").[68]

The council spent much time these days debating the predicament of the very craft guild to which the majority of the Herren belonged. In early August all the masters met with the Twenty-four. Nothing was accomplished. The old and new councils decided to convene the entire guild on the dance floor. There were preliminary discussions of the agenda. The Twenty-four submitted their view of things to the council. The problem was inflation and difficulties with the fulling mill. Everything the masters had to buy was dearer than ever before, and they were piling up massive debts, not just within the community but to outside merchants, the dealers in woad, for example. Non-weaver merchants in Zwickau were trading in woad, too.[69] To obtain woad ordinary weavers evidently had borrowed from the guild. The guild itself had about three thousand florins' worth of obligations to pay off at the Leipzig Michaelmas trade fair, and the Twenty-four did not see how this could be done.[70]

For its part the city council set down what it intended to decree at the coming assembly. It would ordain that henceforth woad must be paid for two weeks in advance of the Easter and Michaelmas fairs in Leipzig. As for old debts, schedules of payments would have to be agreed upon with the creditors. The gentlemen would establish dates by which other fees were to be paid. They would inform the masters that they must make up anything members of their household received in alms. In short, they *must* maintain or pay their journeymen and carders adequately. Such people were not eligible for public assistance.[71]

When the meeting of the guild took place, twenty-seven masters were outspokenly displeased with the councillors' heavy-handed approach.[72] They had expected not mere instructions to pay all debts, but aid and sympathetic advice. By our lights both sides were fearfully naïve. The councillors continued to believe that assiduity and moral uprightness would bring the woolweavers individually and the guild collectively out of its shadowy vale; they took no cognizance of any objective impediments facing the artisans. It did not occur to them, either weavers or councillors, that regional or even continental trends might affect them, or that their conservative attitudes toward change might have stood in the way of the adoption of truly useful technology. Early in the century the city had prided itself on having "the first mangler and blackdyer . . . in the entire land," a man called "the old Erhart Starck," who died in 1540.[73] In 1531 only five "wheel-spinners" appear in the tax records, and there is no evidence that their numbers were increasing rapidly. Rather, they seem to have been a sort of oddity.

The guildsmen had mentally come to accept the councillors' implied assertion that by detailed regulation of the economy they could help bring prosperity to the city. The guildsmen were beginning to perceive that they were wrong, but this perception afforded them no relief. They went on meeting on the sly and grumbling against the council, which became sufficiently alarmed—reminiscent of 1525 and after—to forbid gatherings.[74] At the customary ceremony of homage to the incoming council, perhaps postponed until October of 1539 because of the unrest, Wolff Koch, the same bladesmith who had led the people in 1525 in presenting grievances to the magistrates as the peasants stormed outside the walls, told the council that there were things it ought to know but which should be withheld from the common man.[75] We do not get to hear whatever message he imparted to the gentlemen.

On 22 November 1539, the council heard the devastating news from Frankfurt-an-Oder and Stettin (today Szczecin) that many Zwickau cloths were not of the proper length and that the certifying signs were not clear. No further account remains to us. Someone had counterfeited the city's wool marks.[76] Internal difficulties were of a lesser magnitude than the besmirching of the city's international reputation for producing wool cloth of reliable quality. Some weavers were reacting to inflation by literally cutting corners, or rather ends. In 1531 the weavers had told the council that some burghers were buying foreign cloths, finishing them, and selling them as Zwickau products.[77] Perhaps the wrongly marked yardages were not even of Zwickau manufacture. For all the city's bureaucrats, for all its supervision of citizens' activities, substandard woolens bearing a false stamp of approval were unquestionably making their way into foreign markets. General economic decline, of course, but likely also its now undependable wares help explain the shrinking of the city's Advent or Saint Katherine's Day market. In an effort to rejuvenate it, the council moved it in 1540 to the day after Saint Nicholas's Day, in other words, to the first Sunday in December.[78]

In 1541 the council and the woolweavers' guild were able to agree on principles governing the acquisition of woad. Only the Four Masters could buy it, and only enough to supply the needs of the Zwickau weavers. The local master craftsmen were to purchase what they required from the Four Masters. Two councillors would oversee the woad accounts. They added that inferior cloths were not to receive the city imprint. Disobedience would incur a ruinous ten-florin fine.[79]

The weavers' guild may have been worse off than others in Zwickau, but other artisans were bound to be affected sooner or later. In 1542 the shoemakers were found to be heavily indebted.[80] The *Schuster* were never a controversial group. Their complaints at the annual reception of the new council were mild. There are no mentions in extant records of the shoemakers being fined for violations of their guild constitution. They did not press the council to allow them to change their practices. In short, this is the first time that we hear of any trouble among them. They had, we can be sure, been obliged to pay more to the tanners for hides, who in turn had had to pay more to the butchers, on whose dilemma we have ample testimony. Now the shoemakers' indebtedness and inability to free themselves from it brought the threat of punishment. They were given until Michaelmas 1542 to pay their debts. When they failed to do so, the council gave them an eight-day period of grace, after which it said it would act against the Four Masters.[81] At the end of that time, all offending shoemakers were supposed to be arrested.[82] It seems that they were not, for the council threatened again early in 1543.[83] Finally, the council allotted them two additonal years in which to pay.[84] The bakers' guild was being so obstreperous at this time, conspiring against the council, that the gentlemen no doubt appreciated the shoemakers' docility and were lenient.

By the 1540s the entire city was gripped by inflation. The woolweavers were trying to circumvent the woad dealers by buying and using cheap dyes such as *pressilge*, a dyewood producing red or brownish-yellow hues and coming, as its name implies, from Brazil.[85] The Four Masters were themselves leaders of this conspiracy. These officers were George Walther, Heinrich Gebhard, Peter Graff, and Caspar Teucher.[86] Of great interest is the appearance here of two longstanding rebels against conciliar domination of Zwickau, Heinrich Gebhard and Caspar Teucher. Gebhard was connected with the artisan revolt of 1516, and both these men were avid followers of Thomas Müntzer and Niclas Storch. Of the four only Graff, the richest, had suffered a decline in his fortunes between the two Türkensteuer, though when inflation is taken into account, Teucher had, too (see table 11). Their motives are not clear. They were not benefiting personally in any obvious way from the use of the cheap dyes. The presence of two known opponents of the council among the Four Masters indicates a determination to act contrary to the conciliar will and a sense of knowing better than the members of the ruling circle how to lead the guild out of its financial quandary. They had already demonstrated their self-confidence. The council punished them now and did not allow them to serve as Four Masters again.[87] However, the abuses that they had promoted did not thereby cease, and the council admonished the entire guild in late December 1542.[88]

Reports of short lengths and low quality continued to reach Zwickau. The council admitted in 1544 that the reputation of the guild and of the city had been damaged.[89] It set stiff new fines of nearly six florins for weavers who were repeated violators of the rules and of just under three florins for first-time offenders.[90] These measures wrought no improvement.[91]

The names of four individuals appear as opportunists in exploiting the weavers' economic embarrassment. They are Ratsherr Michel von Mila; his brother Melchior, who among other things misused his wife's property; Ratsherr Bonaventura Werner; and Hans Opel, an inveterate and immoderate wife-beater who was finally exiled in 1541 for his

TABLE 11
ECONOMIC STATUS OF 1542 FOUR MASTERS
OF WOOLWEAVERS' GUILD
(In Florins)

	1531	1542
Georg Walther	320	360
Heinrich Gebhard	120	150
Peter Graff	820	750
Caspar Teucher	340	340

SOURCE: Türkensteuer, ZSA, Ax AII 16, Nr.12.

80

domestic transgressions.[92] In 1533 the entire woolweavers' guild, evidently led in this undertaking by a councillor, Georg Hechelmoller, appealed to the elector to intervene. They said that Bonaventura Werner had contrived, to his own advantage, to exclude them from the purchase of raw wool in the administrative district (*Amt*) of Weimar.[93] It is credible that Werner had tried and was now reprimanded by the prince, for the following year the von Mila brethren petitioned their ruler to award them a monopoly of this trade in Amt Weimar;[94] Johann Friedrich declined.

In 1534 the woolweavers complained to the council "that Herr Michel von Mila, city Vogt, and Hans Opel with their violation [of the laws] chase the woolweavers away from the wool buying at the nobles' [estates]. In particular this happened to the Gebhards at the [manor of the] knight von Meussebach."[95] Once again the Gebhard name! Hans Gebhard was just as radical as his brother Heinrich. An unstated number of weavers approached von Mila in 1544 begging for time to remit what they owed him. Herr von Mila's assets grew from 3,163 florins in 1531 to over 6,000 in 1542. This was one of the most dramatic increases in the city. By 1542 von Mila owned much land near Zwickau, at least three rental houses in town besides the one he occupied, and was referred to as a dealer in "oxen, wool cloth, debt, and other." The "debt" is especially intriguing. He bought up debts held by other people and was probably also a primary lender to people who asked him. He sold wool on credit to weavers who were unable to pay outright. The needs of others had clearly become his gain by 1544.

The allegations of some scholars that early capitalists in Zwickau invested money in ways that brought about the subjection of ordinary workers would require much documentation, which has not yet been provided.[96] Von Mila may have attempted such subjection in a crude way, but if he succeeded at all, it was only temporarily. Karl Steinmüller's statement that Zwickau entrepreneurs created workshops (*Verlage*) and employed numbers of weavers is simply not borne out by the sources.[97] There were greedy, shrewd, unscrupulous individuals who turned other people's misfortune into their profit; but they did not succeed in Zwickau in establishing anything resembling factories, nor was their behavior ever anything but exceptional. Moreover, these opportunists were not always city folk. Some of Zwickau's knightly neighbors and better-off peasants saw the gain to be realized in raising wool and livestock for the Zwickau market, and for other, rival markets. The noble Reuss family von Plauen zu Greiz was one of these.

The Reuss slandered Zwickau in 1545, and the council ordered the weavers and the butchers not to buy from them anymore.[98]

Some artisans found their circumstances intolerable and decided to leave the city. The council warned them that if they departed without paying off all their debts, they would lose their citizenship and could never return.[99] It did not add that it would also deny them the usual letter of testimony to their good standing, without which it was hard to enter a trade in any other city.

At the same time, poor people who had left their own hometowns under a similar cloud were regularly arriving in Zwickau, hoping to begin a new life there. They were bringing their wives "and many children," and this was disadvantageous, the council said, to established burghers. The councillors resolved to examine the newcomers' credentials carefully, to interrogate them closely as to their life and morals, and to allow them to settle only if there were room in their particular craft.[100]

Tax records to the contrary notwithstanding, inflation hurt Zwickau badly. The councillors, mostly well-intentioned men, ever saw rigorous discipline, applied by them, as holding out the only hope of economic recovery. Having had no experience of such matter, they knew no other course. They were as befuddled as the masses, even if they as property owners suffered far less. From our perspective the magistrates offered hardly one constructive suggestion to the debt-ridden population. Innovation and experimentation were to be strictly avoided. When a baker wanted to convey his bread to market by means of a horse, he was forbidden since not all the other bakers had horses.[101]

The councillors did not know either what to do about indebtedness. Here they did have personal experience, for many had borrowed from the *neuherrengeld*, from the *unmundige kindergeld* (money held in trust for minor children), from the community chest after its foundation in 1523, and from the assets of the council and the city. Provided they had the consent of a majority of their colleagues, which was by no means always forthcoming, the councillors could borrow from public coffers. They did this perhaps too readily. The modern economist seems ever to be proclaiming that credit is the lubricant of the economic machine; but in Zwickau in the sixteenth century, assets were all in considering credit-worthiness, expendable income nothing. It strikes this observer that many comfortable gentlemen and some well-provided widows had so little cash available that they could hardly pay their property taxes or the Turkish tax; thus, they should not have been allowed to borrow money. Without pecuniary flexibility, not even the magistrates could be relied on to repay what they had borrowed. They often passed their encumbrances along to their heirs, who were obliged to pay. Occasionally the family dwelling itself had to be sold off to obtain cash. Lenders of public revenue seem not to have inquired what a prospective borrower's income was, much less how he proposed to use the loan.

Viewed as a group, the citizens of Zwickau did increase their public indebtedness between 1531 and 1542. The value of debts to the community chest and to the council could be deducted from taxable assets in calculating a person's worth for purposes of the Türkensteuer. It is questionable how accurately such debts were recorded in 1531, for only two individuals, both councillors, took advantage of this right. Had the possibility not been publicized to the whole community? Perhaps the community chest was not yet openly treated as a source of loans. In any case, in 1542 sixty persons of varying station had borrowed from the community chest or from the council, and the total of these debts was slightly under eight thousand florins.[102] As this is a negligible sum when compared with the total value of property in the city at the time, one could not conclude on the basis of the tax records that Zwickauers bore an overly heavy burden of debt. Yet the councillors expressed concern that people were unwisely tapping the communal sources, and under electoral pressure they set dates by which people were at least to have made substantial payments on the principal of their loans. In the end they failed to observe these deadlines.

If citizens were increasingly and injudiciously laden with debts, they must have borrowed heavily from one another. We have only a few examples of people doing so, one of them being the indebtedness for raw wool of a number of weavers to Michel von Mila. This kind of encumbrance was strictly between individuals, and no unified civic record was made of it. These debts were not taken into account when figuring how much Türkensteuer a person owed, and so conjecture on their magnitude and frequency is not possible. All available examples, however, do support the contention that more Zwickauers were indebted in 1542 than had ever been before.

One type of loan with which the citizenry seems to have been familiar all along is the mortgage. People borrowed from one another in order to buy a house. This seems in the main to have been a matter of agreement between the seller and the purchaser, the latter making payments over time to the former. But up until inflation made itself felt in the city, Zwickauers did not often borrow heavily for other purposes. They paid in cash to meet their daily expenses, or they went without. Gradually, as we have seen, an undetermined number of craftsmen were compelled to borrow the raw materials of their trades. If they had been able simultaneously to raise the prices they charged for their shoes or their cloth, they would have been all right. But the council stonily held down prices along with wages. When, as in the case of meat, the city fathers relented at all, they were insufficiently permissive to enable an artisan to cover the costs of his raw materials and realize a profit. Under these circumstances, indebtedness had to be tolerated.

The council occasionally remitted the outstanding city taxes of its friends. This was supposed to be secret, but the people quickly found out. The masses were more than annoyed because they felt terribly burdened by taxes but had no entree into the charmed circle of the magistrates' beneficiaries. In 1519 the people submitted a list of nineteen grievances to the council, item 3 of which was "about remission of debts."[103] Those in power did not change their ways. The council either suborned or rewarded bladesmith Wolff Koch periodically forgiving his debts.[104]

The Role of the Elector

Over-reliance on one product, inflation, and ill-conceived methods of counteracting it were major causes of Zwickau's economic plight. There were others—or if they do not deserve to be labeled causes, they were at least aggravators of the problem. The electors' own efforts to extract ever greater revenues from the cities, and their apparent inability to deal decisively with their knights' and even their own officials' diversion of the major trade route away from Zwickau were partly to blame.

Every level of government regarded all levels beneath it as potential sources of income. This was nothing new in the Reformation era. City account books mention the following taxes with regularity, many applicable to all but some only to persons in a particular craft: *bankzins* (for having a stall in the marketplace); *hauszins* (not defined); *ladenzins* (probably for having a shop on one's premises); *kammerzins* (not defined); *geschoss* (property tax); *circkelgelt* (for guarding walls and streets); *marktgelt* (for selling in the market); *hirtengelt* (for using the community shepherds); *bretengelt* (a sales tax on lumber); *salzgelt* (a sales tax on salt); *thurzoll* (not defined); *tuchzoll* (possibly for offering woolen cloth for sale in the drapers' hall); *ochsenzoll* (for bringing livestock into city domains); and *schlachtzoll* (for slaughtering livestock). Then there were territorial imposts. Frederick the Wise had long since levied on his subjects a forest tax for cutting timber and a beverage tax (*getränkezehnt*) for brewing.[105] Long before the Reformation period, he had collected money (*heerfahrtgeld*) for the war against the Turks (e.g., 1492, 1501). Johann demanded an onerous heerfahrtgeld in 1525 and a Türkensteuer in 1528; Johann Friedrich imposed heerfahrtgeld in 1542 and again in 1546. In 1534 Johann Friedrich, out of money because of his own prodigality and the costs of his military enterprises, raised the forest tax, which had previously ranged between one pfennig and six pfennig a *klaffter*, to nine pfennig per klaffter.[106] Johann and Johann Friedrich announced new Turkish taxes in 1531 and 1542 respectively, just when inflation was severely afflicting the cities. In 1542 Johann Friedrich devalued the Ernestine florin, making it equivalent to twenty-four groschen instead of twenty-one.[107] This had no immediate effect on Zwickau because the people largely ignored it, perhaps until a modicum of stability was achieved again after the Schmalkaldic War.

In their perpetual need of money, the princes had sold monopolies on certain trades to cities. Chemnitz possessed a monopoly on commercial linen production. The elector had allowed Zwickau to establish its own guild of linen weavers in 1500–1501. Peter Schumann recorded that a city bleaching house was erected in 1513.[108] This was done in accordance with an electoral decree.[109] The citzens of Chemnitz vehemently protested the building of this house.[110] The Zwickau guild flourished, and Chemnitz, an Albertine city, never ceased to complain about what it perceived to be a violation of the terms of its monopoly. Consequently, Johann Friedrich curtailed Zwickau's commercial linen production in 1541.[111] In 1542 no journeymen in this profession were identified, and there were fewer masters than in 1531.

Pewter and tin manufacture, which the much jeered Burgomaster Lasan ever tried to promote, met a similar fate. Brunswick and Goslar had enjoyed regional predominance here. When the elector defeated Heinrich von Braunschweig in 1542, Zwickau's councillors hastened to request part of their business.[112] Most of the pertinent documentation is missing. The prince did grant Zwickau one quarter of Goslar's rights, but even so, in 1543 the city's dealers in pewter and tin wares announced to the council that they were giving up the trade.[113]

Most amazing of all Johann Friedrich's interventions in his city's economy was his decision to concentrate in Altenburg the grain trade of the entire administrative district (*Amt*) of Altenburg, which included Zwickau. The councillors in February 1546 vigorously protested to their prince that Zwickau's grain market, which had always done well, was being ruined as a result of the elector's order that neither peasant nor wagoner in the entire Amt could take grain to the Zwickau market until he had offered it for sale in Altenburg. The council pointed out that Altenburg could produce no proof of such a privilege, and that the practice conflicted with all prior custom. Johann Friedrich refused to reconsider.[114]

Perhaps individually these were not ruinous developments. They do, however, point up two realities of early sixteenth-century economic life rather vividly. Even if Zwickau had seen the need to diversify its means of livelihood, it could not simply have taken action to do so. The rigid bonds of tradition held it and other cities tightly, as did the more muscular princely arm. Just as guildsmen were not free to innovate or to outdo their colleagues in creative ways, so neither could cities. Chemnitz held dominion over linen production and would brook no competition. Further, very little could be done without the princely blessing. Nor was his negligence or distraction a certain boon. The land between marketplaces was his to secure, and if his representatives failed to do their jobs, appeals were drawn out and action long in coming.

A number of examples of the electors' imperfect dominion over knights and officials could be cited, but most are not relevant to Zwickau's economic decline. One is, and that is some nobles' persistent and partly successful efforts to divert the main commercial highway away from Zwickau. In the huldung of September 1519, guild leaders denounced to the council attempts to detour traffic to Schonfels and Werdau, six or seven miles to the west of Zwickau.[115] The butchers added that they were being forced to pay the earls of Schönburg *geleit*, a fee for escort and safe passage that had never been demanded before.[116] During the 1520s matters grew worse. The smiths petitioned the council in 1521 "to bring the highway back into the city," as though it had been entirely displaced to the west. In October 1521 the council in turn beseeched Duke Johann to investigate, and he replied in a manner that suggested that he had never been apprised of these developments before. He expressed dismay at the diversion and promised immediate rectification.[117] As no improvement resulted, the council approached Johann again in April 1523.[118] In January 1524 Peter Weingeln, Schösser in Plauen, described the situation from his perspective: "Most of the wagons coming from Hof were accustomed to go to Ölsnitz, and therefore I could not lead them from there to Zwickau on the Plauen Road (*plauensche stras*). And when they came back fully laden from Leipzig, they took the side road, namely through Pegau, Zeitz, Gera to Schleiz." He went on that the nobles in Falkenstein and Auerbach and the Trutzschler family were encouraging this. He himself, he added, always complied with electoral directives.[119]

It took the elector six more years to make a thorough inquiry. In December 1529 the council reported to Johann on negotiations that had just taken place in Zwickau between the councillors and the prince's *Amtsmänner* at Werdau, Plauen, Weida, and Pausa, all local nobles themselves. It turned out, they told him, that there were not one but four alternate routes, all bypassing Zwickau (see the map, p. 88):

1. Hof−Schleiz−Gera−Pegau
2. Hof−Plauen−Ebersdorf−Gera−Pegau
3. Hof−Ölsnitz−Schneeberg−Chemnitz
4. Hof−Plauen−Mila−Werdau−Altenburg.[120]

The council recommended that he punish transporters (*furleute*) who used the illegal byways with a three-florin fine for the first offense, a six-florin fine for the second, and corporal punishment the third time.[121] One of the council's concluding remarks is highly pertinent to the issue of diversion: the gentlemen describe the main thoroughfare, the legal one through Zwickau, as being in such terrible physical condition that the wagoners can get through only with difficulty (*schwerlich*); and they urge Johann to order the cities and Amt officials to improve it, especially "since fees for escort are taken and tolls collected for that purpose."[122]

The shifting of the highway away from Zwickau continued at least into the 1530s. It is impossible to say precisely what effect this had on Zwickau's fiscal state, but this was not a salubrious evolution. How often have we today viewed the wrecks of previously thriving towns along roads left to their potholes after a new freeway opened a mile or two away? Zwickau's innkeepers, shopkeepers, and producers of small goods benefited from the traffic to and fro through their city. If this diminished, so did their livelihood. The habitual use of other routes to

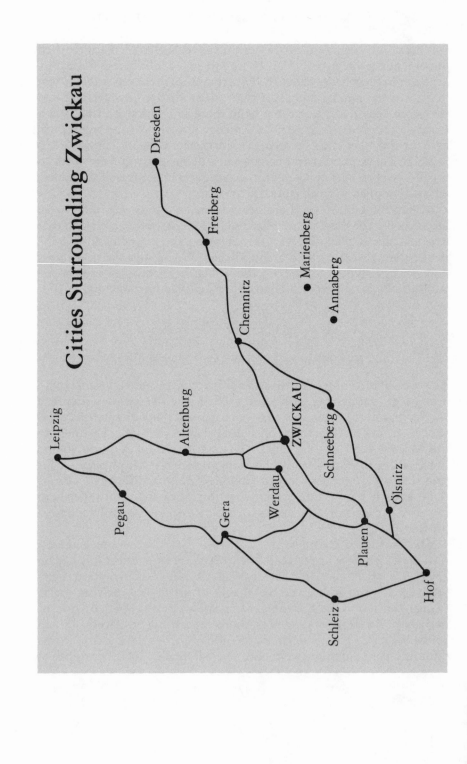

Cities Surrounding Zwickau

and from Leipzig pushed Zwickau back upon its one traditional export, woolen cloth. As we have seen, the woolweavers were less and less able to support Zwickau's economy on their own.

The Reformation and the Economy

Zwickau's problems were besetting and complex. Schneeberg and other Vogtlandish towns were bound to develop their own guilds and markets. Inflation affected everybody in Europe from the 1520s, not just Zwickauers. Fernand Braudel has concluded that all Europe in the mid-sixteenth century came to the end of a long period of prosperity and extraordinarily high living standards and began to decline.[123] The Zwickau council's attempts to find a palliative in discipline were in themselves damaging. Modern economists' theories about inflation, however, have proved to this lay observer not only contradictory but little better able to lead mankind out of its labyrinthine difficulties today. Thus, one can only be humble in pronouncing upon the city fathers' remedies in the sixteenth century. It is entirely clear that their cures did not help the patient.

I cannot maintain that the establishment of Lutheranism in Zwickau effected a revolution in the economic arena. The Reformation does not mark an economic watershed, nor do the alleged attitudes of Calvinist scions in the seventeenth-century Low Countries, England, or New England alter this fact. What did happen in Zwickau was that the city fathers took, along with all other powers, every aspect of economic regulation squarely, openly into their own hands. Whereas in 1500 the guilds had a measure of autonomy in routine matters, by 1530 the council had forbidden guild meetings unless it gave permission beforehand and unless its representatives were present; it either appointed or approved most guilds' Viermeister; it had altered guild articles to make them fully compatible with its authoritarian vision; and it had taken unto itself the direction of every economic decision, every activity. We have seen in part, and shall see more completely, how the crisis of the Reformation led to princely confirmation of conciliar rule. The craftsmen were as a consequence implicitly relieved of any obligation to find their own solutions to economic deterioration. They sensed this, and their attitude toward the preemptive Herren was one of expectation—expectation that the arrogant patricians could and would lead the city out of its woeful condition. When the gentlemen only issued decrees concerning the repayment of craftsmen's debts, pronounced upon weavers' infractions, and threatened the common people with fines and imprisonment, the artisans' already considerable scorn for the magistrates grew apace. The Lutheran Reformation strengthened not only the councillors' certainty of their right to govern absolutely but also their conviction that discipline and the contented, unquestioning, unaspiring, non-innovative production by each man and woman in his or her little corner of the city would ultimately return Zwickau to health. The Reformation was in no way responsible for inflation or the widening chasm between rich and poor, but it played its part in making realistic curative measures more improbable than ever.

The princes for their part were tradition-bound. They looked backward to the familiar rather than around to imaginative innovation in their attempts at ordering the larger Ernestine economy. They protected deleterious urban monopolies granted in ancient charters; or, if they wished, they brought them to an end by fiat. They cared not if their prodigious gambling or war and preparations for war ultimately worsened their subjects' lives. They were men of their day. However hard they, and in particular Johann Friedrich, tried to bring every aspect of government, trivial and local as well as large and territorial, within their purview, they failed to do so. Not even the determined Johann Friedrich, conqueror of Brunswick, could quite make his nobles do his bidding; nor in an age threatened by war could he circumvent his warrior class by turning government entirely over to members of the bourgeoisie. Schösser, of non-noble provenance, did more and more, but the knightly Amtsmänner could not be dispensed with. They and their relatives, doing as they pleased, helped undermine Zwickau's economy. Theirs is not the primary blame, but they helped.

Despite Zwickau's troubles, most of those people who had established themselves financially by 1531 continued to do well enough. Much of what business there was went their way. Those few who could invested in land, and that land gave them flexibility to produce what the market demanded. The few entrepreneurs there were seem not to have specialized in one product, much less to have presided over anything resembling a factory. Few men accumulated great capital or did with it what one expects capitalists to do, invest in a particular enterprise or industry. A handful of unscrupulous men, Burgomaster Michel von Mila among them, manipulated the wool market to their advantage, but the council took at least some measures against such activities. The obstacles to unfettered accumulation were greater than the self-aggrandizers could surmount. Nevertheless, the unprincipled all too

90

often had ties to the council. I suspect some councillors of shedding crocodile tears on behalf of "the poor masters."

Zwickau remained up to the Schmalkaldic War a one-product town in what was becoming ever more an economic backwater. Leipzig was increasingly at the center of the stream. Zwickau's part of Germany had always been profoundly rural; not even the hopes, dreams, and investments of its few cosmopolitan citizens could alter that. Its economy was so fragile that even small misfortunes threatened it. It was already in marked decline by the time Emperor Charles V transferred its territorial matrix from the Ernestine Johann Friedrich to the Albertine Moritz of Saxony in 1547. Moritz's troops may have sealed Zwickau's fate, but they did not bring the city low all by themselves.

Humanist Oratory, Radical
Revelation, Conciliar Resolve:
The Coming of the Reformation

Without the Reformation, Zwickau would never have attracted the attention of modern scholars. Indeed, without the Reformation, patriotic native sons and daughters would have been hard pressed to establish their city's claim to fame. Antiquarian accounts of the town's "blossom time" have always focused narrowly on the glory of the Lutheran victory on the banks of the Zwickauer Mulde during the decade of the 1520s. This crucial period of struggle and transformation demands to be treated in the three portions into which it naturally falls: the early, experimental, still somewhat tentative first five years, 1520 to 1524; the decisive Peasants' War of 1525; and the years of consolidation, 1526 to 1531.

Martin Luther's emergence into the European limelight after 1517 permitted people of every station not just to go on criticizing the Catholic church—already in 1500 a venerable and universal pastime—but seriously to consider alternatives. Luther for a time naïvely believed that all similarly dissident eyes would focus on him, or on the scripture as interpreted by him. His disillusionment took more than a decade to complete.

Luther served as a catalyst for change. In Zwickau a number of individuals entertained varying notions of the form that that change should take. The years from 1518 to 1526 were full of suspense as news of late developments spread by word of mouth and people wondered how the mounting tensions over religion would be released. Some men in ruling circles were early attracted to the Lutheran message. Luther himself regarded Hermann Mühlpfort, a member of Zwickau's city council from 1510, as an admirable Christian magistrate: he dedicated his pivotal treatise of 1520, "On the Freedom of a Christian Man," to

Mühlpfort. Luther was not acquainted with Mühlpfort and misnamed him Hieronymus.

Zwickau was at no time without its ties to Wittenberg. Many Zwickauers knew of all major events there.[1] The elector maintained a residence in Wittenberg, which kept the traffic of government flowing in and out. The presence of one of the three regional universities there from 1502 attracted some sons of Zwickau, though before Luther's ascendance, Leipzig, being closer, was oftener visited. Stephan Roth, studying in Wittenberg, reported to Hermann Mühlpfort on events there, and he married Ursula Kruger, sister-in-law of Georg Rhaw, Wittenberg's printer.

These and many similar anecdotes reveal that Zwickau's educated and governing class had had, and continued to have, knowledge of what was going on in Wittenberg and were more susceptible to its and other cities' influences than the common people were. These individuals made up Zwickau's "scribal" society. Judging by the frequency and intensity with which the guilds petitioned the city council for public scribes and reckoners, we must conclude that the portion of society with direct access to the written word was small, distinctly in the minority.

Bernd Moeller's famous contention that without the book (or pamphlet) there could have been no Reformation needs some modification for rural eastern Germany, but it is perhaps not altogether inaccurate. Subsequent scholarship, notably that of Robert Scribner, has pointed out that pictures too were printed and disseminated among the "simple folk." In addition, preachers and other literate persons conveyed the message of the printed word to analphabetic populations.[2] Hence, sophisticated ideas from Luther and the Wittenberg theologians did make themselves heard by means of their agents, formal and informal, in Zwickau.

The problem was, from the Lutheran point of view, that no method of supervision and control both over the exposition of these ideas and over the agents yet existed in these years of flux from 1518 through 1525. The religious picture in this period was highly individualistic and frequently changing. It must have been a most important psychological moment when word went round in the middle of 1521 that Frederick the Wise was not going to bend the knee to pope or emperor and turn Luther over to ecclesiastical authorities. Wherever the people may have speculated that Luther was during his sojourn in the Wartburg, they must have suspected the elector's collusion. If the church had possessed the renegade Augustinian, it would surely have announced this with pride and severity. That it did not, that it could not, was fraught with significance.

Critics of the church from every level of society now took courage. Circumspectly at first, then with fewer inhibitions, they spoke and they acted as they chose. Anticlericalism was rife. In 1521 there was as yet no reason to regard any of these fault-finders as more libertine than Luther himself. They were true to the spirit of the missing friar. As for his teachings, how could anyone be sure at this early date what they were? How could anyone foresee that once formulated they would receive princely and magisterial backing and would be proclaimed the orthodox and only acceptable doctrines? How could subsequent generations condemn Carlstadt, Storch, or Müntzer for the inaccuracy of their prophetic vision?

Many different voices were heard during this latitudinarian interlude, and the people welcomed the entertainment that the homilists provided. Zwickau being no metropolis, forms of popular recreation were usually of the modest, mundane variety. If the preachers larded their sermons with attacks on the city councillors or on each other, then how much more exciting a break in daily routine attendance at services was. Attraction to preachers who could arouse popular sentiment characterized the late Middle Ages and was not a sixteenth-century novelty.[3]

Johannes Wildenauer Egranus

Within our immediately pre-Reformation setting, the people of Zwickau were entertained and divided by a passionate dispute between the preacher in Saint Mary's Church, Johannes Wildenauer (called Egranus because he came from Eger, on the Bohemian side of the border of the Margravate of Bayreuth), and the Zwickauer Franciscans. Egranus had taken the master of arts degree in Leipzig in 1507 and was very drawn to humanism, particularly humanist biblicism.[4] He objected strenuously to the myth of the three marriages of Saint Anne, mother of the Virgin, which was not only popular in Zwickau but given formal status by its inscription in Saint Mary's Church on the Stoss-Wolgemut altar. Egranus, like Jacques Lefevre d'Etaples before him and Martin Luther after, found the story of Saint Anne unbiblical and denounced it from the pulpit.[5] The Franciscans then castigated Egranus and his views.

Egranus also pressed for simplification of ritual and the elimination of those observances not found in scripture. He urged the city council to stop the custom of burning candles in the church on Saint Sebastian's Day. The gentlemen resolved to burn them anyway, in keeping, they said, with age-old practice; but they agreed not to allow an unseemly "magnificent" display of candles.[6] Egranus's sentiments are fully consistent with his humanist sympathies; they should not be labeled Protestant.

The conflict between Egranus and the Zwickau Franciscans was just one more episode in a thoroughly familiar pattern of intra-ecclesiastical bickering. When it burst upon the scene in 1517, the city council was not yet accustomed to rendering opinions in doctrinal controversies. These were resolved by the bishop's staff in Naumburg. In 1517 and after, the councillors generally sided with Egranus because, as members of Zwickau's small educated class, they appreciated the clergyman's humanistic proclivities, his persuasive delivery, his rational appeal to scripture, his seriousness about his clerical duties, and his upright life. Too, they, along with many non-patricians, wished to narrow the influence of the mighty Franciscans in parish affairs.

The city council consistently went out of its way to keep Egranus, who found the vicious assaults first of the friars, then of Thomas Müntzer, unendurable. It gave Egranus one hundred florins on one occasion to reduce his accumulated debts[7] and forty florins on another.[8] It added a number of fringe benefits to his compensation. It ordered a brand new preacher's house to be built in Saint Mary's parish.[9] It summoned the Franciscans' reading master and their terminary and reprimanded them early in 1518 and periodically thereafter warned them and their community to desist.[10] Throughout, the council had two concerns: to keep a preacher that appealed to it and to maintain public order. It made no effort to determine whether Saint Anne had had three husbands and borne three daughters named Mary.

Thomas Müntzer

The situation became more tense and complex after Thomas Müntzer's arrival in May 1520.[11] Only with the coming of this controversial man can one begin to speak of a Protestant Reformation in Zwickau. Ironically, Egranus may have helped Müntzer obtain a preaching post in Zwickau: Luther introduced Egranus and Müntzer at the Leipzig Disputation, and possibly through Egranus's mediation the council asked Müntzer to substitute for Egranus while the latter was on leave, traveling and visiting Willibald Pirckheimer, Beatus Rhenanus, and other humanists.[12]

When it agreed to hire Müntzer as its preacher, the council can have been in no doubt about his temperament. Before coming to Zwickau, Müntzer had established a reputation as a thoroughly outspoken critic of the church. This was the basis of the temporary, fragile bond between Müntzer and Luther as it was of that between Egranus and Luther. Luther had written to the Franciscans in Jüterbog about Müntzer in 1519,

> I don't know what Thomas preached. But I do know that in this matter too your wickedness has betrayed itself. When he has attacked prelates, popes, and bishops in general, he has [done] not only what is permissible but what ought to be done. [You would not oppose this] if you did not wish to deny and hinder the holy writ. For in [scripture] Christ censures [his opponents as] thieves, robbers, and wolves; you want to make him [Müntzer] guilty for this. You would have been correct if he had mentioned individuals by name. But *you* are the ones who deprive people of their good reputation; you are the slanderers. You neither read nor understand anything. All your arguments amount to what comes into your head, which you then say openly. When will you give him and us satisfaction for such severe defamation?[13]

That same year the Leipzig Dominican Johann von Weida accused Müntzer.

> To the honorable Magister Thomas Müntzer, confessor in Cloister Beudnitz. First of all: greeting such as you deserve and seek with your slanderous writings. For you mix the bitter gall of calumny in with the sweetness of love, love which actually does not exist in you at all. You call a person praiseworthy all the while you find fault with him. It comes out of all this that you are lacking in virtue but are filled with poisonous ambition.[14]

When Müntzer took up his duties in Zwickau in May 1520, he understood that his position was temporary. The council throughout Müntzer's residence discussed persuading Egranus to return, but this apparently had nothing to do with attitudes toward Müntzer. When Egranus did come back brieflly, from October 1520 until April 1521,

Müntzer was content to move over to a vacant preacher's post at Saint Katherine's Church. The council's generally favorable attitude toward Müntzer did not now deteriorate. When it became apparent that Egranus would not stay, and even after relations between the two preachers had soured, the council was willing to contemplate having Müntzer transfer back to the principal church, Saint Mary's, or at least to have him recommend a new preacher.[15] Thus, most councillors remained for some time outside the preachers' fray.

At first Müntzer's sermons were chiefly anti-Catholic. This coincided nicely with the antipathy many citizens were feeling for the Franciscans, whose tiff with Egranus had sharpened public hostility toward them. Müntzer's early opinions, voiced from the pulpit of Saint Mary's, seemed a natural complement to those of the absent Egranus. One of his most famous comments was that the Franciscans had such big mouths that one could well cut a pound from each and they would still have mouths enough.[16] Such declarations struck a sympathetic chord in the minds of certain powerful members of the city council. Foremost among these were Burgomaster Laurentius Bärensprung, who had a master of arts degree from the University of Paris, and one of the city judges, Hermann Mühlpfort.

The friars were not thrilled to have this new, highly articulate, and uninhibited adversary. They reported Müntzer's remarks to the electoral court, whose representatives inquired of the council more than once. On 13 June 1520, the council's secretary recorded that the Rat had had to apologize "again" in reply to a letter from "doctore schmidbburgs des Cantzlers" that had accused Müntzer of "ranging too far and coarsely" in his sermons.[17] These complaints did not alarm the council, which reiterated its wish to retain Müntzer in Saint Katherine's Church even if Egranus should return to Saint Mary's.

In late August 1520, again at the Franciscans' behest, an electoral commission called the contending parties to a hearing. The council now thought it best to tread lightly. It resolved "not to give the master [Müntzer] its support this time but to say to the master that it will see how the discussions go and what the suggestions will be. If reproaches were made that he found intolerable, he could then appeal further to the council. In that case the council would not abandon its support of him and would know how to proceed in a fitting manner."[18]

Although in 1520 most of the councillors were still insensitive to the theological content of sermons, and despite the fact that they were accustomed to criticism from the pulpit, Müntzer's ability to arouse the

97

common man gradually began to make them uneasy. After 19 August 1520, some unsophisticated folk may even have believed that Müntzer had the power to bring disaster upon sinners. During his second "trial" sermon in Saint Katherine's Church on that day—Müntzer gave two sermons there to see whether the congregation would like to have him as its own preacher—a wooden prop being used while the ceiling was being revaulted fell, harmlessly as it turned out. But the listeners were terrified and nearly trampled one another getting out of the church.[19] The incident demonstrated to the somewhat less credulous councillors, most of whom had been in attendance at the sermon, that Müntzer possessed at least sufficient charisma to pack this small church in the woolweavers' district.

Shortly after, on 22 August 1520, both appointed elders at Saint Katherine's Church, members of the city council, asked to be relieved of their posts.[20] Something was making their tenure as elders less than comfortable. Had some development exacerbated the tensions that already characterized relations between the councilmen and ordinary craftsmen? Were these tensions made still worse by the "great dying" that afflicted Zwickau during the summer of 1520? Scholars have long asserted that the radical Niclas Storch was at work specifically in this congregation at this time. Did this onset of an epidemic heighten either his appeal or the masses' volatility? Were Storch and Müntzer coming to appreciate one another during his period? Whatever the case, the council cannot fully have appreciated the dangers, for it was negotiating Müntzer's transfer to the vacant preachership, and Müntzer was favorably disposed (*gutwillig*) to the idea.[21]

During the Christmas season, Müntzer's passion and condonation of violence could no longer be ignored. He directed his invective against the Catholic pastor of the village of Marienthal, Nicolaus Hofer. Hofer had had the audacity to defend himself and his faith against Müntzer's onslaughts. Further, he was visiting Müntzer's sermon. On detecting Hofer's presence, Müntzer verbally unleashed mob violence. Müntzer's adherents slung filth and rocks after the fleeing priest, injuring him badly. In 1523 a follower of Müntzer murdered Hofer.[22]

In itself Müntzer's behavior was not reprehensible to the council. The Rat was not above marshalling popular action toward the attainment of its own ends. Hofer *was* a dogged papist, after all, utterly averse to change. The council could not wholeheartedly disapprove of victimizing such an ardent representative of the church.

The struggle between Müntzer and the returned Egranus enchanted it less. Müntzer launched his attack on Egranus in November 1520. It is to be recalled that Egranus was, and remained, Catholic. But in these years Catholic was a nebulous designation: technically in 1520 everyone was Catholic. Müntzer made a tactical miscalculation, however, in including Egranus among his foes. The Franciscans were one thing; Egranus was decidedly another. Müntzer failed to make the distinction between them; he assailed Egranus relentlessly. To judge by twenty-four articles that Müntzer posted or had posted against Egranus, Müntzer perceived and detested Egranus's basic conservatism and reluctance to overthrow the Catholic church.[23] He found Egranus too cerebral for his tastes, too abstract, too intellectual, too restrained in his presentations, and altogether just too much like Erasmus, whom Egranus greatly admired.[24] Müntzer and his newfound friends in the poorer Saint Katherine's congregation particularly resented the lengths to which the council went to make Egranus happy in Zwickau. Someone in Müntzer's circle wrote openly to Egranus, "You are the boy of the 'fat pennies' [the rich]. You only want to spend time with the 'big Johns' [*den grossen Hansen*, i.e., the rich and mighty]."[25]

Egranus did make reply to Müntzer, but compared with the Saint Katherine's preacher, he was positively retiring. Müntzer was now accused, probably by a partisan of Egranus, of making common cause with "ordinary louts" (*gemeinen Buben*) so that his spirit would waft into every corner of the city, and of so preaching revolt as to make violence an everday event.[26] Johann Agricola, the Wittenberg theologian, wrote to Müntzer in about April 1521, "Persons who desire the best for you have informed us that you misuse the office of preacher: instead of teaching what is right, you attack other people by name slanderously. . . . To put if briefly, they said you pant for murder and blood."[27]

Only late in 1520 is there any evidence of possible dissension within the council on religious matters. Some of the gentlemen may have become concerned about potential unrest among the people. On 12 December the secretary recorded, "Concerning both councillors Dr. Studeler and Vogt Mühlpfort, it is decided that we shall let the matter between them rest for eight days and in the meantime summon neither one to council meetings but wait and see if they seek the council's clemency. If they do not they should be required [to appear] one after the other and be remonstrated with concerning this behavior that they showed to each other in the presence of both councils and about the need for punishment, etc. And the punishment is not to be remitted."[28]

Mühlpfort is not listed as attending a session again until New Year's Day. Studeler was not present again until 16 February, which may have been because he was ill: he died on 2 April 1521.

It is not certain that Mühlpfort's and Studeler's strife had anything to do with religion. I am inclined to think that it did because of concurrent events in Zwickau, because of Mühlpfort's known affinity for Luther, and because Müntzer was Studeler's confessor. Yet the gentlemen may have been quarreling over almost anything else: conflicts between and among councillors were regular occurrences. Unfortunately for us, the councillors did not want the public to be aware of such conflict and went so far as to discourage explicitness in the minutes even though the minutes were accessible to very few. Too, the city fathers all knew what the issues were and thought it superfluous to describe them.

At year's end the controversy between Müntzer and Egranus came once again to the elector's attention. Someone threw a slanderous note through Müntzer's window. On 10 January 1521, the council requested Vogt Sangner to question Müntzer as to who might have done this.[29] Presumably Müntzer accused Egranus, of whom, however, such a deed would have been quite uncharacteristic. Of course, Egranus's followers could have done it. The bishop of Naumburg tried to involve himself, as was still his right and duty: he cited both preachers to appear before the diocesan consistory in Zeitz. Apparently the council intervened, and they did not go.[30]

We catch the tone of Egranus's retorts to Müntzer from one letter that has survived. Egranus wrote in February 1521, "That you so slanderously used me last Saturday at the castle and otherwise speak ill of me among your drinking companions, also that you screech so devilishly about me from the pulpit—all this I must endure with patience. Perhaps this spirit of yours that you so publicize teaches you these things. If so, continue right on." He asks Müntzer to stick to the truth and promises in return not to criticize Müntzer's teachings any more. He begs Müntzer's pardon for not thinking Müntzer has as sound an understanding as he.[31] As was to be expected, the two men's mutual contempt continued unabated.

As the guarantor of public order if not tranquility, the council discussed various means of damping the coals of unrest. On 4 February 1521, the council voted unanimously (*ayntrechtiglich*) to invite the preacher in neighboring Schneeberg, Nicolaus Hausmann, to come to Zwickau as its pastor. Technically the city had a pastor in the person of the aged Doctor-of-Both-Laws Donat Gross, who, however, had not resided in Zwickau for years but preferred to dwell in Nuremberg. The council did possess the right of patronage over the pastoral position. It did not overly concern itself at this moment with the legal problem of whether it could replace a man who did not wish to be replaced without at least what would normally have been thought good cause. The council was of the opinion that absenteeism was an intolerable abuse and that the Zwickau flock now desperately needed pastoral guidance. Furthermore, it had Frederick the Wise's and his brother Johann's approval in making a bid for a resident pastor. As it turned out, Gross accepted the council's terms in 1522: the council was to pay him sixty florins a year for the rest of his life and also support his cousin from the pastoral benefice until the said cousin died.[32]

The gentlemen's unanimity suggests that the council was not as deeply divided at this time as Helmut Bräuer has asserted.[33] The contentious Erasmas Studeler was, it must be recalled, absent, either because he had failed to make his peace with Mühlpfort or because he lay on his deathbed. But there was no noticeable dissent in the decision for Hausmann, a known devotee of Martin Luther and Luther's own candidate for the post. Of course, the use of *ayntrechtiglich* might also imply that before the vote, at this and prior meetings, the council chamber had been the scene of heated debates. Yet if opposition to Luther's views as then understood had been deep in ruling circles, this *Eintracht* would have been hard to achieve. Although the evidence is spotty, councillors Nickel Partt and Christoff Kühn probably were, as Bräuer says (following Karl Czok who follows Paul Wappler), disciples of Müntzer or Storch.[34] Both Partt and Kühn lived in the eastern half of the city, close to the majority of Müntzer's followers. Nevertheless, if they had been uncompromising, they could not have remained on the council. Even had the majority of the city fathers been willing, the elector would hardly have confirmed any partisan of Müntzer or Storch after 1521. Partt continued on as a councillor until his death in 1539, and Kühn disappears from the roster in 1531–32, a full decade after the turmoil of 1521. The elector, it is true, did see fit to reprimand the gentlemen of the council during these months for the discord among them.[35] In addition, we know that Partt took his religion very seriously. In the mid-1530s, whenever the subject arose of whether Carnival (*Fastnacht*) ought to be celebrated, this man was opposed. In January 1535 he proclaimed, "It was the devil who thought up Carnival!"[36]

This is not to dismiss the contention that some comparatively well-off craftsmen supported Müntzer or other radicals. On the contrary. But what united the councillors was their dislike of the Franciscans and other Catholic wielders of power within what the Ratsherren considered to be properly their own sphere. They were already being driven to make finer distinctions within the broad field of critics of the Catholic church.

Outside the town hall a bellicose spirit spread among the people. Unhappily, our knowledge of it is hindered by the absence of the council minutes for this crucial period. According to Wappler, T. W. Hildebrand, in 1817 deacon in Saint Mary's Church, celebrated the three hundredth anniversary of Luther's posting his ninety-five theses against indulgences by destroying all evidence of the council's treatment of Müntzer in the late winter and spring of 1521. This destruction consisted of ripping out folios 23–35 of the pertinent Ratsprotokolle. Wappler surmises that Hildebrand did this in order to make it look as if the Reformation was without strife in Zwickau and to conceal some less than admirable demeanor on the part of the city council.[37]

Despite the lack of these records, the following account may be given with reasonable certainty. By the new year, the elector and his officials clearly had a lower opinion of Müntzer than the city council did. The council perceived more gradually that Müntzer's popularity was not devoid of negative significance for the council and for public order. A tendency toward violence revealed itself among Müntzer's admirers, and though this was ostensibly in the service of a higher, spiritual cause, it could be fed by widespread popular hostility toward the city council and quickly change its target. On 6 March the council resolved to call the entire community together on the pretext of reading them a new order for the school. Above this it desired to "warn them diligently that no one is to create a cohort [for one of the clergymen] nor to cause a riot, on pain of punishment to his body or property." The clergy (*pristr*) were to be admonished separately.[38]

On 10 April 1521, someone caused panic in this city of wood by shouting, "Fire, fire!"[39] Müntzer and his partisans were suspect. Müntzer denied any part in the episode, afterward writing to Luther, "Everyone, with the exception of the deluded heads of the council, knows that during the unrest I was in the bath suspecting nothing; and that the whole council would have been slain (*interfectus*) the next night if I had not prevented it."[40]

On 14 April, Müntzer or his friends posted a ninety-one-verse satire of Egranus on the Franciscan friary. Egranus had long since given notice, and no doubt the mockery depicted him as fleeing the field of battle. Siegfried Bräuer surmises that Egranus's adherents responded with their own doggerel the very next day.[41] The composition of rhymes came easily to our German forebears.

On 16 April 1521, the elector's *Amtshauptmann* stepped in and left the council no recourse but to dismiss Müntzer. The preacher accepted the twenty-five florins owed him in salary up until 1 May, plus the customary gratuity of five florins that testified to his leaving in good standing;[42] he departed without requesting *geleit*, the protective escort given to honorable men and that secured the passage of endangered persons. Müntzer's most enthusiastic followers, who had come to view their leader as a prophetic figure, now rose up, desiring to provide him this *geleit* out of city territories. This unnerved the council. It ordered the arrest and overnight detention of those who could be apprehended. It imprisoned fifty-six men, mainly woolweavers (*knappen*),[43] for one night only.[44] This was a moderate response by the council. It hoped to squelch rebellion with mildness.

Egranus left his own post as planned and shortly took up a preachership in Joachimsthal. Thus, both men went to Bohemia. Egranus cast a last verbal missile after Müntzer in a letter to Luther written in May:

> Your Thomas—for so he styles himself—came here and made everything topsy-turvy with his insane noise and his teachings. The stubbornness and shamelessness of the man are great. He directs himself in accordance with neither the advice of friends nor the authority of scripture, but supported only by his [purported] revelations he causes nothing but factionalism. This is a person who is born to schism and heresy. But in the end the evil falls upon his own head and he into the pit that he has dug for others. In a disgraceful manner he has taken flight. As is his nature, he has (to the disgrace of this otherwise famous city) had fellow conspirators among the people, folk encumbered with debts, law-breakers, persons given to revolt, whom in the main he attracted to himself through his confessional office and through private conventicles. His poison is the heritage he left behind, for the day laborers scream even yet against every person of rank, every preacher and priest. I hear that the wild beast strews about all sorts of lies concerning me. I must bear that; my conscience and my innocence comfort me. I do not believe that any good and educated man can trust this most mendacious human being.[45]

The question of what Müntzer taught while in Zwickau still wants a precise answer, which, regrettably, is not yet to be found. Siegfried

Bräuer is correct that Müntzer was shaping his "revolutionary theology" while in Zwickau; but shaping is one thing and articulating a full-blown doctrine another. Bräuer is probably right in disagreeing with M. M. Smirin that Müntzer was already proclaiming his new principle of a people's reformation.[46] It is clear that Müntzer already claimed to be the recipient of divine messages. Between August and November 1520, Müntzer added an entirely new theme to his sermons: having previously directed his scathing sermons against Catholic church and Catholic leaders, he now added revilement of the rich and of secular authorities. This transformation in his message seems to have happened so fast that the councillors had not fully comprehended its significance for themselves before the electoral official stepped in and forced Müntzer's departure. Those in Saint Katherine's congregation would certainly have welcomed the preacher's new sentiments; their own hostility toward the council reached back over a decade and was becoming part of the pattern of their lives. Egranus's parting comments above do hint, though they do not prove, that Müntzer was already becoming an exponent of social and economic equality during the half-year or so before his dismissal.

The search for the Müntzer of early 1521 is complicated by our inability to differentiate between the views of Müntzer himself and those of the Zwickau Prophets, and even the views of their respective followers, if respective groups there were.[47] Müntzer left a vacuum on his departure that other charismatic types could easily step into. We should avoid the temptation to conclude that Müntzer emphasized revelation to the extent, or in the same way, that Storch did by the time he got to Wittenberg in late December, or indeed that the men's beliefs were identical in any respect.

Radically inclined women in Zwickau preferred Müntzer's teaching on marriage to Storch's. Storch was said to be unchaste himself and to advocate abstaining from marriage but having the sexual favors of as many women as one wished.[48] When in 1529 the church visitation committee questioned several women about their unorthodox denial of sex to their husbands, they replied that marriage was whoredom, that they were married to Christ, and that no one could serve two masters.[49] This resembles Luther's description of Müntzer's alleged teaching "that a man could sleep with his wife only if, as a result of divine revelation, he was certain that a holy child would result from their intercourse; those who did not live in this manner engaged in prostitution with their wives." Luther continued, "His effect was such that several Zwickau matrons publicly confessed, if they had slept with their husbands, 'This night I have been a whore.' "[50]

Three women followers of Müntzer or Storch—Mrs. Martha Teucher, Mrs. Sophie Kratzber, and the wife of Jorg Vetter—were rumored to lead other women toward this reputedly Müntzerian point of view. Georg Spalatin's collection of their opinions on 26 January 1529 just might inform us about Müntzer's doctrines in 1521. Mrs. Vetter and Mrs. Kratzber denied everything (Mrs. Kratzber later confessed) but Mrs. Teucher described her outlook in some detail. Well-intentioned archivists have concealed portions of her remarks under brown tape, but something can be gleaned from Spalatin's scribbled notation.

Mrs. Teucher professes to follow Christ alone. She cannot obey two masters and belongs to Christ, not her husband. Christ called her in the vineyard and wants her to be his. Christ says, "Dispute and overcome and I will set you upon the th[rone?]."[51] Even if she is many miles away, she is with God. The sacrament is a representation (*pitscher*). The city must be worthy that God is supposed to enter. She knows that she has her faith. She desires to die for Christ's sake and would wish [martyrdom] even if she had three thousand necks. She does not like to go to confession. She admits that she has preached.[52]

One has to be very cautious in drawing conclusions about Müntzer from this summary. By 1529 Austrian Anabaptist ideas were spreading into the area, and if Frau Teucher had preached in the countryside, she might have absorbed some of them. Indeed, Hans Sturm from Freistadt, in Upper Austria, was apprehended inside the city in February 1529, not long after Spalatin's examination of Mrs. Teucher and others.[53] But this woman had been known to the authorities for her dissidence since 1521. Her views had been established in that year or the year before though they could have been modified later.

It is tempting to find in her statement about a city having to be worthy before God entered it a mild version of Müntzer's violent millenarianism. If Müntzer did yell, "Fire, fire!" from his window at 3:00 A.M. on 10 April 1521, can he have hoped to create such a disturbance that he could take over Zwickau and reform it to his liking? Had he thought God said to *him*, "Dispute and overcome," or even "Struggle and conquer, and I will set *you* upon the throne"? Had he perhaps got this notion when the prop had fallen from the church ceiling some months earlier and made the people hysterical? Melanchthon recollected in 1529 that Storch had maintained something similar in 1521:

saints and the elect would rule after the destruction of all the godless, and under his leadership all the kings and princes of the earth would be killed and the church purified.[54] Without further information than we now possess, certainty about the interaction between Müntzer and Storch and their respective ideas must still elude us.

The Zwickau Prophets

A curiosity of Müntzer's sojourn in Zwickau is that until he departed, in fact until several months later, we hear almost nothing about the trio who by December would be calling themselves prophets of God and claiming to enjoy direct communication with the Deity. Niclas Storch was known to Müntzer, for Müntzer praised him from the pulpit of Saint Katherine's Church. He declared that Storch was "raised above all priests as the one who best knew the Bible" and that he was "highly perceptive (*erkannt*) in spirit."[55]

Storch was a member of a fairly numerous family of that name in and around Zwickau. The family probably originated in the surrounding countryside, for the surname appears from time to time in the Schultheiss's records. A Jacob Storch had enrolled in Leipzig in the winter of 1487. A Jacob Storch owned a house in the infamous Hundsgasse in or about 1521. Most of the Storchs lived outside the Tränkthor, near the Paradise Bridge.

Niclas was a woolweaver.[56] He may well have traveled into Bohemian territory as a journeyman and there picked up Waldensian, Hussite, and other nonconformist ideas; yet many local knappen did not travel at all but continued on after apprenticeship perfecting their weaving skills right at home. He nevertheless could have been exposed to heretical notions since German-speaking journeymen came from Bohemian and near-lying lands to work in Zwickau. A number came from Eger, Joachimsthal, and Kadan, for example. Bohemian traders regularly offered their wares in Zwickau's marketplace.[57] Zwickau lay near the border and was never immune to currents affecting its southeastern neighbors.[58]

Niclas claimed to be unlettered, and Melanchthon believed him. His claim was probably not true, although he did have a prodigious memory. Melanchthon and Nicolaus von Amsdorf were most impressed by his knowledge of the Bible, and most likely Storch had consulted that authority personally and often.[59] As he forged a link between himself and Zwickau's craftsmen, he found it advantageous to mention his ignorance. A friend of Storch's later described him during his Zwickau years: "I cannot say whether he had special spiritual powers (*einen sonderlichen fliegenden Geist*). He went among the people in such an easy, friendly, and humble manner; he was able to transpose words and make himself appear as devout and holy as one of God's angels. He was a rather slender person who put on no airs whatever, but let himself ever be seen as a simple man, in a long gray gown without folds and wearing a wide hat on his head. But he was an unchaste man."[60]

Insofar as extant documents allow us to examine the situation, Müntzer's influence among the people was greater. Max Steinmetz's conclusion that Müntzer was the more important of the two, not just from the historian and ideologue's point of view but in the eyes of the radicals' Zwickau contemporaries, jibes with available evidence from that city.[61] Karlheinz Blaschke, a non-Marxist historian familiar with the sources, concurs with this.[62] Local dissidents claimed to be Müntzer's adherents first and Storch's second or not at all. In 1522 the council labeled all the dissidents "Magister Thomas's following," and there is altogether less frequent mention of Storch in the documents from 1521 and 1522.[63]

As we know, Luther stressed the sufficiency of the Bible in providing man with knowledge of God's will, whereas Müntzer and Storch came to believe that the Holy Spirit revealed truths superior to those in the Bible to certain people. Both Müntzer and Storch were certain that they enjoyed this divine blessing. In their very self-confidence lay the cause of their ultimate disaffection with one another: at any moment the Spirit might reveal something to one that was incompatible with its alleged message to the other. Luther, who was not inclined to study the details of what he thought were the outrageous tenets of Müntzer or any of the Zwickau Prophets, nonetheless remarked to Spalatin about the irreconcilability of Storch's views with those of Marcus Stübner or of Müntzer in the late summer of 1522, "And the man [Storch] is on nearly every point in conflict with Marcus [Stübner] and Thomas [Müntzer—or perhaps Drechsel!]. He deals only with the issue of baptism and seems to be carried away by a frivolous spirit that does not pay close attention to his own ideas."[64]

Thomas Drechsel was a prominent, home-owning member of Zwickau's smiths' guild. Melanchthon was wrong in calling him a woolweaver.[65] Like most of the other radical leaders of the city, Drechsel was not a member of an oppressed, downtrodden class. He had been a Viermeister of the smiths' guild in 1505–6, 1510–11, and 1517–18.[66] He was a brother of the priest Peter Drechsel (both men were uncles of Stephan Roth) who endowed Zwickau's School Brotherhood in 1519. As such, Thomas seems to have been persuaded, perhaps in the name of family solidarity, to allow himself to be included among that society's founders; his name appears thirty-ninth and last on the list of the Drechsels and their relations by marriage. He was married to a woman whose maiden name was Voit, and he and his wife had at least three sons and a daughter.[67] Thomas Drechsel was not a young man when the Reformation began. Like so many of his neighbors, he must have found aggravating and radicalizing the obvious, often successful efforts of the town councillors to gain in wealth and power at the expense of their fellow citizens.

Drechsel lived in the Tränkviertel, a densely populated artisan district, along the Mulde and susceptible to flooding, where many of Müntzer's disciples were to be found. His home was outside the city gate and probably not very large. He had trouble paying the many taxes demanded of him and was in debt to the city before 1510, in 1510, 1511, 1512, 1517, and 1518. The sums he owed were large if he was just scraping by: an accumulated stall fee (*bankzins*) of 4.29 florins in 1510, payment of which had to be divided over several years; and five groschen in property tax for 1517. Drechsel clearly made an effort to meet his obligations and ultimately did eliminate his debts, yet the record suggests a somewhat precarious economic existence and a continual threat of insolvency.[68]

Marcus, son of Thomas, was called Stübner because his father owned a bathhouse in Elsterberg. Marcus was not a citizen of Zwickau. He came from an adequately comfortable background: the bathhouse owners of Zwickau were quite well off, and one may suppose that this was likewise the case in Elsterberg. Also, sons of truly poor families rarely attended a university, and Stübner had studied in Wittenberg, where he probably met Müntzer. His family could afford the tuition and was motivated, as most of the poor were not, to send its son on for higher education.

Perhaps Stübner was attracted to Zwickau because of his close acquaintance with Müntzer, even though Müntzer was no longer present. Stübner was probably in Wittenberg during some part of June 1521, for in late December, Melanchthon remarked that he had debated with this man six months earlier.[69] Müntzer thought he was in Elsterberg "in the bath," for on 15 June he wrote him there.[70] Stübner accompanied Müntzer to Prague and must have come to Zwickau after that. He was not considered a permanent resident.

Stübner was said by Melanchthon's biographer Joachim Camerarius to be the brains of the Prophets and even to play the dominant role behind the scenes. According to Camerarius, Stübner formulated the Prophets' basic doctrines; but if Luther is correct about their fundamental disagreement, then this could not be true.[71] In any case, Melanchthon respected Stübner's learning.[72]

During the summer of 1521, a lack of beer, everyone's main beverage, rendered the populace even more open to the Prophets' message than otherwise. According to Schumann, the city almost ran out of beer after the council had shortened brewing times for the third time. The city fathers were forced to order more than a hundred barrels in such places as Zschoppau and Schneeberg in order to forestall great suffering among the people.[73] No doubt the masses were furious and volatile.

Nicolaus Hausmann

After Thomas Müntzer's dismissal and departure for Bohemia, such radicals as Storch and Drechsel, shortly joined, we gather, by Stübner, kept the Müntzerian storm from subsiding. At first the new pastor Nicolaus Hausmann, who had arrived in May and had not yet oriented himself, could be of little help. He could as yet command little respect in discontented circles. Too, Storch was an articulate adversary. Hausmann and the council made various attempts to ensure that the members of Saint Katherine's congregation heard regular preaching. In an effort to come up with a permanent preacher who would appeal to the masses and counter the influence of Storch, the council wrote to "Wittenberg and to Leipzig." No wholly satisfactory occupant for the position was immediately forthcoming.

Before the summer was over, however, Hausmann's presence was beginning to alter the religious picture. From the outset the councillors were able to regard the new pastor as one of their own sort. Hausmann's father had been a councillor in Freiberg for years, and his family was highly respected there. In 1492, when Hausmann was fourteen, the father became his princes' *Münzmeister*, overseer of the Wettin mint in Freiberg. Hausmann attended the University of Leipzig and received the bachelor of arts degree in 1499 and the master of arts in 1503.[74] His privileged upbringing may help to explain his spendthriftiness while in Zwickau; but this tendency combined with a deep generosity: he burdened himself with maintaining several poorer clergymen and others. At the time that the councillors voted unanimously to invite Hausmann to Zwickau, he was a preacher in Schneeberg. He was already committed to Luther, and the council was beginning to distinguish between a truly Lutheran position and those of Egranus and Müntzer. Hausmann would not waver during his lifetime.

Hausmann combined self-confidence with trepidation. He often seemed unable to come to a decision in ecclesiastical matters in his new home city without consulting Luther, which eventually irritated both Luther and the city council. Luther wrote to his friend on 24 March 1526, for example, responding to a request from the Zwickau cleric, "You ask me to make a general order of [church] ceremonies. But how can I handle so many matters? I wish that you would draw up a form and send it to me. Do this so that you may contribute something in this business in accordance with your God-given gift."[75]

Having served as a pastor, Hausmann had a grasp of conditions in the parishes that for its realism was superior to Luther's own. It was Hausmann who asserted to Frederick the Wise, Johann, and Johann Friedrich the need for parish visitation in order to eliminate both Catholicism and various abuses. In this Hausmann influenced Luther, who initially believed that sheer preaching of the Word would effect desired reforms.

By August 1521 Pastor Hausmann was so distressed by the "false belief" in Zwickau that he proposed to write a summation of prevalent errors and use this as an aid in holding formal interrogations of those suspected of adhering to wrong doctrines. He begged the council's assistance in these undertakings "in case the people do not wish to be examined."[76]

During 1521 the differences among Egranus's humanistic Catholic, Müntzer's revelational radical, and Hausmann's pro-Lutheran outlooks became apparent, not only to the city fathers but also to Luther. Hausmann promoted what we can confidently refer to as Lutheranism. Because of his labors and the sympathy for specifically Lutheran teachings among leading members of the council, the Lutheran Reformation as such began to take hold in Zwickau. Events outside the city abetted the process of making distinctions and imparted to the magistrates a sense of the need to intervene. During the autumn news continued to arrive of events in Wittenberg, of preaching against the mass, of taking communion in both kinds.[77] No one was certain where such licentious acts would lead or what the authorities' response would be.

In Zwickau the council cooperated with Hausmann. During the second half of 1521, council and pastor proceeded to restrict the activities of the Catholic church. The gentlemen resolved to seek the elector's help in compelling priests to reside rather than fill their offices with low-paid vicars.[78] They discussed ways of combatting the Cistercian outpost, the Grünhainer Hof, whose sway over a number of peasants near the city conflicted with city aspirations. The minutes make oblique reference to a request the council had made through the Schösser apropos of the Cistercians and to which it awaited reply. The scribe mentions some secret activities (*haymlickayten*) that the monks had been carrying on and that the councilmen regarded as illegal. The magistrates decided to renew their subornation of a monk to spy on the Hofmeister.[79]

The council showed its dissatisfaction with the age-old privilege of the Antonites, fattening two swine a year within city limits.[80] They composed and defended to the prince and to diocesan officials a new burial order. The Franciscans attacked the new order because it made no distinction between the corpses of clergy and laity.[81] The council undertook an inventory of all church and monastic treasures (*kleynotten*) "as the councilmen consider that it is good and necessary."[82] The Herren outlawed begging from door to door by any friars or monks in Zwickau. All must stand by the churches and ask for alms "just as poor citizens are obliged to do."[83]

Having spent the first two and a half months of the conciliar year trying to confine Catholic privileges and investigating rumors of Catholic conspiracy, in December the gentlemen were startled to hear compelling stories of a "secret brotherhood" in another quarter. It was said to include woolweavers, but the councillors state explicitly that membership is not restricted to that trade: "Secret brotherhood. Because it has come to the council's attention that the knappen, etc., and other people besides them [intend] to set up a secret brotherhood, out of which no good could be expected, one shall with all diligence, true endeavor, and in secret, appoint [people] to get behind this matter so that then the council can do what is necessary."[84] Part of the misbehavior of the accused was openly singing a song against "the clergy, the popes, bishops, monks and friars." The song was also directed against "well known people and residents." The issues were by no means ex-

111

clusively religious but focused too upon people's demeanor in a secular context. Opposition to the city council was a central motive of the dissidents.

The leading suspects were haled before the clergy and conciliar representatives on 16–17 December. The Zwickau Prophets themselves escaped beforehand. The remaining ringleaders were a weaver, Caspar Teucher (not to be confused with stonemason Caspar Teicher), and his wife, and a probable Austrian journeyman weaver, Hans von der Freystadt. The last held some sort of post from the city, for the secretary records his firing on 14 December. The scribe writes, "There are many factors to take into account as it is reported that von der Freystadt is so bold as to represent things as good in order now and again to cause evil."[85] Clergy and councillors cross-examined fourteen people in all, identifying them as "the Hundtsgesser, etc." All were quizzed on their religious beliefs.

One man, Ludwig Reudnitz, declared, "Whatever person is a sinner is also a heretic before God."[86] One can imagine the remark to which this was a response. Pastor Hausmann gives us the most reliable account of the hearings; on 18 December he summarized the nonconformists' "gruesome" tenets. Some, he said, doubted whether the faith of the godparents aided infants being christened. Some thought the scripture had no power to instruct men, that one must be taught by the spirit alone. "If God had wanted people to be taught by the scripture, he would have sent us a bible down from heaven." One should not pray for the dead. Hausmann describes such doctrines as "unchristian, picardish, and heretical."[87]

Hausmann's summary is astonishingly close to Haubolt von Einsiedeln and Georg Spalatin's reiteration of the Zwickau Prophets' beliefs as they found them. Haubolt and Spalatin's use of the word *some* suggests diversity of opinion among the three radicals—or were they a recipient of Hausmann's letter and taking it for granted that the views of those just questioned in Zwickau were the same as the Prophets'?

> Adults alone should be baptized.
> Some doubt whether the faith of a godparent is helpful to a child at his baptism.
> Some were of the opinion that one could be saved without faith.[88]
> Some say that the scripture is not powerful enough (*zur lare der menschen vncrefftig*) to teach men but that men must be taught by the spirit (*geist*). If God had wanted to teach men with scripture, he would have

sent us a bible down from heaven. The dead are not to be prayed for, and other gruesome errors that give the city of Zwickau an unchristian and picardish reputation.[89]

Armed with such incriminating testimony, the council now moved to punishment. Hans von der Freystadt was put out of the city on 1 January 1522.[90] All the others were informed that their cases were being turned over to Duke Johann. Four who were altogether unrepentant— Stephan Hareinweil, Caspar Jorge, Balthasar Ferber, and Georg Beyreuther—were imprisoned. These men had sought aid from the Schösser against the city council, and the council always regarded such action as a most grave offense regardless of the issues in dispute. One of the four (unnamed) was still in prison on 2 January, but he had finally admitted his error and was to be released "in two or three days."[91]

There are two levels of significance to the council's actions against the dissidents. For the first time, the council was acting in the stead of the bishop's consistory as the definer and guarantor of religious orthodoxy. With the pastor's advice, it was deciding what was acceptable belief and what was not, and it was forcing recantation and imposing punishment. To the extent that they understood it at this early date, they were using Lutheran teaching as their criterion of doctrinal respectability, although at this point they would still have tolerated traditional Catholic views. By any admissible standard, the radicals' convictions were figuratively beyond the pale and if not altered must be placed there physically.

Although ostensibly only religious in concern, these hearings also had their secular aspects. The council was now seeing the dangers inherent in encouraging popular opposition to the Catholic church. The line between preaching on a religious subject and rousing the populace to revolt against civil authority was exceedingly fine. By the end of 1521, the council wanted only those preachers who were content with the existing class and economic divisions in society. The councillors could, as they ever had before, tolerate mild criticism of themselves or unfavorable treatment of a few contemporary political issues from the pulpit, provided that neither criticism nor unfavorable treatment concealed any advocacy of a new social or political order. In 1522 the council went through contortions to obtain preachers who as orators had the power to entertain and win the affection of the people; it wanted them as an antidote to the charismatic political disruptiveness of men like Müntzer and Storch.

TABLE 12
Named Rebels of December 1521
Community and Guild Service

Georg Beyreuther
1519–20	Master of ashes
1526	1 of 4 buyers of raw wool
1532–33	Viermeister of weavers
1534	City councillor

Hans Bruschweyn "the Elder"
1518–19	Master of ashes
1534–35	Examiner of drapery
1535–36	1 of 4 collectors of debts
1539–40	1 of 10 committee of common masters

Baltasar Ferber
—	—

Hans Gebhard
1535–36	City overseer of hospitals
1536–37	City overseer of hospitals
1538–39	City overseer of hospitals
1539–40	City overseer of hospitals

Heinrich Gebhard
1530–31	Master of ashes
1531–32	Master of ashes
1535–36	Viermeister of weavers
1539–40	Viermeister of weavers
1541–42	Viermeister of weavers

Stephan Hareinweil
1510–11	Master of ashes
1516–17	Viermeister of weavers
1518–19	Viermeister of weavers
1520–21	Viermeister of weavers
1522–23	Viermeister of weavers
1526–27	Viermeister of weavers
1529–30	Examiner of raw wool
1530–31	Viermeister of weavers

Caspar Jorge (Georg)
1521–22	Viermeister of weavers
1526–27	Examiner of raw wool
1531–32	Viermeister of weavers

Ludwig Reudnitz
1530–31	Examiner of drapery

Michel Rudolff (Rudloff)
1529–30	Examiner of "wide cloth"

Jacof Schneider
1526–27	Examiner of raw wool
1530–31	*Werffenzeher*[a]

TABLE 12

NAMED REBELS OF DECEMBER 1521

COMMUNITY AND GUILD SERVICE

Hans Tech	
1522−23	Master of ashes
1529−30	Examiner of raw wool
Caspar Teucher	
1526−27	Master of ashes
1539−40	Viermeister of weavers
1541−42	Viermeister of weavers

SOURCE: ZSA, *Amtsbücher*. The *Amtsbuch* is missing for 1523−26.

[a]Related to putting warp on the looms.

TABLE 13

NAMED REBELS OF DECEMBER 1521

QUARTERS OF RESIDENCE AND ECONOMIC STATUS

		1523		1531	
	City Qtr.[a]	Form of Property[b]	Value (in fl.)	Form of Property	Value (in fl.)
Georg Beyreuther	7	hyc	460	hyc	510
Hans Bruschweyn	7	hy	106	hyg	126
Baltasar Ferber	—	—	—	—	—
Hans Gebhard	7	hy	250	hy	220
Heinrich Gebhard	7	hy	130	hy	120
Stephan Hareinweil	7	hyca	630	hyca	700
Caspar Jorge[c]	7	?	?	—	—
Ludwig Reudnitz	7	hy	150	hy	200
Michel Rudolff	?	hy	100	hy	100
Jacof Schneider	5	hy	220	hy	250
Hans Tech	7	hy	210	hy	210
Caspar Teucher	5	hy	65	hy	340

SOURCE: WSA, Reg. Pp 368[2−4]:"Vorzeichnus der ligenden grunden vnd gutter Im Weichbilde der Stadt Zwickau Wirderung etc."; Türkensteuer, ZSA, Ax AII 17, Nr. 19a.

[a]I have designated the southeast quarter (Tränkviertel) of the city within the walls quarter 7; and the northeast quarter (Niederviertel) within the walls, where the Hundsgasse has been thought to have been located, quarter 5.

[b]h = house; y = yard; c = cellar; g = garden; a = acreage.

[c]This is a curious case, for Caspar Jorge is listed in the *Ratsrechnungen* as behind in his taxes in 1520, as he also had been in 1519. In 1520 this debt was forgiven him. His name is mentioned in the Ratsprotokolle for 1527; yet he does not appear in the tax registers of 1523 or of 1531, by which year he may have died.

Who Were the Hundsgesser?

As noted above, the city council labeled those followers of Müntzer and Storch who were questioned on 16–17 December 1521 as "Hundtsgesser, etc."[92] The identity of the residents of "Dog Lane" has remained a mystery because of all those rebels questioned in 1521, only three, Jacof Schneider and Caspar Teucher and his wife, lived in the Lower Quarter (Niederviertel) of the city by 1523 when an assessment of all real property was made.[93] The Hundsgasse, according to the oldest available maps, lay in that quarter. Indeed, by 1523 only one other reputed follower of Müntzer or Storch, Hans Tzscheppener, resided in that quarter. This seems to render uncertain the entire identification of the Hundsgasse or its quarter of the city with radical religion. Yet the scribe presumably knew whereof he wrote.

The city's *Lehenbuch* for about 1498–1522, a record of the changes of ownership of property, may offer clarification.[94] Unfortunately, dates are not provided. When property changed hands, the previous owner's name was simply crossed out and the new owner's written in. The order of ownership is, however, sure.

At some time between 1498 and 1522, the following adherents of Müntzer/Storch possessed houses in the Hundsgasse and still had them when this volume ceased to be kept: Hans Gebhard, Peter Hauzu, Franz Reissinger, Hans Bruschwein, and Hans Piger. Other owners and previous owners had the same last names as rebels and may have housed them in 1521: Peter Kratzber, Hans Vetter, Jorg Ferber, Jacof Storch, and Balthasar Schopff. Several of these names do not appear on lists of known and suspected radicals until 1529, when Spalatin made a thorough investigation of heresy, but there was enough continuity between 1521 and 1529 to indicate stability in the membership of the leading nonconformist circle. In 1529 Spalatin personally questioned these persons: Catharina, the *Hebamme* (midwife) at the Niederthor; Martha Teucher, wife of Caspar; the wife of Jorg Vetter; Margareta Neumercker; the wife of Wolff Kratzber; the wife of Ludwig Reudnitz; Jorg Storch; Gregor Schmidt; Peter Hauzu; Franz Reissinger; Kuntz Kramer; Hans Gebhard; Jacof Schneider; and Heinrich Gebhard.[95] Among the additional people he had intended to talk to were Peter von Rossberg; the wife of Hans Vetter; someone called only "Schoplin" (possibly the wife of Balthasar Schopff); and a Mrs. Piger.[96]

Spalatin identifies Heinrich Gebhard and Frau Teucher in 1529 as residents in the Hundsgasse. Curiously, they are both assigned to the

Tränkviertel in 1523 and 1531. The property survey of 1523 reveals that nearly all those who had been or who would be accused of heresy now dwelled in the Tränkviertel and thus presumably away from the Hundsgasse.

The solution to this mystery seems to lie in some modern misconception about where the early sixteenth-century Hundsgasse was, and this misconception has been promoted by the sixteenth-century tax collector's application of that street name only to a small alley adjacent to Saint Katherine's Church that contained a mere dozen houses. Emil Herzog's map of Zwickau as it was in 1836 (see p. 16, above) shows the Niederviertel as a slender slice of the city, not more than an eighth of the intramural space, a quarter whose eastern boundary went right down the middle of the Hundsgasse.[97] The dwellings on the west side of the lane were in the Niederviertel, while those on the east side were in the extensive Tränkviertel. This was already the case in the early sixteenth century. The Hundsgasse was in the Tränkviertel as well as the Niederviertel. Although it looks superficially as if nearly all those who had been or who would be accused of heresy had moved from one quarter to the other, they had not; they were and remained "hundtsgesser." Thus, these leading nonconformists retained a certain geographic as well as ideological cohesion throughout the early part of the Reformation era, until they began to die off. Niclas Storch was surely a relative of Jacof Storch in the Hundsgasse or of Jorg Storch outside the gate, where Thomas Drechsel also resided, or of both.

Whether interrogated in December 1521 or named afterward, the leading rebels were no ordinary citizens. Of those questioned initially, the ten about whom we have economic and other information had held or would hold positions of respect within their guild. One, Georg Beyreuther, would actually enter the city council later on, in 1534, as in that same year did Hans Sommerschuh, another admirer of Müntzer.[98] Most of the posts that they held were ones to which their fellow guildsmen, and not the city council, named them. Is this one reason why the council eventually forced the woolweavers' guild to submit a list of candidates for the office of Viermeister and allow it the final choice? Up until that time, guildsmen who had proved their mettle through public nonconformity enjoyed a prestige among their colleagues that showed itself in frequent election to guild offices.

The majority of the rebel leaders were solid citizens. They owned property, took part in guild governance, and sooner or later would outwardly conform in the practice of the Lutheranism that was in the

TABLE 14
Followers of Müntzer/Storch Named after December 1521
Quarters of Residence and Economic Status

	1521		1531		1542	
	City Qtr.[a]	Wealth (in fl.)	City Qtr.	Wealth (in fl.)	City Qtr.	Wealth (in fl.)
Christoff Burghart (Bernfuhrer)	—	—	—	—	—	—
Mrs. Geiger "in der Hundtsgasse"	—	—	—	—	—	—
Peter Hauzu	7	90	7	100	7	110
Georg Jacob	—	—	—	—	—	—
Kuntz Kramer	—	—	—	—	—	—
Sophie (Mrs. Wolff) Kratzber	7	500	7	610	5	800
Margarete (Mrs. Augstin) Neumarcker	3	435	3	340	3	400
Mrs. Hans Piger	7	40	7	50	1	0
Mrs. Ludwig Reudnitz	7	150	7	200	—	—
Peter von Rossberg	—	—	—	—	—	—
Franz Reissinger	7	110	—	—	7	180
Gregor Schmidt (Barbirer)	1	250	1	286	3	200[b]
Mrs. (Balthasar?) Schoplyn[c]	7	425	7	420	7	425
Hans Sommerschuh, Jr.	7	600	7	1,277	—	—
Jorg Storch	8	60	8	50	8	50
Mrs. Strauss	5	215?	—	—	—	—
Hans Tzscheppener	5	80	5	80	5	60[b]
Mrs. Jorg Vetter[d]	7	40	—	—	—	—
Wolff Vogelsang (Fidler)	7	230	7	250	7	250[b]

Source: WSA, Reg. Pp 368[2–4]: "Vorzeichnus der ligenden grunden vnd gutter Im Weichbilde der Stadt Zwickau Wirderung etc."; Türkensteuer, ZSA, Ax AII 17, Nr. 19a; ZSA, Ax AII 16, Nr. 12.

[a] 1=Oberviertel within the walls; 3=Frauenviertel within the walls; 5=Unterviertel within the walls; 7=Tränkviertel within the walls; 8=Tränkviertel outside the walls.

[b] Widow's estate.

[c] Possibly wife of councillor 1516 till his death 2 January 1523. Next door to Hans Piger and thus close to many followers of Müntzer/Storch.

[d] In 1529 the parish visitors forced Mrs. Vetter to sell all her property and move away.

process of being established (see tables 12–14). As a group they were decidedly not the downtrodden and miserable victims of the city fathers that Marxist scholars would prefer. More likely they enjoyed a provenance similar to that of the councillors themselves and aspired to the same status as the councillors. They may have felt frustrated as they witnessed the council's self-aggrandizement, which was directed as much against members of their own social class as against society's lower levels. The notion that in Zwickau the self-perpetuating elite was viewed with a covetous eye is not farfetched.

Evidence is too spotty to allow firm conclusions, but it is noteworthy that a list of men who became burghers in the early part of the sixteenth century contains the names of five religious dissidents: Wolff Vogelsang (1504), Georg Beyreuther (1510), Heinrich Gebhart (1510), Michel Rudolff (1512), and Caspar Teucher (1514).[99] Were newcomers less ready to acquiesce before the entrenched elite than those whose families had long dwelled in Zwickau?

Some of the rebels of 1521 had revolted against the council in 1516, before the Reformation had come on the scene. The names of still others appear among those who helped create unrest and sympathized with the peasantry during the Peasants' War in 1525. In 1516 neither the "infamous" Stephan Hareinweil nor Caspar Jorge had willingly accepted the council's responses to the list of grievances presented by representatives of the citizenry at large.[100] In 1525 Hans and Heinrich Gebhard were obliged to apologize publicly to both elector and city council.[101] Their precise offense is not stated. In the context of other business dealt with at that moment, their transgression most likely was having mocked the council and having advocated providing none of the two hundred foot soldiers demanded by the prince for the battle against the peasants. And they generally stirred up others. The Gebhards, still Müntzer sympathizers in 1529, continued to identify themselves as adversaries of the council.

The common theme underlying the crises of 1516, 1521, and 1525 was hostility toward the city council and its efforts to hold alone the reins of government. Resentment was widespread among the lower echelons of society; this is not to be dismissed. However, these sentiments were also well established among property owners and that middling group that fed Zwickau's bureaucracy and wished to rise higher within it. People from this group, the councillors' own class, led opposition in all its forms to the oligarchy. They let no opportunity slip by. Without them to arouse other burghers and to focus popular dissatisfaction, the unrest of 1516–17, 1521, and 1525 would have been so diffuse as hardly to unsettle the council. Storch and Drechsel, the two native Zwickau Prophets, show every sign of belonging to this group.

In view of the socioeconomic similarities between the troublemakers and the councillors before they entered the council, it is not surprising that some councillors, too, were drawn to what we now call radical religion. Nickel Partt and Christoff Kühn, both woolweaver masters, opposed the hearings of 16–17 December and were banished from council meetings for several weeks. On 8 January 1522, the secretary recorded, "Pardt and Cristoff Khun. It is decided to leave them out [of coming meetings] until the Leipzig fair. Then they are to be called and the matters on account of which they were temporarily left out and not summoned to meetings seriously discussed with them, etc. And their reply is to be heard."[102] Hausmann alleged that there were others though he provided no number. He lamented to Duke Johann on 18 December 1521, "Although the burgomaster and some of his colleagues spare no effort and labor every day to root out and quiet these matters, it is nevertheless a concern that some members of the council are involved in this matter and openly further it, [that] against God, honor, and law they protect, shelter, represent, and actively stir up [the heretics]." Hausmann begged the prince to investigate and to aid the beleaguered magistrates and the clergy.[103]

Overbearing though they often were, the councillors understood the benefit to themselves of displaying mildness. Over time they were even able to forgive and forget. Partt and Kühn were soon reconciled with their colleagues; eventually the council even elected George Beyreuther to its ranks. The patricians barred forever from the urban presence only the most intractable, unrepentant rabble-rousers. A Storch wrote to the burgomaster in January 1525, perhaps asking to return to his hometown. He had written previously. The scribe notes for 11 January, "Storch. Because he has written to the burgomaster, the same answer is to be given him and he is to be made to stay out and one is to have nothing to do with him."[104] This may have been Franz Storch, the rebellious journeyman baker. But high-ranking individuals did think of Niclas Storch when the Peasants' War broke out. Melanchthon wrote to Camerarius in 1525:

> I wish to know if Storch, the flagbearer of the new prophets, is among the peasants. He claims for himself dominion over the earth, and the

120

people say that within four years he will come into power, arrange the service of God [to his own specifications], and turn the nations over to his saints to possess. They report that an angel appeared to him and told him that he would occupy Gabriel's throne. That means, in their opinion, that the Empire has been promised him.[105]

One is inclined to think of Niclas Storch, too, in view of the fact that his fellow radical Hans von der Freystadt sought permission to return to Zwickau just before the Peasants' War, in March 1525. According to Wappler, Freystadt had led the journeymen weavers who were determined to give Müntzer escort in 1521. On 22 March 1525, the scribe recorded, "Hanssen von der Freistat. One is to write again and remind him of the council's last reply [to him] and stand by that. Unless he were to undertake something improper, in which case the council would not forget the distress he had caused it."[106]

The council heard rumors in 1534 and 1536 that Storch was in the area. By now the spread of Austrian Anabaptism into the Erzgebirge had elicited an official and hard line from the elector, and the council no longer regarded Storch as a mere troublesome individual. It searched for him in vain.[107]

For all its self-serving biases, the council showed great skill in defusing its potentially most explosive adversaries. It displayed this skill most clearly in troubled hours, when public anger might have got out of hand. In times of peace it dispensed with tact and did as it pleased, often treading very heavily.

Progress toward Reform

Despite small and temporary divisions in the ranks, the council proceeded to create a Lutheran church for the entire city. Disagreement does not appear to have slowed it. Civic interest triumphed over the compunctions of councillors who otherwise tended either to the Catholic right or to the radical left. Even the dullest councillors were glad of an opportunity, provided by the Reformation, to hasten and facilitate the city's accumulation and consolidation of jurisdiction over all persons and properties within the walls and many without. For decades the council had struggled to acquire more power, at the expense of nearly every other type of corporation. The Reformation represented to all the city fathers a chance not just to punish Catholic moral and

121

fiscal abuses but indeed to eliminate this mighty institution entirely and to absorb its functions. This was a gigantic windfall of power for ambitious men.

It has been customary to give Hermann Mühlpfort most of the credit for orchestrating the Reformation from within the council. Mühlpfort had first entered the governing circle as an electoral appointee in 1510. He was burgomaster during that crucial year from Saint Michael's Day (29 September), 1521 until Saint Moritz's Day (28 September), 1522. He held the same office in 1523–24, 1525–26, 1527–28, 1529–30, 1531–32, and 1533 until his death. His was no small part in Zwickau's ecclesiastical "purification." He worked hand in hand, however, with his counterpart in alternate years, the Paris master of arts Laurentius Bärensprung, first a councillor in 1504. In these years the council in office and the council theoretically out of office strove together to build a Lutheran church polity.

How Bärensprung became attracted to Lutheran teaching is unfortunately not known. Very likely he was first drawn to humanism and disapproval of the institutional Catholic church; when Egranus, whom Bärensprung admired, made his final exit, the councillor found his personal evolution into an advocate of Lutheranism quite natural within Zwickau's setting. Bärensprung was ruling burgomaster in 1520–21 and was clearly as decisive as any of his colleagues in moving toward civic control of the local church. He died on 19 April 1533. The man was laden with debts, but Johann, first as duke, then as elector, insisted that his colleagues tolerate his precarious financial state.

The year 1522 was a turning point for the Catholic church in Zwickau. In most respects, at year's beginning church structure was unchanged. By year's end the church, though still alive, was a shadow of its former self. The changes were overwhelmingly the doing of the council, whose larger, often worldly purposes coincided with Nicolaus Hausmann's spiritual ones. For a time council and pastor were allies. Nevertheless, it would be shy of the mark to say that the Lutheran Reformation had been carried out.

In the early weeks of 1522, the populace was still in turmoil as a consequence of Müntzer's, Storch's, and others' work of marshalling public opinion against the council, not a difficult task. The council's burdens, partly self-made, became at once so enormous that any notion of half the councillors being out of office in alternate years now became and remained ludicrous. The council took on, for example, the hearing of all cases of slander among the citizens, which, it admitted, had become so frequent that "the council has practically enough to do every day with these matters."[108] Of course, it made hardly any difference whether the council *qua* council presided over slander hearings or whether it assigned them to the courts: the judges and jurymen were all councillors.

Citizens daily harangued the councillors to their faces. Even though sixteen student supporters of Müntzer/Storch had been dismissed from the grammar school in January, some students or their families apparently sassed Burkhard Waldauff, one of the two councillors appointed to oversee the academy.[109] Some citizens did not take pride in the school, regarding it as a perpetrator of humanist intellectualism, which was alien to them and linked to the city councillors. In August 1523 the council had to arrest people who stood outside the school and mocked the students.[110]

In spite of all the council could do, Zwickau knew little peace in these days. There were three leading factions. First was the party of the city council and Pastor Hausmann, which labored not only for law and order but for the confinement, if not the abolition, of Catholic institutions, to the advantage of the city government. It is probable but not presently demonstrable that many of Zwickau's better educated, humanistically inclined citizens were sympathetic to this group and that Egranus's admirers might have felt more at home here after their leader's departure than in association with the other parties. Second were the so-called sectarians, sometimes referred to as Storchites, but who in fact continued to identify strongly with Thomas Müntzer. These were mainly artisans and their families, but they ran the gamut in their economic status from exceedingly comfortable to poor. They shared a deep resentment of the council's usurpations at their expense, an attraction to less authoritarian religion, and a cultural orientation not toward southwest German humanism but toward the environs of Zwickau itself. Third were the Catholics, clergy and laity. This is the group that has been largely overlooked by scholars, yet evidence of its existence and of its strength is considerable. One reason that the council launched a veritable campaign against the secular priests, the Franciscans, and the Cistercians early in 1522 was that their hold on the people was strong. Numerous persons of unidentified socioeconomic condition went regularly to the Franciscans to confess, to hear mass, and to listen to sermons that were becoming intensely political.[111] When on 20 March 1524 communion in both kinds was first offered to the laity, only twenty citizens received it.[112] The council found that

123

moderate measures did not adequately discourage members of this tradition-bound Catholic sector, and, as we shall see, it quickly turned to
concerted action.

A minority of Zwickau's residents actively involved themselves in
these controversies that so arouse our interest. They no doubt had their
opinions, but they did not take to the streets or join conventicles. Even
if, as was rumored, Müntzer or Storch had succeeded in enlisting
"twelve apostles and seventy-two disciples," it is to be remembered
that eighty-four is not a high percentage of approximately 7,500.
Zwickau's main industry was woolweaving; and if indeed many of the
city's religious radicals were affiliated with this craft, this was only to be
expected. Most of the councillors themselves throughout the first half
of the sixteenth century were woolweavers or wool merchants by profession. It is perhaps remarkable that two of the three Zwickau
Prophets were not associated with cloth production at all. Certainly
conditions in Zwickau do not lend credibility to the widely held belief
today that there has ever been a strong link between weaving and religious nonconformity.[113] None of this lessens the significance of the
Zwickau radicals' appeal, but it may help to keep that appeal, and the
nature of the Reformation for that matter, in proper perspective.

Against this background of partisan strife, the council proceeded
undaunted against the Catholic church in Zwickau. So far as the secular
priests were concerned, of which Zwickau's churches and chapels had
several dozen, the council gave Hausmann permission to bring them to
order and delegated a councillor to assist him.[114] It took measures to
retain Johann Zeidler, Egranus's successor, as preacher in Saint Mary's
Church.[115] It also at this time wished to keep Wolfgang Zeiner as
preacher at Saint Katherine's.[116] By June, evidently with Duke Johann's approval, the council instructed its secretary to write to every
benefice holder and tell him that if he did not reside in the city and
personally carry out the duties of his office, he would no longer receive
income from "his" endowment.[117] Fortunately for the council, Johann
regarded Lutheranism in general and reform of clerical abuses in particular far more favorably than did his conservative brother Frederick
the Wise. The council, in consultation with Hausmann, forbade
Zwickau's several lay fraternities to receive further moneys from testaments, but it specifically exempted the hospitals and churches from
this provision.[118] Here again it encountered no resistance from Duke
Johann.

Dealing with the regular clergy was more challenging. The Franciscans and the Cistercians were corporations of literate and determined men who had behind them not merely their local colleagues but the authority and tradition of the Catholic hierarchy. They were not so easily divided and conquered. They met the propagandistic and legal maneuvers of the council with like ploys. Thus, without the condonation of the princes, it is not certain that the council would have been victorious.

The princes, however, had nothing to do with the way in which the council's problems with the Cistercians in the Grünhainer Hof were solved. This was a case in which the common folks' proclivity toward violence served the council's own purposes. Indeed, according to Peter Schumann, whose father took part, some councillors themselves joined right in.[119] For unknown reasons the Cistercians imprisoned a peasant in March 1522. The people were incensed. If any element bound the majority of Zwickau's residents throughout the Reformation era, it was disgust and anger at the corrupt, arrogant, self-serving behavior of the clergy, particularly of monks and friars. Popular resentment easily ignited. A poem composed anonymously at the time tells the story— well, most of it![120]

Why, How, and By Whom the Grünhainer Hof Was Stormed

> Be quiet, hark, and listen too!
> A brand new tale I'll tell to you.
> I shall try to tell you why
> In Zwickau was heard a great outcry.
> Near six in the evening (as they say)
> —it happened on Mardi Gras Thursday,[121]
> From Our Lord's birth, the thousandth year,
> Five hundred and twenty-two it were—
> Some one of us did undertake
> A Carnival play for to make.
> A Grünhain monk he took no rest
> Till poor folk he in his stocks oppressed.
> He tormented many who were in need
> And added his scorn to injury.
> He captured an innocent peasant son
> And ruined his bodily health in bonds.[122]
> Such deeds as these do not befit
> A man whose life is to God commit',
> Who should show mercy to his neighbor
> In order to gain Almighty favor.

THE COMING OF THE REFORMATION

When the people saw what was going on,
Off to the council they did run.
Through courtyard they in furious tempers
With pikes, axes, and other weapons
Right up to the convent door did race.
The monks were sitting in perfect peace
When noise of the action in hearing came.
Now all was wreckage; men spoke without shame.
The monk he got his just deserts:
All that was there was fast dispersed.
The doors were broken into two,
The beds ripped up, some stabbed right through,
Benches, cushions, chests and all.
Each person acted quite at will.
Many books were torn and spoiled,
Dragged in filth and thoroughly soiled.
Candles, sausages, bacon and cheeses,
Cowls and hoods all torn to pieces.
To pewter pots and household things
A bitter death the night did bring.
Silver cups were taken as prize
By whoever found them, of whatever size.
Every person took his share—
'Twas put to better use, I swear!
The images people hacked to pieces;
God-outlawed worship of idols ceases.

When people began to quiet down,
They saw the stock and the peasant bound.
God helped the poor man from this seat,
But men's arms moved the stocks to the street.
A monk by the name of Valentine (Herr)
Had to carry the thing to the market square.
With mockery and many a blow
They beat the man till his blood did flow.
This Shrovetide game amused for sure.
It wasn't excessive but only fair.
The stock was carried out again
By means of Mr. Valentine.
The monks ne'er entered that convent more,
A considerable blessing to the poor.

Enough has now been said of this:
To tell it at all entails a risk.

A part I've told you nothing of,
Avoiding punishment from above.
If someone really did too much,
The Hand of Justice him will touch.

The effects of this uprising constituted for the council a giant step toward gaining control of the urban church. The city fathers' implicit, if not explicit, approval of the riot is borne out by the total lack of discussion of it in the minutes. Indeed, few minutes on any subject were taken during the second half of March and all of April, suggesting that whatever was talked about was ultra-secret in nature. Normally, whenever widespread popular dissatisfaction threatened to erupt into violence, the council's secretary took up much space in the minutes book recording the discussions. In March 1522 this was strikingly not the case. Public ire had coincided with conciliar ambition, and mob action achieved what might have taken the bureaucracy years. A master glazier, Hans Wimmer, who had personally smashed all the monks' windows (had he installed them?), enjoyed lasting renown for his boldness, not just among ordinary citizens.[123]

The council hastened to try to obtain the vacated monastery and the Cistercians' rural jurisdictions near Zwickau. The prince did not match their haste. Elector Johann Friedrich conceded the building in Zwickau to the council only in October 1542. Even so the council was obliged to pay the elector four hundred florins for this property. The Hof was thenceforth to house the city grammer school.[124] The city failed to gain the rural jurisdictions.

During April 1522 the council had its hands full. Having seen the masses in action against the Grünhainer Hof, and feeling daily the barbs of the Franciscans, the gentlemen worried about further riots. On the evening of 8 April, someone assaulted a friar with a tankard.[125] A spirit of rebellion lay very near the surface. On hearing that Luther was in the vicinity and aware how effective his sermons had been in restoring order in Wittenberg, the council enthusiastically invited him to detour to Zwickau. He arrived the very next day and stayed at the home of Burgomaster Hermann Mühlpfort. Between 29 April and 2 May, Luther preached four times: twice at the Franciscan friary, once at city hall, and once at Schloss Zwicker, in that order.[126] The first location no doubt galled the Franciscans, who were powerless to prevent him from speaking on their premises.

127

The reformer's sermons were on the following subjects: (1) that good works flow from faith; (2) good works and marriage; (3) the true way (Christ) and the false way, Christ's atonement for the sins of mankind; (4) faith and love, the duties of the priest (to preach and to pray), baptism, and prayers for the dead.[127] In view of conditions in Zwickau, it is to us nothing short of astonishing that Luther failed to address the matter of civic unrest. It is unlikely that he had not been apprised of the enthusiasm for Müntzer/Storch that persisted in the city. Rather, he was still convinced that the word of God itself would convert and pacify. Simply summarizing his beliefs, based in scripture as he saw them to be, would reform and tranquilize the population.

Peter Schumann, who got the information from his father, states that fourteen thousand people turned out to hear Luther speak at the city hall.[128] Such a figure is not unthinkable: Zwickau's resident population was about half that, and an additional seven thousand could well have come in from the surrounding countryside and neighboring towns. The *Geleitsmann* of Borna, one of the officials who were to oversee and facilitate the movement of people and goods on the highways, told the elector that there had been twenty-five thousand in the audience.[129] Some sort of outburst occurred among the listeners as Luther delivered his sermon from city hall. Primary evidence of this unrest and of its nature is now lacking. T. W. Hildebrand makes the intriguing comment, "To be sure, while Luther was preaching from city hall a tumult broke out among the listeners who were here from Schneeberg, Annaberg and other places. But Luther being stoned out of town over the Paradise Bridge is a fairy tale."[130] The council paid Luther an honorarium of ten gold florins.[131]

The quelling of public display against the council was owing less to Luther's appearance than to the absence in Zwickau of a leader for the sectarians. Among the partisans of Müntzer and Storch feeling ran strong against Luther as well as against humanism and those attracted to it. In late November 1522, the council had one Christoff Burghard (or Bernfuhrer) apprehended and questioned about his *"ratio fidei."* He was accused of being inclined toward religious enthusiasm (*schwirmmherrey*) and the ill-behavior "of the spirits" and of being a member of Müntzer's sect. He was supposed to have written a song against Luther and Erasmus, and others were rumored to be in complicity with him.[132] He was banished early the next year for five years, a very severe punishment designed to set an example.[133]

The council now concentrated on the Franciscans. Earlier in the year it had backed away from its half-hearted attempt to assume governance of the friars. The brothers had refused to hand over a key,[134] but to resort to force at this point would have produced princely reprobation. As the spring wore on, the gentlemen found intolerable the hold of the friars on a number of residents who went to them for spiritual ministration. In early June two councilmen went to the monastery and told the "guardian" that "Werner" was not to preach any more.[135] The result was less than satisfactory, for the scribe remarked just two weeks later that the Franciscans would have to elect another custodian and another guardian because the behavior of the current ones "will lead to a riot."[136] Finally, at the end of June the entire council solemnly walked to the cloister, removed the guardian "and others" and imposed its own member upon the brothers. Who this was is not stated, but it could have been Herr Michel Sangner, whom the friars had rejected earlier. The council intended to put the old guardian out of the city.[137] This did not produce harmony. The Franciscans labored all the harder to arouse the public against the magistrates, who finally appealed to Duke Johann.[138] Technically, Johann permitted them only to reprimand the friars; nevertheless, in October they banned from the city a friar who had preached "hard" against Hausmann.[139] A debate between the Franciscans and the reformed clergy in the presence of the Rat on 21 November 1524 was for show only, giving the council a chance formally to excoriate the brothers.[140]

At some point in its various discussions of ecclesiastical matters with Duke Johann and Elector Frederick the Wise in 1522, the council obtained formal jurisdiction over priestly endowments. The city secretary noted that income from the Felix and Adauctus altar in Saint Mary's Church could not be paid out without the knowledge and approval of the council, for the council now had jurisdiction (*gerichtigkeit*) and intended to use it.[141] Regarding the All Souls benefice, a member of the council was to go to the administrator or to the testamentaries and tell them that the interest from the endowment would be better used by the hospital or the school.[142] The council also began to put pressure on the Calend Fraternity, whose wealth it wished to use for the city's philanthropic purposes. The prior and elders of that brotherhood were to be made to render an account to the council so that the money could later be diverted from financing masses for members to maintaining the poor "etc." Such a radical change required princely assent, and the council sought it.[143] It did not obtain final permission to dissolve the organization until 1527.

During the fall of 1521, Hausmann wrote an "Ordinance for Priests." This work is evidently not extant, but his broader, more comprehensive assessment of the church in Zwickau, probably composed early in 1523 at the behest of Duke Johann, is.[144] Hausmann considered the first order of business to be circumscribing, if not wholly eliminating, the participation of dozens of altarists in the life of the parish. In this the council could hardly have agreed more fully, and vowed its cooperation.[145]

Hausmann worked closely with the councillors during this period. He went to Zeitz several times in the company of one or more of the gentlemen to inform diocesan authorities of what the council and he were doing in Zwickau. This cannot have been a pleasant task, but it was one that Frederick the Wise's reluctance to permit innovation made necessary. The councilmen's sense of comradery with Hausmann is given expression by the patricians' invitation to him and the two preachers, Johann Zeidler and Wolfgang Zeiner, to join them in their private Mardi Gras festivities.[146]

Despite the councillors' personal liking for both preachers, Magister Zeidler could not reconcile himself to the far-reaching changes being wrought in religious practice and governance. On 4 July 1523, the council resolved to ask him secretly if he would resign so that it could fill his position with someone else.[147] The man complained to the bishop of Naumburg to no avail, and the council fired him on 18 July. It commissioned Burgomaster Mühlpfort to ride to Thandorf and invite Paul Lindenau, then of Ebersdorf, to come to fill the vacancy in Saint Mary's Church. In the meantime, it was delighted to welcome back its former preacher, now an ex-Augustinian Eremite, Caspar Güttel as guest preacher. During June 1523 Güttel gave at least seven sermons in Zwickau. Since Güttel was an articulate, outspoken advocate of the Lutheran variety of reformation, his presence aided the causes of both Luther and the council. On 25 June the council awarded him an honorarium of twenty florins for four weeks' labor.[148] Among other guest preachers during 1523–24 were Wenzel Link, then pastor in Altenburg, and Friedrich Myconius (Mecum), the future superintendent in Gotha. As for Zeidler, he was recalcitrant. He was forbidden to enter the pulpit from 8 August 1523.[149]

It is virtually impossible to assess the impact of the sermon on the people of the city. The preaching position was instrumental in many German cities in starting reform.[150] In Zwickau, where the Rat called for reform before anyone else, the burghers were not so keen to espouse the movement. Preachers of every variety passed through town, from the erudite, humanist Egranus to the inflammatory Müntzer; from the blunt, anti-popular Conrad Cordatus to the weak-voiced Christoff Ering. The people judged them more than anything else by the sheer theater of their delivery, and, secondarily, by the degree of their antipathy for the council. The theological convictions of the homilists counted as a distant third factor, remarkably behind the first two. The council's best hope for calming and converting the people lay in attracting absolutely spell-binding preachers of Lutheran doctrine, of peace and respect for the law. Güttel was such a one, but men of his caliber were rare, and he was happily employed elsewhere. The council always had its eye peeled for similar preachers who might be brought to Zwickau.

During the autumn of 1522, the council named a committee from its own ranks to suggest how school and parish might be financially sustained. The members were Mühlpfort, Vogt Wolff Schicker, Schultheiss Gotthard Büttner, and Burkhard Waldauff.[151] Inspired by Luther's outline of a community chest for the city of Leisnig in 1523, the committee evidently suggested adopting such a mechanism. The first pertinent reference in the council minutes is to "dy gemayne Buchsen" on 8 August 1523, and the second to "der gemeyne kasten" on 19 August.[152] All church funds were to be channeled into this chest.

Beginning in 1523 the council actively sought to remove tax exemptions from clerical properties. The secretary expressed the monetary motive quite freely, along with other reasons. The council opened negotiations with the Dominicans of Plauen to shut their depot in Zwickau. It offered to buy their house for a fair price or to let them sell it to a burgher. In any case, the black friars were to be informed, their property would no longer be free of tax.[153] In contrast to the Franciscans, the Dominicans did not undertake the cure of souls in Zwickau. Their purpose there was exclusively economic. On 6 April 1524, the Dominicans sold their house to the council for two hundred florins.[154]

At the time of the 1533 visitation, there were still twenty-three occupied priests' houses in the city.[155] The unanswered question is whether their inhabitants were working clergymen, former priests, or people whom the council had allowed to reside in them. The available data suggest that these dwellings were free of property tax, but even that is not certain. As for the altarists themselves, many were irate from the start over changes being carried out. Hausmann and the council would have been pleased to see them all leave the city, which, however, they were usually financially or physically in no position to do. A conciliar decree of October 1524 that altarists did not have to be paid at all unless they deserved to be, that is, unless they submitted to the reformed church, was unrealistic. The council had to find ways of maintaining those who stayed even though, private and individual masses being more and more restricted, the men could render only small service to the church over which Hausmann presided. A few who were not averse to cooperating with the Lutheran-minded authorities were given elementary clerical tasks to perform and were generally accorded better treatment. Most were not turned out of their homes in any event. In this regard both pastor and council conceded that a complete transition from old to new would take time. Yet the need to sustain so many priests was one factor hindering smooth operation of the community chest.

There were other, more telling ones. Although the council minutes for 29 September 1523 to 28 September 1524 are missing, it is apparent from other sources that during this period the councillors intensified their efforts to buy out or confiscate ecclesiastical endowments and to concentrate all their incomes in the new community chest. Only in early 1524 did Egranus, now in Joachimsthal, stop receiving income from a Lehen in Saint Mary's Church, for example; and the excuse for denying it to him was "because he does not reside."[156] The School and Corpus Christi fraternities met their doom in 1523 along with a number of endowed masses. Problems arose because principal sums were not returned either to members or heirs of endowers. This produced a certain ambivalence, particularly in well-to-do quarters. One colorful example involves the chantry of Saint Helena in Saint Mary's Church. Founded by Heinrich Mühlpfort, deceased uncle of Hermann and a long-time city councillor himself, this endowment produced sums annually that Heinrich's descendants, including the Lutheran stalwart Hermann, were reluctant to see turned over to the community chest. The council had no little conflict with the burgomaster over this. Mühlpfort began pressing his colleagues in late October 1526.[157] Less than a year later, the council sentenced him to brief, patrician-style imprisonment in the town hall. Whether this was carried out is not clear; Mühlpfort appealed to the elector.[158] Johann's decision is not known, but he was inclined to allow lay endowers and their families to receive one third of the income from benefices. In 1529 two heirs of Heinrich Mühlpfort were awarded ecclesiastical "silverwork and treasures" from a benefice.[159] Johann Friedrich would not be as permissive, but his rule was some years off.[160]

Many other endowers or their heirs appealed attempts to deny them income from benefices. The Römer descendants won some concessions in 1529 and 1545.[161] In 1545 Burgomaster Oswald Lasan apparently succeeded, with the help of Luther, Bugenhagen, and Melanchthon, in having a portion of the revenue from the Jacob and Laurence endowment, established by his forebears, earmarked for the support of student members of his family.[162] Some claimants on benefices even tried to take back the principal.[163]

We do not know what percentage of all revenues from pre-Reformation endowments was diverted as a result of such efforts. As usual, much documentation is missing. More important—a second affliction of the community chest from its inception—accounting practices in connection with these moneys were severely flawed.[164] From the start a councillor served as administrator (*fursteher*) of the community chest, and he was obligated to present an annual account to the council.[165] But the council itself—and this constitutes a third impediment to the success of the fund—came to view the chest as a source of loans to its members and their friends and relatives. Previously the gentlemen had borrowed chiefly from the "new councillors' money," which every man elected to the city council for the first time had to pay before taking his seat.

A fourth obstacle to the smooth functioning of the community chest was the fact that Zwickau citizens were no longer as free with their alms as they had been under Catholicism. The council repeatedly deliberated the question of how to get the people to continue the level of donation that they had made before. Luther finally perceived the magnitude of the problem when he took part in the general visitation of 1528–29. He wrote, "Under popery the people were charitable and gave gladly; but now under the gospel, nobody gives anything but only fleeces his neighbor. Each person wants to have everything for himself alone. And the longer the gospel is preached, so much more do the people drown in greed, arrogance, and luxury, just as if the poor begger's sack was supposed to stay there forever. The devil has indeed made two inroads among the people."[166]

The years 1523 and 1524 were particularly full ones for the reformers of the church in Zwickau. Working closely together, the city council and Pastor Hausmann had virtually concluded the process of

TABLE 15
Some Religious Changes in Zwickau, 1523–1545

1521		Priests, monks, and friars may not beg from house to house.
1523	4 June	Corpus Christi procession moved from afternoon to morning, severely curtailed; sermon in St. Mary's churchyard.
	2 July	*Salve Regina* eliminated.
	8 July	St. Mary's Church, Host no longer borne around.
	16 July	St. Katherine's Church, Host no longer borne around.
1524	Lent	Several couples wed; citizens privately eat meat though Rat forbids sale, confiscates two slaughtered calves.
	22 March	Hausmann has *Frühmesser* altar and choir screen removed from St. Katherine's Church.
	24 March	Mass said in German; communion offered in both kinds.
	25 March	Passion sermon eliminated.
	26 March	Reformed baptismal ceremony introduced; Old Testament readings in German.
	25 December	New Testament readings in German.
1525	30 April	Entire service in German.
1526	Lent	Meat may be freely sold.
1529	January	Visitors permit Latin mass and vespers on high feast days; Saturday bell ringing for souls of dead eliminated.
1545	5 August	On Luther's order, elevation of Host and Chalice ceases.

establishing Lutheranism and eliminating Catholicism before the outbreak of the Peasants' War in their area. The power of most Catholic corporations had been broken, and a new ecclesiastical administration with the council at its top had been created. The council met every expression of opposition with decisive suppressive measures. Nonetheless, opposition remained. Even if they did not exactly flourish, both Müntzerites and Catholics were still present.

The single major goal that the council had failed to attain was the abolition of the Franciscan community. Success was soon to come, but its achievement was an accompaniment to the Peasants' War and must be described in its proper context. So long as the Franciscans remained, even though they no longer enjoyed any formal authority, they constituted a symbol of traditional religion that could arouse antipathy toward the council in some quarters.

By the death of Frederick the Wise in early May 1525, a great many details remained to be worked out, but the city council had made those major revisions in policy and practice that lay at the heart of the Lutheran Reformation. Working with Hausmann they had eliminated male (but not female) monasticism and were treating with their prince to obtain monastic holdings and jurisdictions. They had accepted Hausmann's "Ordinance of Priests" and reduced Saint Mary's staff to a pastor, a preacher, and two deacons. Saint Katherine's clergy, always less numerous, was similarly reduced. The council had only to buy out, or await the deaths of, a few priests.[167] The preachers in both Saint Mary's and Saint Katherine's churches were committed to Lutheran teaching. Hausmann had markedly reduced the number and purposes of masses, though negotiations with some endowers remained in progress. Hausmann and others had finally convinced Luther of the need for a German mass. A short version (1524) and a longer version (1526) were finally forthcoming and were adopted by Zwickau's pastor, as were Luther's other revised rituals as they came off the printing presses of Wittenberg and then of Zwickau itself. A community chest now existed, out of which clergy, teachers, the poor, and the ill were to gain sustenance. This community chest was never the fiscal success that it might have been in better, more honest managers' hands, but it was not a total failure either. The destitute could no longer beg from house to house or in the marketplace, but if they appeared on Sunday after the sermon, they got their dole.

Governance of the church by mid-1525 lay in the hands of the city council. The councillors thought that it did, and for the time being, at least, they were not wrong. Pastor Hausmann had to seek their consent for every sort of innovation. The gentlemen so readily gave it that the pastor quickly came to think of himself as the highest local authority in church affairs. These differing views of the source of power would soon lead to a collision between council and pastor, and in turn between elector and city, as we shall see. Unmistakably, however, the Catholic church was finished in Zwickau before the summer of 1525. The council had put widespread popular antipathy toward Catholic clergy to its own use, had seized control of religious institutions, and had imposed its political as well as its theological will upon a people that had not entirely anticipated the outcome. The years of flux, during which persons with widely varying opinions on religion were bold enough to speak out, now came abruptly to an end. The Peasants' War so frightened those in power, of every sort at every level, that it ultimately reinforced an already growing authoritarianism in ruling circles.

The Reformation came far sooner to electoral cities like Zwickau than it did to outlying hamlets and villages. Zwickau compelled the peasants directly under its rule to accept pastors to the council's liking, that is, Lutheran. Yet it could not alter overnight the common people's own private convictions. Nor could it affect independent congregations or parishes within noble domains. Fully another decade would elapse before the elector, through his appointed representatives and in his name, would end Catholicism in the countryside. In 1533 the parish visitors commented about peasants in "the council's villages": "Because some are still papists and have not been to the sacrament in many years, they are supposed to improve their ways or not be tolerated in the community any longer."[168] Convert and conform or get out of the elector's lands!

Pockets of quiet resistance lived on within Zwickau itself. The visitors had to ordain "that no one who would not receive the Lord's Supper under both kinds may henceforth serve as anyone's godparent nor may he be buried with the customary ceremonies."[169] Blasius Walter, an impecunious weaver, died on 25 January 1540. He had refused ever to receive communion in both kinds and had openly decried the practice. He was buried in Saint Moritz's cemetery, which lay outside the walls, "*sine crux, dux, et lux et sine Campana*" (without cross, procession, light or knell).[170] The city was moderate by sixteenth-century standards: it did not force all recusants into exile.

Discretion as the Better Part
of Sympathy: The Urban Response
to The Peasants' War

The eruption of the Peasants' War in Ernestine Franconia and Thuringia early in 1525 and its spread into the Vogtland in the spring pushed discussion of religious alterations into second place in Zwickau's city council meetings. Zwickau had established a modus vivendi with the peasants in its hinterland. True, the path to this condition had not been entirely smooth. In 1524, for instance, a force of four hundred armed Zwickauers had confiscated some Schneeberg beer from the peasants of Kulitzsch, a village in the domains of the knight Rudolph von der Planitz.[1] As in other spheres, during the two generations preceding the Reformation, the council had sought every opening to expand its authority over the rural communities nearby. Most resentful of this ill-concealed effort were the nobles, who correctly saw in Zwickau's advances an impinging upon their own prerogatives.

In 1531 the council administered twenty-five peasant families in the village of Reinsdorf; eleven in Weissenborn; and sixty-two in Stangengrün.[2] Apart from these the Rat collected taxes on a handful of properties in other villages. By the next assessment to aid in the fight against the Turks, in 1542, the council had added Marienthal, rights to which it had acquired from the nuns in Eisenberg. In 1542 seventeen peasant properties were listed for Marienthal as well. One of these, however, belonged to the councillor Dr. Stephan Wilde.[3]

As we have seen, the council administered justice to its peasants by means of a Schultheiss, whose jurisdiction was called *Osterweihe*. This Schultheiss was always a member of the council, as were his *Schöppen* or jurymen. There were also village magistrates (*Dorfrichter*) who handled minor matters and who in any case were in close communication with the council.

A rapid perusal of the Schultheiss's records gives the impression that under Zwickau's rule the application of customary village law was increasingly discouraged. The vocabulary changes markedly during the late fifteenth and early sixteenth centuries. The term "vor gehegter Dingbank" had all but disappeared even before the Reformation. A closer examination of court records would need to be undertaken before one could safely conclude that Zwickau was as consciously attempting to impose Roman law upon the rustics as it was upon urban dwellers. Still, throughout the period under study, the common people within the city as well as without repeatedly complained that the council was neglecting traditional laws and applying new ones of its own invention.

The major issues that had existed between Zwickau and the peasants of the whole immediate vicinity were the products of two prohibitions. First, within an imprecise area called the *bannmeile*, encompassing more than thirty villages, only Zwickau beer could be sold. This regulation guaranteed a market for the "Zwickisch" beverage. This angered the peasantry, and the nobility as well, who abetted their tenants in violating it.

Second, within the bannmeile practicing the skilled trades was, as noted, severely restricted, as it had been from the early fifteenth century. This, too, applied to nobles' domains and was supposed to remove competition with Zwickau's crafts. Rural hamlets could have only the number and sorts of craftsmen that were absolutely essential to their daily operations; otherwise they were to fill their material needs in Zwickau.[4] The peasants even had to sell their surplus crops and homemade foodstuffs in the Zwickau marketplace.[5] Strangers and Zwickauers alike were prohibited from buying from the peasantry in the countryside.[6]

During the frequent disputes over these two issues, the prince came down squarely on Zwickau's side. He saw this as a way of nurturing this urban center, which he recognized as a source of money and soldiers superior to landed estates. And Ernestine domains were lacking in noteworthy cities. Frederick the Wise wished to foster his few cities' growth and well-being.

Whenever neighboring peasants had difficulties with the knights, they sought aid and advice from Zwickau. This occurred often, even immediately before the Peasants' War. On 16 January 1525, the men of Pölbitz, Auerbach, Pöhlau, and Hohndorf complained to the city council about Hans von Weissbach's usurpation of (unspecified) water rights.[7] He also ran his sheep on their lands.[8] The city fathers were only too happy to be of service. On 29 March they wrote to their prospective legal advisor Georg Komerstadt in Leipzig and asked him to seek redress for the peasants from "the territorial prince."[9] The scribe, quoting representatives of the entire Zwickau gemeinde, would shortly refer to local nobles as "enemies" of the peasants.[10] The council petitioned their prince on 24 April 1525 on behalf of the peasants of Schneppendorf and Oberauerbach regarding Hans von Weissbach's running sheep on their lands.[11]

When many peasants in proximity to Zwickau broke into violence in April and May of 1525, they directed their ire principally against noble and clerical landlords. They did not admire the patricians of Zwickau, but they acknowledged them as their sometime champions. There is a certain irony in the peasants' relatively friendly attitude toward the council: it contrasts sharply with many urban residents' accurate perception that the councillors sought their own advantage at almost anyone's expense. It must be recalled that the councillors' advantage did lie, and had long lain, in cultivating the peasants' cooperation against the knights. Despite several vigorous legal clashes with peasants and even one armed confrontation over beer, viewed as a whole relations between the councillors and their peasant neighbors were satisfactory.

The expectation that Zwickau's government would side with villagers against nobles and prelates may be seen in a letter that the rebellious citizens of Reinsdorf directed to the council on 7 May 1525.

> The word of God endures forever. . . . Because of late the word of God is everywhere on the rise and has come into the bright sunshine, as a result of which we poor people have received instruction as to how greatly we have been led astray by our spiritual lords, pastors and clergymen. And in part this has not yet wanted to stop. Similarly our overlords (*lehnhern*), who are supposed to protect and defend us, utterly and completely ruin and consume us and despoil our land and possessions through their manifold impositions, labor service, [forced] loans, and many additional things, etc. Whereas, then, throughout the lands here and there revolt has taken place and has spread, as one can see, we have also committed ourselves; and each man binds himself to the twelve articles [of Memmingen] which have gone out in print, and swears to uphold the same along with the holy gospel and the word of God, etc. For which, with God's help, we all together in our assembly intend to strive as long as body and life last, etc.

On this account we come to you. We ask and we implore you, for the sake of God's holy word, Christian love, and neighborliness, to assist us poor people with advice and deed, food and drink, manpower (*leuthen*), protection, and everything else that we need for this our Christian undertaking. Such to the best of our ability do we poor people ever diligently strive to deserve from you, our kind (*gunstigen*) lords, brothers, and neighbors. Therefore, we ask your honors to send back your written and consoling reply with the bearer of this letter; we shall conform ourselves to it.[12]

This message is addressed "to the reputed, honorable, and wise burgomasters and both councils of the city of Zwickau, our kind, dear lords, brothers and neighbors etc."

The residents of Stangengrün humbly asked the council to ease their tax burden. For reasons that are not clear, the council summarily refused and dispatched their request to the prince.[13] To the Reindorfers, however, the councillors were positively gentle, and they seem not to have informed Johann, at least not in writing. The council's reply went out not only in its own name but in that of the craftsmen and the whole community. Under the circumstances, though, it is doubtful that any but council members actually worked on it.

Assuredly you as pious Christians will act in this matter with God's help and the foreknowledge of our Christian, most praiseworthy prince, a lover of the word of God, in such a way as to please the Almighty, as not to disobey your prince, and as to promote the well-being of your body and soul, which in our view is highly necessary. To that end and in peace we gladly desire to support you so that in no way is anything begun or discussed that is against those in authority, in accordance with God's word. In addition, you must consider that we have to afford protection to our city, which has need of it. But food, insofar as we have extra, we would be happy to supply at a fair price.[14]

This missive is addressed "to our dear and good friends, the assembly at Reinsdorf." The council was not being gracious entirely out of sympathy for the Reinsdorfers. The events of early May were complex and dangerous to Zwickau, and the councillors exerted themselves to navigate between Scylla and Charybdis. The Reinsdorfers may have attracted as many as three thousand warriors to their army (*haufen*), the largest in the area, and the Rat saw the need to pacify them for the city's security.

Many local knights were seeking refuge behind Zwickau's walls. This worried the council. These nobles were always an unruly lot, arro-

140

gant, badly behaved in town, regarding themselves as exempt from any laws save the elector's and often even from his. They came armed and with numerous relatives and retainers. Zwickau was already crowded and had few places to put the guests. More important than this was the possibility that the rebels might come to the conclusion that Zwickau had welcomed these sojourners, their foes. Like the peasants, noblemen had approached the council for help against the rustic onslaught. On 6 May the nobles of the Vogtland collectively appealed for assistance. In this and all other cases like it the council politely demurred.[15] It added a separate note to its response to the "Adel vff Milaw": "In addition, we cannot conceal from you that several and more than one assembly of the rebellious peasants in the same way have asked us for help and support, to whom we gave the reasons [we gave you] together with others. Not improperly, we denied their requests too."[16]

The presence of a number of knights in Zwickau created so manifest a danger for the city, a danger that every level of society could perceive, that the council consulted the heads of all the guilds, representatives from the rest of the artisan community, and "the doctors" on what to do. On 5 May they came to a decision. They agreed to give the nobles verbal sympathy, to acknowledge the difficulties that the peasant revolt was posing for the knights. However, they would not wish to keep from the noblemen that the peasants had heard of their flight into Zwickau and resented the city's harboring them, their enemies (*ire feinde*), who had for so long "flayed and scraped them and laid so many plagues upon them." If the knights remained, the peasants could well attack Zwickau. Under these circumstances, then, the nobility would know what was the proper course of action.[17]

It was wishful thinking to hope that the knights, now in personal danger and wholly unaccustomed to defer to the city council in any matter, would heed this low-key request to depart. Still, the city had declared its refusal to become the partisan of the nobles. The council exhibited no little skill as it negotiated the treacherous path between the two armed camps. Reflecting its desire for detachment, the council labeled the struggle in the countryside "the peasants' and nobles' matter."[18]

We know that in the end the council's policy succeeded, but not without electoral and other princely intervention to subdue the peasants. If princely military might ultimately quelled the rebellion, other electoral practices beforehand actually increased Zwickau's danger. First of all, the elector allowed his Schloss Zwicker to be placed at the disposal of high ranking nobility. Though the city played no part in this, the castle, whose ramparts made up part of the city wall, was identified with Zwickau proper. The city had to provide food and other emergency necessities for the castle's temporary occupants whoever they were.

Second, the elector required Zwickau to contribute a battalion of two hundred men, fully equipped and suitably commanded, to aid him against the peasants.[19] The city had to comply. Any reluctance it attempted to convey to the peasants (and to no one else!) may have been missed in the confusion.

Third, Johann compelled the city council to raise a tax (*heerfahrtgeld*) in aid of his armies.[20] In the process of obeying, the councillors, delegated as tax collectors, had to demand money not only from those urban artisans whose sympathies lay with the peasants but from the very peasants themselves. Although evidence is lacking, this enterprise cannot have enhanced the city's image among the beleaguered peasants.

Zwickau's danger in this period was thus very real, and every member of the council was acutely aware of it. The council named a committee to make provision for Zwickau's defense.[21] Anyone who even verbally resisted the council was not to be reasoned with but punished straightaway.[22] Trustworthy butchers were for a fee to spy on the peasants and learn their plans, reporting to the councillors and to no "common man."[23] The gates were shut promptly and extra watchers put on the walls.[24] A contingent of soldiers was to reinforce the customary authorities during the Trinity Market (*Jahrmarkt*) in June.[25] The council sent messengers to Johann in Weimar whenever it had any information to impart.[26]

The council's precautions were designed partly to protect the city against revolt within the walls. Sentiment favorable to the peasants was widespread among the citizens, and not just among the "poor and downtrodden" who might have thought of the peasants as their rural counterparts. Niclas Reynoldt, related by marriage to the Mühlpfort family and one-time member of the council, received a conciliar reprimand for running around town "saying certain things that are rumored to serve rebellion."[27] Bartel Forster, whose taxable worth in 1531 was 230 florins and in 1542 300 florins, wrote a letter to all artisans and the entire community of Zwickau. He declared that the Twelve Articles (of Memmingen) were in accordance with scripture and that he himself wished to stand by God's holy word.[28] Forster was briefly imprisoned.

On 1 May, Walpurgis Day, the council received the duke's order to send two hundred infantrymen to him in Weimar. His missive further instructed the gentlemen to admonish the populace to obey their ruler and not to make common cause with the peasants.[29] The councilmen were very wary of large gatherings at this point and summoned the guilds one at a time to tell them.

The bakers and the shoemakers accepted Johann's command without further ado. The butchers, however, said that they would submit only if Zwickau's other craftsmen, both with and without guilds, were of the same mind. The smiths were even more emphatic: they would agree to nothing behind the other artisans' backs. Those from the community (*gemein*), that is, craftsmen without guild organization, being called as a group, likewise refused to give any answer to the prince without first consulting their fellows in all trades.

On 1 May, then, the council, seeing the possibility of discord grow, did not convene the largest trade, the woolweavers, at all. It nervously decided to gather all the craftsmen of the city together at 5:00 the next morning. They were to meet in the recently built drapers' hall (*Kaufhaus*), the pride of Zwickau's citizenry, an edifice long desired by the weavers' guild. These councillors were becoming experts in managing those subject to them: they knew that the woolweavers would hardly revolt and despoil this gem of their profession. But the patricians were uneasy just the same. Their scribe observed, "In today's negotiation much aversion was noticed and detected within the community against the monks and against several members of the council." When violence had plainly been averted, the same secretary went back and added, "But, praise be to God, it all went well, as per what comes after this."[30]

The antecedent of "it" is the early morning assembly of 2 May. All craftsmen were present. The doctors, whatever their professional expertise, were there too; on account of their superior education, they were considered appropriate advisors of all sides. The following councillors presided: ruling burgomaster Laurentius Bärensprung; past burgomaster Hermann Mühlpfort; past burgomaster Ludwig Preuss; former Stadtvogt Simon Sangner, a man of advanced age and long public service who evidently died later that year; and Burkhard Waldauff, overseer of the school and earlier the object of some burghers' revilement.[31]

Bärensprung began with a summary of events to date, including some artisans' reluctance to comply with all parts of the duke's instruc-

143

tion. This had given the council no recourse, he continued, except to call the handworkers together. First he would have the ruler's order read out and then a reply that the council had drafted. He went on that if the craftsmen found parts of this response "too sharp," they should so indicate so that the language might be softened! Part of the council's self-protective strategy was to seem to resist the princes' command. In fact, it was never its intention to resist. The chief magistrate also urged his listeners, if they wished to add something, to present it "in a modest manner." He inquired of them how many foot soldiers they intended to send to their prince.

After some general discussion, all consented to letting a committee take up the issues and speak for the entire community of tradesmen. The doctors, the previous and present Viermeister of the guilds, and the official spokesmen for the nonguild artisans made up this committee. All agreed to have the highly respected blade maker Wolff Koch present the committee's proposals to the whole gathering. The committee went to work immediately. The throngs did not disband; they waited.

Finally Wolff Koch and his colleagues were ready. He said that one point on which citizens had achieved concurrence the previous day was that none of them would join in rebellion or riot (*empörung ader aufrur anfahen*) but that each would be an obedient citizen. This, Koch said, was the view of the committee as well. No person should conspire with another behind the back of the princes, and the citizenry should tell Johann this in writing so that any punishment from him would be set aside.[32]

Whatever other grievances the people had, whether against each other, the council, or the princes, they should let rest until the end of the Leipzig fair in June. Then they might appeal to their rulers to investigate and provide relief. Koch declared, on behalf of the committee, that the decision as to how many footsoldiers to send, whether one hundred or two hundred, should be left to the council. But, he went on, the officers, the men, and the princes should be informed that although they as citizens were willing to fiight against seditious mobs and sacrifice life and limb to defend those in authority, they would by no means move against poor peasants who had once again (*widerumb*) risen up, since in no other way were the peasants able to obtain the justice and liberties (*gerechtigkeit vnd freiheiten*) that were theirs from God and in accordance with His word.

The scribe noted that the city council accepted this statement.[33] The gentlemen mitigated the harshness of this message in order not to bring the princes' wrath down on Zwickau.[34]

Later the same day, as the councillors were composing a formal answer to Frederick the Wise and Duke Johann along these lines, representatives from the community petitioned the Rat assiduously to order the monks to leave town. People were unwilling to tolerate them any longer, they said. They lived contrary to scripture, they tried to raise rebellion, and "many of the old followed them."[35]

This statement ought not to be taken entirely at face value. It is true that there had long been public antipathy toward the friars, who were frequently the butt of popular ridicule. In December 1524 people had hung an effigy of Saint Francis in the marketplace and reviled it.[36] In January 1525 some young men had broken into the cloister and thrown stones at the brothers at their very altar.[37] During Carnival 1525, just prior to the spread of the Peasants' War into this region, some people had dressed themselves up as monks and nuns and allowed themselves to be chased by others into rabbit nets.[38]

But what about the community's allegation on 2 May that "many of the old people" adhered to the friars? Can it be that in Zwickau there were generational differences in religious views? Were the elderly disposed to keep the old, familiar practices and the young desirous of change? Modern psychology and sociology would affirm this possibility, yet without birth and death data or the names of the tradition-minded, we cannot be sure if or how the ranks divided in Zwickau. The council itself mentioned some burghers' affinity for the Franciscans but did not refer to age. Instead, the scribe increases our knowledge of the underlying political issues: "The citizens. Some go to the monks [and] have much fellowship with them. The monks likely stand with the [knight] of Schönburg, in every matter take a position against the council and do not want to obey the council. The citizens are concerned that through their [the friars'] efforts a revolt could be prepared and produce most undesirable results."[39] In some quarters, then, Catholic commitment remained strong; and opposition to conciliar aggrandizement could take the form of resolute attendance on the Franciscans. The gentlemen of the council were not above orchestrating a "request" for the brothers' removal and suggesting specific arguments for inclusion in it.

Although it had detested the friars' presence for years, the council was unable until early May 1525 finally to expel the monastic brethren. It had taken a number of preliminary steps, however. In 1523 the friars' numbers were forcibly reduced from about ninety to twenty-two; and on 19 September 1523, the council told them that by Easter 1524 they must diminish their ranks by two additional men. They were forbidden to take on novices.[40] The councillors hoped to remove the mendicant thorn in their side through attrition. They forbade the Franciscans to beg from door to door, but the friars continued to do so. Pastor Hausmann and the preachers Zeiner and Lindenau put their opposition to the brothers in print either late in 1523 or early in 1524.[41] On 11 February 1525, the council shut the Franciscans up in their friary to keep them from arousing public sentiment against the council still further—an unlikely possibility if the brothers had had no hold on the people; they were forbidden ever again to preach.[42] On 13 February the scribe wrote, "The draft of the council's reasons for having to shut the cloister is to be sent out to the advisors of our gracious lord and ruler."[43] The council had been considering how best to approach the territorial wielders of power.

Why only on 2 May 1525, as the peasants raged in the countryside, did the council think itself in a position to cast out the friars, ostensibly in response to a popular appeal? Why did the magistrates wait so long? In the first place, as we have seen, the councillors were acutely aware of many craftsmen's sympathy for the peasants. Many of the same craftsmen also held both the Franciscans and the councillors in contempt. The scribe had noted only the day before, "In today's discussions much aversion that the community feels against the friars and against several members of the council was noticed and sensed (*vormargkt vnd gespurt*)."[44] Was the expulsion of the gray friars an effort in one dramatic move to placate restive citizens and simultaneously to attain their goal of the brothers' removal? This does seem to be the case; it constitutes a parallel in 1525 to the riot against the Cistercians three years earlier.

But surely the council would not have been reluctant to push out the friars sooner if some other obstacle had not stood in its way. Frederick the Wise died on 5 May 1525. Although the evangelical inclinations of his brother and heir Johann had long been known, Frederick was conservative in religion. He commanded all his subjects to abide by the decree of the imperial *Reichsregiment* at Augsburg in March 1523, according to which no further innovations in religion were to be made.[45] For several months prior to his death, Frederick's demise had been expected. Word of his weakening condition traveled from the elector's hunting lodge at Lochau, where he spent his last weeks, to his officials in cities. The council in Zwickau, knowing that the Lutheran-minded Johann would accede momentarily to full rule of Ernestine lands, felt free at last to act against the Franciscans.

Peter Schumann's assertion that the friars departed without hostility or resistance is inaccurate. That they were *gutwillig* does not jibe with the unrelenting antagonism that had recently characterized the relationship between brothers and councillors. The council minutes show that at the last moment the friars demanded a written list of the reasons why they were being exiled. Burgomaster Bärensprung refused to comply, saying that there had not been many Franciscans on earth three hundred years before and that they existed by papal privilege only. The gospel, he went on, gave them no legitimacy.[46] The friars were gone by the morning of 3 May.[47] The next day a group of councillors took possession of the empty friary and began to distribute its household supplies to Zwickau's poor. They stationed guards around it to prevent looting and vandalism.[48]

The Franciscans would scarcely have consented to leave at a time when every person was nervous about setting foot outside the protecting city wall. They knew that exodus just now, with the peasants in uproar and furious at every symbol of ecclesiastical, as well as of lay, oppression, placed them greatly at risk. No wonder several of the refugees sneaked right back into town to be hidden by the beguines.

In addition, the newly displaced Franciscans communicated their plight at once to Elector Johann. Perhaps ironically, in view of the councillors' expectation of a princely blessing, Johann did not greet the relegation of the brothers with applause. His first order of business was to subdue the peasants, but that having been accomplished, in July he wrote to the council to inquire why and how the friars had been excluded from Zwickau. The gentlemen composed a tightly knit reply describing the Franciscans' intolerable behavior and their own "moderate and patient" responses.[49] Their crowning argument, irresistible to any prince who had just experienced the revolt of his peasants, was that since the brothers' exit, the citizens had been "united and peaceable." These words persuaded Johann, and he contented himself with making the council pay each brother a sum of money as compensation. In 1526 he modified this directive such that only those friars who accepted their secularization were to receive grants. The sums ranged from less than six florins up to two hundred florins.[50]

Not everyone in town was placated by the Franciscans' ejection, by the guild leaders' verbal defense of the peasants in their collective re-

147

sponse to the princes, or by the council's cautious pragmatism in accepting this sentiment. On 6 May the secretary noted, "Those people who speak ill of the council and slander the Four Masters of the woolweavers are not at this time to be argued with but, in accordance with the letter from our prince, they are to be sent for, their deeds recounted, and punishment meted out. [This is] in order that fear [of authority] and obedience may be maintained."[51]

The council's position in Zwickau was strengthened on 8 May when the new elector directed his retort to the craftsmen's leaders' epistle not to his humble urban subjects themselves but strictly to the council. This reassured the council; but still not entirely confident of peace, it read Johann's reply to the community representatives as well as some letters of unrecorded content to the council from peasants and nobles, presumably those requesting succor.[52] The gentlemen agreed to distribute copies of the elector's letter to the Viermeister, to be read out in each guild assembly. Prince and councillors alike proscribed city folk's mixing in "the peasants' and nobles' matter."

Despite the council's precautions, the elector became aware of the dissidence in Zwickau. He wrote to the council and citizenry at about the end of the first week in May. Only the Zwickauers' response is extant. On 11 May they said to their ruler that they had received his letter accusing some of them of intending to join the peasant uprising. This was "entirely unlike us and painful for us to hear." They wondered who would spread such a tale about "us poor people." They recounted to him their meeting in the new drapers' hall and how everyone there had publicly exclaimed and wanted it forbidden to take part in riot or revolt or in any violation of Christian charity, from which acts they themselves would refrain or lose life and property. They begged him not to let false reports alienate him from Zwickau.[53] They were not, as we know, telling Johann the whole story. Later in May the council admitted as much when it urged the prince to be patient "insofar as possible" until his own officials had had a chance to look into matters, and since "we hope to God that we may be able to quiet the people entirely."[54]

As it turned out, within the walls the council was able to do just this. By Saturday, 13 May, two days before the Battle of Frankenhausen, the city was sufficiently calm that the patricians could dispense with guards at city hall. They removed them, they said, "in view of the fact that a good and friendly will prevails within the community and that on their own account they [the people] wrote to the territorial lord that they would sacrifice body and life [for him] and help to punish any who might rebel."[55] Thus, there were two replies to the elector's accusations: one from the council and one from the community. When the community was hammering out the text of theirs, the council encouragingly provided refreshments at public expense.[56]

Outside Zwickau, however, there was little tranquility and small spirit of accommodation. The elector sent the council instructions to assist the Schösser in compelling the peasantry of the area to give their noble landlords taxes and services as before and to desist from driving their sheep on prohibited land and from fishing in forbidden waters. If the peasants had grievances, they were to seek redress from their prince in a legal manner. The prince *would*, the peasants were to be told, investigate allegations of noble impropriety.

After some debate the councillors agreed to do their ruler's bidding, that is, to urge the peasants to accept an investigation of their complaints. The city fathers remarked, nevertheless, that they too, just like peasants, had "no small difficulty" with the knights, and they affirmed that there was an urgent need for the elector to look into the nobles' behavior. They told Johann that it would be best if the city stayed out of the conflict as much as possible "in view of the fact that the council would arouse the ill will of the peasants and would make its own affairs more difficult to manage."[57]

On 25 May 1525, the councillors informed those with grievances in Zwickau that they could congregate to voice them on 16 June, three weeks hence. The councilmen were playing for time, hoping that by then the grumbling would have ceased. They knew of the massacre of the peasants at Frankenhausen by then, and they must have hoped that by mid-June a climate would prevail that made complaint ill-advised. In this they were entirely correct. By the middle of June, Johann had begun his sweep through affected territories in quest of escaped rebels. Urban malcontents could achieve nothing now, but the council put extra guards on city hall during the Trinity Market just in case.[58] The next week Johann arrived in Zwickau in person. The council made him and accompanying dignitaries gifts of wine.[59] It sent its servants scurrying from house to house in search of stabling for horses and extra beds for Johann's guests and approximately 2,200 troops.[60] It had beds moved from the vacant friary up to the castle and hoped it would get them back.[61]

Although on 2 May Pastor Hausmann, apparently oblivious to the uproar in and around his city, had shut himself up in his study to write his second lengthy evaluation of the condition of religion in Zwickau—his so-called second *Gutachten*—in June this intelligent, serious, studious, mild, and somewhat retiring cleric became his adopted home's benefactor. Princely cohorts had rounded up some eighty peasant belligerents and intended to deal severely with them. In keeping with what had been done elsewhere, many were to be beheaded; the executioner had been ordered. Hausmann and the preacher at Saint Katherine's Church, Wolfgang Zeiner, beseeched the princes for the rustics' lives. They stood upon the ancient Saxon right of pleading for the life of a condemned person, which was still often honored, even in the early sixteenth century. Hausmann's motives were overwhelmingly spiritual and compassionate, though his deed would confer political benefits upon Zwickau.

We do not know what Hausmann's arguments were. It would have been wholly consistent with the views of his colleagues on the city council if he had emphasized the unremedied troubles that the peasants had experienced on account of the knights. It would have been in keeping with Hausmann's temperament and religious convictions if he had preached to the court on the quality of mercy. However, Saxon law did not demand sermons; all he needed to do was to beg for the peasants' lives. One hardly requires written testimony to believe that the rescued peasants and their families were grateful to the pastor. His act of Christian charity may even have aided them in accepting Lutheranism.

Hausmann's intercession annoyed Luther. Aware of this, the pastor defended his action to Stephan Roth in August: "It is complained about me that I behaved badly and improperly in speaking out for the peasants. I saw and heard that innocent men had been seized. What I observed was no just proceeding; torture was used whenever the hearings weren't producing results. They were being accused without being given any time to respond [in their own defense]."[62]

The peasants failed to improve their political, social, or economic circumstances by their uprising. Peter Blickle has called the Peasants' War the "revolution of the common man," and in western regions he finds some ameliorating consequences of it.[63] In Ernestine lands the peasantry was and remained the powerless, disregarded mass of the age. The elector did not now set out to right the wrongs perpetually done the peasants; any subsequent inquiry into noble abuses came to naught. Not only did Johann have what were in his estimation far more consequent matters to attend to, but disparaging attitudes toward workers of the soil were imbedded in late-medieval burgher and noble culture. Devout man that he was, he could find in Lutheran teaching further justification than was already at his disposal for leaving the peasants in the positions of subjugation to which God had assigned them.

The city fathers, for their part, acted throughout in what they thought to be their own, and by extension the city's, best interest. They were the great gainers from the Peasants' War. A trend toward greater magisterial control of the population was already visible by the end of the first decade of the sixteenth century; and whenever the people expressed concerted opposition, even when this opposition took a non-violent form, the outcome was further princely confirmation of the council's advancing might. The Peasants' War, in presenting a *violent* challenge to established hegemony, brought the new elector Johann more firmly than ever down on the gentlemen's side. Save only his regalian rights, they were to rule without popular cavil or interference, over "their" peasants outside the city, as inside over the urban masses. The councillors were to be guarantors of peace and stability, and they could perform this function best the more complete their powers—save again, the electors' own prerogatives. The peasants' and the citizens' unrest handed the lords of the city nearly all that they desired, on a golden platter, as it were, obviating their need to watch for single, small opportunities and move at carefully calculated moments. In their minds—whether consciously or not—the commune as an organic whole was dead. But in the end, they had not had to dispatch it. They could blame the people for that—and relish doing so.

As for the knights, they went on as before encroaching on peasants' traditional rights. The peasants could hardly take comfort in the elector's simultaneous steady infringement of noble privileges, which may have made the knights bear down even harder on their village subjects.

Given the complexity of Zwickau's situation during the Peasants' War, taking into account the city's long and continuing controversies with local nobles over water and forest rights, the sale of beer, the diversion of highways, and a number of other issues affecting Zwickau's health, we can grasp the predicament in which the city found itself in May 1525. It *did* have grounds for sympathizing with the peasants. It was not entirely playing a role for purposes of remaining unscathed. Hermann Mühlpfort's and others' negative reaction to Martin Luther's brutal condemnation of the rebels in his diatribe "On the Murdering, Robbing Hordes of Peasants" is fully comprehensible.[64] Mühlpfort testified to Roth on 4 June 1525, "Doctor Martin's reputation has fallen greatly among the educated and uneducated."[65] A teacher at the Latin school, Valentin Hertel, wrote to Roth, "It is amazing how bad the multitude feels toward him."[66] In this violent age, Mühlpfort's disenchantment could hardly have been a result simply of Luther's advocating the killing of peasants. People in that day did not castigate a man of the cloth for advocating the taking of human life. But Luther revealed his detachment from the problems of daily life in the countryside, problems of which even members of Zwickau's city council were aware. Luther's response, then, in its extremity and its lack of realism was inappropriate; his remarks were unsuited to the circumstances as the councillors knew them.

Mühlpfort did not convey his disillusionment to the reformer. Ever the pragmatist, he realized that it would not be wise to alienate Luther. In March 1527, when he wrote to Roth, who was studying in Wittenberg, he asked his friend to relay greetings to Luther and his wife.[67] Thus, the aftermath of the Peasants' War does not precipitate or foreshadow the eventual split between Zwickau and Luther.

Only belatedly, in August 1525, did the council publicly berate its peasant neighbors for their violent insubordination the preceding spring. On 23 August it resolved to send the Reinsdorf peasants a stern message of disapproval "so that many people may detect that the peasants' revolt did not please the council and so that the peasantry may develop a [proper] fear of the council."[68] It decided at the same time not to take the Kulitzsch peasants' side any further against the knight of Wiesenberg, "so that the council can maintain its good reputation for not ever having applauded the peasants' misbehavior."[69] It continued throughout to defend peasant communities against nobles if the peasants in question had taken no part in the uprising.[70] By 1526, however, the council had dispensed with even this distinction: it was aiding both former rebels and non-rebels against knightly oppression. At the same time, in those villages under its dominion it had to collect the sometimes huge fines imposed by the prince as a penalty for the revolt. Reinsdorf alone paid one hundred florins.[71] Yet Zwickau's peasant survivors of the war came away from the judicial aftermath with their lives. Mildly put, this was better than many.

The Council Triumphant . . . and
Then the Elector:
The Reformation in Place

Two major themes dominate Zwickau's ecclesiastical development during the remainder of the Reformation era, up until the surrender of the city to the Albertine Duke Moritz of Saxony in 1546. The first of these is consolidation of the municipal council's power over the church and all religious matters. The second is conflict, conflict between the clergy and the council, among the evangelical clergy, between the council and Martin Luther, and between the council and the elector.

The Peasants' War and the ripples it created among urban worker populations stiffened the resolve of the Zwickau council—and its resolve had not been flaccid before—to supervise every aspect of public life. From the princely point of view, city councils throughout electoral domains were now very important instruments in preventing other such uprisings. On 23 August 1525, gladly obeying a directive from Johann, the city council told the Viermeister of all the guilds and the appointed representatives of the rest of the artisan community that Zwickau's craftsmen were never to assemble en masse again. The promised congregation of late June never having taken place, the Viermeister had just composed some grievances (their nature is not disclosed) and wished to read them to all craftsmen "and others" and to come to a collective decision. This was exactly the kind of self-governing impulse, tolerated of necessity during the peasants' uprising, that the councillors were determined to nip in the bud. The patricians replied that the Viermeister knew what the prince had commanded, namely that the council was henceforward by no means to permit the people to come together. In the future the Viermeister should tell the council that they wished to convene; the council would summon the four representatives of the non-guild craftsmen (*gemein*) to join them. They could discuss any articles, and then each could take them to his respective guild for opinions. After that the Viermeister might report their constituents' views to each other, modify their grievances, and finally submit them to the council.[1]

In reality the Rat strove to impede the workers' cooperating on their list of grievances, which were after all directed against the council. Some bold craftsmen organized an unauthorized secret meeting in "the Platner's" house and intended to forward their complaints directly to Elector Johann. The council, in quick, pre-emptive action, had Hermann Mühlpfort speak to Johann in Torgau. Mühlpfort told him these people were being "hedge-councillors" (*wingkel Rethe*), that is, pseudo-city councillors, acting surreptitiously, without any qualification or the slightest right to do so.[2] In this instance, nevertheless, the craftsmen somehow succeeded in composing their petition and sending it off to Johann by year's end. On 7 January 1526, the prince wrote again to the council that the people were not to meet. He nonetheless demanded a response from the gentlemen to the artisans' "articles."[3]

In 1527 the Herren forbade the bearing of arms at any time by anyone but themselves.[4] We assume that citizens could bring firearms to shooting practice, which was encouraged so that the city would be able to defend itself if the need arose.

The following year the council adopted a formal policy (in contrast to informal practice prior to this) of keeping separate from ordinary burghers. Councillors were no longer to drink with common folk. "After serious consideration," the scribe wrote, "the council finds that in these deceptive, treacherous times it is not good that members of the council should be all too friendly with other burghers, nor that they go with them frequently to drink wine or beer." On Sunday and holidays after this, the councillors should come to the "little old room" in the town hall and socialize among themselves.[5]

After the Peasants' War, the city fathers undertook to make examples of selected craftsmen who during the spring of 1525 had especially strongly and publicly criticized them. One of those singled out, "the old" Hans Sommer, a smith, had distinctly opposed the peasants. Sommer lived outside the city wall, in the external Frauenviertel, and was thus vulnerable to peasant attack. He was sentenced to eight days' imprisonment in the *Rosselturm*, a tower in the city wall, for having said, "The council hinders the nobility against the peasants." If he suffered any injury from the peasants, he had declared, he would go to the council for reparations. He knew no master but God, he added.

When the councillors now reminded him about the elector, he boldly retorted, "Who knows which master will endure." He had been unwilling, despite his stated animosity toward the peasants, to help defend his prince against the rebels.[6]

In extending and tightening their dominion, the councillors took a number of major steps over the next several years. Any individual coming to live inside the walls, even a young girl coming in from the suburbs to be a serving maid, now had to appear before the council itself and swear an oath of obedience. Furthermore, these oaths had to be repeated each year. One might be lax on the matter of renewals where they pertained to members of the feminine sex but not of the masculine.[7] From 1525, as seen, the guilds could meet only with conciliar permission. From 1528 members of the council had to be present at, and throughout, their convocations.[8]

Fines for transgressions of any sort were increasingly stiff. In 1529 Dittrich Balbirer "used some words against the council's emissaries" and was put in prison and made to pay a penalty of ten florins, for any but the wealthy a ruinous sum.[9] Asmus Richter spoke against Burgomaster Bärensprung in a woolweavers' assembly and was immediately jailed.[10] The councillors had ever been objects of ridicule and lament, but in earlier times they had contented themselves with a reprimand or a public retraction. The era of lenience was now over. A totalitarian spirit prevailed in governing circles.

During the years from 1525 to 1530, the council assumed almost entire control over religious affairs in Zwickau. Whenever it needed a pretext it could point to persistent "heresy." It is true that the council had failed to quell the fires of religious nonconformity. On 20 January 1528, the Herren resolved that because enthusiasm (*schwirmerey*) was so widespread and revolt a danger, the people should urgently be called together quarter by quarter and most sternly warned of the consequences.[11] The preacher Paul Lindenau was furious because even though the citizens' transgression was spiritual, the clergy were not asked to administer the dressing down.[12] No doubt Spalatin's thorough investigation of the situation a year later was a product of the failure of admonition. In 1528, in conformity with Johann's pronouncement against "enthusiasts, Anabaptists, and sacramentarians," leading suspects were called before the council and the pastor and questioned.[13] Spalatin, head of the visitors for Stiftland Meissen and the Vogtland, covered much of the same ground. The council condemned two women, Mrs. Kratzber and Mrs. Vetter, to exile, not only for their religious beliefs but because they were assertive and had converted other women. The authorities later relented and allowed Mrs. Kratzber to remain.[14]

Anabaptism was present in the vicinity of Zwickau in the late twenties, but so far as extant documents permit us to see, the magistrates did not apply this label to recusants within the walls until 1536. At that time the scribe noted that some woolweavers "and others" secretly met in houses and practiced their Anabaptism and preached. They lived, he said, mainly around Saint Katherine's Church. Just at this time a rumor circulated that Niclas Storch was back.[15]

The contrast between the council's position vis-a-vis the church in 1520 and in 1530 could hardly be more stark. In 1520 the council's strategy, as it had been for generations, was to maneuver among the multifarious subdivisions of Catholicism's vast bureaucratic network, among prelates, canon lawyers, patrons, monks, nuns, priests, preachers, and altarists. It could count a number of small victories among its attainments and even a few large ones like the acquisition of patronage over the pastorate. It had honed its opportunistic skills in the process.

By 1530 the council had even the details of ecclesiastical life in its disposal. The one serious exception to this lay in the limitations on its jurisdiction over a declining number of patrons and beneficiaries. Some patrons balked at releasing their endowments to the council; some occupants of benefices refused to be bought off. Elector Johann, evangelical though he was, was unwilling to abrogate all existing contracts. He was inclined to allow endowers and their heirs one-third of the income from church benefices, with the remainder to go into urban community chests. Or he permitted contracts to be terminated through negotiation. This was a lengthy procedure, one nearly but not quite finished by 1546. In addition, both Johann and his son Johann Friedrich were ever watchful to promote their own interests. Thus, in the end the city council had to pay both the Cistercians for the ravaged Grünhainer Hof *and* their prince for the right to add it to the urban domain. Johann otherwise did allow the council virtually full power over the daily operation of the church, interfering only occasionally. The council steeled itself against these exertions of sovereignty.

Zwickau's leading clergy—Pastor Hausmann, his successor Leonhard Beyer, and the appointed preachers Paul Lindenau, Lorenz Soranus, Conrad Cordatus, and Christoff Ering—failed to grasp political reality. So did Martin Luther. This brings us to the theme of conflict over the church in Zwickau. Although there were peaceful interludes

and peaceable clerics, strife was so frequent after 1525, when Lutheranism was already the established faith, that it may be called characteris-
tic of the entire Reformation era in this city.

Most widely known of all the episodes of confrontation is that between Nicolaus Hausmann and the council. The reason for this celeb-
rity is that Hausmann was Martin Luther's close friend and frequent
advisor. When Hausmann and the council clashed, Luther stood firmly
on his follower's side. The reformer unleashed a barrage of invective
against the councillors (as against all who disagreed with him)[16] and
refused to be reconciled with Zwickau's governors afterward.

Hausmann's relations with the councillors had deteriorated gradually after reaching their high point during 1525. So often had the city
fathers taken the pastor's advice between 1521 and 1525 that Hausmann enjoyed a sense of being in charge of the fledgling Lutheran
church there. Hausmann and the councillor cooperated, their motives
being partly the same. In its large dimensions, the transformation into
an evangelical church was complete by the end of 1525. At the same
time, as already observed, one consequence of the Peasants' War was
the council's determination to rule totally and alone within the walls.
For both these reasons, Hausmann's and the council's perspectives diverged. Hausmann, from 1527 designated superintendent, thought he
presided over Zwickau's religious establishment, whereas the councillors were certain that they did.

The collision is first apparent to the historian early in 1527.[17]
Zwickau's populace surely caught wind of it sooner. One of the issues
producing confrontation was oversight of the school. The council had
ever played a part in this, whereas the emerging Lutheran view was
that in Zwickau, as everywhere, teachers were lower level clergy and as
such subject to the pastor in whatever parish they worked. On 16 December 1527, the scribe wrote, "It was decided that the pastor and both
preachers shall be summoned and told how negligent they have shown
themselves in the matter of school fees (*Schulgeld*), [18] and added to that
our desire that they state their views [publicly] and from the chancel
help to further this cause."[19]

There was more to the problem than Schulgeld collection. Inserted
without pagination between two folios of council minutes, and dated
28 December 1527, is a list of subjects presented to Hausmann and his
aides for their consideration and reply.[20] The topics are not elaborated
upon, and we are left with only a very general knowledge of the difficulties. Still, the list is somewhat informative.

First of all:

1) What the council agreed to with the pastor and the pastor with the council, etc.
2) On the school
3) On holidays and bell ringing
4) Dissension between the council and the preachers and then between the preachers
5) Community chest
6) On religious enthusiasts (*schwirmer*)

Answer:

1) They [the pastor and the preachers] do not intend to resist the council in anything having to do with good order.
2) On the school, they will do it if it is consistent with the word of God. Poor children.[21]
3) Community chest, if some equipment (*gereth*) [was taken?] it did not occur as a result of bad feelings. It was told him [the pastor?] in general that the person suspected of having taken the equipment should be talked to about it.[22]
4) On holidays and bell ringing, they have discontinued it on account of drunkenness (*vollerrey*). In view of the fact that above that, some people get stabbed and beaten up. Feasts of the apostles have been forgotten. They want to retain the feasts of Circumcision [1 January] and Epiphany [6 January].
If on religious holidays the great bell [of Saint Mary's Church] is rung, it should also take place on Sundays.[23]

A few weeks later, Burgomaster Mühlpfort and Saint Mary's preacher Paul Lindenau were at each other's throats, and the rest of the council had to mediate between them.[24] The issues between them are not stated. Whatever they were, Lindenau attacked Mühlpfort from the pulpit, and the council ordered him to desist "so that nothing disadvantageous might follow out of it."[25] This phrase is, of course, a euphemism for public unrest. On 22 February 1528, the council denied pastor and preachers permission to do something unspecified since it was almost carnival time (*Fassnacht*). The gentlemen indicated that even if entreated again, they would hold fast.[26] Whether related or not, the council on the same day reprimanded Mühlpfort and reminded him of his oath and duty.[27]

Tempers waxed hotter by the autumn. Hausmann refused to wed a couple who had pledged their troth in secret, without their parents' consent. Private betrothals had long been forbidden by both church and state; this was not a Lutheran innovation, although Luther had already published his condemnation of such vows.[28] But other scholars in Wittenberg were known to disagree with Luther, particularly Hieronymus Schurf, and the council may have been aware of this and felt justified.[29] The gentlemen had motives of their own, however. They had asked Hausmann politely to marry the pair, and in November they lost patience. They said that the prohibition on secret engagements had not yet become law, which was not true except in the technical sense that Elector Johann may not yet have confirmed every one of his deceased brother's decrees. "In particular both councils have decided to have the pastor told that he is to give the young woman to the journeyman and to do nothing but that (*vnd solchs In keinen weg anders halten*)!"[30] Hausmann remained intransigent. On 16 November 1528, the council resolved to order a deacon, Adam Schuman, to perform the ceremony.[31]

Hausmann did not attempt to save the embattled, demagogic preacher Lindenau. On 30 January 1529, the parish visitors examined him for doctrinal competence and found him qualified to preach.[32] Curiously, in their official account the visitors did not show any awareness of schism among the leaders of Zwickau's church. They did know, however, and investigated further. Lindenau left in early March, and the council gave him a written testimony to his satisfactory performance in the city.[33]

The bone of contention was in fact not Lindenau's familiarity with or adherence to Lutheran teaching. It was rather that he preached in an inflammatory and relentless way against certain councillors, especially Mühlpfort. He was accused, too, of constantly using profane language.[34] Mühlpfort wrote to Stephan Roth in Wittenberg on 15 March 1527 describing Lindenau's demeanor.

> What a drama is unfolding in Zwickau, not unlike that of Thomas Müntzer. Pretentiousness, envy, and hate want to burst forth. . . . Never in my life have I heard more excessive, coarse, and unreasonable slander or such impropriety as that which he [Lindenau] practices and has practiced for a long time.
>
> The sworn masters of the bakers' guild . . . went astray, as a result of which some were jailed. This was during my administration. Paul took offense at this and preached, "The old fool [Mühlpfort] should be slugged in the mouth," etc. On account of this I summoned him, together with the pastor and [preacher] Zeiner and asked him [to stop] and reasoned with him in a brotherly fashion. When the Turks were creating

such an outcry in Hungary, I sent him a message to have the people pray to God for blessed peace and for the success of the estates' and our most gracious lords' matters (*sachen*), to the praise of God. He took offense at this and did not want to do it.

This very day he publicly preached, "Woe, woe, woe to you and all your children. You had foreign guests at your [son's] wedding and erected a shrine to Venus (*eynen fenus perck*)! Are you a patron of the gospel? What a fine patron you are! You have advertised pleasure at your front gate! The word of God endures forever.[35] Have that torn off and write: You have erected an altar to Venus, Here it is in Zwickau! You whore, you lout, you proud wretch, you haughty boob, you highfalutin donkey. You let yourself think that no one is more clever than you. . . . You hold council against me, you brought me here and want to drive me out again because I won't condone your airs, misdeeds, knavery, shitting around, thievery, and whoring! Note well, your power hangs by a thread, and when it is broken, your power will well and soon come to an end." . . . I gave him no cause [for this attack] and held [a] decent wedding party with no more than seven foreign guests. . . .[36]

The congregation loved this. Spalatin reported that the masses in Zwickau would rather hear Lindenau than "Martin himself."[37] Even the other councillors were favorably disposed to Lindenau. On 19 January 1529, Spalatin quoted his informants as saying, "The entire council was nearly in agreement with Paul."[38] On 4 February 1528, the council spoke of the matter as if it were a conflict between Mühlpfort alone and Lindenau, and it set up a committee to mediate between them.[39] The gentlemen asked Hausmann's assistance in persuading Mühlpfort to let his wrath toward the preacher subside.[40] This well-intended gesture availed them nothing.

Luther wrote personally to Lindenau on 10 February 1528, "I have begged you previously in letters, my Paul, to teach the word of God in peace and to refrain from [references] to persons and to all those things that rouse the masses, which is usually without [positive] results."[41] At about this time Lindenau had even come to the elector's attention. He ordered Georg Spalatin to go to Zwickau to investigate. When Spalatin arrived, in March 1528, Hausmann had taken Lindenau to Wittenberg "for his [Lindenau's] improvement."[42] Thus, Spalatin did not get to interview the controversial preacher. He and his companions must have spoken with other people, however, for they recommended to Johann that Lindenau be replaced. They wanted to give the preacher a chance to study theology futher. Lindenau had a formal hearing in Wittenberg in early April. Luther wrote to Hausmann that he had defended himself well and that Mühlpfort, too, had been vindicated.[43] But by then Lindenau was no longer an employee of the Zwickau church. After his departure, in May 1529, he wrote a letter to the elector denying any wrongdoing. He protested that his accusers had rarely if ever heard him preach.[44]

Mühlpfort was surely glad to be free of this unrelenting critic, but the people, among whom Lindenau had been very popular, were not only deprived of a favorite entertainment but were given one more demonstration of Mühlpfort's seemingly limitless power to control them.

Luther nominated Conrad Cordatus to replace Lindenau, and his recommendation was accepted. Cordatus was installed in his new office on Easter Saturday and was told how he ought to deport himself.[45] He did not take the advice.

Lindenau's removal produced not a whit of tranquility in Zwickau. The council now focused its attention on Lorenz Soranus, preacher in Saint Katherine's Church. Further, Cordatus proved immediately unpopular. Zwickau's elite considered him nothing but a "coarse Austrian."[46] The folk in Saint Mary's congregation who had enjoyed Lindenau's preaching were not disposed to welcome Cordatus with open arms. According to Ernst Fabian, who has studied the rift between Zwickau and Luther in detail, on 4 April 1529 Cordatus "proceeded in his maiden sermon to attack the Zwickauers without restraint, so that right from the start a general bitterness arose against him, and Luther himself thought it advisable to warn him to be moderate."[47] But Luther also told Cordatus on 9 April, "It's all right with me if those wicked folk are annoyed by you,"[48] Virtually from the beginning, those in authority, including conciliar scribe Stephan Roth, whom Fabian calls the heart of the resistance to Cordatus, refused to attend his sermons.

Cordatus attacked every level of the citizenry and alienated them all. Lindenau had directed his invective toward the magistrates and thus had been able to remain popular with many ordinary folk. Cordatus disaffected nearly everyone. He accused his listeners of being "sacramentarians, Anabaptists, blockheads, oxen, fools, lovers of falsehood,[49] and adulterers."[50] In September 1530 the shoemakers told the council, regarding both Soranus and Cordatus,

It annoys the [guild] masters and in fact the entire community that the preachers press the magistrates so hard to punish the citizens. They [the preachers] punish them [the people] from the pulpit. They are all too hasty, without shame, spiteful, envious, emotional, showing no leniency or friendliness, etc. [Does] it well behoove them so to teach the simple people and laity? What ideas such [demeanor] gives the common masses and why this should be of concern, the Honorable Council in its high wisdom and prudence may well consider, etc.[51]

By July Cordatus was ready to call it quits. Luther urged him to "be strong in Christ so that you can bear your hard and ungrateful Zwickauers. . . . Remember that the world is the world, that is, hostile to the word of God and an enemy of God."[52] The next month Luther wrote to Cordatus that he was willing to help Hausmann and him leave Zwickau for good. Luther acknowledged that his advice to Johann regarding the city had been "useless."[53]

The city council, meanwhile, wished not to spoil its relationship with Luther, but it would not compromise its jurisdiction over the church. During a lull in the contest between patricians and clergy, the council wished to make Luther a present of a decorative silver chain to wear. Luther told Hausmann that he had declined the gift as such ornaments were for the nobility and the like.[54]

By the autumn of 1530, Luther was once again counseling Hausmann and Cordatus to leave their posts. He revealed to Cordatus how widespread were attacks on Lutheran clergymen: "I neither know nor have anything to reply to your letters, my Cordatus, so heavily do complaints of this sort from our prince's entire dukedom weight me down. For our ministry to be thus scorned, regarded with hate and malediction, and then extinguished by hunger is a hidden and most noxious sort of persecution."[55]

Then on 25 February 1531 the council summarily informed Lorenz Soranus that after Walpurgis, 1 May, his services would no longer be needed, because, it said, "the congregation was not attracted to him as a person nor to his sermons."[56] As the council would later write to the elector, part of the reason was Soranus's alleged unchastity and attested beating and abuse of his wife. Soranus, according to the council, had tried to bring another woman into the bedroom he shared with his wife, and he did this in his wife's very presense. He was accustomed to take his walks in a suspicious area outside the walls called the Whores' Ditch, which gave rise to the obvious rumors. When criticized he said he would walk there all the more often.[57] When Soranus wrote his own defense, he declared that the accusation that he was unchaste was a "monstrous lie."[58]

The council's policy was to retain as preacher for Saint Katherine's Church a man who did appeal to the congregation but who was in no sense inflammatory. Lindenau had fostered popular scorn of the councillors. Soranus was not, as he himself ruefully noted, accused of this. He had not, he said, been wildly popular because he had admonished his listeners to obey those in authority.[59] The council had planned the firing in advance; it had drawn up a letter of reference (*Abschiedsbrief*) on 17 February 1531, vouching for Soranus's satisfactory performance and good character.[60] But Soranus preferred to depart immediately, without waiting to be given this letter to take along. The council paid him his salary to 1 May, plus a five-florin bonus.

Hausmann took Soranus to Wittenberg with him. Hausmann and Luther were incensed less by Soranus's dismissal than by the council's imperiously having taken such action without the advice and consent of its pastor and superintendent. Now at last the real issue comes into the open: who under the new religious order was in charge of the church, its teachings, its functions, its properties, and its personnel? The council, having long since obtained rights of patronage over Saint Mary's and Saint Katherine's, thought that its power was ultimate. Hausmann, having been named superintendent not only over Zwickau's clergy but also over others outside of town, was convinced that his was the highest local authority.

According to Fabian this issue gave Hausmann the energy for the first time to assert his rights as pastor.[61] There had indeed been a certain lethargic quality in Hausmann's oversight of his subordinates, yet he was not lethargic in drawing up lengthy recommendations for the implementation of Lutheranism. He also displayed amazing vigor in his frequent trips to Wittenberg to consult Luther. His was not a lazy or lackadaisical temperament. It would be nearer the mark to see in Hausmann a man of compassion and relative tolerance who found it hard to castigate those who sincerely professed the same faith as he. It is also possible that he took a certain private pleasure in the invective that the preachers slung at the councillors, some of whom truly were, we know, most self-important individuals.

The council itself characterized Hausmann as follows: "He doesn't look after or watch any preacher, deacon, or vicar but lets them deal with one another and perform as it pleases them. . . . In addition, if they discuss a subject in a sermon or otherwise, too much or in an improper manner, he lets on as if he did not notice in order not to anger them. [The result is] that they do not think much of him, for he is more in fear of them than they of him."[62] Roth and Mühlpfort called him the little saint (*sanctulus*).[63]

Stephan Roth remonstrated with Luther, who by now had openly vented his rage against Zwickau. Roth pointed out that in nearly every sermon Soranus had employed language such as "you thick skulls, you blockheads, you rogues, you villains, you boors, you oxen, you coarse Zwickauers, you godless people," and other similar epithets.[64] He asked Luther, "Why do you damn us without a hearing?" and he quoted to him the saying that was inscribed over the entrance to Zwickau's courtroom in city hall: "One man's story is no story; one should hear both sides."[65] The council as a whole wrote sternly to Luther on the same day, advancing many of the same arguments as Roth. The men ended with a threat to reply to Luther with a printed pamphlet proving their innocence of the charges directed at them by the reformer and explaining why they had dismissed Soranus. They hoped, they added, that such a step would not be necessary.[66]

As one might expect, this in no way blunted Luther's attack. Nor did the council exhibit the slightest remorse for its high-handedness. Indeed, it had already proceeded in March to invite Stanislaus Hoffmann from Pressnitz in Bohemia to come to Zwickau to deliver a test sermon. It liked what it heard, and Hoffmann took up Soranus's former position on 1 May. Luther duly upbraided him.[67] Cordatus, just returned from Wittenberg, did likewise from the pulpit. Hausmann, too, was back in Zwickau. Following Luther's instructions, he wrote to the council on 13 May requesting it to bring the entire controversy before the visitors in the forthcoming general visitation of parishes.[68] On 17 May he threatened to preach against Hoffmann himself,[69] which he proceeded to do, weeping in the pulpit.[70] The congregation, far from being sympathetic, was disaffected. Hausmann then made another trip to Wittenberg.

In the pastor's absence, the council commanded Cordatus to cease preaching altogether. Cordatus claimed to be acting pastor while Hausmann was away; this the council emphatically gainsaid. On this note Cordatus, too, took Luther's advice and left the city, returning briefly on 5 June to pick up his family.

Hausmann likewise relinquished his position in Zwickau that summer. Having left in mid-May without taking formal leave, he was still in Wittenberg in late June. The councillors finally wrote to him and reminded him that there was no one to perform his ministerial duties.

164

"We demand herewith," they told him, "if you wish to be our pastor, that you return between now and July 8 or the following week and take up your office as is proper. If you do not, you should know that we will make provision according to our opportunity and our needs. . . ."[71] In August the elector made the cleric's *de facto* resignation *de jure*.

During the summer Luther made a concerted epistolary effort to marshall popular and clerical support in Zwickau for his side in the dispute. He wrote to the people of the city.[72] He hinted to the three deacons, Johann Göbel, Liborius Magdeburg, and Adam Schumann, that they leave Zwickau.[73] They did not; Luther was not in good standing among Zwickauers at this time.

Both Luther and the council appealed to the elector in their conflict. He would have been apprised in any case of a schism so deep within his lands. Both sides made their preliminary cases verbally, to the prince's advisors, and in writing. On 30 June Johann invited both parties to a hearing before his counsellors, to be held starting 3 August in Torgau. This hearing lasted about three weeks. Zwickau sent Burgomaster Bärensprung, Councilman Gothard Büttner, Secretary Johann Hofmann, and lawyer for the council Dr. Andreas Frank of Kamenz. Mühlpfort joined them later on. On the other side was a formidable group: Hausmann, Cordatus, Luther, Melanchthon, and Justus Jonas. By now the question of whether Soranus had been wrongly dismissed had faded into the background. Soranus seems to have had few defenders at any point.

Testimony included not a few insults and intentional exaggeration of the truth. Mühlpfort called Luther "the German pope" and accused him of lusting after power.[74] Luther was least dignified of all. Cordatus wrote to a friend in Zwickau that the elector's counsellors had twice gone to Luther and begged him to compromise just a little.[75] During an intermission in the hearings, yet in the presence of the commission, Luther delivered his famous excommunication:

Accursed be every one who preaches in Zwickau. . . . May I die an enemy of this city. . . . For myself I have excommunicated Zwickau and I have cursed her because she will remain impenitent. Not only this but she wants us to approve impious deeds. Other cities in this land have also undertaken things against me but have crawled back repentant. But those from Zwickau are great lords and have many good benefactors at court. For that reason they do not allow themselves to be scolded nor do they need to obey. I had disciplined myself so that I would not rage. But those from Zwickau have made me break my rule. Zwickau, as pertains to those who govern you, I have especially cursed you in the name of God. At their drinking parties they could not keep quiet about us.

He added, turning to the commissioners, "From this you can understand how wolves are able to preach to us against the Shepherd's will."[76]

Luther obviously foresaw that the outcome would not be the one he desired. He was on the defensive, personally affronted by the commissioners' inclination toward Zwickau's delegation and their failure to be moved to submission by his own emotional if fluent harangues. He was trying to save face. There is some irony in the fact that Luther had argued just eight years earlier that congregations must be allowed to hear, choose, induct, and dismiss their own pastors and other spiritual teachers.[77]

The elector delivered a decision late in August. It was, as anticipated, a defeat for Luther. It was not, however, an unqualified victory for the city council. Luther might have taken comfort in that, but he did not; he harbored his grudge against Zwickau for several years. The elector designed and proclaimed his *own* triumph. First of all, Hausmann's and Cordatus's departure from their posts in Zwickau was confirmed. More important by far was Johann's enunciation of the new principle that only the ruler himself could permit either the hiring or the firing of clergy of all ranks. This applied thenceforward to every nook and cranny of the Ernestine domains. It was a major theoretical setback for all those city councils who for generations had striven to gather control of local churches into their gentlemanly hands. Bärensprung, Mühlpfort, and their colleagues can hardly have rejoiced at this. Catholic prelates and noble patrons had been seeing their rights of patronage erode steadily, and initially the elector and towns had been the chief gainers in this process. Now the prince was announcing in effect that he alone had dominion over the church within his territories, in city as well as countryside, and that he would brook no interference. Furthermore, nothing was to be considered too minute for his personal scrutiny, not even the selection of a minister for a rural hamlet of a dozen families. The legal stage was now set for Johann Friedrich's scrupulous supervision in the late 1530s of even trivial events in his subjects' lives. Johann Friedrich already assisted his father in governing in 1531 and may have influenced his father's verdict in the struggle between Zwickau and its clergy.

In practice the council went on making its own dispositions of clerical posts and in most respects ruling its church. Normally it had only to go through the formality of obtaining Johann's and then Johann Friedrich's assent before changing its ecclesiastical guard. Still, it realized that its territorial overlord could step in without notice.

Because of Luther's truculent animosity toward Zwickau as well as the city's deserved reputation for being hard on its clerics, the city did not easily replace Hausmann. Magister Christoff Ering soon took Cordatus's place as preacher at Saint Mary's Church. But the first thirteen men who were offered the pastorate turned it down.[78] Perhaps for this reason, as much as for sentimental ones, members of the council sought reconciliation with Luther. They did this to no immediate avail. In the council's initial negotiations with master-of-arts Leonhard Beyer, the man who finally succeeded Hausmann, the candidate made conciliar reestablishment of friendly relations with the reformer a precondition of accepting the post in Zwickau. Since Luther himself would not relent, however, Beyer finally agreed to come to Zwickau anyway. The elector approved the choice, and Beyer entered office on 3 June 1532.

Concord was not yet to prevail in these contentious circles. When strife with the new pastor reached its peak in 1536, both of the Reformation burgomasters were dead. Laurentius Bärensprung, who had entered the Rat in 1504, succumbed on 18 April 1533, and Hermann Mühlpfort, a councillor since 1510, followed on 25 August 1534. Their deaths marked the passing of a generation, the close of the period of religious change. Overcoming a range of impediments, they had established Lutheranism in Zwickau.

In the mounting tension between the council and the new pastor, the main issue was the same as before: who calls and governs the clergy. By the time the visitation committee began its work in Zwickau on 22 November 1533, relations between the council and the pastor had so deteriorated that the visitors remarked, "The council has been rather strongly in opposition to its pastor." The scribe continued that the visitors had worked hard to reconcile the parties.[79] The council accused the pastor of not performing his tasks assiduously, of going for many walks, and of seldom visiting the sick. They said that he rarely inspected the two schools (a school for girls had been founded in 1526) and that he held mass not more than once a year.[80] Above all, it complained that Beyer would not permit the council to be the highest overseer of churches and schools.[81]

No doubt in their dealings with the disputants, the visitors exhorted Beyer to greater industry. They also saw fit to write down in the instructions (*artickel*) that they composed for each community they inspected that "the council, as ordained in the last visitation as well, shall not hire any preacher, deacon, schoolmaster or sexton without the pastor's knowledge and consent. Instead it should direct and present them to the pastor. And the above-named servants of the church shall be duly obedient to the pastor."[82] At the same time the visitors enjoined "pastor, preachers, and deacons" from using "vexing, barbed, or uncalled-for language against authorities who do not act in accordance with God's word, in order so much better to maintain Christian peace and unity."[83]

One wonders whether the failure to achieve this Christian peace and unity had anything to do with the resignation all at once in 1535 of three members of the Gymnasium faculty, the schoolmaster Johannes Neander (Neuman), his assistant Bartholomeus Sylesius, and the cantor Wolfgang Schleiffer.[84] Whatever the reasons for their leaving, the council exacerbated the differences between Beyer and itself by unilaterally naming Petrus Plateanus rector of the boys' school and then replacing the other *baccalaureus* Hieronymus Nopus with Niclas Rudolf.

The resignation of a deacon, Liborius Magdeburg, in 1536 occasioned the formal rift between Beyer and the gentlemen of the council. Beyer, persuaded of his right to select a new deacon, nominated Sebald Forster, called Schutzenmeister, a Zwickauer born and bred, to the council on 30 June. Schutzenmeister had enjoyed the income from a local church benefice for seven years while he studied. The council, defending its right of choice, rejected him, whom it personally found no fault with, and reasserted its exclusive privilege to name new clergy and teachers. Each quoted to the other the appropriate article from the visitors' instructions of 1533.[85] Beyer finally relented and accepted a promise from the council not to force clergy or pedagogues upon him. Partly as a token of good will and partly because they had favored Beyer's own choice all along, the gentlemen on 8 July unanimously elected Sebald Forster Schutzenmeister deacon. It presented him to Beyer to be examined for doctrinal competence. All the councillors personally congratulated Schutzenmeister and wished him health and happiness.[86]

After this the council did consult the pastor when a clerical post fell vacant. When in 1539, for example, Stanislaus Hoffmann died, the magistrates discussed candidates with the pastor.[87] Yet it alone elected. This is apparent in its deliberations and attempts to attract Paul Rephun as preacher for Saint Mary's Church in 1541.[88]

Nevertheless relations between pastor and magistrates were not harmonious. On 13 August 1536, the council was incensed at Beyer's sermon of the previous day and of other occasions, in which he had needled (*ansticht*) the councillors, the schoolmaster, "and others." The gentlemen threatened to report him to the elector if he ever did it again.[89] At issue here was the council's failure to consult Beyer before hiring school teachers. Within weeks of the first apparent accommodation over Schutzenmeister, by August 1536, Zwickau's chief clergyman and the city fathers were again at odds.

In the midst of this summer storm, Luther, Bugenhagen, and Spalatin wrote Beyer a letter against the Rat, and Melanchthon added a postscript. One passage in particular now seems ironic because the sentiment it contains contrasts so starkly with the reality of church government wherever Protestantism was officially adopted: "Our gospel and teaching press upon us as of the highest importance that one should distinguish between the two regiments, secular and spiritual, and not mix the two unless extreme need or lack of personnel force one to do otherwise."[90]

The council's relations with Luther had been, to say the very least, strained since Hausmann's departure, and the city fathers did not wish to plunge into even more profound estrangement from the man whose faith they had espoused. In 1535 Stephan Roth had verbally prostrated himself at Luther's feet in an effort to lift his own and Zwickau's "excommunication." Thus, this new schism with Beyer was doubly embarrassing. Nontheless, Luther was beginning to soften after five years' contempt for Zwickau. In September 1536 he received Roth in Wittenberg. He did this in part because on 26 August the council had relented and agreed to include Beyer in its deliberations about new church and school personnel. Its own motivation was surely not to effect a reconciliation with the reformer, under whose curse it had managed to function well enough. It must have realized or been informed, perhaps by the elector himself, that the visitors' intention had been to have the council include the pastor in major decisions touching the church. The council could not escape this intention forever; it had been only a question of time before it accepted this comparatively minor infringement of its sovereignty.

Yet the council was not indifferent to Luther's wrath. This was so even before Bärensprung's and Mühlpfort's deaths. Under their regimes the council had written to Luther and received no replies.[91] On 22 September 1536, Luther having finally spoken to Roth, the council wrote to the reformer in tones of relief and joy:

> When our city secretary Magister Stephan Roth recently came home from Wittenberg, he said to us the Lord's Prayer that Your Reputable Worthiness wished; and he reported that it is Your Reputable Worthiness's request and wish to us that we live peaceably with each other and with our pastor. And so, in a spirit of friendship and thankfulness, we have taken up the greeting and wish of Your Reputable Worthiness, our especially gracious and beloved lord and friend. And we would like to tell Your Reputable Worthiness in truth that we are extremely desirous (God grant us grace, and in accordance with Christ's commandment) of living in peace and harmony not just with our pastor but also with all men.[92]

The council could not resist adding its old refrain, that it hoped that in the future, Luther would not judge it without a hearing.

The late summer or autumn lull that the elector's representatives effected in the tumultuous relationship between Beyer and the council was soon only a memory. On 26 February 1537, the superintendent submitted to the patricians a formal complaint. The council was not living up to the terms of its agreement, the pastor said. The schoolmaster Plateanus had hired five bachelors to read in the grammar school without Beyer even being aware of it. He accused the council of making improper use of tuition from non-Zwickau boys and of not passing out free rolls to poor lads. He said that the council was violating the visitors' mandate in its use of the community chest. He asked that clerics' salaries be paid out in the parish in a uniform way.[93] The council replied point by point and made no evident concessions.[94] Despairing of creating harmony between Beyer and the schoolmaster, the city fathers wrote to Justus Jonas and Philip Melanchthon. Apparently these luminaries mediated between the two and persuaded them to sign a written treaty.[95]

In February 1538 Beyer focused on the patricians' obvious neglect and abuse of the community chest.[96] The councillors made each other ill-secured loans from its resources and did not hasten to collect its unpaid debts. They had detached the two richest sources of income, the "Rich Alms" foundation (*Reiche Almosen*) and the Saints George and Margaret Hospital, which now received mainly the well-to-do within its walls. Although Beyer was correct in most of his assertions, and although Johann Friedrich would later demand to see the account books of the community chest, this problem was not resolved during the Reformation era.[97]

On 24 May the vistors appeared in Zwickau to look into Beyer's allegations. They ordered the city to put the two rich foundations back in the community chest. The council appealed to the elector,[98] but the decision was against them.[99] The loan of Beyer to the city of Freiberg upon its conversion to Lutheranism in 1538 quieted the dispute temporarily, as, of course, did the elector's intervention.

In 1542 the pastor gave the council a long list of its transgressions in administering the community chest.[100] Roth wrote, among other colorful marginalia against Beyer, "If the devil came out and *told* people he was black, all the world would flee."[101] Beyer argued, in keeping with his view of his pastoral and superintendential offices, that the council should not be able to draw from the community money without his consent. The council refuted this vehemently.

The controversy dragged on until it was part of the city's normal pattern. Beyer was not above petitioning the elector to grant him a garden near Saint Moritz's Church outside the walls to the north. As a reward for Beyer's recent service as chaplain to the Saxon armies invading Braunschweig, the elector did, thereby withdrawing forty groschen in taxes that had gone from the property into the community chest each year.[102] Roth was appalled and exclaimed in the margin of the council minutes, "Oh, the insatiable avarice of the clergy! May the Lord not give his blessing since this garden has been seized out of the gullets of poor people; by means of this [garden] the custodian of the church [sexton] has been fed for many years."[103] Beyer could be greedy. In 1545 he asked for a fifty-florin raise in his two-hundred-florin annual salary. He would have been content to let the additional sum be contributed by the other pastors in his superintendential district out of their slender maintenance.[104] The council balked, but Johann Friedrich insisted that the raise be provided, out of the community chest.[105]

It must be told that Roth himself petitioned his ruler for an annual income, complaining that he could not live on what he had. However, Roth did not already have, as Beyer did, two hundred florins a year in cash plus a garden and free housing. Roth, who by this time was a member of the city council and no longer its secretary, was now appointed council treasurer, which carried a compensation of fifty florins a year.[106] This together with the fifty florins annually that he received from his uncle's benefice gave him an income of one hundred florins.

He received other minor revenues from editing and for undertaking special assignments for the council. He spent much of his disposable income on books, and in his will he donated these to the grammar school library.[107]

There was constant strife, too, between the preacher Christoff Ering and Beyer. Ering originally preached at Saint Mary's Church for one hundred, fifty florins a year and then transferred to Saint Katherine's, where he wished to stay. However, the preachership at Saint Katherine's paid only one hundred, twenty-five florins, and Ering refused to allow his salary to be cut.[108] Beyer wanted Ering to preach at Saint Mary's, but the preacher thought his voice too weak to carry well in the larger sanctuary. The council relented and paid Ering the higher wage, but still the two would not cease their quarreling. Ering's window was smashed with a rock one night in 1543, and the council rounded up eight suspects. Each had to swear that he or she (one of the eight was a woman) had not done the deed "so help me God and His holy word."[109] Two of the suspects were Wolff Koch and his son.

Bugenhagen, Caspar Cruciger, Georg Major, and Melanchthon at length begged the two clerics to stop their bickering.[110] The council finally appealed to Johann Friedrich to step in once again.[111] This conciliar resort to electoral authority, voluntary as it was, weakened still further the council's aspiration to govern its own church.

Not even the Schmalkaldic War cramped the contentious style of Beyer and Ering. The transfer of Zwickau and the Vogtland to Moritz of Saxony in 1547 did effect a certain reconciliation between the pastor and the city council. Beyer quickly annoyed his new prince by failing to conceal his affection for the defeated Johann Friedrich. During 1547 and 1548, the gentlemen defended Beyer, who nevertheless left his post in December 1548. In February 1549, when he departed the city, a number of Zwickau's most prominent citizens gave him escort.

The Nature of the Reformation in Zwickau

The Reformation in Zwickau was a change that facilitated change. Strictly speaking, of course, it had to do with religion. We all know that in Zwickau as elsewhere the sway of the pope and bishops came to an end, monasticism went out of existence, the Lord's Supper was dispensed in both kinds, the seven sacraments were reduced to two, and the sermon became the centerpiece of church services. Yet to define the Reformation only in terms of the alterations it wrought in the ecclesiastical sphere is to tell but a fraction of the story.

In contrast to the twentieth century, when we are left reeling from "future shock," transformations in human affairs in the sixteenth century usually took many years. In their coming they were evolutions, not revolutions. The Wettin princes had yearned for greater influence over their domestic churches throughout the fifteenth century and had taken some small but perceptible steps in that direction. The towns, such as they were, were asserting themselves against their noble neighbors, who were concomitantly declining. City councils made every effort to expand their authority while urban artisans, perceiving this, prepared to resist. The knights' success in multiplying and replenishing the earth probably worked them greater hardship than urban encroachment because their lands were further divided with each generation. The Ernestine territories were overwhelmingly rural, and the peasants by the late fifteenth century had often arranged quite favorable terms with their landlords. They then found themselves carried by a new current in a disadvantageous direction, toward greater subjection. Once again, all these processes were from our perspective anything but speedy.

The Reformation, intended at the conscious level to touch only religion and the institutional church, set everything in uncharacteristic motion. It pumped adrenalin into religious veins to be sure. But the political circulatory system was not discrete from the religious, and people began to dream of attaining immediately what had been the subjects of vague and distant visions. Traveling mentally now at a faster pace, people's ambitions collided more often and with far greater likelihood of injury to some party. Too, as we are mere mortals, the desires of our hearts sometimes present themselves to us in disguise. Hence, peasants and artisans could imagine that the proper new religion would right civil wrongs, and they sought to promote their worldly interests in their selection of religious teachings and leaders. God did not favor the doctors of theology, they felt sure. The unlettered could approach the Deity, talk with him personally, and be the instruments of his will. How strange that we scrutinize everything around us in the modern world and acknowledge religious admixtures in politics and economy, yet regarding the past we want each strain, each element, pure and unalloyed.

Whether the possibilities inherent in the Reformation ever became conscious to any party, all most distinctly felt the loosening of the stays

173

that its advent brought them. In Zwickau the city council, not at first unanimously, saw a chance to eliminate a rival jurisdiction, the Catholic church's, and it did so with gusto. In view of society's normally slower metabolic rate at the end of the Middle Ages, five or six years was a short time, not incompatible with gusto. And one did have to observe the duty to obey one's conservative, elderly elector, Frederick the Wise.

The council also found in the Reformation a rationale for tightening its grip on the city population. Did not Luther teach and emphasize the obedience owed to princes and magistrates? The council's infringements on popular participation in government were more rapid and concerted now, though they had definitely begun earlier in the century. The progress of these infringements is a steady accompaniment to religious themes throughout the Reformation decade.

It is foolish to maintain, since evidence is almost wholly lacking, that Zwickau's privileged classes only or even mainly favored Lutheranism. On the one hand, Catholics abounded until at least the visitation of 1533. Catholics were handicapped by the relegation of their Franciscan spokesmen in 1525, but they were hardly defeated. When the council sent women into the empty friary to remove household items, sell what was saleable, and distribute the rest to the poor, public jeering and abuse nearly halted the operation.[112] The council wanted it thought that the friars had been ejected by popular demand, and many did want them out; but other views were well represented among the populace.

Nor was Thomas Müntzer's following to be found exclusively among the poor and downtrodden. Well-to-do people living near Saint Katherine's church and in other parts of the city were acquainted with Müntzer and with Storch. Among the few of their partisans whose names we know were many of a middling economic station and some who were well off.

A majority of councillors, whatever their private religious inclinations, were moved by their public office to desire the city's and their own best advantage. This clearly lay, as it had for generations, in narrowing the sphere of the Catholic hierarchy. Suddenly the Reformation presented the gentlemen with that entire sphere, or so it seemed to them for several years, up to the summer of 1531. This windfall of power and money was enough to dispel almost anyone's doubts about the correctness or appeal of Luther's message.

Whatever their own creedal proclivities, nearly everyone eventually realized that the triumph of Lutheranism meant almost unlimited au-

174

thority for the council. Only belatedly, perhaps, did a few perceive that the prior multiple jurisdictions, each rivaling the others, may have prevented any one from exercising thoroughness of oversight and becoming as a consequence too severe. There was no going back. After 1525, thanks in part to the peasants' uprising, the elector confirmed to the council what it so desired, namely, an almost unrestricted power to control the citizenry. Reformation and revolt each contributed much to this outcome. The councillors collectively were the great domestic victors of the Reformation decade in Zwickau.

They triumphed outside the walls as well. With Johann's patronage of Lutheranism and his support of Zwickau's city fathers, the knights could hardly resist further curtailment of their rights. They held out with all their might, and holding out often meant opposing Lutheranism energetically. Their station gave them a degree of protection not afforded the common man, but by the 1540s they too had succumbed to their overlord, the Protestant elector, now Johann Friedrich. Save only in name, *jus patronatus* had fallen into the lap of their prince.

The lowly of the countryside caught what they thought was a whiff of liberty in early reformist messages. The Reinsdorf peasants thought that scripture freed them from traditional servitude whereas others imagined that the Holy Spirit absolved them of the need to submit in matters affecting their souls to those who could read the word of God. They were to be greatly disillusioned, most dramatically concerning the former and gradually concerning the latter. There were, it is to be remembered, always some Catholics among them. Catholics in this setting were presumably the submissive, the conservative, the quiet. We shall probably never know how numerous they were, but the visitors said they were there.

Martin Luther experienced particular frustration in his dealings with Zwickau. Initially gratified that the council and his dear friend Nicolaus Hausmann made common cause in establishing "purified, scriptural" religion in the city, he had at the end of the twenties to face the reality that the magistrates intended to accept his judgments on theology and liturgy but to reject his views on the more practical aspects of running the urban church. Neither Luther nor Hausmann was prepared to concede a difference between the theoretical and strictly ecclesiastical and the administrative aspects of the new faith. The decision against their point of view in August 1531 was an especially bitter pill.

From 1531 the figure of the elector looms over all. Zwickau's council, as it leapt from gain to gain, finally ran up against the princely aspirations. It had always deferred to him, of course, but it had apparently not conceived of his ambitions as stretching even to the management of the city's everyday domestic affairs. The squabble between Hausmann and the councillors strikes us as hardly surprising. The development of the Ernestine Reformation during the 1520s should prepare us for it. All parties had been on a binge of acquisitiveness. The council and even Frederick the Wise and Johann had harkened to Hausmann, had taken his advice. Each had envisioned himself at the head of a church, a city church.

Conflict was inevitable. Even Luther sat back on his heels in Torgau in August 1531, when it became clear that he would not have his way about the role of pastors in urban parishes. The conciliar representatives mistakenly thought they were winning. Victory lay, however, with Johann, or more likely, since Johann died in 1532, with Johann Friedrich. This duke gathered the threads of sovereignty, even local sovereignty, into his hands and would not let them go. Only he could approve pastoral candidates, no one but he. Only he could dismiss them. He could intervene in the work of his consistory in Wittenberg in marriage or morals or any sorts of cases. He could investigate the allegations of misuse of funds belonging to community chests. The Ernestine church became his personal church, his *Eigenkirche*, and none could gainsay him. The single area in which he did not intrude was that of doctrine. Only here was Luther, as long as he lived, in no danger of contravention.

The Erzgebirge
versus Nuremburg: The Defeat
of Popular Culture

When in 1911 Karl Holl wrote about the significance of the Reformation for culture, he had a different theme in mind than I. His is a theological analysis of such topics as Luther's and Calvin's views of the relations of church and state, the nature of the state and the (political) individual, and Luther's attitudes toward the peasants, the poor, and free enterprise.[1] By contrast, I write under the influence of anthropology, in particular of ethnography. From this standpoint, culture is as much non-intellectual as intellectual and includes social attitudes, tastes, the sense of space and time—the values, practices, and the cosmic outlook of a people or a group. I am not uninterested in what Luther wrote on these subjects, but I wish chiefly to discover what effects if any his teachings may have had on the lives, in this case, of Zwickauers. Even before that, however, I wish to determine, so far as extant sources permit, what the culture of Zwickauers was like.

Historians of the Middle Ages have long since acknowledged that there existed clerical culture and lay culture; noble culture and peasant culture; and, with the growth of urban centers, burgher culture as well. Of course, these had reciprocal effects upon one another, hard though it may be to identify, much less to measure them. Although everyone permanently resident in Zwickau fell into the category of burgher, there were burghers and then there were burghers. It is tempting to divide them along economic lines—the have-lots versus the have-less. It is true that there appears to have been a wealth component in the division of Zwickau's populace into broad cultural groups; yet financial security alone did not lay down the lines along which people separated. The crux of the matter was attraction to urban humanist attitudes as opposed to satisfaction with the indigenous values derived from the surrounding countryside and modified to meet the requirements of town life.

The Common People

Urban humanism was the novelty and the intruder. Indigenous culture, by definition, was present first, the matrix within which the humanist infant developed. The reader will realize that documenting the outlook and even many of the daily practices of nonscribal groups in any society is an arduous, sometimes an impossible, task. The fortunate researcher possesses snatches of material which she can only marshall and offer as the slender index that it is. Judgment based on many months of scrutinizing the disparate sources is forced, unfairly perhaps, to fill the gaps.

As with all medieval cities, Zwickau's population grew as much by immigration as by natural reproduction. One reason that Zwickau artisans sympathized with the plight of nearby peasants in 1525 is that these guildsmen and some of the journeymen were acquainted with, and may have been related to, the rebels and their confreres. The taxes levied for the war against the encroaching Turks in 1531 and 1542 reveal, through the use of place names where last names were unknown, that many of Zwickau's journeymen in every guild (1) came from the villages in the city's locale if not its immediate hinterland, and (2) rarely came from distant places but even when of urban origin came almost exclusively from neighboring towns. In the 1531 Türkensteuerregister, one hundred, twenty-three journeymen were identified by place of origin. At least ninety came from within seventy-five miles of Zwickau. Fifteen did come from farther away. I have not been able to identify the eighteen remaining place names; they probably belonged to rural villages now no longer in existence or are only wide spots on a country road. Of the ninety whose provenance was in Zwickau's vicinity, nearly all journeymen came into the city from some point along the Nuremberg-Breslau trade route passing through Zwickau. Zwickau's strongest ties were with the people of its own region; it was in no sense cosmopolitan.

Paul Wappler,[2] Heinrich Boehmer,[3] Anne-Rose Fröhlich,[4] and Günter Mühlpfort,[5] to name only a few, have all asserted the religious radicals' indebtedness to more eastern currents without offering proof. I take them to be relying on annalist Lasan's account of the hearings of

16–17 December 1521, in which he attributes Storch's views to this knappe's travels in Bohemia.[6] Subsequent annalists seem all to have adopted this explanation. Not that I think they are wrong; so far as we can tell from what we know of the Zwickau dissidents, there were doctrinal similarities between them and the latter-day Hussites. Müntzer and Storch may, however, have been as oblivious to such connections as Luther was in 1519 when in Leipzig Johannes Eck accused him of being a Hussite. One treads on thin ice in affirming the existence of bonds either between Luther and Huss or between Storch and the Taborites when proof consists only of doctrinal similarities and of references to wars against invading Hussites or the trials of a few Waldensians in the 1460s.

Siegfried Sieber's article, "Geistige Beziehungen zwischen Böhmen und Sachsen zur Zeit der Reformation," employs a different tack in listing individuals who at some time during their lives were in both Bohemia and Saxony.[7] Not only radicals moved in this way. Egranus came from Eger and after departing Zwickau took up a post in Joachimsthal.[8] Georgius Agricola went to Joachimsthal after leaving Zwickau for the second time in 1527.[9] Stephan Roth was schoolmaster in Joachimsthal as a young man, before returning to his home town. Lorenz Soranus's replacement, Stanislaus Hoffmann, with his Slavic given name, came from Pressnitz.

Political boundaries did not coincide with cultural ones. People of all sorts came and went daily between Bohemia and the Wettin domains. There is nothing to suggest that Czech was spoken in Zwickau; German speaking people lived east as well as west of the Erzgebirge, and translators were easy to come by. Müntzer needed one when he preached in Prague in 1521. There is much evidence of Zwickau's interchange with Bohemian lands. Goods traveled to and from Bohemia through Zwickau. Blaschke mentions Bohemian grain coming to south Saxony at the beginning of the sixteenth century, and salt from Halle passing through Saxon territory to Bohemia.[10] Bohemian hawkers regularly traded in the marketplace.[11] Kolatches were well known in our city and were not a foreign delicacy. A number of journeymen stemmed from western Bohemia. When the journeymen bakers rose up in 1521–22 and, not getting satisfaction from the council, left town, they went to Kadan in Bohemia.[12] The Saxon electors at tax collecting times considered themselves beset by Bohemian pennies and in vain proclaimed against this currency.[13] Their collectors did not mean to disobey them, but many people possessed only these coins and

179

could pay in no other. During Lent 1542 the councillors collected the first installment of Johann Friedrich's latest impost for the war against the Turks. Of a grand total of 1,705 florins, 5 groschen, 11 pence paid, 1,613 florins, 6 groschen was in Bohemian pennies.[14] This is approximately ninety-five percent. In all the elector's lands including the western Franconia, forty-two percent of the tax was received in this currency.[15] The farther east one went, the more of these pennies there were.

When Zwickau first had a printing press, and especially from its establishment in 1523 until about 1526 when Jorg Gastel gave up the trade, either the printer or literate citizens or both were most interested to know the beliefs of the Bohemian Brethren. Luther, too, in these years, having explored his affinity with Huss, investigated the Brethren, and his quest may have influenced the Zwickau printer. Whatever the reasons, works about the Brethren issued from the press and were sold.[16]

An additional sign of the Zwickau population's sense of relatedness to its own region, in particular to the Erzgebirge, is the people's flight to Schneeberg in January 1547. The new elector, the Albertine Moritz of Saxony, became incensed with even prominent citizens' disinclination toward him and exiled almost the entire populace. In what must have been a poignant scene, the people trekked the twelve miles to their southern neighbor Schneeberg and sought refuge with her. Schneeberg would have been hard pressed in that trying winter to sustain herself and several thousand Zwickauers, yet she cared for them as best she could until Moritz relented. There is surely some significance in the Zwickauers' choice of city. This kind of intrusion required a spirit of kinship between the hosts and refugees to make it acceptable.

Further research may enable us to define with precision the relationship between the German and Bohemian portions of the Erzgebirge region. The information that we presently possess indicates a cultural, social, and economic cohesion in that area, of which religious similarities are but one manifestation. If this is so, then all the people of the vicinity, not just Müntzer or Storch or even Luther, were at least unconsciously familiar with what we label Hussite themes.

Zwickau's ordinary folk were illiterate. The guilds repeatedly pressed the city council to provide them with a public scribe and reckoner, a request that would hardly have been necessary if the ability to write and add had been widespread among craftsmen.[17] This lack heightened their vulnerability to lettered entrepreneurs. When the journeymen bakers revolted in 1522, they surely chose the most scribally competent person they could to record and transmit their grievances, yet the resultant document is hardly a masterpiece of prose.[18] The peasants of Reinsdorf did better in their petition to the council for aid in 1525.[19]

Despite the illiteracy of most of the citizens, it cannot be maintained that the written or printed word had no impact on the lives of Zwickau's humble folk. In 1525 everyone knew at least the general content of the Twelve Articles of Memmingen, which were printed in town. Legal documents continually used the phrase "read or hear read," (*lesen oder horen lessen*).[20] Those who could read put their skill at the service of their brethren. Orders from the elector were ever being read to the populace in front of the town hall or in church. Without doubt information and sentiments reaching Zwickau via the printed word were also disseminated among the men in taverns, where the male population spent much of its leisure time.

The reason for most Zwickauers' analphabetism was not simply either a lack of leisure or of tuition money. The attitude appears again and again that book learning is a waste of time and leads only to vapid pedantry or to participation in oppression. In view of the curriculum of the day, this attitude was not unwarranted. What meaning could the comedies of Terence, read or acted out in Latin, have, many must have thought, for the lowly who slaved their days and part of their nights away carding wool or baking bread? If these comedies had been presented to the public in the vernacular, the common man might have been more entertained, it is true, than by other classical works, but they were not translated. In contrast to our own day, in the early sixteenth century grammar school faculty did not ask whether their instruction could be made more relevant to life's concrete tasks. Most of the artisan class did not wish to educate their children, not even their sons. They did not share in the allegedly universal admiration of Zwickau's grammar school, and as we have seen, some of them were occasionally willing to stand outside and mock the boys until the councillors had to interfere.[21] The cerebral life was not for them. Hence, they may have rejected both Luther and Erasmus as too abstract and impractical. No doubt there were a number who did not go to this extreme. We lack the sources to show whether or not individuals or families with ambitions, however modest their circumstances, may have seen in the education of their sons a means of gaining entree into the circles of those with at least a modicum of political clout. An undetermined number of local burghers did send their sons to the Gymnasium and thus saw some point in exposing them to Terence.

If most ordinary people did not fill their free hours with reading or listening to books, what did they do for recreation? They liked their good times, which were avenues of momentary escape from the generally grim reality of late medieval and early modern life. Women's recreation consisted of getting together with other women, arranging parties either for fun or in celebration of a wedding or other festive event, and attending dances. An indication of the social importance to women of marriage, birth, and baptism is the city council's complaint around 1490 about the amounts women were spending on refreshments for the parties they held after a baby's christening, the mother's later return to church, funerals, and similar occasions. The women "invited many people [to these observances] and in the process have almost consumed [their families financially]." Thereafter they could invite no more than twelve guests. The councillors declared that at the traditional feminine gathering that marked a woman's return to society six weeks after she had borne a child, nothing more than bread, cheese, and local beer could be served.[22] The Reformation eliminated this rite of the new mother's purification and reentry into the life of the community.

Women associated with the production of woolen cloth—carders, spinners, and *kneppinnen*—were often unavoidably together as they worked, or they got together and through chit-chat relieved the tedium of their routine. They gossiped and retold the tales that they themselves had first heard from older friends and relatives. Martin Luther, in his condemnation of all types of popular oral literature, gives us some insight into the nature of these tales:

'Fools' tales' are the fables and fairy stories and other prattle, in the making up of which the Greeks were more able than others. Among us it is the fairy tales that the women and maids recite while spinning. Also, the vagabonds have their sayings. Besides that, worldly songs are sung, some of them shameful, some on worthless subjects. Here belong those of the Priest of Kalenberg [a trickster priest], Dietrich of Berne [a chivalric knight of yore], and countless other such things. It is particularly unchristian where one tells such stuff to the congregation that has come together to hear God's word and to learn the scripture; although it often happens, when many have gathered, even if they begin with serious matters, that they soon fall into frivolous, loose, amusing babble, with which they waste their time and avoid something better.[23]

Men recited and listened to this type of tale, too. Parish visitors in Saxony tried to do away with the gatherings at which stories were recited, but it is doubtful that they succeeded.

Men's social life had two focuses, the guild and the tavern. Originally craft guilds had had almost as many social functions as economic. Guildsmen organized games and meals, endowed altars, marched in their special places in the annual Corpus Christi processions, and cared for their sick and widowed. Guilds were a major determinant of companionship. As we have seen, the growth of authoritarianism in Zwickau resulted in a diminished role for the artisan guilds in social life. Particularly after the Peasants' War, when gatherings of every sort were suspect, the council forbade some traditional guild activities. The journeymen of the joiners' guild, for example, had always been under an obligation to provide a meal of roast meat for all the masters before advancing to master's status themselves. Most of the other guilds had similar social rituals attached to the induction of new members. In 1526 the council abolished this practice, admitting its fear that such events would lead to revolt.[24] The council applied this prohibition generally, not just to the joiners.

Men consequently resorted with greater emphasis to their other age-old site of relaxation, the tavern. For nonguildsmen the public house had ever been the repair of their leisure hours. Beginning in the late 1520s, the only sure way that guild members could circumvent the council's rulings against assembly was to frequent the same drinking establishments as their guild fellows. For their penny or three, men could imbibe their beer in the company of their peers, yet stay within the new conciliar bounds. As always, women were barred from the taverns.

Holidays may have been frequent under Catholicism, but work days were long. The bakers were up as early as 2:00 A.M., followed shortly, at 3:00 or 3:30, by other artisans, laborers, and servants in general. Often they did not stop working until 6:00 or even 8:00 P.M. It is thus comprehensible why taverns were closed on workdays. On holidays men might drink till 7:00 P.M. in summer and till 8:00 P.M. from Saint Bartholomew's Day (24 August) to Easter. They could remain sitting, however, until 9:00 or 10:00 P.M., depending on the season. Food could not be served along with the beverage.[25]

In and out of taverns men gambled, legally and if need be illegally. They won and lost money at such games as Fifteen (*Mendeln*), Tails (*Schwantzen*), Rats (*Retzen*), Cakes (*Tholhoppen*), Ruptures (*Car-*

noffel Spiel), Thirty-one Sewers (*Neher*), and Write 101 (*Schreyben Ayns vnd Hundert*). The forbidden games were Poor-Make-Rich (*Arm-Mach-Reych*), Rich-Make-Poor (*Reych-Mach-Arm*), Grab (*Rumfen*), New Fifteen (*Nawh Mendeln*), Buck Fifteen (*Bockmendeln*), Dig In (*Rawschen*), and Fifteen Sewers (*Neher*).[26] All dice games were illegal, but board games were permissible if the stakes were kept very low, at two pfennig a sitting or less.[27] Such pastimes, if unrestrained, threatened to add new families to the public dole, the councillors of 1524 thought.

From at least 1348, when we first hear of a brothel in Zwickau, until its closure in March 1526, unmarried men could and did seek another kind of sport among the officially tolerated women of pleasure.[28] The city regulated prostitution, and the inhabitants of the bordello rented their business premises from the council and wore the distinctive apparel prescribed for them. The late medieval guild system fostered prostitution in two ways. Although Zwickau's guilds by 1500 did not forbid journeymen to marry, many cities still did. As the ranks of the masters closed and fewer journeymen could feel certain of advancing to the highest status, journeymen had either to be allowed to wed or at the very least be provided some accepted means of slaking their sexual thirst. Secondly, the position of journeymen was typically so little remunerative that supporting a family on so slender an income would have been very difficult indeed. Journeymen normally resided in the households of the master craftsmen for whom they worked and were dependent on those masters for their sustenance. Masters would not have wished to maintain a growing brood of journeymen's offspring even if good use could be made of the wives as carders or general household help.

Syphilis arrived in Zwickau in 1497. There is no evidence that fear of contracting this malady altered many people's behavior. In 1524 Zwickau's *Franzosenhaus*, the "house of the French" (sickness), had only fifteen to twenty inmates of both sexes in it, but this was owing to the practice of allowing syphilitics to live in society unless or until they had obvious symptoms of the disease.[29]

Society's constraints on sexual liberties may or may not have been stronger than they are in the West today. Councillors occasionally impregnated serving women in their homes, and this was an embarrassment not only to their families but to the city, which was technically obliged to punish adultery severely. Councillors usually got off with a fine "for friendship's sake."[30] As a matter of fact, however, a cursory reading of the council's ledgers shows a growing lenience—that is, a

184

more frequent imposition of fines and a less frequent infliction of capital or other corporal penalties—in punishing sins of the flesh committed by people of every station. This contrasts with the council's banning of condoned sex in the brothel. In keeping with Lutheran teaching, promiscuity could not be tolerated; privately, however, transgressors were dealt with more lightly than before, far more lightly, indeed, than the law allowed. But what went on in the overcrowded households of lesser citizens is anybody's guess. At the very least, as Erik Erikson has said of young man Luther, children saw and heard a great deal.[31]

Public festivals provided the citizens with another type of diversion. Of these *Fastnacht* or Mardi Gras, which fell on the Tuesday after the seventh Sunday before Easter, or the day before Ash Wednesday, was the most universally enjoyed. Technically part of the late medieval church calendar, Fastnacht must be treated as within the realm of secular recreation because it represented the very opposite of the sober, ascetic piety of Lent. Carnival stands in the starkest contrast to religion, which is precisely why Martin Luther and his associates so objected to it. Peter Berke errs in asserting that "Luther was relatively sympathetic to popular traditions . . . and he was no enemy of Carnival or Johannisnacht."[32]

The cold and drab of winter in Zwickau being what they were, people looked forward to Fastnacht with great anticipation. Spirits rose and inhibitions shrunk days in advance. In contrast to other European cities, Zwickau had no official carnival to mark this day, no recognized "world turned upside down." Nonetheless, there was plenty to do. At all socioeconomic levels, the men grew restless and rowdy while the women planned dinners, dresses, and dances. There were always some events that had been thought out in advance. School boys put on Latin or (after 1519) Greek dramas, usually comedies, to show off their scholarly prowess. There were public games and shooting contests, sword and hoop dances. The chronicler Peter Schumann has left us an account of a particularly long and festive Fastnacht celebration in 1518, more elaborate than usual because Duke Johann and his entire household had fled plague-infested Weimar for the newly refurbished Schloss Zwicker. Schumann describes the recreations of every level of urban society plus the nobility. The peasants came into town to share in the fun and witnessed many (unnamed) plays and games in the main marketplace. In one that is described, eighteen men dressed as storks "read nuts" and were eliminated one by one, as perhaps in musical chairs, until only one was left, the winner. In another, a big shaggy dog was harnessed to a sled or small sleigh and made to pull a child back and forth through the evidently snowy streets. There were numerous foot-races and contests with swords—whether blood flowed as a result of the latter is not stated. There were also sword dances.[33]

The nobles favored military entertainments, and the citizens did their best to oblige their duke and his high ranking guests. On Monday, 15 February, six hundred fully armed burghers paraded past the re-viewers and arranged themselves in battle formation. This was no empty pastime. The Zwickauers were assuring their prince, who very much wanted to know, of their readiness to fight for him, come the Turks, the French, or Albertine cousins though they might. Later at the castle, twelve cuirassiers, albeit without their mounts, demonstrated their skill to the noble audience. At other times the nobles held tour-naments of their own and sometimes admitted burghers to the lists: citizens were encouraged ever to hone their martial capabilities.

In 1518 Zwickauers put on other unusual displays for the nobility. One evening twenty-six members of the coopers' guild performed their special hoop dance, during which each wore a burning candle affixed to his head. The butchers were even more impressive. They were well known in the region for repeatedly tossing a man up in the air on the hide of a cow and catching him. This exhibition never failed to amaze an audience. Johann Friedrich demanded to see it in 1535; and years later, in 1561, the butchers were ordered to perform their feat in Leipzig for the wedding of Anna of Saxony and William of Orange.[34] However extraordinary this display may have been in eastern Ger-many in the sixteenth century, primitive societies have been known to attempt to hasten the delivery of a baby by throwing a laboring mother up in an animal skin in this way.[35] In fact, such a practice has been attested for the Erzgebirge.[36] After the butchers' show on this particu-lar evening, a peasant, Hans Wickel, amused everyone by allowing himself to be so tossed.

On this occasion the nobility and their bourgeois guests at the Schloss had an opportunity to view both high and low comedy—high, that is, if the Latin language made it high. Unnamed Zwickauers pre-sented Terence's comedy *The Eunuchs*. They then proceeded to rhymed dramatizations of the proverbial battle between the sexes, de-picting in one case seven women quarreling over a man, and in another seven peasant men struggling over one young woman.[37] Love is not the only subject of these little plays; attitudes toward the lower classes are treated as well. In Schumann's account as a whole, we see very vividly that Zwickau's was a class society and that everyone knew his place within it. Be that as it might, there existed among all classes a mutual enjoyment of the license of Fastnacht, a distinct sense of shared pleasure. This reciprocity, this spirit of the wholeness of the citizenry of Zwickau, was soon to disappear.

Absent during 1518, but prominent in the Mardi Gras festivities of other years, were displays of contempt for monks, friars, and nuns. This phenomenon is not as transparent as it seems. Although many people from every rank in society scorned the regular clergy for their interference in city affairs and for their oppression of peasants subject to them, many others quietly sought their spiritual ministration and attracted little notice in so doing. People were of at least two minds in Zwickau and were not uniformly anticlerical or even anti-Franciscan. Things surely did get out of hand in early March 1522, when feeling against the local Cistercians and the liberty of Fastnacht combined with politics to ignite into violence. The Cistercian depot in Zwickau, the Grünhainer Hof, was, as we have seen, overrun, looted, and vandalized. From then on the city fathers, political beneficiaries of that uprising, were more cautious about Carnival and eager to prevent similar outbursts, which another time, they well knew, could easily make targets of them. The storming of the Grünhainer Hof had at one level been an expression of urban dwellers' sympathy for the abused peasantry. Thus, it was not surprising that in February 1525, on the eve of the Peasants' War, the council proscribed the customary gatherings. At most a few neighbors could get together and drink, but not more than "1 *firtel bir.*" There could be no dancing or ruckus, and they had to get the council's permission beforehand. The people were incensed. Little did they then realize that they would never be allowed to celebrate Fastnacht in the old way again.

After the abolition of Fastnacht, which had served to unite the citizens in a common release of inhibitions and pent-up aggressive impulses, people importuned the council each and every year on record to relent and permit some sort of celebration. Only in the mid-1530s did the magistrates let people have private parties—which confined people to their own socioeconomic group.[38] Violators met with a stiff one-florin fine.[39] Disregard of this regulation was nevertheless so frequent that in 1540 the councillors further limited the number of guests to "three, four, five, or six burghers" and their wives.[40]

The move, after a general prohibition of most of a decade, to private celebration and away from the earlier community games, both repre-

187

sents and coincides with the shift that we have observed elsewhere away from identification as a united citizenry of Zwickau and toward a sense of relatedness to one's own class. The governing elite initiated this movement in all its aspects. The ordinary folk, who naturally perceived that they were viewed as unworthy, deeply resented it.

The elector supported the city fathers completely, not just in their elimination of the public Mardi Gras but in their measures to restrict even guild meetings and every sort of spontaneous gathering. As we have seen, guild masters were forbidden to meet without express permission from the council, and councillors physically oversaw every sort of artisan assembly.[41] Finally Elector Johann Friedrich prohibited the masses in all his cities from congregating for any reason, "for seldom or hardly does any good come of it."[42]

The Elite

At some time during the fifteenth century, incipient German humanism made itself felt in Zwickau. There are two likely ways in which this strain of intellectual life reached Zwickau. The first is from Nuremberg. When in the 1470s Martin Römer vastly enriched himself by means of silver mines near Schneeberg, he expanded his cloth and metal trade and opened an office in Nuremberg. Nuremberg was already the object of some admiration in Zwickau, but this leading citizen's stories and artifacts brought home from his visits there, coupled with his generous philanthropy at home, reinforced the favor with which everything connected with this *Weltstadt* was regarded. News of the printing press reached Zwickau only in 1470, and a few incunabula came into the possession of Zwickau's small literate circle along with other goods traveling the highway from Nuremberg to Breslau.[43] Erasmus's reputation could well have arrived in this manner.

The other probable route taken by early humanism to Zwickau was that from Leipzig. Curiously, nearly all the staff of Zwickau's grammar school and most of the university-trained clergymen prior to the Reformation received their higher education at the University of Leipzig and not at Erfurt or the southwest German universities. After the founding of the University of Wittenberg in 1502, a fair number of burgher sons attended that institution. In all, 436 Zwickauers visited the universities of either Erfurt, Cologne, Leipzig, or Wittenberg between

1470 and 1550, an average of 5.38 new enrollments per year. Karl Steinmüller errs in his assertion that between 1533 and 1536, thirty-seven Zwickau sons studied at the University of Cologne.[44] In fact, none studied there during that period.

As tables 16 and 17 show, surprisingly many of the Zwickauers who enrolled at universities continued on to a bachelor's degree in arts. Very few individuals attended other universities. The Reformation burgomaster Laurentius Bärensprung had taken the master of arts degree at the University of Paris, but in doing so he was highly unusual among his home-town contemporaries.

However it came on the scene, humanism accompanied Zwickau's rise after 1470 from a town of little consequence to one of noticeable affluence and regional importance. Its receptive audience was made up chiefly of the resident partakers of the new wealth and status, and also of a few clergymen and teachers at the grammar school.

The earliest reference to a school in Zwickau dates from 1330.[45] The annalist Peter Schumann put the student body at nine hundred boys at the end of the fifteenth century; the city council told Johann Friedrich in 1546 that there were then eight hundred pupils.[46] Either of these is an impressive figure for a town with not far over seven thousand inhabitants. In 1479 Martin Römer had donated to the city a large, three-story building to serve as a school, and this could accommodate many lads. Some must have been housed on these premises while others, including many who were not native to Zwickau, boarded in town. In October 1542 the city finally obtained electoral permission to take over as a sturdier, more capacious school building the former Grünhainer Hof. It was ready for use in 1548.

As observed, most of Zwickau's artisan population did not think book learning essential for its children, and most could not have afforded the high tuition, which varied during the years under study. According to Emil Herzog, the historian of the grammar school, tuition was one florin a year for city boys and two florins for "foreigners," not such a lordly sum.[47] But the register of city officials (Amtsbuch) for 1520 refers to a two-florin tuition that had to be paid three times a year, at the beginning of each quarter, for an annual total of six florins, a large sum. It is nowhere stated that this high fee applied only to the short-lived Greek school, though that is a possibility.[48] Few scholarships were available. Assistance to the poor took the form of free rolls on Fridays, paid for by the Borner endowment of 1504. A further burden, the school constitution (*ordnung*) of 1523 required boys to

TABLE 16
ZWICKAUERS' UNIVERSITY ATTENDANCE, 1470–1550

	Erfurt	Cologne	Leipzig	Wittenberg
1470–79	8	7	40	—
1480–89	1	9	36	—
1490–99	2	13	46	—
1500–09	7	2	62	24
1510–19	2	1	44	22
1520–29	1	1	4	11
1530–39	0	0	2	21
1540–50	4	0	24	42
Totals	25	33	258	120

SOURCE: *Acten der Erfurter Universität*, ed. J. C. Hermann Weissenborn, 3 vols. (Halle, 1881, 1884, 1899); *Die Matrikel der Universität Koln*, Hermann Keussen, 2 vols. (Bonn, 1892, 1919); *Die Matrikel der Universität Leipzig*, ed. Georg Erler, vols. 16–18, 2nd main pt., *Codex diplomaticus Saxoniae Regiae* (Leipzig, 1895, 1897, 1902); *Album Academiae Vitebergensis ab A. Ch. MDII usque ad A. MDLX*, ed. Carolus Eduardus Foerstemann, 1 (Leipzig, 1841).

TABLE 17
ZWICKAUERS EARNING ACADEMIC DEGREES IN ARTS
LEIPZIG AND WITTENBERG, 1470–1550

	Leipzig			Wittenberg		
	B.A.	M.A.	%[a]	B.A.	M.A.	%[a]
1470–79	14	4	45	—	—	—
1480–89	14	2	44	—	—	—
1490–99	16	2	39	—	—	—
1500–09	19	6	40	5	4	38
1510–19	22	4	59	5	1	27
1520–29	1	0	25	1	1	18
1530–39	0	0	0	1	4	24
1540–50	0	2	8	3	16	45

SOURCE: *Die Matrikel der Universität Leipzig; Die Baccalaurei und Magistri der Wittenberger philosophischen Fakultät 1503–1560*, ed. Julius Köstlin, 4 vols. (Halle, 1887–91).

[a]Percentages are based on the number of students that enrolled during the same decade. The decade is something of an artificial unit; nevertheless, the figures suggest a higher frequency in the taking of degrees than I had anticipated.

commit themselves to a full six years of study.[49] Clearly, only boys from families with discretionary income could afford to attend.

An early sixteenth-century curriculum reveals the profound impact of humanist educational ideals upon Zwickau's pedagogues. The *schulordnung* containing this curriculum dates from 1523—it was one of the first books to issue from Zwickau's printing press[50]—but it assigns religion only a marginal place in the boys' formal studies. Religious instruction began in the Gymnasium only in 1530.[51]

In 1523 the sixth class, the lowest, learned to write in Latin and in German. The fifth class studied arithmetic and Donatus's grammar "from memory," some colloquies of Erasmus, and Cicero's letters. They began to learn Greek; they had daily homework assignments. The forth class moved on to Aventinus's Latin grammar, Greek declensions, Aesop's fables, Cicero's "On Friendship," Virgil's "Bucolics," Terence, Erasmus's *Paraphrases* and *De copia verborum*, and Lucian's dialogues. They too had daily homework. The third class applied themselves to Cicero's "On Public Office" and his orations, to Livy, more Virgil, Horace, and Quintilian; to Lucian, and to the comedies of Aristophanes. They read the New Testament in Greek. They acquired the rudiments of Hebrew grammar. They strove to write letters in accord with Erasmus's advice on the epistolary art, and they read Valla's praise of the Latin language. They had daily memorization. The second and first classes were combined and therefore had the same course of study. They read the Old Testament in Hebrew as well as in Latin and Greek translations. They took up Homer, Euripides, Aristotle, Pliny, and Seneca. As a finishing touch, the first class received instruction in good management (*wirtschaft*), applied architecture (*baukunst*), the military arts, and a bit of law and medicine, the latter two offered by the city lawyer and its physician respectively.[52]

Reminiscent of Guarino and Vittorino, the boys were not subject to corporal punishment. Lesser penalties were applied, and in cases of extreme insubordination or ineducability, students suffered expulsion. Later on humanistic ideals were no longer so completely in vogue. The establishment of Lutheranism in Zwickau brought no major revisions in the curriculum; its humanistic content continued to appeal to those in power and indeed to represent the epitome of gentlemanly knowledge. However, Lutheran overseers added religious instruction—belatedly, it strikes one—and stricter discipline. A new school order incorporating these changes was drawn up by the rector, Magister Petrus Plateanus, in 1537, and confirmed by Philip Melanchthon, Johann

Bugenhagen, Justus Jonas, and Caspar Cruciger.[53] Plateanus was such a stern taskmaster that the people began to call the grammar school "the whetstone" (*die schleiffmühle*).

The city fathers desired, partly under the influence of the Reformation, to provide an opportunity for girls of the town to gain a rudimentary education. The council retained a former nun as schoolmistress. It opened a school on 14 November 1526, which it shortly thereafter housed in the newly vacant beguinage. Girls were to be taught to read and write in German, to sing, sew, and behave properly.[54] Any more substantive education was thought unsuitable for the "intellectually weaker sex."

School curricula inevitably reveal the ideals of their framers. Where they are successful, they also produce graduates who are ready to propagate those ideals. This classical education was not, nor was it intended to be, practical in the sense of preparing one for a trade. This is why Zwickau's craftsmen as a group were indifferent to it. Only those who aspired to the position of the men at the top saw purpose in sending their sons to the Latin school. Unfortunately, we do not know how large that group of aspirants was. In the main, learning of the sort to be acquired in the Zwickau school functioned as a barrier between the governing classes and the unlettered populace at large. This condition predates and is independent of the Reformation though it was a component in the struggle among religious factions during the early Reformation era.

The circle of men who were not only drawn to humanism but who engaged in literary or scholarly activities of their own was very small. Despite patriotic antiquarians to the contrary, Zwickau's intellectuals could not hold a candle to Nuremberg's or Strassburg's—there were no Pirckheimers, no Dürers, no Wimpfelings in our town. Still, the city is none the less fascinating just because it was an economic and cultural center of smaller size and lesser brilliance than has often emotionally been asserted.

The names of those literati who worked in Zwickau in the early sixteenth century are well known because often recited. Erasmus Stüler, Studeler, or Stella as he romantically preferred to be called, was a Leipzig-trained doctor of medicine. Frederick the Wise imposed this immigrant on a resistant city council in 1501, and except for times of his incapacity due to illness, a councillor he remained until his death in April 1521. Studeler deliberately distorted the history of Zwickau. He strengthened the myth of Zwickau's identification as Schwanenstadt

(Swan City), a notion that must have originated because of the city's several branches of the Mulde, its lakes, its moat, and the residence of a population of swans thereon. Beginning about 1515 the university immatriculation registers refer to Zwickau as Cygnea, the lads being now "young swans." Studeler's contemporaries did not object to his embroidery on the city's not especially remarkable past. Indeed, his work appealed to the patricians, and they adopted, or at least consented to, his myths.

Studeler was one of the council's most fractious members during the first two decades of the sixteenth century. He engaged in personal verbal attacks on his fellow councillors and got involved in litigation with his neighbors. There is still considerable mystery surrounding his relations with Thomas Müntzer, for the councillor accepted the preacher as his confessor in 1520, a time when Studeler was ill and knew that his end approached. What may have transpired between them or whether Studeler did indeed defend the rabble-rousing Müntzer in the council remains conjectural. Strangely, in both his public and his private life, Studeler appears to epitomize all that Müntzer came to disparage. He hardly meets our ideal of humanist behavior. But Lauro Martines has observed, apropos of Italy, that we need to modify our ideal. According to him, humanists were consistently elitist and antipopular, and they used the past to create an ideology in support of their predominance in society and government.[55] They were frequently cantankerous and always self-serving. Studeler was surely cast in this mold.

Georg Bauer, alias Georgius Agricola, is representative of the type of scholar who sojourned in Zwickau as a teacher at the Latin school and then went on to bigger and better things. Agricola was born in Glauchau, about eight miles from Zwickau, in 1494. Where he obtained his early education is unknown, but he enrolled in the arts faculty at the University of Leipzig in 1514. In 1518, a fresh *baccalaureus artium*, he came to Zwickau, first serving as assistant schoolmaster and in 1520 as head of the Gymnasium. He composed a small Latin grammar for his students.[56] He left Zwickau in 1522, returned to the University of Leipzig, studied in Italy, became a physician, met Johannes Froben in Basel, and through him became acquainted with Erasmus. He briefly came back to Zwickau in 1526. The work for which he is best remembered is *De re metallica*, translated into English in 1912 by our own future president, Herbert Clark Hoover, and Mrs. Hoover.[57] This magnum opus, a description of mining processes, had not suggested itself to him when he taught in Zwickau, and his later activities owed nothing to his youthful employment. Zwickau provided him with a good first position, but it had little with which to satisfy his ranging curiosity. It should be noted, too, that from his trip to Italy on, Agricola's special interest was science. This was not a consequence of his exposure to humanism, though no intellectual sphere was immune to the effects that humanism had on all areas of scholarship. While teaching in Zwickau, Agricola presided over a general curriculum; he was not yet the scientist. Zwickau's teachers in any case showed scant inclination toward anything resembling science.

Agricola remained a Catholic to the end of his days. He initially favored reform within the church and wrote some antipapal epigrams. One of these ran,

> If nothing but a coin put into a small box can save us,
> Alas! Poverty, you are too much for me!
> If, Christ, you have saved us by your death,
> Then, Poverty, you are not at all a misfortune.[58]

Even so, he found Luther and Lutheranism not to his taste.[59] He disliked the apparent tendency in Lutheranism to make God responsible for man's sin.[60] The affinity of prominent city councillors for Lutheranism may have helped him come to his decision to leave Zwickau. During 1521 the tempest raged over Müntzer, Storch, and the Erasmian preacher Johannes Wildenauer Egranus. Karl Steinmüller is correct in maintaining that in the fray, Zwickau's previously receptive soil for Erasmianism suffered erosion.[61]

Stephan Roth was Zwickau's single native, resident, and productive humanist. He probably received his earliest education in Zwickau, but for reasons unknown he transferred to the Chemnitz grammar school, where he stayed from about 1506 to 1508. He attended the University of Leipzig from 1512 and received the B.A. in 1513 and the M.A. in 1516. He studied with such figures as Richard Crocus and Peter Mosellanus. From 1517 to 1520 the young Roth served as schoolmaster in his home town. He encouraged the founding of a separate Greek school, which, however, was very short-lived: in 1520 it was merged with the Latin school. Roth at that time accepted an offer to teach in the Bohemian city of Joachimsthal and remained there for three years.[62] In 1523 he went to Wittenberg for further study. From there he continued his voluminous correspondence with his friends.[63] He was apparently entertained in Luther's home and was enormously attracted by the reformer's message and erudition. He also greatly admired the Wittenberg city pastor, Luther's colleague, Johann Bugenhagen.

Roth's interests and allegiances are best revealed by the list of works that he edited and translated.[64] Items on it range from *Joannis Francisci Pici Mirandulae domini et comitis Staurostichon* (Leipzig: Valentine Schumann, 1517), to *Ein gesprech zwayer Ehelicher weyber, die eyne der andern vber den man klagt, von Erasmo Roterodamo lateynisch beschrieben, allen eheleutten, zu mercklichem nutz vnd frommen, gedeutschet. 1524.* The latter appeared in Wittenberg in the year in which Roth married Ursula Kruger, sister-in-law of Wittenberg printer Georg Rhaw. From 1524 on Roth edited exclusively works of a religious character, including a number by Luther and by Bugenhagen. The labor for which he is best remembered now is his compilation of Luther's postils for the entire church year.[65] Roth maintained connections with many printers and scholars, a preponderance of them in Wittenberg, Leipzig, and Nuremberg.[66]

Roth was drawn to the Reformation. He became associated with the city council first as a scribe in February 1528, and then, near the end of his life, in 1543, as a full-fledged councillor. Others of the humanistic figures that appeared in and then disappeared from Zwickau may, like Agricola, have found Lutheranism unappealing, even when, like Agricola and Egranus, they had publicly found fault with Holy Mother Church. Magister Johann Zeidler was another such person. He served as schoolmaster in Zwickau from 1510 to 1515 and then became an altarist in Saint Mary's Church, and from 1521 he was a preacher there.[67] He favored reform but not the Reformation and was consequently forced to leave in 1523 even though the councillors liked him as a person. Magister Johann Neander (Neumann) studied in Wittenberg and spent most of his life teaching in Lutheran cities, but in his old age he retired to a monastery.[68]

No absolutely clear pattern emerges. It looks as if of those men coming to Zwickau prior to the firm establishment of the Reformation, as many decided for Luther, or at any rate chose to stay, as remained true to the Catholic faith. One cannot well evaluate Bernd Moeller's theory about the temporary bond between humanism and Reformation on the basis of only Zwickau examples, but in fact one finds in Zwickau modest support for Moeller.[69] Those humanistically oriented men who would remain loyal to Catholicism were briefly in accord with those who we now know would adhere to Luther, in opposing Catholic corruption. The period of unity was brief, lasting from about 1518 to 1523 at the latest. In this particular group one does not see the generation gap that Moeller posits, following Herbert Schoffler.[70] Yet, as the councillors observed in 1525, within Zwickau's population as a whole there was a tendency among the old to continue to visit the Franciscan chapel.[71] Some of the councillors themselves who had passed from humanism to Reformation were not young, among them the instrumental Lutheran burgomaster Laurentius Bärensprung. One encounters notable exceptions to every hypothesis that one constructs, which keeps historians humble before what Paul Oskar Kristeller has called historical pluralism.[72]

Likewise, the relationship of the printing press to humanistically oriented circles was not what one might expect. In negotiating with a printer, the city councillors envisioned the office as one that would bring glory to their city and pleasure to themselves. This was not invariably the case.

In 1523 Hans Schonsberger the Younger of Augsburg offered to set up a printing press and paper mill in Zwickau. The city council reacted with alacrity. It signed a contract with Schonsberger in June, giving him a monopoly in the city for twenty years as well as an attractive exemption from property tax.[73] Schonsberger did not oversee the printing himself but delegated that task to Jörg Gastel. There shortly appeared a number of works with which the authorities could hardly have found fault: treatises by Luther and sermons of the popular preacher Dr. Caspar Güttel, formerly of Zwickau but at this time preacher in Eisleben. There were others of Andreas Osiander, then of Nuremberg; Wenceslas Link, then of Altenburg but originally from Nuremberg; Johannes Oecolampadius, called "Ecclesiasten zu Adelnburg [sic]"—had he visited Link in Altenburg?—and Friedrich Myconius (Mecum), a former Franciscan in Annaberg who had preached in Zwickau. But several other works issued from the press, some without attribution, that did not strictly support the council. The council was, after all, completely inexperienced at playing the censor, and it was determined to keep a printer in Zwickau. A certain Johann Locher "von München," a wandering evangelical preacher, wrote uninhibitedly against the Franciscans and the cult of the Virgin. This he could have done with impunity; but Frederick the Wise and his brother Johann, even if not the city council, found especially irksome his expressions of sympathy for the peasantry.[74] In reality, Locher urged the peasants not to take any hasty action; one could hardly label Locher, or

196

Gastel, unrestrained.[75] The princes saw things differently. They disliked the fact that several editions of the peasants' articles had issued from the press.[76] They thought that the best treatment of the peasants was no treatment at all. They commanded the printer to submit everything he proposed to publish to the electoral court for scrutiny. The council complained that such a stricture would drive the printer away from the city and begged for mitigation. Whatever the reply, Locher disappeared from town by mid-May 1524, and Gastel seems to have stopped printing.[77]

Dealings between Schonsberger and the council became complicated after this. Gabriel Kantz, another Augsburg printer, set up shop despite Schonsberger's monopoly, which, however, Schonsberger evidently was not using. Kantz printed in Zwickau from 1526 until his death from sweating sickness in 1529. His widow married Wolff Meierpeck, the first printer in Freiberg, who took over as stationer and remained until 1550. For the remainder of the sixteenth century, Zwickau had no press.

A striking feature of the list of first books printed in Zwickau is that an overwhelming majority of them have to do with religion. Scarcely any are the kinds of works associated with humanism. What is to be made of this? In 1523 in Zwickau there was very great interest in religion. Polemics continued to fly, but by now a Lutheran outcome was assured. The city was in the midst of its transformation from Catholic to Lutheran, and whatever side individuals stood on, this was the topic of the day. In view of this, there was quite a market for sermons, treatises on the Bohemian Brethren, translations of Psalms into German, and parts of the Lutheran liturgy as these emerged from Wittenberg. Despite the continued presence of loyal Catholics, in governing circles the Catholic church as a worldly corporation was *institutum non gratum*, and the publication list reflects this. Too, the titles lead us to conclude, along with Moeller, that "after 1520 the evangelical movement began to escape from humanism."[78] But like a rebellious youth leaving home, however much it desired to, the Lutheran evangelical movement could never shake loose of its humanist roots. The Lutheran reformers carried their linguistic skills and their memory of thousands of passages from the writers of antiquity around with them forever.

Unquestionably, the printer himself determined which works went to press, and Gastel was personally interested in religion. It seems business logic to us that he would have modified his personal tastes to accommodate public demand and make a profit. But perhaps he did

197

not. As before 1523, the products of other printing firms were sold in Zwickau, and so the book-buying public could select the titles that appealed to it whether among Gastel's wares or not. In 1538 Meierpeck and another, unnamed, bookseller complained to the council that "foreign booksellers" were ruining their trade.[79] As a means of protection they demanded to be formed, along with "one and one half" bookbinders, into a guild.[80] The council retorted that there were too few of them to justify creating a guild. It ordered the "foreigners" to sell only at the biweekly local markets and the three large annual fairs.[81] The reading public clearly sought out those who dealt in books and pamphlets not published in their midst, and any who wished humanist literature could eventually get it.

If Zwickau's elite regarded itself as superior to the humble masses because of its better education and its humanistic values, it attempted to demonstrate in the material realm its high station in the earthly hierarchy. Sumptuary laws in Zwickau, as elsewhere, greatly aided the high and the mighty in looking distinct from their poorer, less powerful neighbors. However much they may have affected humble folk, sumptuary laws were part of elite culture. Throughout the late Middle Ages and the sixteenth century, the rich—and especially the city fathers and their families—could wear more lavish and plentiful clothing and more valuable jewelry, and could have larger weddings with more guests, more dishes, and better wine than their lower ranking fellows. Female members of their families could have longer, fuller skirts. Some undated sumptuary laws, assigned to the period 1475 to 1510, grant councillors' wives and daughters the right to own up to four dresses of "foreign" material (that is, not manufactured in Zwickau), and each of these could be worth a maximum of thirty florins, more than the cost of a modest cottage. They could have two everyday dresses, besides. Ordinary women and maidens were restricted to three dresses of foreign cloth, none valued at more than twenty florins. They might wear silk in their hair, but only "common" silk. Servingwomen were allowed to wear no silk at all except to tie up their tresses, and their clothes were to be appropriately plain. The council declared to all classes, "Henceforth women may wear no wreaths or feathers."[82]

Such rules were typical all over Europe and bear witness to everyone's assumption that God had created human society as a hierarchy. Human nature ever moved the lower echelons to try to better their position, even if the only way they could do it was to have a gown that exceeded the limit by a centimeter or two in length. Human nature ever moved dominant citizens to confirm their superiority by keeping their underlings from rising. This cast of mind took on a tinge of urgency in the sixteenth century as serious inflation beset the city.

Other material symbols of social prominence in Zwickau were several. First of all, one owned as large a house as one could afford. Rich and poor dwelled close together in every quarter of Zwickau, but the main thoroughfares and the marketplace were lined with the imposing stone-and-stucco homes of the well-to-do. These were the houses with several storys, numerous rooms, water piped into the courtyards, and even bathrooms. Far more common were the modest residences of poorer property owners and of landlords. These houses had only one or two floors and probably often had more than one family living in them—the family of the artisan owner and perhaps the family of his married journeyman. But the rich also shared their households with people to whom they were not related, particularly with servants; owing to this practice, the affluent were as little likely to enjoy privacy as the poor. Less grand homes were usually made of wood and did not have stone foundations. The poor had no courtyards or gardens and little in the way of heating facilities.

There is no longer evidence of the arrangement of rooms in the houses, of fixtures or furnishings. If only it had been possible to examine the ancient edifices before they were razed in 1975! Sixteenth-century housewives prized a certain white-glazed pottery, described simply as "white ware." Some shopkeepers, among them women, dealt exclusively in this commodity, yet there are no examples of it in the current collection of the Zwickau City Museum. Perhaps future excavations will turn up some shards. Ordinary pottery was predominantly plain brown and wheel turned, with the occasional piece crudely glazed in unctuous green. There was in Zwickau nothing to rival the fine faince and glassware of Italy and the southwest German cities though rich families must have owned an imported example or two.

This much is certain: the well-off looked to Nuremberg and the southwest cities of the Empire for styles of public architecture, art, clothing, jewelry, and dance. Luther himself said of Nuremberg that it "shines all over Germany like a sun amid the moon and the stars."[83] Fernand Braudel has recently used similar language in describing Nuremberg in the early modern period, calling it a "sun city."[84] Two of

199

Zwickau's leading goldsmithing families, the Gaulenhöfer in the fifteenth century and the Schröter in the sixteenth, came from Nuremberg.[85] Young Zwickauers traveled to Nuremberg or Augsburg to learn
this craft.[86] Sexton Paul Greff left a touching account of cultured citizens' yearning to be like their counterparts in Nuremberg. In June
1522 a trio of singers from Nuremberg visited Zwickau. Greff was
practically overcome with pleasure. He described the singing of the
soprano and the alto as "such richly artistic and lovely singing as we
have never heard here, with modest gestures [and] with pure, lovely
high notes such that there was not the slightest movement of her [the
soprano's] mouth that the text and words did not require." They performed along with the singing "beautiful, refined dances that were
unknown to us, not as we coarse blocks of wood run and crawl as
though out of our minds."[87]

Civic leaders frequently sought some improvement for Zwickau, and
when they did, they usually looked to Nuremberg or one of the other
southwestern metropolises. When in 1453 Saint Mary's Church
needed a new choir, the city fathers may have had it modeled on that of
Saint Laurence's Church in Nuremberg.[88] Saint Mary's impressive altar was the work of Michael Wolgemut and Veit Stoss, both citizens of
Nuremberg in the late 1400s.[89] Peter Breuer, sculptor of Zwickau's
lovely *Pieta*, was born in Zwickau in 1473 but studied in Würzburg.
Michael Heuffner, creator of the imposing *Holy Sepulchre* in Saint
Mary's Church, was born in Eger but was a member of the so-called
Nuremberg school.[90] When the councillors desired a better midwife
than was available locally for their wives and daughers, they wrote to
Nuremberg, which had a veritable guild for midwives.[91] When they
wanted to know how goldsmiths' and candlemakers' guilds should be
organized, they wrote to Nuremberg.[92] The city's first printer came
from Augsburg. A paucity of sources hinders us in ascertaining
whether this emulation of Nuremberg was a late medieval development or a consistent strain in Zwickau's history. Helga Baier's account
of the decoration of Saint Mary's Church suggests that after mid-
century the influence of Nuremberg waned. This would be entirely in
keeping with other aspects of Zwickau's history at the time.

The less affluent of Zwickau aped in turn those to whose station they
aspired, unaware of the provenance of their models. In no respect did
Zwickauers quite meet the standard set by the successful of Nuremberg. How could they when their city had only a small fraction of the

200

population of the metropolis, when Zwickau was located away from Europe's centers of creativity, politics, and commerce? Dates of origin aside, compared with Nuremberg, Zwickau developed very slowly and even at its zenith, after 1470, never attained the variety or sophistication of the southwestern city.

Members of Zwickau's small elite class liked to think of themselves as more different from the common people than they really were. In their outlook on the world, the various groups in society had more in common than the privileged would have cared to admit. The city fathers along with the Protestant clergy professed disdain for the superstitions (*Aberglaube*) of lesser folk.[93] They were horrified to hear of a quack in an outlying village applying fried onions and incantations to a peasant's head in an effort to cure him.[94] They punished a young woman for taking money for her promises to find various items that people had lost.[95]

Hugh Trevor Roper had remarked that one age's rationalism is another age's superstition.[96] Perhaps that is why the councillors seem to us just as superstitious as those whom they scorned. They believed that infants in utero might be deformed if their mothers chanced to encounter a certain man with a "monstrous visage." They therefore showed this unfortunate to the city gate.[97] They and the masses believed that witches did exist and did have the power to make the healthy ill, to ruin crops, to kill children, and all other deeds widely attributed to witches during the sixteenth century.[98] In 1522 the future burgomaster Oswald Lasan recounted with feeling how a witch had been apprehended in 1510:

> There was a very aged woman here in Zwickau, a painter of that name [Mahler], an enchantress or mistress of the black arts, who through her unchristian skill performed works that were amazing to hear about. She made well people infirm, blinded the seeing, poisoned the newborn to death, crippled strong limbs, and—an [even more] excessive vice— through her false way gave the little whore girl an abortion. And above all this lamentable and horrifying artistry, she left her evil, erroneous, very damaging seeds behind her. For these and many other bad deeds she finally received her reward. She was burned with her books and [other artifacts of her] trade hung around her neck.[99]

The educated believed along with the illiterate that the appearance of a comet or other celestial phenomenon portended disaster.[100] However, with the coming of the Reformation, the city council prohibited the practice of ringing the church bell during thunderstorms, which had been thought to prevent storm damage. One stormy night in 1512, it had been rung continuously for eight hours until it cracked.[101] The council in 1540 threw out of town three individuals for hawking beets that they said were mandrake roots ("sie falsche alraunen, so von rotten ruben gemacht, vor rechte vorkaufft haben").[102] There is more to this incident than meets the eye. The people obviously believed in the legendary powers of the mandrake: to confer upon its owner sexual potency, riches, and power, among others.[103] The councillors were not disputing that the mandrake root could do these things; they too believed that it could. They were only acting against a dishonest business practice, the misrepresentation of a product offered for sale.

Martin Luther shared the attitudes of the urban magistrates. Like them he scorned his fellows' superstitions, their resort to soothsayers, mediums, diviners, magicians, and witches. He affirmed the existence of all of these based on biblical mention, but he considered them all to be allied with the devil. Indeed, he drew up a rather complete and altogether fascinating taxonomy of the various aides of Lucifer.[104] To use their services was, he warned, to employ the evil one. Only somewhat less dangerous were the sages who purported to interpret comets, eclipses, earth tremors, and other extraordinary natural events. Luther did not condemn them outright, but he did not wish Christians to pay them any mind. He rejected Philip Melanchthon's dear astrology altogether.

Both Luther and the city fathers held the view that although mortal beings could manipulate nature and interpret to others the meaning hidden in natural phenomena, Christians should acknowledge the sufficiency for their own lives of God's providence. To trust God was demanded of all believers. Superstition lay not in impiously consulting reputed experts alone but in presuming to exert control over God or his creation by buying potions, ringing church bells during storms, or wearing mandrake roots. The difference between the elite and the average citizens of Zwickau lay not so much in what they believed to exist—good angels, bad angels, sorcerers, fortune tellers, alchemists, and witches—but in their willingness or unwillingness to employ them. The poor and unlettered did not feel themselves to be in secure enough a position in life to be able to dispense with these potential aids.

The Religious Culture

Educated and uneducated alike participated in the dominant religious traditions of the late Middle Ages. A small number of nonconformists should not cause us to doubt this; they are the exceptions that prove the rule. Members of every class regularly invoked the Virgin Mary and the myriad other saints, the wealthy endowing altars or charitable foundations in their honor, all citizens naming their children after these holy figures. The vigor and constancy with which Luther attacked the cults of saints lends additional credence to this generalization. He accused priests and monks of turning Mary into a goddess and declared, "No one curses this mother and her fruit so much as those who surround her with rosaries and who always have the 'hail Mary' in their mouths (*ym maul*). Above all others these are the ones who most vehemently curse Christ's word and faith."[105] He attacked the legends of some of Zwickau's, and indeed Germany's, most beloved saints, among them Anne, Elizabeth, Peter, Nicolas, the apostle Thomas, George, Margaret, Christopher, Barbara, Michael and the other archangels, Apollonia, Laurence, Sebastian, and Anthony.[106] He radically altered the church calendar, wishing to diminish the attention it obviously drew to saints, and focused it instead on the career of Jesus.

Because of the cooperation of the electors Johann and Johann Friedrich, Luther's dicta were implemented throughout Ernestine lands during the late 1520s and the 1530s. In Zwickau a convinced Lutheran council acted with dispatch, forcing the abandonment of shrines, dismantling altars, and razing dedicated chapels. As we have seen, its motives were pragmatic as well as ideological: it was intent on acquiring the Catholic church's local property and might. Pastor Hausmann and the councillors publicly defended these acts strictly by religion, however. Magistrates and clergy now rejected the intermediary powers of saints and not only forbade people to worship them but circumspectly removed most of their images from the churches and sold off any of value. This alone represents a significant change in popular culture. Johann Huizinga was of the opinion that no one resisted. In *The Waning of the Middle Ages*, Huizinga says, "A hundred years after Gerson wrote, the Reformation attacked the cult of the saints, and nowhere in the whole contested area did it meet with less resistance. In strong contrast with the belief in witchcraft and demonology, which fully maintained their ground in Protestant countries, both among the clergy and the laity, the saints fell without a blow being struck in their defense. This was possibly due to the fact that nearly everything connected with the saints had become *caput mortuum*."[107]

This assertion needs examining, not only as it may apply to Zwickau. Within Zwickau the women were not quick to stop venerating the patroness of women in childbirth, Saint Margaret. Caspar Güttel, former preacher in Saint Mary's Church, returned to Zwickau at the council's behest during the chaotic summer of 1523. In one sermon this former devotee of Saint Anne admonished, "Women would also often very much like to have husbands, but they fear the pains and danger in the time of birth. Because of this they insist on Saint Margaret's little book and have more recourse to Margaret than to Christ himself. They struggle against the will of God."[108]

Even respected citizens were dismayed whenever it came to their attention that the council was disposing, secretly as always, of the Catholic treasures of the local churches. Some objected on the grounds that they were uncertain where the money gained from this enterprise was going. Pastor Leonhard Beyer was among these, tattling to the elector. Johann Friedrich was angry that the valuables had been disposed of without his approval; but as it was by then a *fait accompli*, he instructed the council to use the money only in aid of the poor and to give Beyer a key to the chest where it was kept.[109] Other people felt strongly that to meddle with holy objects—and some still regarded them as holy—was sacrilege. Peter Schumann was openly incensed when writing about the 1539 melting down of gold and silver objects. He concluded, "Robbers of the good of the church. Woe to you who plunder, you yourself [*sic*] will be robbed."[110] Fabian Busch, the locksmith appointed by the council to melt the artifacts, declared before he began, "May it be God's will that I melt [these]! If I am sinning, may God forgive me!"[111]

We may suppose that the Wolgemut-Stoss altar in Saint Mary's Church, with its many images of saints, survived because it was the creation of citizens of illustrious, emulated Nuremberg and was dear to the heart of Zwickau's humanistically and southwest oriented governing circle. This altar had been since its installation an object of civic pride. Even so, with the coming of the Reformation, the golden, glowing Stoss figures were kept covered except on high feast days.[112] The *Pieta* by Peter Breuer and the *Holy Sepulchre* by Michael Heuffner were moved out of the sanctuary.[113] Just after mid-century, Pastor Johann

Petrejus found the saint-filled altar so offensive that he nearly persuaded the city council to dispose of it.[114]

Luther, and after him the patricians of Zwickau, decried traditional feast-day observances on two grounds: first, as in the case of the saints, that they were unauthenticated by holy writ, and second, that they were occasions of immoral, self-indulgent, even riotous behavior. He was aware of and despised the fact that certain festivities held in association with the old church calendar were near and dear to the common people's hearts. A number of his pronouncements on the German proclivity to eat and drink excessively are dated in late January and February, the season of Fastnacht. The magistrates, as governors of a sinful society, charged by God to punish transgressors, must see to it that their subjects restrained their base impulses. Unruliness was unruliness whether it was a product of the spirit of political insubordination or of celebration. For both religious and civil reasons, Fastnacht could not be endured.

Many other venerable observances throughout Ernestine lands went the way of Fastnacht. Luther did not appreciate the splendor or the civic pageantry and unity displayed in the annual Corpus Christi processions. On the day of Corpus Christi in 1523 he preached, "I am not in favor of this feast because the sacrament is wrongly and ignominiously treated. . . . We want to cover it over with dirt and bury it."[115] In Zwickau Corpus Christi processions had taken place in the afternoon, beginning at Saint Mary's Church and moving through the Frauenthor.[116] On the very day that Luther preached in Wittenberg, this observance was transferred to morning and went only as far as Saint Margaret's Cemetery, right outside the city gate, near the Saints George and Margaret Hospital. There passages were read from the gospels. Luther's homiletic statement against the old practice was among Zwickau's earliest printed books, evidently intended to reinforce this change in the ritual.[117] Nicolaus Hausmann was behind the innovation. In his first evaluation of the church and religion in Zwickau—his first *Gutachten*—of early 1523, he harshly criticized the old ceremony:

> Oh, eternal God, what offenses are committed on this day! There is such a drinking in the guilds the whole week long, just as around carnival! Outwardly we bless God as the Jews did on Palm Sunday, we run around with green olive branches, that is, we stick around a lot of May blossoms, strew every pavement with grass, and, probably dressed in priestly

205

vestments, we carry large silver images, goblets, monstrances, pacems—
we haven't mentioned [still] other [objects]. God is supposed to be especially well pleased by all of this, but more likely he is angry with us; he
desires to be honored and called upon not with outer adornment but in
living faith, love, and forbearing patience.[118]

Under Hausmann's direction and with the council's approval, Zwickau
buried its procession and covered it over with dirt.

We cannot know how many burghers favored this change and how
many regretted it. Some did regret it. In 1584 an old man, now perforce
Lutheran, looked back, wistfully it seems, upon the Corpus Christi processions of his boyhood in Catholic Zwickau:

> On those feast days, they had a magnificent procession, . . . the images
> of the saints and the Virgin Mary were borne around the city or church-
> yard, . . . just as we bear the dead [today] . . . and I helped often and
> a great deal to carry out this procession. . . . The way over which one
> went around the city was almost entirely strewn with grass. Inside the
> church the altars were spread with Saint John's wort, curly mint, and
> pheasant's eye, which were pleasantly fragrant and lovely to look at.
> When one came back into the church, all the altars were hung with
> letters of indulgence. Two offerings were made. They took place as fol-
> lows: The council and the most important [citizens] went one after the
> other into the choir around the altar, . . . they laid down what they had
> and wanted to give. . . . The pastor stood and watched what each gave,
> accepted each offering, and with his hand drew it toward himself.

Whether as an afterthought or not, this man added that he missed the
preaching, for there had not been any in those days.[119]

Other sacred holidays prior to the Reformation were typically
quieter. On Palm Sunday a wooden donkey was brought into the
church, and the clergy acted out Christ's entry into Jerusalem and his
subsequent betrayal.[120] Easter was a time of rejoicing for the common
people because of its religious meaning, because the privations of Lent
were over, and because warm weather was on its way. Celebration took
the form of eating meat if one could afford it. Zwickau was far enough
north that the favored vernal custom of decking the inside of the
churches with green branches and flowers had to await Pentecost.

On the Thursday of Christ's ascension, five and a half weeks after
Easter, the clergy dramatized Christ's elevation. After the mass they
brought into the sanctuary a wooden figure of Christ, which was made
physically to triumph over an effigy of the devil, which was cast to the
ground. The boys of the congregation literally tore the devil to pieces

with sticks and kicks, while the clergy threw quantities of little cakes, raisins, and almonds among the people and were amused to watch them scramble and shove one another to get at the goodies.[121] The Reformation brought an end to such theater. In 1527 the council also eliminated a traditional Easter Eve observance, but the secretary did not describe it.[122]

At Pentecost there were religious plays for the public. An annual marksmanship contest was also held. A wooden bird was positioned safely away from the neighborhoods, and all contestants attempted to shoot it down. The winner was proclaimed the new King of the Marksmen (*Schützenkönig*), and he was freed for one year from payment of property tax, watch tax (*wachtgeld*), and the tax on beer and wine.[123] These financial dispensations must have provided a strong incentive to practice.

Luther had a low opinion of every Catholic effort to make some ceremonies comprehensible to the illiterate masses or to involve them in services in any pleasurable way. He mentioned in particular that on Easter priests had mingled in their sermons "foolish, laughable prattle" in order to wake up the drowsy.[124] At Christmastime presiding clergy had displayed a model of the Christ child in a cradle.[125] He complained that there were rhymes and monkey business too, just as on Three Kings Day, Good Friday, and certain saints' days.[126] He wished all such activities done away with. Luther criticized Erasmus, Sadoleto, Italians, "etc." to his dinner guests for giving in to the crowd. "It is their opinion that one should always incline to the populace and for the sake of public peace believe what the common people believe, even if the faith of the people is obviously nothing; for it is certain that they don't believe in God the Father, Son, and Holy Ghost."[127]

One aspect of religious culture that originated long before the Reformation and bound together society's wealthier and middling members was brotherhoods. On the eve of the Reformation, there were approximately eight of these. Some were so ancient that the dates of their foundation were no longer certain; the most recent, the School Brotherhood, dated from only 1519 and testified to the humanistic proclivities of the educated. These organizations were social and philanthropic as well as religious in nature. Every late medieval city had them, and they were a parallel in the socio-religious world to guilds in the socio-economic and councils in the political sphere. Late medieval society was indeed a network of corporations.

In both Saint Katherine's and Saint Mary's congregations there were

207

Corpus Christi brotherhoods. The one at Saint Katherine's consisted of woolweavers; their society had endowed an altar there that was popularly referred to as the *Knappenaltar*. They held periodic meetings, maintained their altar, and took care of members who suffered misfortune. The Corpus Christi brotherhood at Saint Mary's Church and the Saint Anne Brotherhood at Saint Katherine's were each made up of artisans from various guilds. Although it is nowhere stated, it is likely that these associations sponsored special events on the day of Corpus Christi in June and on the feast of Saint Anne (26 July) respectively.

The Fraternity of the Calends (it met on the calends of every month) had a chapter at Saint Mary's and one at Saint Katherine's. Of all the confraternities of medieval foundation, this was the one that admitted women. Some clergy also belonged. The society had masses said for the souls of dead members and sponsored others on certain feast days. It undertook acts of charity for Zwickau's poor and sick, and it held a monthly banquet. This was a prestigious and well-off fraternity, one that refused to cooperate when the council moved to disband it in 1527. It must have been hard for the members to grasp the disfavor into which, collectively, they had suddenly fallen. As recently as 1518, Elector Frederick the Wise and his brother Johann had honored the society by presenting the Saint Katherine's chapter with a Lucus Cranach painting. The princes themselves at that time clearly looked with favor on the activities of such organizations.

An uncle of Stephan Roth, the priest Peter Drechsel, founded and endowed the School Brotherhood. To this fellowship women as well as men were admitted. Most but not all of the female members were designated *uxor* or *filia* of some man on the list of contributors.[128] Women could belong in their own right. All the members intended by their joint efforts to maintain and improve their town's renowned academy and to assist poor and foreign students. Four times a year, in December, February, May or June, and September, they sponsored masses for the dead. The council brought this fraternity to a precipitate end in 1523. This action, though not explained in the council minutes, resulted partly from Lutheran conviction among the ruling gentlemen and partly from their reluctance to see proliferate such potentially rich and influential associations. This one, having just been created, could be nipped in the bud with little trouble.

About the three other brotherhoods we know very little and assume that at least two of them met their demise with the coming of the Reformation, along with those above. They were the Fraternity of

Priests (*Priesterbruderschaft*) and the Jacob Brotherhood at Saint Mary's Church, which cared for pilgrims passing through Zwickau.[129] The only society which may have survived the early sixteenth century was the Fraternity of Marksmen, the *Schützenbrüderschaft*. Its raison d'etre was to encourage its members to improve their shooting skills, something that the times demanded and that their prince strongly urged. In 1468 this association had endowed an altar in Saint Nicholas's Chapel dedicated to Saints Andrew, Christopher, Fabian, Sebastian, and Ursula.[130] Chapel and altar were torn down after the establishment of Lutheranism. However, this society continued to play some part each Pentecost in the city's annual shooting contest.

Martin Luther took a dim view of confraternities and their activities and early preached against them. He said in 1519,

> First of all we want to look at the evil custom of [having] brotherhoods, under the auspices of which one organizes gluttony and drunkenness, has a mass or several celebrated, and afterward the whole day and night and the next day is given over to the devil. Nothing goes on but what displeases God. Such a raging manner was introduced by the evil spirit and called a brotherhood. It is more of a game and is entirely heathen, even sow-like. It would be better if there were no brotherhoods in the world than that such offences should be tolerated. . . . What should Our Lady, Saint Anne, Saint Sebastian or other saints have to do with your brotherhood, which does no more than eat and drink to excess, throw away money, bawl out songs, scream, chatter, dance, and waste time? If one were to make a sow patron of such a brotherhood, even she would not put up with [such behavior].[131]

Religious confraternities were a salient feature of their members' spiritual and social lives. Those who belonged to them identified with one another, came to one another's aid before they came to an outsider's, walked together in processions, performed together upon the visits of dignitaries and on appropriate holidays, and held periodic meetings accompanied by meals and recreation. In the course of the Reformation, they too came to an end. After this there was no formal channel through which women could take part in public life.[132]

The attitude of Protestant historians has been that all these and other similar changes made in popular religious practice as the Reformation progressed constituted a move away from the evil and toward the godly; they have taken it for granted that most of the population welcomed this abandonment of popery. Insufficient attention has been paid to the disorientation that must have accompanied such rapid and sweeping removal of the old ways. All these observances were part of the ancient practice of the people. Popular antipathy toward money-grubbing, interfering clergy need not be translated into hatred of all the church-related customs that had been part of Zwickauers' lives for generations. More to the point, few festivities arose during our period to supplant those taken away. With the establishment of Lutheranism in Zwickau, only instructive religious drama was allowed, as for instance Paul Rebhun's play *Susannah*, which was performed "to great acclaim" in 1537.[133] Schoolboys still put on their Latin and Greek exhibitions, but these were linguistically impenetrable to the masses, who may still have enjoyed the pomp and circumstance for their own sake: a festive atmosphere is satisfying by itself. Passion plays were not permitted any longer. Luther thought them utterly papist, stressing as they did the suffering Saviour rather than the resurrected Christ.[134] He did not approve of drama at all unless it fostered upright living in the common man.[135]

A Turning Point

The early sixteenth century was a watershed in the history of popular culture in Zwickau. Prior to the 1470s there had been, to be sure, differences in wealth and influence among the population, but the people felt themselves generally to be part of the same urban collectivity. The city and its needs united them. Even politically the will of the citizenry, as expressed at stipulated times through guild leaders and other elected spokesmen, was willingly taken into account. The people formed a *Gemeinde* in every sense of the word.

A number of changes occurred in the late fifteenth and early sixteenth centuries that emphasized the distinctions among burghers and that ultimately created rather defined groups. The most obvious change was economic. As Zwickau became a boom town, suddenly there were several *very* wealthy individuals present who sought the rare and refined material accoutrements appropriate to their station. They looked to the flourishing, sophisticated cities of southwest Germany for their models. A psychological accompaniment to this trend was that the nouveaux riches and their offspring came to look down upon their less fortunate neighbors, while for their part, and no doubt independently, Zwickau's merely ordinary residents came to desire a similarly secure if not indulgent life style and to resent those who were able to achieve it. The late fifteenth century was a time of economic and social differentiation within Zwickau.

Humanism heightened the distinctions between elite and nonelite groups. The better off, certainly including a number of solvent though not outright rich master craftsmen, sought education for their sons. As elsewhere in Germany, that education was increasingly of a humanist character. It imbued its partakers with a classical conviction of the capacity and dignity of man. Such an attitude harmonized nicely with the vigor and optimism that already permeated that group of citizens who were benefitting most from their city's new prosperity. Meanwhile, the poor, generally untutored, felt no sympathy for the new learning. They retained the culture of the previous era, one not so far removed from that of the peasant stock of the surrounding villages. Only when the humanistically oriented took up the cause of the city against the institutional Catholic church did the populace enjoy a coincidence of interest. Those holding the reins of government and desiring to raise their city above its unspectacular past saw in the church a greater obstacle to progress than they had before. They now sought to eliminate rival jurisdictions with greater speed and intensity than earlier. The manifest corruption of many clergy gave them an excellent excuse to take action. If only Frederick the Wise had been more cooperative! Not even those who would in the end remain Catholic objected in the pre-Reformation years to efforts to curb ecclesiastical aggrandizement. Except for this interlude, however, humanism widened the gap between those with power and those without. The "haves'" sense of superiority, of knowing what was best for themselves and for the whole community, showed itself in their move to exclude the masses from their small but nonetheless real part in city government. The craftsmen meant it when in the annual presentation of grievances to the incoming council they begged the gentlemen to make no further alterations but to allow them to retain their own customs. The common man may have been untutored but he was not stupid. He was hardly oblivious to the innovations of the city fathers.

The Reformation changed the old relationships irreversibly. How many of those in authority turned to Luther spontaneously, with their whole hearts, we shall never know. Humanistic education prepared them to acknowledge that Luther was correct when he pointed out the Catholic church's blatant departures from scripture. It may well be that in moving against public festivals, saints, superstitious rites, and confraternities they truly believed themselves to be the valiant soldiers of

211

Christ. Certainly Pastor Hausmann thought them so. Popular resistance to these changes may only have convinced them that the devil had taken greater hold among the people than they had guessed.

By abolishing or confining most of the old corporations that had given late medieval society its order, the city council elevated itself over an increasingly undifferentiated mass. Since individuals alone could hardly oppose the council's will, those at the pinnacle of city government could act virtually unhindered—or so they thought. In practice, the patricians found that they had to deal with their prince.

In his far-ranging book, *Popular Culture in Early Modern Europe*, Peter Burke has noted the hostility of the Protestant reformers to popular culture.

> The reformers objected in particular to certain forms of popular religion, such as miracle and mystery plays, popular sermons, and, above all, religious festivals such as saints' days and pilgrimages. They also objected to a good many items of secular popular culture. A comprehensive list would reach formidable proportions, and even a short list would have to include actors, ballads, bear-baiting, bull-fights, cards, chapbooks, charivaris, charlatans, dancing, dicing, divining, fairs, folktales, fortune-telling, magic, masks, minstrels, puppets, taverns, and witchcraft. A remarkable number of these objectionable items could be found in combination at Carnival, so it is no surprise to find the reformers concentrating their attack at this point. In addition they banned—or burned—books, smashed images, closed theatres, chopped down maypoles, and disbanded abbeys of misrule.[136]

Although in some of its particulars Burke's list is not accurate for Zwickau, as a generalization it is correct. By 1540 Zwickau's citizens had not only a very different civic and church polity than had existed twenty years earlier, but major parts of their cosmos had been swept out along with excessive and exploitative Catholic clergymen. The people no longer had a role in town government. All the activities of guilds, whether economic, social, or religious, had been markedly curtailed, for these had depended on the right of craftsmen to assemble. Collective civic ritual was no more. Recreation was *private* recreation, divided along class lines, and confined to taverns, where women and councillors did not imbibe, and to homes. Mary and the saints, those holy figures who had populated and helped to control the universe, were proclaimed to be powerless or mythical, and the people were not to invoke them.

212

There is no evidence that popular fables and tales suffered any disadvantage just because Luther thought them worthless and visitors held forth against them. They had always been recited in a private setting, in the home or the cottage workshop, which was now the focus of recreation. Since, however, the average person in Zwickau was not literate and after 1550 the city had no printing press, we are left with few means of glimpsing, much less of measuring, this aspect of popular culture after mid-century. This handicap notwithstanding, it seems indisputable that the people of Zwickau greeted the second half of the sixteenth century with a radically diminished culture. Citizens remaining after the destructive Schmalkaldic War had to adjust not only to the loss of all their suburbs but to self-important councillors who, insofar as the elector had let them, had taken all urban authority into their own hands; to a more staid, noncommunal, private, class-confined social life; and to an altered cosmos.

The Reformation certainly did not *destroy* late medieval popular culture in Zwickau or elsewhere. Culture has so many facets that nothing less than the elimination of a people could in short order eradicate their culture. Clearly this did not happen in Zwickau even though change accompanying the Reformation was considerable. Too, there must have been regional and local variation in the impact of the Reformation on popular culture. In more cosmopolitan and urban southwest Germany and Switzerland, where stronger humanistic strains, a range of life styles, and numerous territorial divisions moderated the severity of the Reformation, the consequences of religious change may have been less pronounced. The Ernestine lands, by contrast, were still predominantly rural, their cities fewer and smaller, like islands in a sea of profound rusticity. Except at certain border points, Catholics with their more consistent practices did not dwell nearby to serve as counterweights to strict Protestant magistrates. Finally, the greater literacy of common people in the western cities may have afforded the reading public a means of preserving their customs. The printing press may have given popular culture a degree of indestructibility, even respectability, in western towns that it could not in the far less alphabetic Wettin lands. In Strasbourg, for example, Miriam Chrisman had documented an astonishing extent of book ownership among the lower strata of society. Her tables reveal that a tremendous variety of literature was available throughout the century. Whereas Zwickau had only three or four printers during the entire Reformation

213

era and none at all after 1550, Strasbourg had fifty-six printers during the sixteenth century, several of them specializing in the production of vernacular books.[137]

In his already classic *Religion and the Decline of Magic*, Keith Thomas has pointed out that the English people's beliefs in saints, magic, rituals, and amulets served as a means of control over the dangers that surrounded them. The traditions performed needed functions in society and were not dispensable.[138] This was true east and south of the English Channel as well. The loss of major cultural features in the course of the Reformation meant that gaps were left that could not immediately be filled. Society had to recover; it had to be healed of its wounds. How did this recuperation occur? Having been deprived of their traditional "crutches," were people now worn down by evangelical preachers and magisterial pressure? Did the transitional generation thrash about (whether or not it resisted), and did its sons and daughters then readily accept the only faith with which *they* were now acquainted, facing, in other words, a universe different from that of their parents? Shortly after mid-century in Zwickau, there would have been few burghers still living who had taken part in Corpus Christi processions or who could recall the old-style Fastnacht.

In any case, people generate culture; so long as human beings occupied this point on the banks of the Zwickauer Mulde, they would inevitably fill holes left in their social and political life and in their cosmic view. But the new would be different from the old. Apart from Lutheranism, the form and content of which we are acquainted with, what would the nature of the new be? Did the family benefit from the death of communal recreation and ceremony? Did the ruling elite now provide even more than before a model of life style, their manners and values to be aped by lowlier folk?

Did the Reformation produce in places other than Zwickau, beyond the borders of the Ernestine domains, a restructuring of the popular universe? Peter Blickle has recently restated, at a time when not all scholars agree, that the Reformation was a milestone in German and European history.[139] Culture, even the culture of simple people, is an aspect of history, and it may be that here, too, the Reformation marks the end of one age and the beginning of another. It is to be hoped that future research will yield answers to these and other obvious questions.

On the Fringe of Society:
Treatment of the Unfortunate

ne way of gaining insight into the values of a society far removed from our own is to ask how it treats the unfortunate. In rural Germany in the late fifteenth and early sixteenth centuries, the poor, the sick and handicapped, the orphaned, and the elderly all had to depend on their families for sustenance. The cities, by contrast, developed both agencies and fiscal means to care for their own. Of all those whom we today label unfortunates, only criminals were included in formal jurisdictions whether they committed their forbidden acts in town or in the countryside. If apprehended they would be punished.

In thinking about the urban poor, we need to differentiate between those who were or pretended to be impoverished as a religious act, and those who were penniless because they could not help it. Every late medieval city had its many and varied mendicant friars who begged from door to door as a way of life. They engendered no little resentment among the people, who nevertheless gave their alms. Zwickau had its Franciscans, its Dominicans, and its Antonites, as well as mendicants of any other habit who happened to wander through.

In some places students were permitted to beg. No less a person than Martin Luther had, as a boy in Eisenach, gone through the lanes with his bowl crying, "*Panem pro Deo!*" For him this was a student's ritual and not an economic necessity. Schoolboys in Zwickau apparently did not beg, or at any rate not after 1504, when Johann Borner, the pastor in Wernsdorf, endowed a weekly distribution of rolls to those lads who could not afford to buy them.[1] Bread truly was the staff of life in those days, the major part of the diet of both the poor and the not-so-poor.

We are here concerned only with the involuntary poor. During the

215

fifteenth century, Zwickau developed charitable organizations, one of whose functions it was to provide modest nourishment to citizens lacking it. The brotherhoods catered chiefly, but not exclusively, for their own members whom fate had flattened. Those who have never enjoyed elevated means did not qualify for regular help, and these begged in the marketplace, by the church doors, and from house to house. Where these last slept and how they clothed themselves are questions our imaginations must answer. An alms distribution house (*spendehaus*) stood in Saint Mary's churchyard, and the clergy gave out small sums there every Sunday morning. But such amounts were designed to prevent starvation and could hardly have paid anybody's rent.

The provision of food was done in a more regular way, particularly for those poor who had no affiliation with fraternal associations, after the endowing of the so-called Rich Alms (*Reiche Almosen*). This is first referred to in extant sources during 1480, under the label "Rich Dole" (*Reiche Spende*). This was a fund for the poor that modest and well-to-do persons contributed to during their lives. It also benefited greatly from testamentary donations. As elsewhere in Europe, it was the practice in Zwickau for individuals to stipulate in their wills that certain sums or goods purchased with those sums be distributed to the poor.[2] Stephan Roth did this in his will.[3] It was not a practice that entirely died out with the advent of Lutheranism. Others instructed their executors to deposit a stated amount in the Reiche Almosen. Before the Reformation all considered this a pious deed that God and man would regard kindly. Indeed, one's immortal soul *and* one's reputation among the living were widely thought to be at stake. With the coming of Protestantism and Luther's rejection of works as an aid to salvation, one needed only to worry about one's standing in the community.

There are at least three major reasons why the Reiche Almosen, alias Reiche Spende, came into being in the late fifteenth century. One is the enrichment after 1470 of a number of Zwickau's citizens as a result of the mining enterprise to the south. The prosperous could obviously afford to make larger gifts than the financially humble. Also, it seemed that throughout Europe the ranks of the destitute were swelling. Luther's diatribe against the mendicants (*die Bettelmönche*) should be seen against this background. Finally, one of the characteristics of late medieval urban life is the attempt to rationalize and order what had previously been unanalyzed and haphazard. The city fathers sought regular, orderly ways of caring for the disadvantaged.

216

The overseers of this wealthy endowment invested its pecuniary assets with an eye to having a steady income in the form of interest. They loaned ten thousand florins to the city of Erfurt at four percent interest. The four hundred florins produced annually by this arrangement was quite a princely sum to put at the service of Zwickau's poor. However, Erfurt was having troubles of its own and did not remit payment from 1510 to 1517.[4] Lengthy negotiations, involving even the Holy Roman Emperor, resulted in the resumption of payment in the autumn of 1517, but Zwickau never recouped its loss of the seven previous years. The city council could not simply suppress this endowment after it had adopted Lutheranism as the official creed of the city. It put the fund's diminished revenues to the same uses as it had under Catholicism.

The church itself engaged in poor relief before the Reformation. How much of its wealth the parish expended in this way is not known. Every Sunday after the morning masses, the needy gathered at the old *spendehaus* and received their dole. The Lutheran councillors continued this practice—only now, after November 1523, most funds came from the new community chest.

The community chest was in part a new wineskin for old wine. The inspiration for a community chest came from Martin Luther. The magistrates of Leisnig had asked him how they were to deal with ecclesiastical benefices that were coming into their hands. In response Luther composed "An Ordinance for a Community Chest. Advice on How to Handle Ecclesiastical Properties."[5] In accordance with the reformer's suggestion, revenues from endowments, rents and taxes from any remaining church lands, and offerings collected in church were to go into a single fund, from which were to be maintained Protestant clergymen, school teachers, clerics' houses, and the poor. This was a good idea, but it did not function well in Zwickau, for reasons that we saw in chapter 4. In practice, resources available to the community chest declined after the coming of Lutheranism. Inasmuch as charity of all types diminished too, the poor must more and more have been thrown back on their own devices and their relatives' generosity. The city *had* to pay the pastor and repair the roof of Saint Mary's Church if it sprung a leak; but whence came any compulsion to help the poor deal with rising inflation? The council tried to find ways of forcing the citizens to give more, but it failed.[6] By the 1530s the bloom was off Zwickau's economic rose, and fewer were able to give. During the late 1530s, at the latest by 1538, the council attempted to detach the two clearly solvent benefices, the Rich Alms and Saint Margaret's Hospital, from the community chest, a maneuver that Pastor Beyer publicly decried.[7] The dispute over the community chest went on into the 1540s. First the visitors and then the elector stepped in and compelled the council to leave both thriving endowments in the community chest.[8] Even so, the poor were feeling the effects of Zwickau's reduced philanthropic means.

Like the poor, the sick relied heavily on the aid of their families. In every age, including our own, most of the earth's population has known that at any hour it might be struck down by illness or accident. For most the struggle between life and death took place on their own premises. The city gradually created alternatives for those with contagious diseases. For the good of the whole community, such people had to be segregated. The communicable disease that occurs to one first is bubonic/pneumonic plague. Zwickau enjoyed the good fortune of not being visited by this dread affliction between 1472 and 1552.[9] There were other epidemics, however, to some of which the word *pest* was attached. One of these struck during the summer of 1521, for the council purchased a house for the *"pestkranken."*[10] Duke Johann's wife died that fall, whether or not of that disease, but in one breath the council forbade all dancing, drumming and piping "till Saint Katherine's Day [25 November] or Christmas," both out of mourning for her and because of widespread illness in Zwickau.[11] In 1525 medical doctor Sixtus Kolbenschlag must have had good reason to write a treatise for the council, published by Jörg Gastel, on how to deal with "the burdensome and horrifying sickness of the pestilence."[12] The city fathers in 1521 changed the rules that governed who could be buried where; the new rules discriminated against and angered many clergy and common people.[13]

In earlier plague years, the city council had made temporary quarters outside the walls to which the affected had to be removed. And receiving them may have been an earlier role of the hospitals, which in the sixteenth century did not normally take such people. Early in the sixteenth century, the council, the weavers' guild, and the bakers' guild founded "sick houses" (*siechenhäuser*) for their ill members. The council's and the weavers' houses were free of property tax, but for some reason the city fathers refused the same advantage to the bakers.[14]

The date of the founding of the leprosarium is not known. As leprosy waned during the late Middle Ages, lazar houses could be put to other uses. Syphilis arrived in our city in 1497. In either 1519 or 1520, the council saw that this malady had to have special treatment. It removed the few remaining lepers to two of the older and smaller hospitals, the women to the Hospital of the Holy Ghost, and the men to Saint John's Hospital, which were, like all such institutions, outside the walls. It now began to refer to the leprosarium as the *Franzosenhaus*, after the French, on whom it blamed this illness, and it hired a doctor to minister to the inmates. This hospital had a bathhouse and a garden. In 1524 there were only fifteen to twenty residents because of the fact that many syphilitics stayed in their homes.[15] Only when the symptoms of their disease became obvious were they forced to move. On the eve of the Reformation, syphilitics were among those begging from house to house and at the church doors. They were told to stop in 1525, but as a result an alternate means of feeding them had to be found.[16]

As for the lepers, of the women there were just twelve left in 1528 and of the men, nine. Each person paid a sum to get into a hospital and had to bring his own bed, bedding, clothing, and dishes. Before the Reformation each hospital had its priest to say mass and a chapel for him to say it in. Friedrich Myconius preached briefly at Saint John's. These hospitals had endowments of their own from which the residents were fed. They were also, as said, beneficiaries of people's wills. Furthermore, they had some garden space in which the inmates could raise some of their own food.

The richest and most multipurpose of the institutions for the sick was the Saints George and Margaret Hospital, usually called after Saint Margaret alone. It housed chiefly women. The hospital was a large edifice just outside the Frauenthor on the west side of the city. It was surrounded by gardens and outbuildings, and it also possessed far-flung estates. During the late fifteenth century, this hospital came to be very generously endowed and required a sizable staff and full-time administration. Saint Margaret's Hospital had originally constituted its own parish, but it was incorporated into the city parish with the advent of reform. From roughly the middle of the fourteenth century, this hospital had an overseer (*Vorsteher*) who managed its finances and all its activities. By the late fifteenth century, there were two such administrators. This wealthy institution was able to lend the council 1,200 florins in 1519.[17]

Saint Margaret's Hospital had some of the features of a religious confraternity. Healthy citizens could pay a fee (*pfrundengeld*) of between two and twenty florins, according to their means, and become a sort of associate of the hospital. These *pfründner* were usually female but occasionally male. This affiliation conferred upon the pfründner the privilege of being cared for at Saint Margaret's if the need arose. This was a medieval insurance policy, one that the very poor could never afford, but middling families could. During the Reformation era the aristocratic councillors radically reduced this hospital's accessibility in two ways. First, by 1529 the council voted on each applicant for admission to the institution.[18] Second, in 1540 they decreed that thenceforward pfrundengeld would be a flat one hundred florins.[19] Whereas twelve years before they had rejected the application of a couple on the grounds that they were too wealthy and that the hospital was only for "poor citizens,"[20] now they intended to prevent people from the middle ranks of society taking up residence there. Ironically, even many of the gentlemen themselves would have been hard pressed to produce one hundred florins in cash in 1540.

Prior to 1540 Saint Margaret's Hospital opened its doors to women who were not readily recovering from childbirth. Mortality among mothers as well as infants was very high. The city was aware, for instance, that it terrified women, especially the enceinte, to see the graves of those who had died giving birth or of complications afterward. It ordained that a special out-of-the-way part of the cemetery should be reserved for them and that they should be interred hastily, without the usual fanfaire.[21]

Attached to Saint Margaret's Hospital was the so-called Cripple House (*Krüppelhaus*). In one room the deranged of both sexes were kept. This must have created a hellish scene. Less severely impaired people lived out their lives in the community. We who are inclined to see human beings on a continuum of mental health, running the gamut from fully healthy through many degrees and types of neuroses to extreme psychoses, may find it hard to imagine how a society lacking such concepts might come to the conclusion that someone was in need of confinement. As far as I can tell, Zwickauers did not take possession by demons very seriously, though they firmly believed in the devil's existence. Presumably the decision was of a practical nature: a person required hospitalization who was so retarded as not to be able to function in society or so violent that deliberation over his lunacy was unnecessary.

Other than in Saint Margaret's main house, life in the hospitals of Zwickau was not pleasant. Conditions were noisome even by unhygienic sixteenth-century standards. Pastor Hausmann told the council before his untimely departure from Zwickau in 1531 that the poor in the hospitals did not have enough bed linen and urged the supplying of "many clean beds and sheets." He deplored the placing of all the sick together in "one or two beds." He advised airing out the sheets occasionally.[22] From our point of view, the afflicted were better off out among their families and friends.

Up until its dissolution in 1526, there was in Zwickau a house of beguines. On the eve of the Reformation, its inmates did not number over a dozen. These beguines had at some time in their history come under the supervision of the Franciscan friary, and from that time on the women were variously called beguines, Franciscan tertiaries, or simply "the nuns." They took in laundry and made candles to support themselves, and they also tended the house-bound sick. It is unknown whether they asked fees or contributions for this last, but even if they did, they were an invaluable aid to those who had no friends or relatives to wait upon them. The sisters were not attempting to enrich themselves: there is not a hint of self-indulgence about them.

The Reformation eliminated this beguinage and with it this service. The reformers regarded monasticism as unmitigated error. The nine elderly women who remained in 1526 were allowed to go on living together, in a cottage that they purchased with the money they got from the council for their former dwelling and their wash hut. The council thought that it was being magnanimous in letting the women reside together and provided that "they are supposed to be completely satisfied with their work as seamstresses [sewers or menders, not dressmakers] and not to [follow] the rule of [Saint] Francis or that same enthusiasm (*schwirmerej*), under threat of the council's displeasure."[23] Perhaps they continued to visit the sick, but there is no proof of it.

The two or three medical doctors in Zwickau were honored citizens, who, if they stayed in the city, were likely to end up on the ruling council. Even when they did not, the cliquish councillors at least regarded them as suitable friends and drinking partners. Better-off Zwickauers sought them out whenever they were ill. They paid the doctors for services rendered. Medical doctors never appear among the poor or middling citizens in the two extant Türkensteuerregister. They are invariably well-to-do, the owners of large houses and acreages.

The poor, too, may have called upon the doctors, and for all we know the medical men treated them without charge as a compassionate act. But more often ordinary folk visited barbers and apothecaries. Barbers served everywhere during the late Middle Ages as surgeons and dentists; indeed, they were alternately called "wound doctors" (*wunderzte*). Zwickau had too few barbers to form a guild, however. Apothecaries are distinguished in the tax records by their possession of sizable gardens around their houses and comparatively large staffs of servants. They produced quantities of medicinal and aromatic herbs, from which they concocted various medications. They were Zwickau's equivalent to the dispensing pharmacist. The ill often came directly to them for remedies and advice.

It is not certain from the few remaining references whether midwives, too, engaged in the manufacture and prescription of herbal medicine. Zwickau had only between two and four midwives during the first half of the sixteenth century, and in general these were women of modest socio-economic standing. The one exception is the wife of Hans Dawm Barbirer, who was a man of some means and who nearly got in trouble for severely beating the wife in question.[24] During the entire period under study, midwives were not overtly suspected of malevolent deeds—of killing babies or bewitching neighbors—though the authorities did interrogate other women as possible witches. In Zwickau the midwives formed part of the network of legitimate means of treating the sick. They enjoyed tax concessions and occasionally received money or firewood from the council; after all, the councillors' own wives and daughters had to make use of them.

The deformed and the handicapped remained with their families until such time as close relatives died out. Then the council paid a small fee to an adult willing to take on the care of these persons. The handicapped could not marry.[25] This prohibition originated under Catholicism and continued under Lutheranism. It seems to reflect a notion of the inheritability of physical and mental defects.

Orphans were similarly cared for. If they had no accommodating relations, either they took up residence in the Saint Margaret Hospital or the city fathers paid someone to care for them. The foundling was not so fortunate. Any infant left by the wayside was presumed to be illegitimate. Indeed, any stranger was tainted with the suspicion of bastardy until he or she presented a formal letter to the council testifying to his legitimate birth. The foundling, thus, could never enter a guild or practice an organized trade, nor could he or she inherit anything. In one curious case, Elector Johann Friedrich legitimated a certain Barthel of questionable origin and forced his admission to the hatters' guild.[26] This is a unique decree and raises the question whether the prince himself or a high-ranking person known to him may not have sired Barthel during one of the court's sojourns in Schloss Zwicker. Normally, the stigma of illegitimacy clung to a person for life.

The documents no longer exist that would allow one to study the frequency of births outside of wedlock in Zwickau. Emil Herzog compiled a table showing the total numbers of births in the city from 1537 to 1837, and he then destroyed the evidence—according to archivists, along with a sizable portion of the medieval contents of the city archive. He provides the following data regarding illegitimate births from 1537 to 1549:[27]

	births	*illegitimate*
1537	352	11
1538	402	9
1539	370	10
1540	333	4
1541	319	5
1542	369	3
1543	355	5
1544	374	4
1545	350	3
1546	341	4
1547	271	1
1548	279	3
1549	297	6

As for the elderly, we lack data on age distribution as well as on life expectancy in Zwickau. The tax registers provide very few reliable data here. They do tell us that old women (labeled "the old" followed by last name) frequently resided in younger burghers' households. They do not tell us whether they were relatives (unless, rarely, they have the same surname as the property owner), whether they were widowed, or whether they worked at a trade other than homemaking within the household. Their status was low. Neither their own first names nor those of their husbands were usually noted. Widows clearly did occupy a lower social station than they had when their spouses were alive. For one thing, even a widow with money to invest was offered four instead of the customary five percent interest by the council. For another, the widows of nobles around Zwickau were taxed at a much higher rate on their widows' portions than living knights on their assets.[28] Widows, it was apparently thought, should devote themselves to lives of virtue and have little desire for the pleasures that money could buy.

Tax documents fail to identify old men awaiting the angel of death in younger people's homes. Surely there were some, but then as now women were likely to outlive men. Schumann remarked concerning the year 1537 that there had been eighteen widows of city councillors still alive.[29] Women occasionally entered into formal agreements with younger householders, sometimes relatives, sometimes not, whereby the aging party turned all or a portion of her wordly possessions over to another in exchange for support and modest weekly pocket money, until the former died. These contracts were called *leibrentenverträge*. Anything left at the death of the elder became the property of the younger. The obvious danger was that the caretaker or other residents of the domicile might skimp on maintenance or not give out the allowance. Every now and then the elderly brought complaints about such misdeeds before the magistrates. The courts evidently did enforce the terms of the contracts.

The economically better-off aging had alternatives of their own. No doubt many lived comfortably among their grown children, who had commodious dwellings and scarcely noticed one more mouth at table. Others, including a few married couples, entered into leibrentenverträge with the Saint Margaret Hospital. They deposited a large sum of money with the administrator of the hospital, and he in turn paid them a stated amount for their support each year, probably a reasonable interest. When the depositor or depositors died, the principal or the balance became the property of the hospital. By this arrangement the depositors lived out their days in the city, not in the hospital itself, unless, of course, they became disabled.

Some others, however, almost always women, became formal Pfründner of the "rich hospital," before 1540 paying a pfrundengeld in proportion to their assets. They moved into the hospital sooner rather than later. They took desired clothing, a bed, bedding, furniture, and dishes along with them, which became the hospital's on their demise. This class of inmate lived in style. Surrounded by familiar objects, waited on by the plentiful staff of this prosperous institution, they ate very well. They kept busy by spinning flax, the linen being used in the hospital. They also made Easter candles.[30] Life was very different in the main house of Saint Margaret's than it was in the associated Krüppel-haus.

224

Perhaps it is curious that we today classify criminals among the unfortunates of society whereas late medieval man himself did not so regard them. We consider lawbreakers to be the victims of cruel fate, usually having been deprived of the right sort of parental affection and discipline, without the advantages that mitigate life's harshness and reconcile the majority of us to a necessary degree of altruism. Our Zwickauers would have had no sympathy for such a view. Criminal behavior threatened their bodies and their property. Felonious deeds violated God's provision for order in the human community. They were the product of man's moral deformity, inherited from Adam, and a reminder both of the power of Satan and of man's need for the ministrations of the priesthood if he were ever to attain salvation. This basic attitude toward criminality changed little with the coming of Lutheranism. Luther was even more adamant than the pope in averring man's depravity. Ever sinful, man could gain no assurance of salvation, no intercession from priests or saints, no aid from indulgences. All lay in God's hands. The pastor, to be sure, comforted by reminding of God's infinite love for his human creatures, but the cleric offered no assistance.

It is hard to say whether Zwickau's magistrates had Christian cosmology in mind when meting out punishments. They seem to have been very rooted in considerations of this world. The courts—which is to say members of the city council—heard all cases, delivered verdicts and sentences, and saw to it that their employees imposed the stipulated penalties. By our period Zwickau's courts had jurisdiction in both high and low justice and authority inside and outside the walls. Crimes against property were at least as serious as murder. In 1529 a robber baron and his complicitous wife were publicly beheaded for their highway predations.[31] Their daughters, too, were condemned, but someone successfully pleaded that their lives be spared.[32] First and small offenses met with public flogging or banishment, but habitual thieves were shown no mercy. Despite his "very young" age, Gallus Blumenstein from Annaberg was ordered to be hanged "for stealing things" but was then beheaded instead at his own request. The scribe stated that there was no hope for improvement in him.[33] Cleptomania was always a fatal disease. In 1543 Margarethe Bawersfeindin was beheaded for repeated small theft even though the legal experts in Wittenberg, who had been consulted, suggested hanging and had left room in their judgment for the council to choose flogging and exile instead. Stephan Roth, who characteristically opposed capital punishment, remarked, "Councillor [Michel von] Mila and I did not agree [with the others] that a person's life should be taken for the sake of a little old rag that she took and gave back again. But the majority had its way, etc."[34] The council invariably inquired of external authorities—the Wettins' *Oberhofgericht* in Leipzig and the Ernestine branch's *Hofgericht* in Wittenberg—in potentially capital cases, but it could reject the advice received. Interestingly, the city councillors frequently chose a lesser sentence even when death was recommended by both the higher jurid-ical panels. And although a few instances of branding and the lopping off of hands can be found, they are rare. Zwickau did not slit noses or cut off ears. By sixteenth-century standards, the magistrates were mod-erate. Counterfeiters were always executed, and this was because the territorial princes took a very dim view indeed of this transgression.

Murder, on the other hand, was not always a capital offense. It is jarring to modern sensibilities to see how often crimes against prop-erty merited the ultimate punishment whereas crimes against persons frequently did not. Saxon law influenced this mild attitude toward murder. The Zwickau law code from the fourteenth century prescribes several alternatives to the death penalty in cases of murder, including the ancient payment of *manngelt* and the taking of an oath that one had acted in self-defense. This age-old Saxon principle was still in effect in the Reformation era.[35] The Schultheiss's record book contains numerous examples. In 1489 Matthis Wayner murdered Nickel Seydell and was ordered to pay Seydell's sons eight silver schock as satisfaction (*vorgenugen*).[36] In 1537 Paul Mühlpfort, brother of the Reformation burgomaster, stabbed a man named Hans Bucher, who died a week later. The court fined Mühlpfort 22.86 florins, of which it secretly re-mitted to him 2.86 florins. He had begged the court to take into account his dead brother's long service on the council, and the court freely ob-liged.[37] This Paul Mühlpfort was prone to violence and was always dealt with leniently. Hermann himself had not shunned frays. In 1531 he and Paul got into a fight at the Golden Lion Inn with "other big-mouths," and more than one of the belligerents was badly wounded.[38] In 1538 Joachim Döring killed somebody and was merely put out of the city without escort.[39] The court tried to take intent into account. When in 1526 Martin Wagner, the city carpenter, went to strike his wife in a temper and accidentally took the life of his child in its cradle, the coun-cil gave him a choice of eight years' exile, six weeks' imprisonment, or a fine of six *gute schock* (17.14 florins).[40] Needless to say, he chose the fine.

The city fathers were noticeably less compassionate toward the poor and those unrelated to themselves. In 1527 a Stangengrün peasant murdered his wife and was executed with the sword.[41]

The privilege of begging for the life of a condemned person still existed in the early sixteenth century. In 1525, four knights whose crimes are unspecified were about to be dispatched in Schneeberg when an unidentified person or persons begged that they be spared. They were.[42] Only a few months later, Pastor Hausmann invoked the same privilege in gaining the release of the condemned peasant rebels from the surrounding villages. In 1522 a rapist was about to die for his crimes when someone, again unidentified, implored the authorities to spare his life. The man was consequently flogged instead.[43]

Physical abuse of other persons short of murder was usually rewarded with whipping, brief incarceration in one of the towers along the city wall, or a fine. However early modern society approved of some acts of violence that we today do not. Men were expected to chastise their wives, to strike them when they were insubordinate. As women were viewed as similar to children, men should spare the rod in dealing with neither. Technically, men should not exceed the undefined bounds of propriety. In practice, though, men were punished in only the most extreme circumstances, and lightly at that. In 1540 Hans Dawm Barbirer nearly killed his wife "again." The council rejected the wife's entreaty to be divorced from her husband; she was compelled to go on living with him.[44]

When it came to murder and pilfering, men and women were nearly equal before the law. In theory it would have been permissible for men and women to be treated differently. The title page of the Schultheiss's *Gerichtsbuch* for 1486–91 bears the following statement:

> A man to another man, a whole penalty.
> A man to a woman, a half penalty.
> A woman to a man, a whole penalty.
> A woman to another woman, a half penalty.[45]

But what penalties courts actually imposed did not conform to this tidy formula.

Slander elicited quite a uniform response from the authorities. Slanderers of either sex had to retract their words before the injured party and any others who wished to observe. One hundred citizens of both sexes turned out to witness one formal abjuration in 1543.[46] Only councillors and their relatives were certain of enjoying some privacy while admitting their error, this by collusion among the gentlemen and not by law.

The city scribe kept an account of retractions (*abtragbuch*). About half the entries involve women, a much higher proportion of reference to females than can be found in any other document from this period. In 1522 members of Gregor Goldschmidt's family and his neighbors got embroiled in namecalling. Sophia Schubel had to recant before Margaret Goldschmidt as follows: "Dear neighbor, in an agitated and angry mood I called you a field mare[47] and accused you of having done away with a child. In this I did you wrong, and I ask you to forgive me; for I know nothing about you except what is honorable, honest, and good."[48]

In the council's opinion, this public humiliation was not serving its purpose, which was to discourage verbal attacks on one's fellow citizens, especially on the councillors and their staff. In 1545 the city fathers enunciated a new policy: "Slander among the people. Since it does not stop and the council's faithful warning in accordance with God's command is not respected, fines shall not be imposed but instead, for men imprisonment and corporal punishment, and for women wearing the stone around the marketplace."[49] "Wearing the stone" was a traditional penalty for fractious women, one apparently not very frequently employed as the council seems to have been reviving it. The "shame" stone was worn around the neck, like a medallion on a cord, and on it were painted faces of shrewish women.[50] When Wolff Arnold's and Andres Haueisen's wives scolded and abused one another over a long period and the neighbors repeatedly complained, both had to wear the stone. The scribe noted, "Many people came to see it."[51] When "Red Margaret" Hammerschmid, a wool carder, attacked another women named Amaley with a bread knife, both had to wear the stone. Margaret was then imprisoned in addition but quickly released "because of her age." The councillors declared that if she transgressed again, she would have to leave Zwickau.[52] If women inveighed against city officials instead of merely their neighbors, they were more often jailed.[53]

The dungeons provided by the major towers in the city wall were generally for brief incarceration. The weavers who tried to give Thomas Müntzer escort out of town were held for only one day and night, technically for creating a disturbance in the streets. Zwickauer's attitude, firmly grounded in Saxon law and tradition, was that criminals should incur a penalty to their person or property or both. If removal from society was desirable, the offender should be executed or banished, with a marked preference for the latter. Thus, even in peacetime the notion that one was safer within the walls than without was very realistic. The suburbs could have abounded with various people who had been shown the door. Some were not dangerous, but others were. A practical reason for favoring exile over detainment was that those jailed had to be fed and guarded at public cost. The easiest way to avoid such expenditures was to keep the towers empty.

This was the traditional view. A perceptible change occurred during the period under study. During the 1530s and 1540s, the councillors made more and more frequent use of imprisonment as punishment. In 1535 they had one Wolff Schalenreuter held on suspicion of responsibility for the presence in Zwickau of large numbers of "bad Bohemian pennies." They kept him in a tower for over five years, during which time they had him tortured twice. He made no confession despite this ordeal and was finally released on 1 June 1541.[54] In 1539 they ordered a young couple held for ten days for becoming engaged secretly and for having sexual relations, all against the wishes of the woman's parents. The pair were released on their wedding day.[55] In 1544 the city executioner Hans Spitzing badly wounded Caspar Osterlandt, who later died of his injury. Spitzing was imprisoned for thirty-five weeks.[56]

In line with this development, Burgomaster Oswald Lasan in 1537 had decorative iron grillwork removed from Saint Mary's Church and converted into a huge cage. From this time any citizen of tender age who would not obey his parents or who stole fruit from a neighbor's tree, a sin even Saint Augustine confessed to, was made an example by imprisonment in this public structure near the parish church. Adults were placed there as well. In one two-week period shortly after its erection, three people were confined in the "bird cage."[57] The councillors decreed that anyone misbehaving during a sermon would suffer this humiliation.[58] In 1540 they threatened to place there for a day and a night any musicians who played improper melodies and dances or who unduly prolonged their performances.[59] Whether such shaming achieved its goal is doubtful. Certainly the councillors lamented public disorder as loudly in 1546 as they had twenty years earlier. Both bird cage and lamentations are evidence of the councillors' enhanced sense of divine mission and their feeling that they stood in a parental relationship to those under them, who, they thought, were all somewhat childlike even if adults. That a person had passed the age of twenty-one and therefore attained his majority made no difference. Women, of course, were always thought of as akin to children.

In their treatment of their unfortunate fellows, Zwickauers of the Reformation era showed that they were people with a moderate conscience. General prosperity during the waning fifteenth century resulted in more than private self-indulgence. It brought forth philanthropy on an unprecedented scale. On the eve of the Reformation, the city afforded the poor, the sick, and the helpless elderly more avenues of relief than it ever had before. This is not to say that self-sacrifice characterized the relations between rich and poor or that the quality of the care provided was high. But Christianity imposed upon the citizens—and they were willing to accept a certain burden—the obligation to give alms and to help others. Of course, the pre-Lutheran hope that through giving one might smooth his path to paradise is not to be discredited. Fear does help a person to be generous. For the better part of a millennium Christian preachers had stressed to their listeners the need to perform deeds of charity, and that message had taken root. What the populace so objected to at the end of the Middle Ages was a tendency toward parasitism among the clergy and the intensification of demands for contributions during a time of economic contraction. Still, in general the burghers agreed on the nature of their Christian and civic duty.

The progress of inflation from the 1520s on made it increasingly difficult for those near impoverishment to stay off the dole and for those less than wealthy to give. Harsh economic realities may have encouraged certain types of crime, above all theft. At least as important as the effects of inflation and the city's gradual economic decline, however, is that with the coming of Lutheranism and the founding of the community chest, people felt less compelled to give. Beggars no longer stood in the marketplace and at the church doors, taking advantage of any impulsive generosity among the passers-by. Those in need were forbidden to seek alms from door to door. Although the poor were everywhere and visible, the creation of official channels for gaining public assistance shielded the citizenry from daily importunity.

When the council did away with the popular confraternities and put the income from ecclesiastical benefices into the community chest, the line between philanthropic treasuries and the aristocratic councillors' pocketbook blurred. What were the people to think in September 1524 when the council suddenly refused any longer to allow the community's representatives to reveal what they had learned at the presentation of the council's accounts? Only eight carefully chosen delegates of the *Gemeinde* were now admitted to this ritual, and they were sworn to secrecy. How were public moneys being spent?

The ruling gentlemen made various efforts to force the people to give to the community chest. In 1540 they appointed two men to the task of collecting alms from all members of the woolweavers' guild.[60] Their success is dubious in view of the fact that the guild, like many of its members, was just then in straitened financial circumstances. In 1544 the council named a committee of six to gather monetary donations from the weavers, masters and journeymen alike.[61] The population as a whole was at first requested and then in 1545 commanded to give their pennies to the community chest. The people were consistently reluctant to do so. Why, they may have wondered, did the pastor need an income of two hundred florins a year—indeed, he was about to ask for another fifty—in addition to free housing? Giving money for his support did not relieve the sufferings of the poor. During this era of transition from Catholicism to Lutheranism, the people may not have seen the clergy as markedly less self-enriching than their predecessors had been. Nor did all take pride in the grammar school, whose teachers too were paid from the unified fund. To give was to sustain the sons of the rich! Through its consolidation of funds for church, schools, and charity, the governing circle unwittingly discouraged contributions to the poor and disabled. Here socio-political resentments came into play. Nevertheless, wills did continue to specify which groups should receive alms. Testaments were a way of circumventing the community chest.

When all is said and done, Zwickauers displayed less compassion to the poor after the Reformation than they had before. Firing his penultimate shot at the council in the summer of 1530, Nicolaus Hausmann told the patricians how bad things were for the city's impoverished— this although he himself had no high esteem for the common man, who to his mind was apathetic about the "coming of the gospel." He observed that the woolweavers' and other guilds gave nothing to the support of the church. Indeed, in his judgment the entire community should be made to contribute to the community chest for the maintenance of the hospitals and other relief agencies. He asked, "Are not many hands supposed to make light work?" He lamented that although nobody gave anything, every unfortunate *wanted* something, and the existing resources of community chest and parish simply could not stretch far enough. He described the filthy conditions in the hospi-

231

tals and decried the practice of putting all the sick, whatever their affliction, in "one or two beds."[62] A scribe appended his unfriendly opinion
of this whole document: "Advice [rendered] after the fact which was
needed before."[63] All evidence points to a general decrease in aid to
society's needy at a time when more people required help than in recent memory.

By modern Western standards, Zwickauers could be shockingly
cruel. It was as true here as it was, according to Huizinga, in northern
France and the Netherlands, that one could detect the mingled scents
of blood and roses—and several other pungent substances. The executioner was kept busy, not so much with capital punishment or with
branding or torturing as with publicly flogging lawbreakers. Still, he
did kill, brand, torture, and maim when requested to do so, and for
these he was paid a bonus beyond his weekly wage of eight groschen.
He also dispatched dozens of stray dogs each year and by dark of night
removed the contents of people's overflowing latrines and dumped
them in the river, *below* the town.[64] But it is only fair to add that as
much as Zwickau required his services, so much did it despise a man
who would perform such acts. Executioners could not enter craft
guilds.

Judicial violence was a regular though not a daily occurrence in this
city. When it was to be administered, the people turned out to watch.
Most of the time citizens were in accord on the necessity of keeping
public order. The evil in human beings could not be allowed to weaken
the fabric of urban society. Nonetheless, as the first half of the century
wore on, complaints were heard more and more often of the severity
and arbitrariness of the penalties meted out to the little folk whereas
the rich or well connected escaped with fines or just warnings. The
councillors were sensitive to this accusation, but this did not stop them
from looking out for their own. Growing security in their power after
the Peasants' War made them all the more complacent in their partiality. No one but the prince could touch them, and that luminary had only
to hear rumors of popular unrest to get his hackles up. Whereas a
Schultheiss of the early sixteenth century could note in the front of his
summary of proceedings, "Moderation is of more value than all knowledge of the law," by 1545 the city council had entirely rejected this
concept in favor of harsh and summary justice.[65] In its mid-century
eyes, the people were synonymous with disorder. The gentlemen
placed the blame for Zwickau's economic problems squarely on the
shoulders of the undisciplined common man.

The End of an Era:
The Transfer to Moritz

*Z*wickau was already in decline before the 1540s. We have seen the damage that inflation inflicted on the people and the economy, for which a determined and domineering council could find no palliative. By 1541 complaints were reaching the city about the low quality of its wool yardages and about false marks affixed to them. If its main industry, woolweaving, deteriorated, Zwickau was doomed. It had no other sizable manufacture on which to build, or to rebuild, its fiscal health.

Princely policies did not help. Johann Friedrich in 1542 invaded and conquered Brunswick. The terrific cost of fielding an army and occupying a new territory, in combination with his irresistible attraction to high-stake gambling, left this elector's treasury nearly empty despite the sequestration of Ernestine monasteries. Furthermore, this occurred just at a time when the political tensions that would produce the Schmalkaldic War were rising. Johann Friedrich was monetarily unable at this crucial moment to prepare as he ought to have prepared. He was leaving his geographic inheritance exceedingly vulnerable. Neither the special tax imposed for the war against Brunswick nor a new Turkish tax was able to relieve him. German princes ever insisted on carrying on their costly feuds of honor or for petty acquisition when, from our perspective, they would have been better off garnering their small resources against a major, unavoidable confrontation.

When compared to other sixteenth-century potentates, Johann Friedrich was an admirable man. Happily married to Sibyl of Jülich-Cleves for nearly twenty-seven years, he and his wife seem to have been genuinely devoted to Luther's religion and did much to promote the new teachings. Johann Friedrich hated the Jews, ostensibly for their refusal to embrace Christianity, but then so did Luther and most

233

of their contemporaries.[1] Johann Friedrich took a keen interest in governing and gained valuable experience working with and for his uncle Frederick the Wise and his father Johann the Constant. He was no shirker. On the contrary, he was inclined to want to oversee and eventually to decide everything for himself. He had a number of distinguished advisors, and he gave them plenty to do. Nevertheless, he insisted on hearing or seeing all the documentation and opinions that they had marshalled for him and on altering their drafts to suit himself. This devotion to duty, or to power, depending on one's point of view, taxed him greatly. Perhaps it and the political threats looming taller around him explain his crotchety temperament from the late 1530s. He took tasks away from his superintendents that they had long performed and regarded firmly as theirs.[2] And he grew temperamental and more preemptive in his dealings with his cities than ever before.

Zwickau was not the only Ernestine city to notice the waxing overbearance of its prince. In early November 1537, the council received a letter from Plauen's city councillors, written for themselves but also, they said, on behalf of "the other cities in the Vogtland." They observed that in conflict with their ancient charters of liberties and venerable traditions, the elector was intruding more and more into their election of councillors and their annual rendering of accounts to the incoming councils. In particular, Johann Friedrich had been having his *Hauptmann* in Plauen investigate the financial circumstances and personal behavior (*wandel*) of the nominees before deciding whether to confirm them, and he had ordered the same official to be present when the accounts were summarized by the outgoing gentlemen. Such action was without precedent. The governors of Plauen, therefore, were joining with their counterparts in "Olsnitz, Adorff, Pausa, etc." to petition their ruler for redress. They enclosed a draft of their petition.[3]

Zwickau's council discussed the draft at some length. The gentlemen were fully in sympathy with their neighbors. In fact, they thought the petition "somewhat entirely too gently phrased" and that it could "well be more vehemently worded."[4] They had their own legal advisor draw up a stronger petition, strictly in Plauen's name, however. In case Johann Friedrich reacted angrily, Zwickau's magistrates wished to be dissociated from this coalition.

The council's draft, sent with an approbational covering letter back to Plauen, argued that the prince's interference in the election process would bring the councillors into disrepute among the masses. It would imply, for one thing, that nonreelected councillors had not functioned

234

in compliance with their solemn oaths of office. It would also suggest that an *Amtmann*, a high electoral official drawn from the nobility and therefore not an integrated citizen, was better able to judge a candidate's abilities and character than the urban electors themselves. The draft noted that the *Amtleute* as a group were not always His Most Gracious Elector's most loyal subjects and that it might not be to the prince's advantage to have these nobles know all about the cities' food supplies and arms.

The draft concluded in a humble, submissive key. Plauen and the others should say to Johann Friedrich that they did not wish to tie his hands, that they knew their rightful place and would do his bidding. If they had erred, he should instruct them and not take offense.[5]

In its accompanying letter to Plauen, Zwickau's council expressed the opinion that the petition should be carried personally to the elector by an embassy of highly respected councillors. Zwickau's governors also thought the cities of the Vogtland should lodge their appeals separately rather than jointly.[6]

Zwickau had its own problems with Johann Friedrich. The council wanted too much, he apparently thought. In 1538 it wished to expand its linen bleaching industry and may have requested this too often in the prince's judgment. When Burgomaster Oswald Lasan presented this demand to the elector in Torgau in January, the prince completely lost his temper and had to be calmed down by his treasurer and trusted advisor Hans von Ponickau.[7]

Zwickau protested its own treatment at the elector's hands on 23 January 1546: it sent Johann Friedrich twelve articles having to do with the prince's innovations. It is, of course, ironic that the council itself had shown no compunction in altering the practices of the common man in and around the city, but when its territorial lord treated it according to his desire, it objected strenuously. Its grievances may be paraphrased as follows:

1) Zwickau cannot afford to contribute yet more men and money for war against the emperor. The recent exactions and conscription for the war with Brunswick exhausted people's resources.[8]

2) Zwickau always had a good grain market. Now to our great disadvantage and contrary to all right and precedent you are requiring all grain to be offered for sale in Altenburg before coming here.

3) You ordered us to send two members of the council to you to report on the salaries of councillors. We have no salaries as such, only

from the special offices that we fill. Being a councillor endangers our livelihood, and we need salaries.[9]

4) Please allow us to make stipends available from the community chest to enable four poor burghers' sons to study in Wittenberg and to provide trousseaus for poor young women.

5) The grammar school has eight hundred pupils and we cannot feed them all. Please give us some grain for this purpose.

6) You directed us to pay the pastor fifty florins more a year for his duties as superintendent. The community chest cannot afford this. Please let the pastors [in the superintendency] contribute or find another source of money.

7) It is an old custom to let the coopers and wagoners have wood for their craft from your forest near Werdau. Now they have been barred from that forest.

8) You gave us title to the Burkhart Forest in Amt Schwarzenberg. But you let the peasants keep and graze animals there even though the village has its own woods. Please do away with this innovation.

9) Whenever we have to outfit soldiers (*kriegsvolk*), the people living on palace (Schloss Zwicker) land (*burglehner*) are exempt. They should have to contribute six groschen or four groschen, depending on their status.

10) We have asked many times for a decision on the matter of floating timber in the Schonburg territories. Please give us one.

11) We have legal title to Hoyer's mill, which was part of the Saint Martin benefice. Now without our knowledge an agreement has been reached with Hoyer's widow and heirs. Please see that we keep this mill. It belongs to the community chest.

12) Previously, as in ages past, when you ordered your chancery to do something in connection with this council, you have informed us. Now you have stopped this. Please order that this ancient practice be resumed.[10]

In short, the council echoed to the territorial ruler the perennial plea of the populace to *it*: protect our traditional rights and practices! Overall, in the form of uncompliant responses, the elector administered to the councillors a dose of their own medicine. However, neither party saw it this way at the time. Johann Friedrich answered as follows:

1) The council must remember that the prince must defend his lands. In the last war [against Brunswick] your men were practically the least well equipped of all the cities.

2) I can understand why you are upset that grain must go to Altenburg. If the nobility had a choice, they would sell their crops neither in Zwickau nor in Altenburg. You must be satisfied with this.

3) The city will be weakened if we increase councillors' salaries. Allow our advisors to examine your accounts. We shall then think about this.

4) and 5) We are glad that you have such a large school. I have ordered university stipends for all my cities, and you are allotted four. Give me a complete account of your community chest.

6) When we have examined the account of your community chest, we will be able to judge what you can afford. We will not have pastors making contributions as under papal tyranny and oppression. Your pastor can well be content with two hundred, fifty florins and housing as that is about what our other superintendents are earning.[11]

7) The coopers and wagoners must pay [for their wood] in accordance with our wood ordinance.

8) We are commanding the peasants to stay out of the Burkhart Forest.

9) You recently came to a formal agreement with the Amt whereby the Amt and not the city would tax those residing on castle land.

10) We are still considering the damage done by the lords of Schonburg to the floating of timber. Be patient.

11) We will reply soon regarding Hoyer's mill. There is much correspondence on this, and we have much else to attend to just now.

12) We shall see that you are given instructions too.[12]

It was an understatement that Johann Friedrich had many other matters on his mind early in 1546. He had been laboring to extend his and his family's authority over a number of cities and territories and had achieved notable successes. Even though he relied on the neutrality of his Lutheran cousin, the Albertine Duke Moritz, in any conflict between the German Protestant princes and the Catholic emperor and his allies, he saw war on the horizon. As the list of articles shows, he was in the process of raising troops and provisions. Charles V perceived, however, that Moritz, who wasted no affection on his rival Johann Friedrich, was susceptible to persuasion. On 20 June 1546, he promised the Protestant Moritz the position of official protector of the Magdeburg and Halberstadt cathedral chapters. Just months before this Johann Friedrich had won for himself and one of his sons the role of coadjutant in those very two cathedrals. Now Johann Friedrich was certain of armed confrontation, and he was determined to take part himself. The troops mustered in Wittenberg, Ichtershausen, Torgau, Buttstädt, Zwickau, and Coburg and marched off in the summer to join the Hessians and other Protestant battalions. Zwickau was at no time an eager participant in the struggle. On 7 July 1546, the council implored Johann Friedrich not to demand much of it because, it said, the city had neither money nor supplies. "For the citizenry in these deceptive years have come into such poverty that they have not been able to pay the Turkish tax, the Grimma military tax, the wall tax, the most recent military tax against the Brunswicker, or the [regular] property tax and their other debts."[13]

Meanwhile, Moritz, who had at first resisted the temptation to join the imperial forces in the hope of gaining the upper hand at last over the Ernestine branch of his family, finally succumbed to King Ferdinand's inveiglement. Johann Friedrich's downfall was nearly assured, although this elector did enjoy some small triumphs over Albertine and allied troops in western Thuringia.

Zwickau was forced to submit to Moritz in November 1546. Adorf had been taken and plundered on 30 October. Ölsnitz and Plauen surrendered to Moritz immediately afterward, hoping to escape the same grisly fate. On 2 November a trumpeter brassily announced himself and relayed Moritz's message to Zwickau's city fathers: Zwickau had the choice of giving itself over to the duke or being seized by King Ferdinand's Bohemian, Hungarian, and Italian troops. Moritz reminded them through this emissary that he was Johann Friedrich's blood relative. He would guarantee them their Lutheran faith. He gave them three days to decide.[14] On Friday, 5 November, at 3:00 P.M., having spent the intervening time deliberating, the gentlemen agreed to accept Moritz's ultimatum. Their consciences were just sufficiently pricked to compel them to justify their action in writing, both for the burghers and their contemporaries in general and for Johann Friedrich in particular. The populace was furious and regarded the magistrates as traitors for not resisting.[15] The patricians wrote an impassioned and apologetic letter of explanation to the Ernestine elector himself.[16] They had, they said, no provisions either for resisting or for holding out against such a numerous and determined foe. Even should they take up the fight, they knew that there was no hope of relief from electoral forces. They desired intensely not to cause the shedding of blood, "above all innocent blood." The clergy had assured them that in a case such as this they were not violating the oath that they had sworn to their prince. Furthermore, they would not be compelled to abandon the word of God.[17]

They opened the gates to their new ruler. They feared, and with good reason, that Moritz would not be able to restrain the ill-paid, booty-hungry foreign and Catholic soldiers. Moritz did amazingly well, though in the end all the villages around and all the neighborhoods outside the walls were ravaged and destroyed. On Sunday, 7 November 1546, under comprehensible duress, the people swore allegiance to Moritz. He in return conceded to them the right to believe in accordance with the Augsburg Confession. He promised to uphold the city in all its rights and liberties.[18] But many had left the city in order to avoid taking an oath. Moritz knew this and demanded a list of their names. Among them were the two burgomasters, Oswald Lasan and Michel von Mila, who on other matters could not agree. In this instance, however, both lay down their offices and moved away from Zwickau.

As soon as it appeared likely that their lives would be spared, Zwickauers of every condition engaged in recriminations. Never before had so many inhabitants expressed such admiration of Johann Friedrich. In the weeks following Zwickau's submission, many voiced their feelings of loyalty to their "old" and beleaguered prince. They were not entirely cautious in their utterances, and Moritz quickly learned on which side their hearts lay. Furthermore, burghers avoided trading with the Bohemian occupiers and were reluctant to give up their weapons.

With no warning, on Monday, 31 January 1547, Moritz had the larger part of the populace driven out of the city en masse. The one major concession he made was that three councillors and the chief scribe could stay behind to guard city hall, explicitly including the wine cellar.[19] A number of essential craftsmen also were permitted to remain. Nevertheless, now in cold mid-winter, several thousand Zwickauers trudged the dozen miles south to Schneeberg. Only after Johann Friedrich had surrendered, in April, did their new ruler relent and allow them to return. Not all were back until June. The first council meeting after the exodus took place on 18 June 1547.[20] The city by then had a wholly different aspect. Its suburbs no longer stood, and much damage had been done to the city within the walls. The list of citizens' property losses fills one hundred, twenty pages (sixty folios).[21] Johann Friedrich himself was in Altenburg at the end of January, faring badly. He could do nothing to help Zwickau, nor could Zwickau aid him.

Council minutes and other extant documents would lead one to think that as soon as Johann Friedrich was defeated and Moritz firmly in possession of the electorate and other lands ceded to him, life in Zwickau returned to normal. The council went on setting meat prices, regulating guilds and markets, overseeing the administration of justice, and collecting taxes. Pastor Leonhard Beyer went on as before, engaging in bitter verbal strife with the preacher Christoff Ering and with the council itself.[22] Moritz set aside his grudge against Zwickau and invited the entire council to his brother August's wedding in Torgau in October 1548.[23] Life was not the same, however. Pastor Beyer never could reconcile himself to the change in territorial governance. He had first resigned in July 1547 but had let himself be persuaded to change his mind. On 1 December 1548, he was adamant.[24] No lesser men than Johann Bugenhagen, Georg Maior, and Philip Melanchthon tried to dissuade him. Elector Moritz, however, insisted that this time Beyer depart. The reports of Beyer's antipathy had continued to reach him, and Moritz did not want such a man stirring up public opposition to him from the pulpit.[25] Beyer, the council told the venerable Wittenbergers, would not bend in the slightest matter. Having been paid till June, and with a letter giving him toll-free passage, Beyer exited the city in February 1549.[26] He was given the escort of an honored man.

The preacher Ering carried on Beyer's tradition of invective. He maligned the new elector from the pulpit, mainly for accepting the Leipzig Interim. This clergyman nearly landed in prison. The open expression of his views brought an eight-thousand-florin fine down upon the city.[27]

Zwickau's population did not recover the level that it had reached during the city's "blossom time." That is, it reached it again during the nineteenth century but for reasons wholly unrelated to the Reformation era. The heavily populated quarters of the city that had grown up outside the wall and that Moritz's troops had burned were not rebuilt. Gradually, over several years, only essential extramural facilities, such as the Paradise Bridge, dyeing sheds, and Saint Margaret's Hospital, were reconstructed. Zwickau's inhabitants now found the space within the walls quite sufficient for their reduced numbers. Zwickau was the sleepy little town with a reputable grammar school that, with the interruptions of the Thirty Years' War and subsequent wars, it would remain until coal mining and spreading industrialization reinvigorated it centuries later. In 1800 Zwickau's population was only 4,189.[28] The once crowded grammar school could boast of only eighty-six students in 1839.[29] Leipzig in the meantime, with its greater accessibility, its famed markets, and its excellent university would surpass its sister without bounds. In 1500 Zwickau and Leipzig had been remarkably similar. The advantage, the prosperity, and the renown lay with Leipzig. Zwickau was left to treasure the fading memory of its short-lived springtime. As the realities of the Reformation period paled, Zwickauers gladly forgot the turmoil, the conflict, and the unrest that had characterized that age. They reminisced only about the vigor and the blossoms.

The East-Elbean Reform: Conclusion

𝕿hat change is inevitable is a platitude. Zwickau would have been different in 1550 than in 1500 even if the Reformation had never come there; every place was different in 1550 than in 1500. Historians, often tempted to speculate on "what would have happened if" events had taken a course other than they did—scholars who tell themselves and their students that it is fruitless to explore such conjectures—ought to refrain from such guesswork in their writings. However, lest I be taken to imagine that the Reformation all by itself caused a break in Zwickau's traditions, I shall indulge the impulse to ask, "What if Zwickau, the elector of Saxony, and Ernestine territories had remained true to the Catholic church?"

The artisan revolt of 1516–17 brings into clear relief the arrogant, usurpious behavior of the city councillors before Martin Luther was known to any but his friends and students. Laurentius Bärensprung and Hermann Mühlpfort had already emerged as important personages in the struggle between commoners and those gentlemen entitled to be addressed as *Herr*. At odds were the communal ideal of reciprocity between governors and governed, the old political ethic of advice and consent, and the new that placed all local control (save only the rights of the prince) in the hands of the few. Inasmuch as the brother of the elector fully supported the councillors, there is every reason to suppose that even without the Reformation, the burghers would, by mid-century, have been subject to the privileged circle. Subjection was the trend for the many, domination the trend for the magisterial elite.

What the Reformation did by its initial disorder and uncertainty was to hold out to craftsmen, still smarting from their defeat in 1517, the hope that they might now reverse that trend, that they might return to

242

what they thought a golden age of guildsmen's collective dignity. In calling the established order into question, the Reformation seemed to give a general license to act out against corruption and oppression in all their forms: against the Cistercians, the Franciscans, doctrines of papal supremacy and indulgences, abuse of the peasants—and against conciliar preemption of rights accorded over generations to the citizenry. The exercise of this perceived license in turn allowed the magistrates and the prince to take drastic punitive measures and to formalize the disadvantageous relation of mere citizens, whether urban or rural, to those in charge of them. In short, an authoritarian spirit was already waxing and would have expanded still further by 1550 even without the Reformation; but religious reform speeded that spirit along its path and gave it formal legal status earlier than would otherwise have been the case.

The economy was evidently deteriorating everywhere in Europe from about the end of the first quarter of the century. Complaints of higher prices for staples and people's inability to pay were ubiquitous. With or without religious change, this was bound to happen. Whether inflation was caused by the influx into Europe of precious metals from the Spanish conquests of Mexico and Peru or by the pressure a burgeoning population put on resources does not matter so much at this level of generalization. In addition late medieval guild rules militated against innovation and flexibility. There are no grounds for supposing that Zwickau's economy would have been in a salubrious state if Lutheranism had failed to appear.

Were the effects of the Reformation, then, totally apart from the world of sweat and lucre? I think not. The Lutheran Reformation added its weight, the force of its teaching, to the already rigid principles governing manufacture and marketplace in Zwickau. It did this in two ways. First, by its reinforcement of the notion that princes and magistrates speak and subjects step lively to obey, it tacitly relieved the craftsmen of any need to help in finding their own way out of economic conundra. If the domineering councillors are so smart, many a Zwickau artisan must have thought, let them direct us to renewed prosperity. And convinced of the God-given nature of their privileges, the councillors tried: they *ordered* the economy to right itself. However, decrees alone could not work miracles.

Second, Luther's emphasis on vocation, to the extent that it was taken seriously, rendered even more remote an imaginative, pragmatic response to society's economic ails. The idea that God had called each person to the task at which he found himself and even to the manner in which he carried it out cannot have promoted a creative search for solutions. The Lutheran reform may have blessed man's labors, but it also enhanced the rigidity of Zwickau's economy. Mentality is as severe an impediment to finding a cure as the complexity of the illness itself. This is not Max Weber stood on his head; the Zwickauers of 1530 were not, after all, the English Puritans of the next century.

To say that the Reformation facilitated religious change in Zwickau is to subject the reader to a tautology. However, the movement did prove bigger and more pervasive in its impact than many who favored it could have foreseen. It proved to entail much, much more than simply the elimination of venal and excessive Catholic clergy or even of indefensible myth built up over centuries. It ushered in a period of uncertainty during which all comers felt at liberty in accordance with their individual lights to define ultimate truths. It initiated a period of unprecedented religious conflict and governmental reprisal in Zwickau and created divisions that were only mended by magisterial compulsion and the passage of decades. Reality soon dawned on people: the council's vision of reform would prevail. The council enjoined all citizens to conform. Conformity most specifically included acceptance of its headship over the entire church as well as the state. The gentlemen now became outspokenly "Ratsherren by the grace of God." Without the Reformation we can be quite sure that by mid-century the council would have made further progress than it had by 1520 in bringing ecclesiastical jurisdictions into its hands, but each gain would, as before, have had to be tediously wrung from church and prince. And under the influence of a humanism unstressed, according to our fantasy, by the Lutheran challenge, some of the most fanciful doctrinal inventions of the Middle Ages might have been disposed of, much in the same way that Lorenzo Valla discredited the Donation of Constantine. Otherwise, Catholicism would have retained a recognizable shape.

That Catholicism was abolished in Zwickau had serious consequences for popular culture, for throughout the medieval period and on through the sixteenth century, religion was central to people's outlook on the universe. In Zwickau the Lutheran creed, as put into place by the city councillors, altered that outlook by forbidding the rituals that were expressions of it. Thus, a number of major facets of medieval popular culture did not survive the first half of the century. It is easy to speculate on the nature of popular culture without the reform movement, for so much of Europe did not experience, or experienced only to a limited degree, the trauma of creedal division. The extensive survival of ancient Christian rituals down to today must be sought in Catholic parts of Europe, places that did not undergo the crisis of the Reformation. To be sure, Counter-Reformation authorities demanded more upright behavior from the people in their charge, but they usually left saints and civic ritual intact. Catholic rulers could be thoroughly dictatorial, but they left more of the familiar in place than the magistrates in Zwickau did.

If the Reformation had not come to Zwickau, philanthropy and care of the unfortunate would still have suffered. As seen, inflation made nearly everyone less able to contribute to "mild" causes than before. However, the Reformation exacerbated people's stinginess by sparing them the daily importunity of beggars and by removing the pressure of one's peers in guilds and confraternities to give alms. The councillors' substitute for the many and varied funds to which burghers had donated under Catholicism, the community chest, was so closely identified with the gentlemen's personal finances that the many citizens resentful of conciliar high-handedness lacked a motive to give. The city fathers only thinly veiled their efforts to benefit personally from available institutions and resources.

It seems elementary that if the Reformation had not taken place, there would have been no Schmalkaldic War; that without the Schmalkaldic War, Zwickau would have stayed Ernestine and not lost all its suburbs; that it would have remained at mid-century a significant urban center. But this is just too simplistic a statement of cause and effect, for it overlooks the great economic fragility of Zwickau before the war. The forcible transfer of Zwickau from Johann Friedrich and his family to Moritz of Saxony and his, and all its immediate results revealed and aggravated weakness; they did not bring it about. As a part of the Albertine domains from 1547, Zwickau could hardly contend for the position of most important city. Leipzig with its location, its university, its many printers and other amenities was already far ahead, and Dresden was the favored princely residence. Simply by its transfer Zwickau became a third-rate city.

The great beneficiary of the Reformation era was the prince himself, Johann and then Johann Friedrich. Moritz was able to take over the position that his predecessors in the office of Saxon elector had already created. The 1520s were the heyday of the city councillors, not solely in the religious sphere. The term *Ratsreformation* must be understood in its broadest possible sense to mean the rationalization of all urban life under the direction of the patricians—from the perspective of those gentlemen, a reform of all society. It was no coincidence, either, that they took their cues from Nuremberg, which has provided us up till now with the best example of a Ratsreformation. Yet Zwickau's Rat was if anything ahead of Nuremberg's in installing the new faith. We cannot speak here of Nuremberg serving as a model. Developments in Nuremberg probably convinced Zwickau's admiring governors after the fact that they had been correct in their course of action.

But the Ratsreformation was only a solid beginning. In August 1531, with Johann's decision to approve all clerical appointments in his lands, the council suffered a major setback, an adumbration of princely domination to come. Under Johann Friedrich the "east Elbean princes' Reformation" (*Fürstenreformation*) took shape, in Zwickau and beyond. All jurisdictions that the council had laboriously accumulated for itself now belonged to the elector. The councillors were rapidly transformed into agents of their territorial lord, exercising powers delegated by him. The medieval era of cartulary liberties granted to cities for their free or nearly free exercise was at an end. The charters were null and void; a new polity prevailed.

If the Reformation had not come to eastern Germany, would the elector have had to content himself with the network of overlapping jurisdictions that constituted medieval government? I suspect so. I suspect that he, too, as in earlier days, would have had to extend his hegemony through calculation and opportunism, one slow step at a time. Luther's emergency bishop (*Notbischof*) was thus only too happy to be of service, to use the Reformation crisis in the furtherance of his and his family's interests.

Nevertheless, by exposing the ties of religious reform in Zwickau to politics, economy, and society, I do not suggest that all parties cynically set out to profit from the changes and only superficially felt the appeal of Luther's spiritual message. While we cannot see into men's souls, there is every reason to believe that Bärensprung, Mühlpfort, many other residents of Zwickau, and the elector genuinely responded to the call of the Wittenberg nightingale and were convinced that they carried out the will of God in the reform. They could wholeheartedly sing with Martin Luther:

> And though the world, with devils filled,
> Should threaten to undo us,
> We will not fear, for God hath willed
> His truth to triumph through us.[1]

Notes

Introduction

1. Schriften des Vereins für Reformationsgeschichte, no. 180 (Gütersloh, 1962); translated as "Imperial Cities and the Reformation," *Imperial Cities and the Reformation: Three Essays*, trans. H. C. Erik Midelfort and Mark U. Edwards, Jr. (Philadelphia, 1972), 41–115. References hereafter are to the English edition.

2. Ibid., 61; Franz Lau, "Der Bauernkrieg und das angebliche Ende der lutherischen Reformation als spontaner Volksbewegung," *Luther-Jahrbuch* 26 (1952): 119.

3. "Probleme der Reformationsgeschichtsforschung," *Zeitschrift für Kirchengeschichte*, ser. 4, vol. 14 (1965): 246–57; translated as "Problems of Reformation Research," *Imperial Cities and the Reformation: Three Essays*, 3–16. References hereafter are to the English edition.

4. Ibid., 7.

5. A. Geoffrey Dickens, "Intellectual and Social Forces in the German Reformation," *The Urban Classes, the Nobility and the Reformation*, ed. Wolfgang J. Mommsen (Stuttgart, 1979), 11.

6. For an introduction to this concept, see *Die frühbürgerliche Revolution in Deutschland*, ed. Gerhard Brendler (Berlin, 1961).

7. For an introduction to this debate see Peter Blickle, *The Revolution of 1525: The German Peasants' War from a New Perspective*, trans. Thomas A. Brady, Jr. and H. C. Erik Midelfort (Baltimore, 1981); Bob Scribner and Gerhard Benecke, eds., *The German Peasant War 1525: New Viewpoints* (London, 1979); Rainer Wohlfeil, ed., *Der Bauernkrieg 1524–1526. Bauernkrieg und Reformation* (Munich, 1975).

8. Thomas A. Brady, Jr., *Ruling Class, Regime and Reformation at Strasbourg, 1520–1555* (Leiden, 1978); Ingrid Batori and Erdmann Weyrauch, *Die bürgerliche Elite der Stadt Kitzingen. Studien zur Sozial-und Wirtschaftsgeschichte einer landesherrlichen Stadt im 16. Jahrhundert* (Stuttgart, 1982); Olaf Mörke, *Rat und Bürger in der Reformation. Soziale Gruppen und kirchlicher Wandel in den welfischen Hansestädten Lüneburg, Braunschweig und Göttingen* (Hildesheim, 1983).

9. (Stuttgart, 1982), 73–97.

10. Ibid., 79–82.

11. Ibid., 82–87.

12. Ibid., 87–91.

13. Ibid., 92–97.

14. *Archive for Reformation History* 76 (1985): 6–63; bibliography 49–63.

15. *The Reformation in the Cities: The Appeal of Protestantism to Sixteenth-Century Germany and Switzerland* (New Haven, 1975), 2.

16. Brady, *Ruling Class*; Sabean, *Power in the Blood: Popular Culture and Village Discourse in Early Modern Germany* (Cambridge, England, 1984).

17. See, for example, the maps of the first appearance of Lutheran *preachers* in southwest German cities in Manfred Hannemann, *the Diffusion of the Reformation in Southwestern Germany, 1518–1534* (Chicago, 1975), 23–27.

18. *Mitteilungen des Altertumsvereins für Zwickau und Umgegend* (hereafter *MAZU*), 12 (1919): 1–74.

19. *Sächsische Heimatblätter* 20 (1974): 193–223. Bräuer has also recently completed a pamphlet on Luther's conflict with Zwickau between 1527 and 1531: *Zwickau und Martinus Luther: Die gesellschaftlichen Auseinandersetzungen um die städtische Kirchenpolitik in Zwickau (1527–1531)* (Karl-Marx-Stadt, 1983).

20. *The Urban Classes, the Nobility and the Reformation*, ed. Wolfgang J. Mommsen (Stuttgart, 1979), 49–79, esp. 54–62.

21. For example, ibid., 49.

22. Engels, *The Peasant War in Germany*, trans. Moissaye J. Olgin, 2nd ed. (New York, 1966); M. M. Smirin, *Die Volksreformation des Thomas Müntzer und der grosse Bauernkrieg* (Berlin, 1956); Max Steinmetz, "Thomas Müntzer in der Forschung der Gegenwart," *Der deutsche Bauernkrieg und Thomas Müntzer*, ed. Max Steinmetz (Leipzig, 1976), 93–104.

The Venice of Saxony

1. Karl Steinmüller, "Zur Lage der Zwickauer Tuchmacherei zwischen 1470 und 1530," *Die frühbürgerliche Revolution in Deutschland*, ed. Gerhard Brendler (Berlin, 1961), 220–21.

2. Max Rau, "Ueber die Herkunft der Zwickauer Bevölkerung," *Alt-Zwickau* 3 (1925): 10–11: "Auffallend ist die geringe Zahl der aus Norddeutschland gekommenen Bürger, nur 18 [out of 310 for whom place of origin is given], obgleich der Norden ein Hauptabsatzgebiet der heimischen Industrie war."

3. Zwickau Stadtarchiv (herafter ZSA), *Konzeptbuch* 1522–23, fol. 27, for example.

4. See Manfred Kobuch, "Zur Frühgeschichte Zwickaus. Bemerkungen zu Stadt und Vorstadt im 12. und 13. Jahrhundert," *Regionalgeschichtliche Beiträge aus dem Bezirk Karl-Marx-Stadt* 2 (1980): 49–64.

5. ZSA, *Regesten*, IIId, Nr. 8I, fol. 11; *Kopialbuch* Nr. 1: C1a/IIId, Nr. 13a, fols. 3–4. Before this Zwickau had had incomplete and in part temporary jurisdiction.

6. Adolf Laube, *Studien über den erzgebirgischen Silberbergbau von 1470 bis 1546* (Berlin, 1974). It has been customary to say that significant amounts of silver were discovered in 1469. Laube notes (17) that Martin Römer and Hans Federangel received special privileges such as *Münzbefreiung* before 1469, suggesting that certain myths quickly arose concerning the origin of mining on the Schneeberg.

7. Karl Hahn, "Martin Römer der Reiche," *Zwickauer Kulturbilder aus acht Jahrhunderten*, ed. Ewald Dost (Zwickau, 1939). Hahn thinks that Römer gave Zwickau 15,000–20,000 florins but distributed perhaps 80,000 florins besides to other towns (52–53). Ernestine currency during most of the period under study was made up of *heller* or half-pennies; *pfennige* (pennies), of which there were twelve to a *groschen*; groschen, of which there were twenty-one to a *gulden* or florin. After 1542 there were officially twenty-four groschen to a florin, but this did not immediately alter people's practice. A *gut schock* contained sixty groschen, an *alt schock* twenty. As to the value of money, Table 6 shows how much a citizen had to pay for meat during the first half of the sixteenth century. A mean cottage was assessed at 15 or 20 florins in 1531 and 1542, yet a woman of high status might spend up to twice as much on a good dress. Martin Luther believed that every rural pastor needed an annual salary of 50 florins, besides free housing, in order to feed and clothe himself and his family.

8. Emil Herzog, *Chronik der Kreisstadt Zwickau*, 2 vols. (Zwickau, 1839, 1845) 2: 130–31. Herzog intentionally burned thousands of documents from Zwickau's medieval past, evidently believing that his highly derivative and superficial chronicle made them dispensable.

9. Moritz Schwanfelder, *Die Kreisstadt Zwickau und ihre Umgebung, für Fremde und Einheimische historisch-topographisch geschildert* (Hildburghausen and Amsterdam, 1847), 19–20.

10. ZSA, *Regesten* IIId, Nr. 8I, fols. 27–28.

11. ZSA, A^x AII 18, Nr. 29.

12. Rudolf Falk, "Zwickauer Chroniken aus dem 16. Jahrhundert," *Alt-Zwickau* 7 (1924): 28.

13. "Schauspielaufführungen in Zwickau bis 1625," *Neues Archiv für sächsische Geschichte und Altertumskunde* 46 (1925): 113 n.

14. H. Bräuer, *Zwickau und Martinus Luther*, 16. I am grateful to Bräuer for showing me this in manuscript form. See Bräuer's analysis of population density and distribution of wealth, 16–26.

15. ZSA, A AII 11, Nr. 28b, fol. 1; reprinted by Reiner Gross, "Eine Denkschrift des Pfarrers Nikolaus Hausmann an den Rat zu Zwickau von Ende 1529," *Regionalgeschichtliche Beiträge aus dem Bezirk Karl-Marx-Stadt* 4 (1982): 60

16. *The Structures of Everyday Life* 1 (New York, 1981), 70–71; Herzog, *Chronik* 1: 229–32; Carlo M. Cipolla, *Before the Industrial Revolution*, 2nd ed. (New York, 1980), table A-2, pp. 305–6.

17. *Divided Germany and Berlin* (Princeton, 1962), 20.

18. Helga Baier, *Der Dom St. Marien zu Zwickau* (Berlin, 1977), 6. Although called a *Dom* during the nineteenth and twentieth centuries, the church was never a cathedral.

19. Some stalled for years, maintaining that they could not obtain houses there. By the 1540s they all resided in the appointed quarter or in the surburbs.

20. Schwanfelder, *Die Kreisstadt Zwickau*, 53.

The End of Communal Ideals

1. ZSA, *Regesten* IIId, Nr. 8I, fol. 54.

2. See the councillors' bitter complaint and their effort to regulate the hearing of court cases of all types: ZSA, *Ratsprotokolle* (hereafter RP) 1539–40, *1539*, fols. 3–7.

3. It is possible that the councils contained twenty-eight men (fourteen each) during a fourth year, 1537–38, but the relevant Ratsprotokolle and Amtsbücher are missing. By 1538–39 the number was back to twenty-four, where it remained until 1541. At that time the new council was temporarily expanded to thirteen members, but not the old.

4. Frederick the Wise let Burgomaster Lucas Strodel off in 1503 to recover financially (ZSA, A^x AIII 26, Nr. 2, folder 2a, item 17); also Burgomaster Michel Rang (ibid., folder 2c, items 4–5, 1511). Johann said that he would release any men whom public office too greatly burdened (ZSA, A^x AII 7, Nr. 14, 5 March 1524).

5. ZSA, *Regesten* IIId, Nr. 8I, fol. 125. See also the *Calendarium Eberi* accompanying the Schumann chronicle, Falk, "Zwickauer Chroniken," 8 (1924): 32.

6. ZSA, A^x AIII 26, Nr. 2, folder 2a.

7. Konrad Seeliger, "Zur ältesten Geschichte der Stadt Zwickau," *MAZU* 4 (1894): 1; Hugo Ilberg, "Bemerkungen zur Schwanensage," *Alt-Zwickau* 9 (1921): 41; Otto Clemen, "Zu Erasmus Stella," *MAZU* 8 (1905): 177, n. 1.

8. He was too ill in 1516 and 1517, and Duke Johann therefore excused the Rat from electing him (ZSA, A^x AIII 26, Nr. 2, folder 2d, items 3, 6).

9. Quoted by H. Bräuer, "Zwickau zur Zeit Thomas Müntzers," 198.

10. ZSA, A^x AII 11, Nr. 27, 1540. Violators had to pay a stiff fine of one florin.

11. The panel bearing this statement survives and is on display in Zwickau's City Museum.

12. Quoted by Karl Brod, *Rat und Beamte der kurfürstlichen Stadt Zwickau 1485–1547* (Zwickau, 1927), 10.

13. Ibid., 12.

14. ZSA, RP 1510–13, *1511*, fol. 26.

15. ZSA, A^x AIII 11, Nr. 26, fol. 9.

16. *Die Zwickauer Stadtrechtsreformation 1539/69*, ed. Hildegard Berthold, Karl Hahn, and Alfred Schultze (Leipzig, 1935), introduction, 1*–99*. A major issue between Beuther and the council was whether mothers, like fathers, could inherit from their (childless) dead children. The council said no, but the elector intervened on the other, the Saxon, side.

17. ZSA, RP 1510, fol. 26.

18. ZSA, IIIb^1, 54, 1–6, vol. 2, 1517–18. In 1541–42 three are named (IIIb^1, 54, 1–6, vol. 5). However, after that the city attempted to curtail the number of bureaucratic posts, and in 1542–43 and 1544–45 only one is mentioned. After its transfer to Moritz of Saxony, the city's decline hastened and it had little need for legions of functionaries.

19. See ZSA, RP 1522–25, *1522*, fol. 3, for an example of the payment of four percent.

20. ZSA, RP 1522–25, *1525*, fol. 60: "Herr Blasius Schrott shall not move away in view of the fact that he performed [the duties of] his armor office poorly and not at all." Even so, he was one of two armor masters in 1526–27.

21. The city's contribution was two squads (*Fähnlein*) of foot soldiers from inside and outside the walls and four armor wagons. Michel Richter, not Schrott, lead them.

22. See above, p.249, n. 7.

23. ZSA, RP 1516–19, *1518*, fol. 11.

24. ZSA, *Amtsbuch* IIIb^1, 54, 1–6, vol. 6, 1544, fol. 25: "The burghers are supposed to use fishing and hunting and trapping game in an honorable way for their recreation and not, as has often happened up till now, to the ruination of their wives' and children's livelihood."

25. *D. Martin Luthers Werke* (Weimar, 1883–), *Briefwechsel* 8, no. 3319, 9 April 1539. Hereafter WA for Weimarer Ausgabe.

26. For example, ZSA, *Amtsbuch* IIIb^1, 54, 1–6, vol. 4, fol. 92, 1534.

27. See, for instance, the *anträge* for 1529, ZSA, *Amtsbuch* IIIb^1, 54, 1–6, vol. 3, fols. 97–101.

28. ZSA, RP 1539–40, *1540*, fol. 84.

29. Herzog, *Chronik*, 2, pt. 2, 157.

30. ZSA, A^x AI 5, Nr. 3b.

31. ZSA, A^x AII 7, Nr. 13, 3 March 1524.

32. ZSA, RP 1539–40, *1539*, fol. 5.

33. ZSA, *Regesten* IIId, Nr. 8I, fol. 55.

34. ZSA, RP 1519–22, *1522*, fol. 47.

35. The Zwickauer Stadtarchiv contains a long, thin, yellowish-brown envelope bearing no call number or other identifying mark. Within are the *anträge* from 1479, 1482, 1483, 1491, 1495, 1496, 1498, 1499, 1500, 1501, 1502, 1506 (?), 1507, 1508, 1509, 1516, and 1520. The *amtsbücher* (IIIb¹, 54, 1–6) contain anträge for 1517, 1519, 1520, 1521, 1526, 1527, 1529, 1530, 1531, 1532, 1533, 1534, and 1535.

36. The new brewing ordinance is referred to in the council minutes of 1510–11. More revealing are the council minutes of 5 December 1516. Former burgomaster Michel Rang had asked to be allowed to import beer from Chemnitz for his step-daughter's wedding. The council commented that because the restriction on foreign beer had been issued during his administration, he should have to abide by it (RP 1516–19, *1516*, fol. 11). Rang had been burgomaster in 1509–10. A more exact dating of the ordinance and a detailed recitation of its contents are unfortunately not possible.

37. Falk, "Zwickauer Chroniken," 2 (1925): 8.

38. ZSA, *Kopialbuch* 1, C1a/IIId, Nr. 13a, fols. 48–49.

39. "Women's Labor Status in Fifteenth-Century Leiden and Cologne," paper presented at meetings of the American Historical Association, December 1982. See Judith M. Bennett, "The Village Ale-Wife: Women and Brewing in Fourteenth-Century England," *Women and Work in Preindustrial Europe*, ed. Barbara A. Hanawalt (Bloomington, Indiana, 1986), 35, n. 32.

40. ZSA, RP 1510–13, *1510*, fol. 3.

41. ZSA, *Amtsbuch*, IIIb¹, 54, 1–6, vol. 3, fol. 94.

42. ZSA, *Kammerrechnungen*, 1502–12, *1509–1510*, fol. 9.

43. Ibid., *1512–1515*, fol. In the late 1530s the council reversed itself and let every householder brew again, for a fee. Was this a concession to unceasing popular pressure? See ZSA, *Amtsbuch*, IIIb¹, 54, 1–6, vol. 4, fol. 22.

44. ZSA, *Amtsbuch*, III6¹, 54, 1–6, vol. 2, fol. 67.

45. ZSA, RP 1510–13, *1510*, fol. 5. Ironically, when in 1524 Frederick the Wise was thinking of imposing a general tax on salt, the council protested vigorously (ZSA, *Konzeptbuch*, 1524–26, fol. 48).

46. ZSA, *Amtsbuch*, IIIb¹, 54, 1–6, vol. 4, 1535, fol. 125.

47. ZSA, Aˣ AII 7, Nr. 11.

48. The Wettin (both Ernestine and Albertine branches) court in Leipzig.

49. These conciliar replies are also found in ZSA, Aˣ AII, 7, Nr. 11.

50. Ernst Fabian, "Die handschriftlichen Chroniken der Stadt Zwickau: I, Die (Osw. Losanschen) Annalen der Stadt Schwanfeld oder Zwickau von 1231–1534," *MAZU* 10 (1910): 48–49.

51. ZSA, RP 1510–13, *1511*, fol. 1.

52. ZSA, *Regesten*, IIId, Nr. 8I, fol. 55.

53. ZSA, RP 1539–40, *1540*, fol. 77: "Since the council and the city (*Gemeyne Stad*) have assigned (*verschrieben*) properties of the churches and

benefices now and again, one at a time, up to a total value of approximately 20,000 gulden, documents pertaining to which are partly on hand, partly lost, partly never written up at all, etc.," a complete record should be drawn up. The elector had finally ordered an accounting.

54. ZSA, RP 1522–25, *1523*, fol. 67.

55. ZSA, *Amtsbuch*, IIIb¹, 54, 1–6, fol. 148.

56. ZSA, RP 1516–19, *1518*, fol. 25.

57. ZSA, RP 1525–28, *1528*, fol. 34.

58. Paul Wappler, "Inquisition und Ketzerprozesse in Zwickau zur Reformationszeit," *MAZU* 9 (1908): 13–14.

59. ZSA, RP 1539–40, *1539*, fol. 7.

60. ZSA, RP 1525–28, *1525*, fol. 9.

61. Ibid.

62. ZSA, RP 1525–28, *1528*, fol. 44.

63. Falk, "Zwickauer Chroniken," 9 (1924): 35.

64. Ibid., 1 (1923): 35.

65. ZSA, RP 1534–36, *1535*, fol. 8.

66. ZSA, RP 1540–43, *1542*, fol. 53.

67. ZSA, RP 1540–43, *1540*, fol. 1.

68. ZSA, RP 1539–40, *1539*, fol. 2. This is an excerpt from "Pro L. Flacco Oratio." With slight modification I have used the translation of Louis E. Lord, *Cicero, the Speeches* (Cambridge, Massachusetts, 1959), 36, p. 87.

69. "Mag. Stephan Roth, Schulrektor, Stadtschreiber und Ratsherr zu Zwickau im Reformationszeitalter," *Beiträge zur sächsischen Kirchengeschichte* 1 (1882): 74–75.

70. ZSA, *Neue Rathherren Buch*, IIIb¹, Nr. 23b.

71. ZSA, RP 1516–19, *1517*, fol. 29.

72. See Otto Clemen's two-part encomium of Mühlpfort, *Alt-Zwickau* 5 (1922): 20; and 12 (1922): 46–48. Mühlpforts had been in Zwickau since 1303.

73. ZSA, RP 1525–28, *1526*, fols. 6, 9–10.

74. ZSA, RP 1525–28, *1527*, fol. 78. Part of the council minutes are missing here; hence, the outcome is uncertain.

75. ZSA, RP 1528–29, *1529*, fol. 69.

76. ZS, RP 1534–36, *1536*, fol. 41. Ironically, after Mühlpfort's death the Romers attempted to take back the entire property, the city's half, too.

77. Ibid.

78. ZSA, RP 1534–36, *1535*, fol. 19.

79. ZSA, RP 1534–36, *1536*, fol. 24. At his death Mühlpfort had left some sort of letter behind that was "highly injurious" to the council. I have not a clue as to what was in it, unless, perchance, it summarized some other leading citizens' illegal and corrupt actions.

80. ZSA, RP 1536–38, *1538*, fol. 57b.

81. ZSA, RP 1534–36, *1534*, fols. 12, 33.
82. ZSA, *Amtsbuch* IIIb¹, 54, 1–6, vol. 4, fol. 36.
83. "Imperial Cities," 49, 52–53.
84. Ibid., 68–69.
85. Falk, "Zwickauer Chroniken," 10 (1924): 39. The italics are mine. This seems to be a reference to the councillors' not being locked up but rather confined to a room in city hall with the door left open.
86. In 1544 the council lamented that calumny against councilmen, the clergy, "and other burghers" had increased greatly, and that this took the form of calling them names and making up verses ridiculing them (ZSA, RP 1543–44, *1544*, fol. 31).
87. Falk, "Zwickauer Chroniken," 1 (1923): 36.

The Gleam of Silver, the Shadow of Dearth

1. (Stuttgart, 1935; 2nd ed., 1967).
2. Vol. 1 (Leyden, 1936); vol. 2 appeared in 1949.
3. Male children had to be represented by a *furmund* until the age of twenty-one, females, of course, always. Sumptuary laws for adults applied at age twelve.
4. My count from ZSA, A˟ AII 17, Nr. 19a (1531) and A˟ AII 16, Nr. 12 (1542).
5. The number of masters who owned homes has been counted by Paul Kummer ("Gewerbe und Zunftverfassung in Zwickau bis zum Jahre 1600" [Ph.D. diss., University of Leipzig, 1921], 27). His figures are listed in table 5.
6. ZSA, *Amtsbuch* IIIb¹, 54, 1–6, vol. 1, 1503–04.
7. Ibid., vol. 4, 1533–34 and 1534–35.
8. Ibid., vol. 5, 1538–39; vol. 6, 1544–45.
9. ZSA, A˟ AII 7, Nr. 23, 23 October 1542.
10. In 1529, for example, there were twenty-eight (ZSA, RP 1528–29, *1529*, fol. 92). The committee was called the Twenty-four no matter how large it was.
11. ZSA, RP 1522–25, *1524*, fol. 2.
12. ZSA, *Amtsbuch* IIIb¹, 54, 1–6, vol. 2, fol. 151.
13. ZSA, RP 1534–36, *1536*, fol. 62.
14. ZSA, RP 1536–38, *1538*, fol. 80.
15. ZSA, *Amtsbuch* IIIb¹, 54, 1–6, vol. 1, 1509–10.
16. See, for instance, the bakers' complaints from 1543 (ZSA, RP 1540–43, *1543*, fol. 35). On one occasion the entire guild was imprisoned for a night in the various dungeons of the city wall, each member outside the quarter in which he resided.
17. ZSA, X, 49, 127, *Tuchmacher Rechnungen.*
18. In the City Museum in Zwickau is a newly made chart showing the

extent of Zwickau's Bannmeile in the sixteenth century. It reached as far north as Glauchau, about seven miles distant.

19. ZSA, *Regesten*, IIId, Nr. 8I, 1421, fols. 7–8.

20. Weimar Staatsarchiv (hereafter WSA), Reg. Bb 2904, *Jahrrechnung* 1523–24.

21. See summaries of Frederick the Wise's commands of 1508 and 1511 to Planitz: ZSA, *Regesten*, IIId, Nr. 8I, fols. 39, 41.

22. ZSA, *Amtsbuch*, IIIb¹, 54, 1–6, vol. 2, fol. 67.

23. Ibid.

24. WA, *Briefwechsel*, 8, no. 3319, 9 April 1539.

25. This is based on the assets of people named Hennel and Heinel in 1542. That Nickel and Lorenz Hennel really were her sons cannot be proved, and any daughters, having married and changed their names, cannot be identified,

26. Compare with Robert W. Scribner, "Reformation, Society and Humanism in Erfurt, c. 1450–1550" (Ph.D. diss., University of London 1972), vol. 2, almost all of which is tables showing the wealth of councillors, 1509–30.

27. "Zwickau zur Zeit Thomas Müntzers," 194.

28. ZSA, *Amtsbuch*, IIIb¹, 54, 1–6, vol. 4, fol. 34.

29. Ibid., fol. 60.

30. One of the rebel bakers was named Franz Storch.

31. Max Rau, "Zwickauer Bäckerleben im 16. Jahrhundert," *Alt-Zwickau* 9 (1924): 34.

32. Falk, "Zwickauer Chroniken," 8 (1924): 32.

33. Ibid., 11 (1923): 42. On competition for lumber see also WSA, *Findbuch* to Reg. N, fol. 603, where a pertinent document is described that is no longer extant.

34. WSA, *Findbuch* to Reg. N, fol. 609.

35. Elsas, *Geschichte der Preise und Löhne*.

36. WA, *Briefwechsel*, 6, no. 1808.

37. ZSA, *Amtsbuch* IIIb¹, 54, 1–6, vol. 4, fol. 127.

38. ZSA, Aˣ AIII 1, Nr. 14, 28 November 1531, fol. 4.

39. "Klag des armen Manns und Sorgevoll in Teuerung und Hungersnot," discussed by Karl Hahn, "Paul Rebhun," *Alt-Zwickau* 6 (1921): 24.

40. ZSA, RP 1534–36, *1535*, November, fol. 13.

41. ZSA, Aˣ AIII, Nr. 4.

42. Ibid.

43. For example, ZSA, RP 1534–36, *1535*, fols. 2, 29.

44. In regard to table 8, I should note that I disagree with Langer (26, n. 13) that *j* used as a numeral meant *1/2*. Certainly in book pagination it did not.

45. ZSA, *Amtsbuch*, IIIb¹, 54, 1–6, vol. 1, fol. 45.

46. ZSA, *Ratsrechnung* 1521–22, fol. 26.

47. ZSA, RP 1536–38, *1538*, fol. 63; RP 1539–40, *1540*, fol. 60.

48. ZSA, RP 1540–43, *1542*, fol. 63. I have not been able to determine to

what extent the city council curtailed holidays after the introduction of Lutheranism. Artisans traditionally had shortened working hours, for example, on several Mondays ("good" or "blue" Mondays) during the year. In other Saxon cities, after the Reformation magistrates cut these to three or four a year. In addition, they eliminated a number of holidays associated with saints and the Virgin. It is likely that both these changes took place in Zwickau too.

49. Langer, "Zwickauer Lohntaxen," 27, n. 22.

50. Ibid., 35.

51. Unfortunately, the City Museum of Zwickau does not contain one example of this ware.

52. Kummer, "Gewerbe und Zunftverfassung," 101.

53. ZSA, RP 1540-43, *1541*, fol. 27.

54. ZSA, *Amtsbuch* IIIb[1], 54, 1-6, vol. 4, 1533, fol. 63.

55. For instance, ZSA, RP 1539-40, *1540*, fol. 59.

56. Pastor Beyer and the council had a major confrontation on the running of the community chest in the winter of 1538 and another in 1542. See discussion below.

57. ZSA, RP 1522-25, *1525*, fol. 50.

58. Quoted by Max Müller, *Das Tuchmacher-Handwerk*, 46, 85.

59. ZSA, RP 1534-36, fol. 39. Under the council's direction, the guild merely changed its method of accounting: until the guild had entirely exhausted the funds that it had accumulated during all previous years, it was considered to be in the black. Each year's expenditures were calculated and deducted from the guild's entire pecuniary assets. Whether the year's expenditures exceeded the year's income was no longer regarded as crucial.

60. ZSA, RP 1534-36, *1535*, fol. 48.

61. ZSA, RP 1534-36, *1536*, fol. 67.

62. M. Müller, *Das Tuchmacher-Handwerk*, 58-59.

63. ZSA, RP 1536-38, *1537*, fol. 23.

64. Ibid., fol. 44.

65. M. Müller, *Das Tuchmacher-Handwerk*, 39.

66. ZSA, RP 1536-38, *1538*, fol. 49.

67. Ibid., fol. 74.

68. Ibid., fol. 85.

69. WSA, *Findbuch* to Reg. N, fols. 606-7 (document itself no longer extant).

70. ZSA, RP 1536-38, *1538*, fols. 91-93.

71. Ibid., fols., 93-94.

72. Ibid.

73. See Schumann's chronicle, Falk, "Zwickauer Chroniken," 10 (1924): 39.

74. ZSA, RP 1536-38, *1538*, fol. 94.

75. ZSA, RP 1539-40, *1539*, fol. 7, 25 October. I suspect Koch of being two-faced. He was a popular leader who may have brought radical intentions

to the authorities' attention. Perhaps this is why the council occasionally forgave whatever part of his property taxes he had not been able to pay.

76. For an explanation of the grades of woolen cloth in Zwickau and how they were supposed to be marked, see M. Müller, *Das Tuchmacher-Handwerk*, 23–27.

77. ZSA, *Amtsbuch*, IIIb[1], 54, 1–6, vol. 4, fol. 11.

78. ZSA, RP 1540–43, *1540*, fol. 10.

79. ZSA, *Regesten* IIId, Nr. 8I, fols. 129–30.

80. ZSA, RP 1540–43, *1542*, fol. 45.

81. Ibid., fol. 6.

82. Ibid., fol. 9.

83. ZSA, RP 1540–43, *1543*, fol. 32.

84. Ibid., fol. 38.

85. ZSA, RP 1540–43, *1542*, fol. 53.

86. ZSA, *Amtsbuch* IIIb[1], 54, 1–6, vol. 5, fol. 130.

87. ZSA, RP 1540–43, *1542*, fol. 67; *Amtsbücher*.

88. ZSA, RP 1540–43, *1542*, fol. 26.

89. ZSA, RP 1544–45, *1544*, fol. 8.

90. Ibid., fol. 23.

91. The council remonstrated with the guild again at the beginning of Lent, 1545 (ZSA, RP 1544–45, *1545*, fol. 39).

92. Susan C. Karant-Nunn, "Continuity and Change: Some Effects of the Reformation on the Women of Zwickau," *The Sixteenth Century Journal* 12, no. 2 (1982): 33. It is surely just a coincidence that two of these four were among a total of three men whose wives sought divorces during the Reformation period.

93. WSA, *Findbuch* to Reg. N, fol. 602 (documents no longer extant).

94. Ibid., fols. 602–3.

95. ZSA, *Amtsbuch* IIIb[1] 54, 1–6, vol. 4, fol. 93.

96. H. Bräuer, "Zwickau zur Zeit Thomas Müntzers," 194.

97. "Zur Lage der Zwickauer Tuchmacherei," 221–22.

98. ZSA, RP 1544–45, *1545*, fol. 32.

99. ZSA, RP 1540–43, *1543*, fols. 56–57.

100. ZSA, RP 1544–45, *1544*, fol. 1.

101. ZSA, RP 1525–28, *1526*, fol. 38.

102. In 1539 the total of debts to the community chest had been 7,500 florins (ZSA, RP 1539–40, *1539*, fols. 11–12).

103. WSA, *Findbuch* to Reg. N, fol. 592 (the documents themselves no longer exist).

104. ZSA, *Ratsrechnung* 1520–21, fol. 73, for example.

105. See two studies by Otto Kius: *Das Finanzwesen des Ernestinischen Hauses Sachsen im sechszehnten Jahrhundert* (Weimar, 1863) and *Das Forstwesen Thüringens im sechszehnten Jahrhundert* (Jena, 1869).

106. ZSA, RP 1534–36, *1534*, fol. 16.

107. ZSA, RP 1540–43, *1542*, fol. 64. In 1542 collectors of the Türken-steuer inquired of the prince and were instructed to count the florin as twenty-four groschen; they did so, but only in their grand totals! Assessments of real property were the same as in 1531, and throughout "35 schock" (35 times 60 groschen) equals one hundred florins; i.e., the florin equaled twenty-one groschen. This was a shrewd way of saving the better-off citizens some tax. The council was quite willing to neglect taxes that had to be paid into the elector's coffers.

108. Falk, "Zwickauer Chroniken," 12 (1924): 48.

109. ZSA, *Regesten* IIId, Nr. 8I fol. 41.

110. Falk, "Zwickauer Chroniken," 12 (1924): 48.

111. ZSA, A^x AI 12, Nr. 13a. Zwickauers could continue to produce such linen as they could use themselves.

112. ZSA, RP 1540–43, *1542*, fol. 67.

113. ZSA, RP 1540–43, *1543*, fol. 47.

114. ZSA, A^x AII 7, Nr. 27, fols. 2, 12.

115. ZSA, *Amtsbuch* IIIb^1, 54 1–6, vol. 2, fol. 113.

116. Ibid., fol. 116.

117. ZSA, A^x AI, 4, Nr. 9, fol. 3.

118. Ibid., fols. 5–6.

119. Ibid., fols. 7–8.

120. Ibid., fols. 20–21.

121. Ibid.

122. Ibid.

123. *Structures of Everyday Life* 1, pp. 193–94.

Humanist Oratory, Radical Revelation, Conciliar Resolve

1. In 1537 Hermann Mühlpfort, Jr., owned a house in Wittenberg (*Kämmereirechnung* 1537, Stadtarchiv Wittenberg, a photograph of which appears in Karlheinz Blaschke, *Wittenberg die Lutherstadt* [Berlin, 1977], 29).

2. Scribner, *For the Sake of Simple Folk: Popular Propaganda for the German Reformation* (Cambridge, England, 1981), 3. Scribner cites in turn R. Engelsing, *Analphabetentum und Lektüre. Zur Sozialgeschichte des Lesens in Deutschland zwischen feudaler und industrieller Gesellschaft* (Stuttgart, 1973).

3. See ZSA, A^x AII 18, Nr. 37. This is a copy of a letter, dated 7 April 1500, from Frederick the Wise to the bishop of Naumburg, requesting the latter to make the preacher in Saint Mary's Church stop slandering the city council from the pulpit.

4. Otto Clemen, "Johannes Sylvius Egranus," *MAZU* 6 (1899): 1–39.

5. Otto Clemen, "Eine merkwürdige Inschrift am Altar unserer Marien-kirche," *Alt-Zwickau* 2 (1929): 8.

6. ZSA, RP 1519-22, *1520*, fol. 12.

7. ZSA, RP 1519-22, *1519*, fols. 4-5.

8. ZSA, RP 1519-22, *1520*, fol. 24.

9. Ibid., fol. 25.

10. ZSA, RP 1516-19, *1518*, fol. 10; *1519*, fol. 16.

11. See Helmut Bräuer's account from a Marxist perspective, "Der politisch-ideologische Differenzierungsprozess in der Zwickauer Bürger-schaft unter dem Einfluss des Wirkens Thomas Müntzers (1520/21)," *Der deutsche Bauernkrieg und Thomas Müntzer*, ed. Max Steinmetz (Leipzig, 1976), 105-11.

12. Clemen, "Johannes Sylvius Egranus," 16-17.

13. WA, *Briefwechsel*, 1, no. 107.

14. *Thomas Müntzer, Schriften und Briefe*, ed. Günther Franz (Gütersloh, 1968), 351, no. 6, 12 December 1519.

15. ZSA, RP 1519-22, *1520*, fol. 11, 15 December.

16. Laurentius Wilhelm, *Descriptio urbis Cycneae*, 215.

17. ZSA, RP 1519-22, *1520*, fol. 26.

18. Ibid., fol. 34.

19. Wilhelm, *Descriptio urbis Cycneae*, 215.

20. ZSA, RP 1519-22, *1520*, fol. 35.

21. Ibid.

22. Hofer petitioned the council for protection in late December 1520, which it did not grant. Hofer had, it noted, called Müntzer and all his sympa-thizers "heretical rogues and villains" ("*ketscherische schelck vnd boss-wichte*"—ZSA, RP 1519-22, *1520*, fol. 12). Hofer was moving away. The council was glad to be rid of him since it was just now acquiring the right of patronage over the Marienthal pastorate from the Eisenberg nuns, from whom it had purchased similar rights over the Zwickau pastorate in 1505 (RP 1519-22, *1521*, fol. 15).

23. Eric Gritsch, *Reformer Without a Church: The Life and Thought of Thomas Müntzer 1488(?)-1525* (Philadelphia, 1967), 35. On the relation-ship between Egranus and Müntzer, see Walter Elliger, *Thomas Müntzer, Leben und Werk*, 2nd ed. (Göttingen, 1975), 132-66; and Steven E. Ozment, *Mysticism and Dissent: Religious Ideology and Social Protest in the Sixteenth Century* (New Haven, 1973), 61-68. On Egranus, see Hubert Kirchner, *Johann Sylvius Egranus* (Berlin, 1961).

24. For Egranus's reasons for separating himself from the Lutheran movement, see Clemen, "Johannes Sylvius Egranus," part 2, *MAZU* (1902): 20 (letter to Hausmann). Among other reasons, he found Luther too self-righteous and too inclined to outbursts of temperament. He regarded Luther's theology as a new form of scholasticism and considered his diction barbaric and rustic.

25. J. K. Seidemann, *Thomas Müntzer* (Dresden and Leipzig, 1842), document 5c.

26. Ibid., document 5b.

27. *Thomas Müntzer, Schriften und Briefe*, 368, no. 21.

28. ZSA, RP 1519–22, *1520*, fol. 11.

29. ZSA, RP 1519–22, *1521*, fol. 13.

30. Ibid., fol. 14.

31. *Thomas Müntzers Briefwechsel*, ed. Heinrich Boehmer and Friedrich Kirn (Leipzig and Berlin, 1931), no. 20.

32. ZSA, A^x AII 18, Nr. 45; *Kopialbuch* Nr. 1: C1a/IIId, Nr. 13a, fol. 70.

33. "Zwickau zur Zeit Thomas Müntzers," 210.

34. Karl Czok, "Revolutionäre in mitteldeutschen Städten zur Zeit von Reformation und Bauernkrieg," *450 Jahre Reformation*, ed. L. Stern and M. Steinmetz (Berlin, 1967), 131; Paul Wappler, "Thomas Müntzer in Zwickau und die 'Zwickauer Propheten'," *Wissenschaftliche Beilage zu dem Jahresberichte des Realgymnasiums mit Realschule zu Zwickau* (Zwickau, 1908), 24.

35. ZSA, *Regesten* IIId, Nr. 8I, fol. 53.

36. ZSA, RP 1534–36, *1535*, fol. 30.

37. Wappler, "Inquisition und Ketzerprozesse," 83–84.

38. ZSA, RP 1519–22, *1521*, fol. 21.

39. For a detailed account of historians' treatment of this episode, see Siegfried Bräuer, "Müntzers Feuerruf in Zwickau," *Herbergen der Christenheit* (1971): 127–53.

40. *Thomas Müntzers Briefwechsel*, 390, no. 40.

41. "Müntzers Feuerruf," 128.

42. ZSA, *Ratsrechnung* 1520–21, Karton 7, fol. 42.

43. Technically, a *knappe* was a journeyman. But as used in the early sixteenth century, it was a nickname for all woolweavers, including guildmasters. The "Knappenaltar" in Saint Katherine's Church had been endowed by the Corpus Christi confraternity at Saint Katherine's Chruch, to which mainly masters, as settled citizens, would have belonged. Those who rose up to give Müntzer escort included property owners and men of rank within the guild.

44. ZSA, *Ratsrechnung* 1520–21, Karton 7, fol. 38.

45. WA, *Briefwechsel*, 2, no. 345.

46. Smirin, *Die Volksreformation des Thomas Müntzer*.

47. Prof. Siegfried Hoyer (Karl Marx University, Leipzig) has graciously sent me a copy of his 1984 manuscript, "Die Zwickauer Storchianer—Vorläufer der Täufer?" His answer to the question, whether Storch's followers were forerunners of the Anabaptists, is negative. In arriving at this conclusion, he carefully analyzes available literature on the relationship between Müntzer and Storch in Zwickau, which, he agrees, does not permit of any certainty.

48. Wappler, "Thomas Müntzer in Zwickau," 36–41.

49. Georg Buchwald, "Die Protokolle der Kirchenvisitationen in den

Aemtern: Zwickau, Crimmitzschau und Werdau vom 12. bis zum 31. Januar 1529," *Allerlei aus drei Jahrhunderten* 1 (1888): 25.

50. WA, *Tischreden*, no. 1204, c. 1535.

51. "Christus sprech, 'Streyt vnd vberw[inde] so will ich dich setz auf den th[ron],' " WSA, Reg. Ii 245, fol. 31. This can be variously interpreted.

52. Ibid. She was no doubt the one who had preached in July 1521 and about whose activity Duke Johann had inquired (ZSA, *Ratsrechnung* 1519-22, fol. 60).

53. Wappler, "Inquisition und Ketzerprozesse," 21-54. The record of Sturm's interrogation is ZSA, A^x AIII 1, Nr. 10.

54. Quoted by Max Steinmetz from Melanchthon's "Nova scholia in proverbia Salomonis," "Philipp Melanchthon über Thomas Müntzer und Niklaus Storch," *Philipp Melanchthon, Humanist, Reformator, Praeceptor Germaniae* (Berlin, 1963), 138-73.

55. Wappler, "Thomas Müntzer in Zwickau," 12.

56. Franz Storch, possibly a relative of Niclas, was a prominent member of a group of journeymen bakers who rebelled against the council in 1522-23 (ZSA, RP 1522-25, *1523*, fols. 33-34, 43, 50).

57. ZSA, RP 1522-25, *1522*, fol. 19.

58. Siegfried Sieber, "Geistige Beziehungen zwischen Böhmen und Sachsen zur Zeit der Reformation," pt. 1, *Bohemia* 6 (1965): 146-72. Smirin states, without citation, that Luther himself feared that Bohemian religious elements, including radical Taborite tendencies, might affect the character of the German Reformation (*Die Volksreformation*, 101). He says that in contrast to Luther, Müntzer desired to spread Bohemian influence and worked to that end (102).

59. Nikolaus Müller, ed., *Die Wittenberger Bewegung 1521 und 1522*, 2nd ed. (Leipzig, 1911), 139. Heinrich Boehmer, "Die Waldenser von Zwickau und Umgegend," *Neues Archiv für sächsische Geschichte* 36 (1915): 1-38.

60. Quoted by Richard Bachmann, *Niclas Storch, der Anfänger der Zwickauer Wiedertäufer: Ein Lebensbild* (Zwickau, 1880), 4.

61. "Philipp Melanchthon über Thomas Müntzer," 138-73.

62. "Entwicklungstendenzen im Städtewesen Sachsens zu Beginn der Neuzeit," *Die Stadt an der Schwelle zur Neuzeit*, ed. Wilhelm Rausch (Linz, 1980), 256.

63. ZSA, RP 1519-22, *1522*, fol. 36, for instance. Peter Schumann's account, written about 1560 and possibly affected by Melanchthon's intense prejudice against Storch, has Storch as the "archschismatic" who brought his poison home from Bohemia, and as the "master" who led all others into error. Schumann nevertheless refers to Oswald Lasan's version, from which he borrowed, in which an Austrian Erhard Forster calls Müntzer "patronus" and says "se plus credere Mgro. Thomae Müntzer . . . et Nicolao Storch, nisi Storch vinceretur. . . ."

64. Quoted by Bachmann, *Niclas Storch*, 23, 4 September 1522.

65. N. Müller, ed., *Die Wittenberger Bewegung*, 129.

66. ZSA, *Amtsbuch* IIIb¹, 54, 1–6, vol. 1.

68. ZSA, *Stadtrechnungen* 1507–12, fols. 21–22, 29; 1512–15, fol. 26; 1515–19, fols. 94, 98.

69. N. Müller, *Die Wittenberger Bewegung*, 130.

70. *Thomas Müntzer, Schriften und Briefe*, no. 22, 369–70.

71. *Vita Philippi Melanchthonis* (Leipzig, 1723), 42–46.

72. Philip Melanchthon, *Philippi Melanchthonis opera quae supersunt omnia*, ed. Karl Gottlieb Bretschneider, *Corpus Reformatorum* (Halle, 1843–60), 1, p. 182; N. Müller, *Die Wittenberger Bewegung*, 139.

73. Zwickau Ratsschulbibliothek (hereafter ZRB), Schumann's chronicle, fol. 127.

74. Otto Clemen, "Nicolaus Hausmann," *Alt-Zwickau* 1 (1921): 6–8.

75. WA, *Briefwechsel*, 4, no. 988.

76. ZSA, RP 1519–22, *1521*, fol. 49.

77. See Mark U. Edwards, Jr.'s description of the events in Wittenberg, *Luther and the False Brethren* (Stanford, 1975), 7.

78. ZSA, RP 1519–22, *1521*, fol. 8.

79. Ibid., fol. 9.

80. Ibid., fol. 10.

81. Ibid., fol. 13. On the burial order itself see ZSA, RP 1519–22, *1520*, fol. 4. After much discussion of changing burial regulations so that more people could be buried outside the crowded city, the council was forced by serious resistance on the part of craftsmen to come to the following compromise on 29 October 1520: All homeowners and their children, whether their property lay in or out of the walls, were entitled to burial in the city "as for ages past"; propertyless citizens and servants who died outside the city would be buried in Saint Moritz's or Saint John's churchyard, both outside the walls. And burghers were to make sure that the sick and the dying were conveyed to the hospitals and other designated houses outside the walls, which greatly increased the likelihood of death and burial outside.

82. ZSA, RP 1519–22, *1521*, fol. 16; RP 1522–25, *1523*, fol. 50.

83. ZSA, RP 1519–22, *1521*, fol. 15. Friars and monks continued to beg, however, as the council repeated its prohibition early in 1525 (RP 1522–25, *1525*, fol. 28).

84. ZSA, RP 1519–22, *1521*, fol. 16.

85. Ibid., fol. 16.

86. Ibid., fol. 17d.

87. WSA, Reg. N 16. This document is in the form of a letter and in addition to Hausmann is signed by preachers Johann Zeidler and Wolff Zeiner, and by Balthasar Thurschmidt, Mag. Laurentius Ziener, Jacob Bernwalder, Gregorious Stalich (?), and Wolff Meinhart, the last five "city children of Zwickau."

88. Another copy says "without baptism" in place of "without faith" (N. Müller, *Die Wittenberger Bewegung*, 143 n.).

89. Ibid., 142-43.

90. ZSA, RP 1519-22, *1522*, fol. 18.

91. Ibid.

92. ZSA, RP 1519-22, *1521*, fol. 17d.

93. WSA, Reg. Pp. 368²⁻⁴: "Vorzeichnus der ligenden grunden vnd gutter Im Weichbilde der Stadt Zwickau Wirdering etc." A fourth, Hans Bruschwein, owned a house in the Hundsgasse in 1522, but the next year is listed in the Tränkviertel. Yet in 1536 he is listed in the Hundsgasse.

94. ZSA, IIIy, Nr. la: "Lehenbuch 1498 auch Burgerbuch 1498-1522."

95. WSA, Reg. Ii 245, fols. 31, 37.

96. Ibid., fol. 34.

97. Map folded into front of Herzog, *Chronik*, vol. 1. The copy of this work in the library of Karl Marx University contains this map; the copy in the British Library, ostensibly of the same edition, contains a map of Zwickau in 1760 that does not indicate the quarters.

98. See Sommerschuh's letter to Müntzer of 31 July 1521 (*Thomas Müntzer, Schriften und Briefe*, 375-76, no. 27).

99. ZSA, *Lehenbuch*, IIIy, Nr. la.

100. ZSA, Aˣ AII 6, Nr. 4.

101. ZSA, RP 1522-25, *1525*, fol. 78; *Amtsbuch*, 1534-35, fol. 93.

102. ZSA, RP 1519-22, *1522*, fol. 18.

103. WSA, Reg. N 16.

104. ZSA, RP 1522-25, *1525*, fol. 32.

105. Quoted by Bachmann, *Niclas Storch*, 34-35.

106. "Sso wolde der Radt seiner notturft wider Ine nit vorgessen." ZSA, RP 1522-25, *1525*, fol. 48.

107. Wappler, "Inquisition und Ketzerprozesse," 71, says that Storch did visit Zwickau in January 1534. The council minutes are missing. The 1536 scare is attested by RP 1534-36, *1536*, fol. 33.

108. ZSA, RP 1519-22, *1522*, fol. 24.

109. Ibid., fol. 36.

110. ZSA, RP 1522-25, *1523*, fol. 60. Schumann seems to place this event on 9 August 1522, which does not jibe with my reading of the Ratsprotokolle. Did he mix 1522 and 1523?

111. See, for example, ZSA, RP 1519-22, *1522*, fol. 20.

112. Falk, "Zwickauer Chroniken," 2 (1925): 7.

113. Erich Maschke has stated that in every cloth producing city, from Flanders to Florence, weavers, whether of wool or linen, were the most volatile of all the craftsmen. He calls weavers' guilds the "crucibles of conflict" ("die Herde von Auseinandersetzung"). "Verfassung und soziale Kräfte in der deutschen Stadt des späten Mittelalters, vornehmlich in Oberdeutsch-

land," *Vierteljahrschrift für Sozial-und Wirtschaftsgeschichte* 1, 46 (1959): 299. A former student of mine, Diane Booton, in 1982 wrote a term paper on this assertion, in the process collecting citations from a range of modern historians. Zwickau is just not the best place to test this alleged proclivity.

114. ZSA, RP 1519–22, *1522*, fol. 23.

115. Ibid., fol. 28.

116. ZSA, RP 1522–25, *1522*, fol. 10.

117. ZSA, RP 1519–22, *1522*, fol. 45.

118. Ibid., fol. 33.

119. Falk, "Zwickauer Chroniken," 1 (1923): 3.

120. Fabian, "Die handschriftlichen Chroniken," 63–65.

121. Thursday, 6 March 1522.

122. Schumann quotes his father as saying that the peasant's circulation had been so impaired that his toes rotted off (Falk, "Zwickauer Chroniken," 1 [1923]: 3).

123. Ibid.

124. ZSA, A^x AI 14, Nr. 15.

125. Falk, "Zwickauer Chroniken," 1 (1923): 4.

126. WA, 10, pt. 3, 103.

127. Ibid., 103–12.

128. Falk, "Zwickauer Chroniken," 1 (1923): 4. Many soldiers were among them, suggesting a need to take measures against possible uprising.

129. Herzog, *Chronik*, 2, 197.

130. *Das Verhältniss der Stadt Zwickau zur Kirchen-Reformation; bey Gelegenheit des dritten Jubiläums im Jahre 1817, kürzlich dargestellt* (Zwickau, 1817), 52.

131. ZSA, *Ratsrechnung* 1521–22, Karton 7, fol. 34.

132. ZSA, RP 1522–25, *1522*, fols. 15–16.

133. Ibid., *1523*, fol. 29.

134. ZSA, RP 1519–22, *1522*, fols. 19, 24.

135. Ibid., fol. 41.

136. Ibid., fol. 42.

137. Ibid., fol. 44.

138. Ibid., fol. 47, 14 July.

139. Falk, "Zwickauer Chroniken," 1 (1923): 4.

140. ZSA, RP 1522–25, *1524*, fols. 16–17.

141. ZSA, RP 1522–25, *1522*, fol. 12.

142. Ibid., *1522*, fol. 12.

143. Ibid., fols. 21, 23.

144. This "erstes Gutachten" is reprinted in Ludwig Preller, "Nicolaus Hausmann, der Reformator von Zwickau und Anhalt," *Zeitschrift für historische Theologie* 3 (1852): 347–63. It contains a number of recommendations suitable for an "Ordinance for Priests."

145. ZSA, RP 1522–25, *1522*, fols. 20–21.

146. Ibid., fol. 25.

147. ZSA, RP 1522–25, *1523*, fol. 50.

148. Ibid., fol. 49.

149. Ibid., fol. 56. Zeidler enjoyed the income of two benefices until 1525, when the Rat told him that if he wanted to receive it in future, he would have to live in Zwickau (RP 1525–28, *1525*, fol. 6). In the end he accepted the council's terms (fol. 7). There were many Zeidlers in Zwickau, to whom he was probably related.

150. Rudolff Herrmann, "Die Prediger im ausgehenden Mittelalter und ihre Bedeutung für die Einführung der Reformation im ernestinischen Thüringen," *Beiträge zur thüringischen Kirchengeschichte* 1, no. 1 (1929): 20–68; Hannemann, *The Diffusion of the Reformation*, 21–28.

151. ZSA, RP 1522–25, *1522*, fol. 22.

152. Ibid., fol. 56.

153. ZSA, RP 1522–25, *1523*, fol. 54.

154. ZSA, Aˣ AIII 1, Nr. 4.

155. ZSA, Aˣ AII 1, Nr. 23, fol. 101.

156. ZSA, RP 1522–25, *1524*, fol. 6.

157. ZSA, RP 1525–28, *1526*, fol. 6.

158. ZSA, RP 1525–28, *1527*, fol. 78.

159. ZSA, Aˣ AIII 26, Nr. 2, folder 2f, item 27.

160. In 1533 Johann Friedrich wrote to the parish visitors in Thuringia, "Doctor Christian Beyer, our most learned chancellor, advisor, and dear servant, has reported to us that some of you are in error over that article which deals with patrons of church benefices and endowments, and have among yourselves two opinions. . . . Inasmuch as under popery no patron or collator of spiritual benefices was allowed to claim income from benefices that were vacated . . . we believe that it would not be unjust if at present these benefices and their income were used for charitable purposes and taken for the needed support of pastors, preachers, and schools." WSA, Reg. Ii 599.

161. WSA, Reg. Ii 330, fols. 1–5; ZSA, RP 1544–45, *1545*, fol. 35.

162. ZSA, Aˣ AI 6, Nr. 7.

163. For example, ZSA, Aˣ AI 8, Nr. 3.

164. The visitors in 1533 criticized the council for its lackadaisical record keeping. They noted, for instance, that "one third of the ecclesiastical benefices over which the council has patronage are not sequestrated, nor is any separate account of them kept. Instead the records are mixed in with others in a disorderly way." ZSA, Aˣ AIII 1, Nr. 23, fol. 102.

165. See an example in ZSA, RP 1522–25, *1524*, fol. 22.

166. WA, Hauspostille.

167. By 1531 only six priests still received income from Lehen in Saint Mary's Church and three from Lehen in Saint Katherine's. Outside of these

churches, four other ecclesiastical Lehen still sustained clergymen (ZSA, *Tür-kensteuerregister*, AII 17, Nr. 19b, fols. 67–69). In 1542 only seven benefices remained. Before the Reformation there had been twenty-three priestly benefices in Saint Mary's Church and ten in Saint Katherine's.

168. ZSA, A^x AIII 2, Nr. 4, fol. 18.

169. Ernst Fabian, "Die Protokolle der zweiten Kirchenvisitation zu Zwickau vom 10. bis 28. November 1533," *MAZU* 7 (1902): 124–25.

170. Falk, "Zwickauer Chroniken," 10 (1923): 39.

Discretion as the Better Part of Sympathy

1. ZSA, *Regesten*, IIId, Nr. 8I, fol. 64; A^x AII 14, Nr. 2.

2. The council began to divest itself of some peasants late in the Reformation era. In 1541 it "sold" the Stangengrün peasants to the nobleman Hans von Metzsch. At the same time it desired to acquire villages that had been under the control of the monastery at Grünhain, but the elector did not permit this.

3. ZSA, A^x AII 16, Nr. 12, fols. 193–213.

4. See the collection of letters dating from 1483 to 1536 on this subject: ZSA, A^x AII 14, Nr. 3; also A^x AII 14, Nr. 2; and A^x AI 4, Nr. 7.

5. ZSA, A^x AII 12, Nr. 11.

6. M. Müller, *DAS Tuchmacher-Handwerk*, 7.

7. ZSA, RP 1522–25, *1525*, fol. 29.

8. Ibid., fol. 50.

9. Ibid.

10. Ibid., fol. 60, 5 May 1525.

11. ZSA, A^x AIII 26, Nr. 2, folder 14.

12. ZSA, A^x AIII 1, Nr. 6. For a fuller documentary coverage of the entire Peasants' War in central Germany, the reader should consult Walther Peter Fuchs, ed., *Akten zur Geschichte des Bauernkriegs in Mitteldeutschland*, vol. 2 (Jena, 1942).

13. ZSA, A^x AIII 1, Nr. 6.

14. Ibid., 8 May 1525.

15. Ibid.

16. Ibid.

17. ZSA, RP 1522–25, *1525*, fol. 60.

18. Ibid., fol. 63.

19. Ibid., fols. 56, 57.

20. ZSA, A^x AII 16, Nr. 2, "Herfardt geldt von den Burgern eingenomen Inn der Bawernn auffruhr, Anno Dominj 25 eingenomen." This was a heavy tax. A house with brewing rights paid two florins, and houses without this privilege paid one florin. See RP 1525–28, *1525*, fol. 15. Many people experienced difficulty in paying (fol. 21).

21. ZSA, RP 1522–25, *1525*, fol. 61.

22. Ibid., fol. 62.

23. Ibid., fol. 63; *Ratsrechnung* 1524–25, fol. 55.

24. ZSA, RP 1522–25, *1525*, fol. 60.

25. Ibid., fol. 68; *Ratsrechnung* 1524–25, fol. 61.

26. ZSA, *Ratsrechnung* 1524–25, fols. 55, 59. This included telling him that the miners had risen up in Joachimsthal.

27. ZSA, A^x AIII 1, Nr. 6.

28. Ibid. While I am almost certain that I have identified the right Forster, there seems to have been another one in town, a former cleric who complained to the council between 1523 and 1525 about not being paid the interest from his benefice. This matter was settled late in 1525 (A^x AIII 1, Nr. 3). It is conceivable that the two were one and the same person.

29. ZSA, RP 1522–25, *1525*, fol. 56.

30. Ibid., fol. 57.

31. Pastor Hausmann did not help his city in this political crisis. On 2 May 1525, Hausmann was writing his lengthy and famous *Gutachten* to the man who was in three days to become Elector Johann, pressing him to root out religious evils throughout his lands by means of parish visitation. This document reveals no awareness on Hausmann's part of the threat that Zwickau was that very day confronting. This Gutachten is printed, along with the one of 1523, in Preller, "Nicolaus Hausmann," 365–79. See WSA, Reg. Ii 129.

32. Wolff Koch, an owner of a modest home (worth one hundred florins), was viewed by ordinary folk as a courageous man who was willing to tell the council what it did not like to hear. Many were affected by his death in 1540 (Falk, "Zwickauer Chroniken," 10 [1923]: 39).

33. ZSA, RP 1522–25, *1525*, fols. 57–58.

34. ZSA, RP 1525–28, *1525*, fols. 13–14, 6 November.

35. ZSA, RP 1522–25, *1525*, fol. 58.

36. Falk, "Zwickauer Chroniken," 2 (1923): 8.

37. Ibid.

38. Ibid.

39. ZSA, RP 1522–25, *1525*, fol. 54.

40. ZSA, RP 1522–25, *1523*, fol. 67.

41. "Vnterrichdt vnd warnung an die Kirch zu Zwickaw / mit etzlichen Artickeln den Clostervolck doselbst angeboten / vnd von jnen vnbillich abgeschlagen" (Zwickau [written in later: Jorg Gastel, 1523]).

42. Falk, "Zwickauer Chroniken," 2 (1923): 8.

43. ZSA, RP 1522–25, *1525*, fol. 38.

44. Ibid., fol. 57.

45. See two articles by Irmgard Höss: "Georg Spalatins Bedeutung für die Reformation und die Organisation der lutherischen Landeskirche," *Archiv für Reformationsgeschichte* 42, 1–2 (1951): 101–35; and "George Spalatins

Verhältnis zu Luther und der Reformation," *Luther, Mitteilungen der Lu-thergesellschaft* 31, 1 (1960): 67–80.

46. ZSA, RP 1522–25, *1525*, fol. 56.

47. Ibid., fol. 59.

48. Ibid.

49. WSA, Reg. Kk 1566; reprinted in Felician Gess, *Akten und Briefe zur Kirchenpolitik Herzog Georgs von Sachsen*, 2 vols. (Leipzig, 1905), 2, 374.

50. ZSA, A^x AI 8, Nr. 4c.

51. ZSA, RP 1522–25, *1525*, fol 62.

52. Ibid., fol. 61.

53. ZSA, A^x AIII 1, Nr. 6.

54. Ibid.

55. ZSA, RP 1522–25, *1525*, fol. 64.

56. ZSA, *Ratsrechnung* 1524–25, Karton 8, fol. 57.

57. ZSA, RP 1522–25, *1525*, fols. 66–67.

58. ZSA, *Ratsrechnung*, 1524–25, Karton 8, fol. 61.

59. ZSA, RP 1522–25, *1525*, fol. 76.

60. Hildebrand says that 1,500 cavalry and seven hundred footsoldiers came to Zwickau with Johann (*Das Verhältniss der Stadt Zwickau*, 44).

61. ZSA, RP 1522–25, *1525*, fol. 79.

62. Quoted by Oswald Gottlob Schmidt, *Nicolaus Hausmann, der Freund Luther's* (Leipzig, 1860), 47. Schmidt cites evidence that Egranus too thought Hausmann should have stayed out of this matter (48 n.).

63. *The Revolution of 1525*, 187–93.

64. WA 46, 49–55.

65. Reprinted in Theodore Kolde, *Analecta Lutherana* (Gotha, 1883), 64–68. See Clemen's interpretation in "Hermann Mühlpfort," pt. 2, 46–48.

66. Quoted by Ludwig Keller, "Ueber die Anfänge der Reformation in Zwickau," *Monatshefte der Comenius-Gesellschaft* 9 (1900): 176.

67. WA, *Briefwechsel*, 4, with no. 1091.

68. ZSA, RP 1522–25, *1525*, fol. 89.

69. Ibid.

70. ZSA, RP 1525–28, *1525*, fol. 4, the village of Schneppendorf versus Hans von Weissbach.

71. For a list of the fines in Amt Zwickau, see WSA, Reg. N 986.

The Council Triumphant . . . and Then the Elector

1. ZSA, RP 1522–25, *1525*, fol. 88.

2. ZSA, RP 1525–28, *1525*, fol. 21.

3. ZSA, A^x AII 7 Nr. 16.

4. ZSA, RP 1525–28, *1527*, fol. 2.

5. ZSA, RP 1525–28, *1528*, fol. 44.

6. ZSA, RP 1522–25, *1525*, fol. 93.

7. Ibid., fol. 9.

8. ZSA, RP 1525–28, *1528*, fol. 34, 2 March.

9. ZSA, RP 1528–29, *1529*, fol. 155.

10. Ibid., fol. 117.

11. ZSA, RP 1525–28, *1528*, fol. 24.

12. WSA, Reg. Ii 245, fol. 6.

13. ZSA, RP 1525–28, *1528*, fol. 33.

14. ZSA, RP 1528–29, *1529*, fols. 110, 113; Wappler, "Inquisition und Ketzerprozesse," 17–19.

15. ZSA, RP 1534–36, *1536*, fol. 33.

16. Edwards, *Luther and the False Brethren.*

17. For another scholar's account, see H. Bräuer, *Zwickau und Martinus Luther.*

18. Money paid to the teachers by the students, either as tuition or to supplement their salaries.

19. ZSA, RP 1525–28, *1527*, fol. 18.

20. Ibid., between fols. 19 and 20.

21. Hausmann may have argued that many children were too poor to pay Schulgeld.

22. "Ist Ime In gemein angetzeigt solt den furgehalten werden der villeicht solchs gereth ader dorunter vorargkwant." I am unsure of the translation.

23. The pastor desired consistency in the ringing of the church bell. He did not want it sounded any oftener than necessary since he associated bells with Catholicism.

24. ZSA, RP 1525–28, *1528*, fol. 27, 4 February.

25. Ibid., fol. 30, 21 February.

26. Ibid., fol. 31.

27. Ibid., fol. 32.

28. WA, 15, 155–69. In 1488 Frederick the Wise had formally outlawed engagement and marriage without parents' or guardians' permission (ZSA, *Kopialbuch* I, C1a/IIId, Nr. 13a).

29. WA, 30, pt. 3, 199.

30. ZSA, RP 1528–29, *1528*, fols. 16–17.

31. Ibid., fol. 17.

32. Buchwald, "Die Protokolle der Kirchenvisitationen," 25.

33. ZSA, RP 1528–29, *1529*, fol. 65, 27 February; fol. 68, 6 March.

34. WSA, Reg. Ii 245, contains ninety-six folios on the Lindenau case and related matters, including Spalatin's investigation of heresy.

35. *Verbum Dei manet in aeternum.* Like several evangelically minded citizens of Freiberg, Mühlpfort used this as his personal motto and had it inscribed over his front gate.

36. WA, *Briefwechsel*, 4, 183.

37. WSA, Reg. Ii 245, fol. 5.

38. Ibid., fol. 32.

39. ZSA, RP 1525–28, *1528*, fol. 27.

40. Ibid., fol. 29.

41. WA, *Briefwechsel*, 4, no. 1222.

42. WSA, Reg. Ii 245, fol. 32.

43. WA, *Briefwechsel*, 4, no. 1249, 7 April 1528.

44. WSA, Reg. Ii 245, fol. 95. Johann was afraid that Lindenau might spread false doctrine elsewhere in his lands. See ZSA, A[x] AIII 26, Nr. 2, folder 2f, items 29–30. Compare my account with Georg Müller, *Paul Lindenau, der erste evangelische Hofprediger in Dresden* (Leipzig, 1880).

45. ZSA, RP 1528–29, *1529*, fol. 73.

46. Falk, "Zwickauer Chroniken," 7 (1923): 26.

47. "Der Streit Luthers mit dem Zwickauer Rate im Jahre 1531," *MAZU* 8 (1905): 78. WA, *Briefwechsel*, 5, no. 1483, 20 October 1529. Much documentation is located in ZSA, A[x] AIII 1, Nr. 15.

48. WA, *Briefwechsel*, 5, no. 1405.

49. *Affter Köser*, literally sodomites. The Grimm *Wörterbuch* also offers this figurative meaning.

50. ZSA, *Regesten*, IIId, Nr. 8I, fol. 90.

51. ZSA, *Amtsbuch*, IIIb[1], 54, 1–6, vol. 3, fol. 124.

52. WA, *Briefwechsel*, 5, no. 1448, 14 July 1529.

53. Ibid., no. 1458, 1 August 1529; also *Nachtrag, Briefwechsel*, 12, no. 4332.

54. WA, *Briefwechsel*, 5, no. 1515, 3 January 1530.

55. Ibid., no. 1736, 18 October 1530.

56. Quoted by Fabian, "Der Streit Luthers," 85.

57. The council to Elector Johann, 3 April 1531, reprinted in Fabian, "Der Streit Luthers," 149–52.

58. ZSA, A[x] AIII 1, Nr. 15, fol. 5.

59. Fabian, "Der Streit Luthers," 88.

60. ZSA, *Konzeptbuch* 1531–32, no. 11, fol. 8; reprinted by Fabian, 143. Soranus must have been reminded of his early confrontation in Freiberg by Duke Georg, at that time because he would not cease his Lutheran preaching (Gess, *Akten und Briefe*, 1, 775).

61. Fabian, "Der Streit Luthers," 90.

62. Ibid., 83.

63. Ibid., 82. He was not altogether saintly: in 1524 and 1525 Hausmann begged Johann to grant him instead of his brother a cottage and the land on which it stood in Colditz (WSA, Reg. L1 873, fol. 4).

64. WA, *Briefwechsel*, 6, no. 1802, 3 April 1531. Roth does not mention Soranus's alleged promiscuity.

65. Ibid.

66. Ibid., no. 1801.

67. Ibid., no. 1807, 24 April 1531. Hausmann gave Hoffmann his views in person (Fabian, "Der Streit Luthers," 155).

68. Included with WA, *Briefwechsel*, 6, no. 1819.

69. Ibid. Reprinted in Fabian, "Der Streit Luthers," 157.

70. WA, *Briefwechsel*, 6, no. 1819.

71. Fabian, "Der Streit Luthers," 165, 26 June 1531.

72. WA, *Briefwechsel*, 6, no. 1828, 21 June.

73. Ibid., no. 1854, 18 August.

74. Fabian, "Der Streit Luthers," 120.

75. Ibid., 121.

76. Ibid., 122.

77. WA, 11, 401−16. "Dass eine christliche Versammlung oder Gemeine Recht und Macht habe, alle Lehre zu urteilen und Lehrer zu berufen, ein-und . . . abzusetzen, Grund und Ursach aus der Schrift."

78. Fabian, "Der Streit Luthers," 130.

79. Fabian, "Die Protokolle der zweiten Kirchenvisitation," 121.

80. ZSA, A^x AIII1, Nr. 23, fol. 102.

81. Ibid.

82. Ibid., fol. 95. Fabian, "Die Protokolle," 126.

83. Fabian, "Die Protokolle," 127.

84. ZSA, RP 1534−36, *1535*, fol. 43, effective 1 May.

85. ZSA, A^x AIII 1, Nr. 23, fol. 95.

86. ZSA, RP 1534−36, *1536*, fol. 33.

87. ZSA, RP 1539−40, *1539*, fol. 67.

88. ZSA, RP 1540−43, *1541*, fols. 21, 23. Rephun chose to stay in Plauen. The next year he transferred to Oelsnitz as pastor and superintendent.

89. ZSA, RP 1534−36, *1536*, fol. 65.

90. WA, *Briefwechsel*, 7, no. 3052, 24 July 1536.

91. See, for example, WA, *Briefwechsel*, 6, no. 1920, 19 April 1532.

92. WA, *Briefwechsel*, 7, no. 3082. Reprinted in Fabian, "Der Streit Luthers," 175−76.

93. ZSA, RP 1536−38, *1537*, fol. 26. Also A^x AIII 26, Nr. 3, item 8. What the fourth point means is not clear. Perhaps Beyer wanted to pay his subordinates himself given that the council responded by refusing him a key to the chest where the money was kept.

94. ZSA, RP 1536−38, *1537*, fol. 27.

95. Ibid., fol. 32. WA, *Briefwechsel*, 8, no. 3142, 15 March 1537; ZSA, A^x AIII 2, Nr. 8.

96. ZSA, RP 1536−38, *1538*, fols. 53−56.

97. The scribe summarized the elector's order: "Because the council and city had indebted the churches and benefices now and again, approximately up

to 20,000 gulden, and because some of the documents [records of the loans] were on hand and another part lost, a part not ever even carried out, etc. . . . ," a good and complete record was now to be made. ZSA, RP 1539–40, *1540*, fol. 77.

98. ZSA, RP 1536–38, *1538*, fols. 81, 97, 99.

99. I do not know exactly what the elector said, but there are various references to instructions from Johann Friedrich. In 1542 Beyer mentioned the prince's order that two thousand florins' worth of principal per year should be returned to the community chest whence it had been borrowed. ZSA, RP 1540–43, *1542*, fol. 15.

100. Ibid., fols. 15–19.

101. Ibid., fol. 16.

102. ZSA, A^x AIII 26, Nr. 3, item 6.

103. ZSA, RP 1540–43, *1542*, fols. 27–28.

104. ZSA, RP 1544–45, *1545*, fol. 38.

105. ZSA, A^x AIII 2, Nr. 12.

106. ZSA, RP 1544–45, *1545*, fols. 55–56. As nearly as can be judged from the 1542 *Türkensteuerregister*, Roth did not live opulently. His house was sizable, worth one thousand florins, but he owned nothing else of taxable worth. He had two maidservants. He had loaned money to his brothers Bartel and Georg and to cousins, too.

107. ZSA, A^x AI 23, Nr. 48a.

108. ZSA, RP 1539–40, *1540*, fol. 87.

109. ZSA, *Abtragbuch*, IIIx^1, Nr. 138, fols. 120–21.

110. ZSA, A^x AIII 2, Nr. 19; A^x AIII 2, Nr. 20.

111. ZSA, A^x AIII 2, Nr. 11.

112. ZSA, RP 1525–28, *1526*, fol. 29.

The Erzgebirge versus Nuremberg

1. *The Cultural Significance of the Reformation*, trans. Karl and Barbara Hertz and John H. Lichtblau (New York, 1959).

2. "Thomas Müntzer in Zwickau."

3. "Die Waldenser von Zwickau und Umgegend," 38: "The Zwickauer Prophecy may with overwhelming probability be designated a product of Bohemian heretical influences."

4. "Die Einführung der Reformation."

5. "Deutsche Täufer in östlichen Ländern," *Die Frühbürgerliche Revolution in Deutschland*, ed. Gerhard Brendler (Berlin, 1961), 235.

6. Fabian, "Die handschriftlichen Chroniken," 62.

7. Pt. 1: "Pfarrer und Lehrer im 16. Jahrhundert," *Bohemia* 6 (1965): 146–72; pt. 2 (*Bohemia* 7 [1966]: 128–98) deals with the seventeenth century.

8. Clemen, "Johannes Sylvius Egranus," pt. 2, *MAZU* 7 (1902): 4.

9. Introduction to Georgius Agricola, *De re metallica*, trans. Herbert Clark Hoover and Lou Henry Hoover (New York, 1950), vii.

10. "Deutsche Wirtschaftseinheit oder Wirtschaftspartikularismus?" *Die frühbürgerliche Revolution in Deutschland*, 54.

11. For instance, ZSA, RP 1522–25, *1522*, fol. 19. Zwickauers resented the Bohemian presence if it took away from their own business.

12. Max Rau, "Zwickauer Bäckerleben im 16. Jahrhundert," *Alt-Zwickau* 9 (1924): 34.

13. See, for example, ZSA, A^x AIII 25, Nr. 8, folder 1, Johann's warning of 1507 not to use foreign money. At that time a Bohemian groschen was worth 10 d. in Saxon currency. On 13 January 1533, Johann Friedrich declared the use of all foreign coins illegal (A^x AIII 4, Nr. 6). In Zwickau in 1542 the elector told the authorities to exchange Bohemian pennies *before* the collection of the Türkensteuer and for the tax to accept only "good money." Even so, this coin was virtually all the people offered, and the councillors petitioned the elector for leniency. WSA, Reg. Pp 369, fol. 1; WSA, Reg. Pp 369^8, fols. 28–31.

14. ZSA, A^x AII 16, Nr. 12, fol. 215.

15. WSA, Reg. Pp 369$^{1-20}$, fols. 44–46.

16. Fabian, "Die Einführung des Buchdrucks in Zwickau 1523," *MAZU* 6 (1899): 120, 125; Helmut Claus, *Die Zwickauer Drucke des 16. Jahrhunderts* (Gotha, 1985), 116–17.

17. In 1535 the council allowed one Hieronymus Marschalck to organize a *rechenschule* on a trial basis (ZSA, RP 1534–36, fol. 49), but what happened to it we do not hear.

18. ZSA, A^x AIII 26, Nr. 2, folder 2e.

19. ZSA, A^x AIII 1, Nr. 6.

20. See, for example, ZSA, *Kopialbuch* V, Cle, Nr. 17, 1469–1509.

21. ZSA, RP 1522–25, *1523*, fol. 59, 19 August, headed "Spöttr der Schulr addr Knaben dy In dy schule gehen."

22. ZSA, A^x AIII 11, Nr. 26, fol. 6.

23. "Fastenpostille. 1525," "Epistel am Oculi," WA, 17, pt. 2, 208.

24. ZSA, RP 1525–28, *1526*, fol. 35.

25. ZSA, A^x AII 11, Nr. 25, fol. 14.

26. I am not certain of these translations. Not even the Brothers Grimm were familiar with all the late medieval games of eastern Germany.

27. ZSA, A^x AIII 4, Nr. 3, 24 April 1524.

28. Herzog, *Chronik*, 1, 158 n.

29. Herbert Friedrich, *Das Armen- und Fürsorgewesen in Zwickau bis zur Einführung der Reformation* (Würzburg, 1934), 47.

30. For example, Ludwig Eckstein, Jr., apparently a close relative of a councillor, got his maid pregnant in 1520 and paid an extraordinarily large fine of 85.7 florins, but "for friendship's sake" he was neither executed nor banished,

either of which the law would have allowed (ZSA, *Ratsrechnung*, Karton 7, fol. 12). Most such fines were smaller.

31. *Young Man Luther* (New York, 1962), 63.

32. Peter Burke, *Popular Culture in Early Modern Europe* (London, 1978), 218.

33. Ernst Fabian, "Fürstenbesuche und Volksbelustigungen in Zwickau im 16. Jahrhundert," *MAZU* 10 (1910): 121-24.

34. Herzog, *Chronik*, 2, 122.

35. Claude Chidamian, "Mak and the Tossing in the Blanket," *Speculum* (April 1947): 186-90.

36. H. H. Ploss, Max Bartels, and Paul Bartels, *Woman, An Historical Gynecological and Anthropological Compendium* (London, 1935), vol. 3, 72.

37. Herzog, *Chronik*, 2, 185.

38. ZSA, RP 1534-36, *1535*, fol. 30.

39. Ibid., *1536*, fol. 37.

40. ZSA, RP 1539-40, *1540*, fol. 42.

41. ZSA, RP 1525-28, *1528*, fol. 34, 2 March.

42. ZSA, RP, 1539-40, *1539*, fol. 7.

43. Holger Nickel, "Die Inkunabeln der Ratsschulbibliothek Zwickau. Entstehung, Geschichte und Bestand der Sammlung" (Ph.D. diss., Humboldt University, Berlin, 1976).

44. "Agricola in Zwickau," *Freiberger Forschungshefte*, D18 (1957): 38.

45. Emil Herzog, *Geschichte des Zwickauer Gymnasiums* (Zwickau, 1869), 2.

46. Falk, "Zwickauer Chroniken," 2 (1924): 5; ZSA, A^x AII 7, Nr. 27, January-February 1456, fol. 4.

47. Herzog, *Chronik*, 1, 174.

48. ZSA, *Amtsbuch*, IIIb^1, 54, 1-6, vol. 2, fol. 145.

49. Herzog, *Geschichte*, 12.

50. *Ordnung dess Nawen Studij vnd yetzt auffgerichten Collegij yn Fürstlicher Stadt Zwickau* (Zwickau, 1523). This is item 14 in Fabian, "Die Einführung des Buchdrucks," 111; Claus, *Die Zwickauer Drucke*, no. 28, 86.

51. Herzog, Geschichte, 17.

52. Ibid., 14-15.

53. Ibid., 17.

54. Susan C. Karant-Nunn, "Continuity and Change: Some Effects of the Reformation on the Women of Zwickau," *The Sixteenth Century Journal* 13, 2 (1982): 19-20.

55. *Power and Imagination* (New York, 1979), chap. 11, "Humanism: A Program for Ruling Classes."

56. *Georgii Agricolae Glaucii Libellus de Prima ac Simplici Institutione Grammatica* (Leipzig: Melchior Lotther, 1520).

57. The translation retains the Latin title. The work was initially published in 1556, the year after Agricola's death.

58. Steinmüller, "Agricola in Zwickau," 37.

59. Hoover and Hoover, introduction to *De re metallica*, ix.

60. Otto Clemen, "Zwei theologische Abhandlungen des Georg Agricola," *Neues Archiv für sächsische Geschichte* 21 (1900): 265–73.

61. "Agricola in Zwickau," 30.

62. G. Müller, "Mag. Stephan Roth," 56–57.

63. Roth's correspondence resides in the Zwickau Ratsschulbibliothek and is reputed to include around two thousand letters. Only portions have been published.

64. For the fullest possible listing (he was invited to edit other works and may have done so), see G. Buchwald, *Stadtschreiber M. Stephan Roth in seiner literarisch-buchhändlerischen Bedeutung für die Reformationszeit, Archiv für Geschichte des Deutschen Buchhandels* 16 (1893): 6–246. Pp. 26–245 are excerpts from Roth's letters.

65. *Sommerpostille* (1526), WA, 10, pt. 1. sec. 2, 211–441; *Festpostille* (1526), 17, pt. 2, 249–516; *Winterpostille* (1528), 21, 1–194.

66. Buchwald, *Stadtschreiber M. Stephan Roth*, 16.

67. Herzog, *Geschichte*, 73.

68. Ibid., 76.

69. "Die deutschen Humanisten und die Anfänge der Reformation," *Zeitschrift für Kirchengeschichte* 8 (1959): 46–61; translated as "The German Humanists and the Beginnings of the Reformation," *Imperial Cities and the Reformation: Three Essays*, 19–38.

70. "The German Humanists," 32–33; Schöffler, *Die Reformation* (Bochum, 1936): 39.

71. ZSA, RP 1522–25, *1525*, fol. 58.

72. *Renaissance Thought: The Classic, Scholastic, and Humanist Strains* (New York, 1961), 119.

73. ZSA, Aˣ AI 10, Nr. 3.

74. *Ein Claglicher Sendtbrieff des Baurn-veyndts zu Karsthannsen seynem Pundtgnossen mit Radt vnd Trost Die gantz Christenhayt belangendt*; and *Ein vngevonlicher vnd der Ander Sendtbrieff dess Baurn-feyndts zu Karsthannsen Der doch nit allein wider ynn Sunder der Gantzen Christenhayt entgegen ist*. Fabian, "Die Einführung," 123; Claus, *Die Zwickauer Drucke*, 105. Both booklets have printed at the back, "Gedruckt durch Johann Locher von München." Fabian and Claus agree on 1524 as the date of publication for both.

75. *Ein Claglicher Sentbrieff*, passim; *Ein vngevonlicher . . . Sendtbrieff*, passim.

76. Claus, *Die Zwickauer Drucke*, 120–21.

77. Ibid., 15. On Locher's career, see Paul Kalkoff, "Die Prädikanten Rot-Locher, Eberlin und Kettenbach," *Archiv für Reformationsgeschichte* 25 (1928): 128-50.

78. "The German Humanists," 30.

79. ZSA, RP 1536-38, *1538*, fol. 41.

80. Ibid.

81. Ibid., fols. 47-48.

82. ZSA, A^x AII 11, Nr. 25, "Drei Polizeiordnungen der Stadt Zwickau," fols. 10-11.

83. Quoted by the Portland *Oregonian*, 10 April 1983, 18. I cannot locate this statement in the Weimarer Ausgabe.

84. *Structures of Everyday Life*, 1, 482.

85. Karl Hahn, "Alte Zwickauer Goldschmiede," *Alt-Zwickau* 5 (1928): 18-19.

86. Ibid., 18.

87. Curt Vogel, "Einiges zur älteren Musikgeschichte Zwickaus," *Alt-Zwickau* 8 (1922): 30.

88. Helga Baier, *Der Dom St. Marien zu Zwickau*, 6.

89. Ibid., 20-21.

90. Ibid., 22.

91. See Merry E. Wiesner, *Working Women in Renaissance Germany* (New Brunswick, New Jersey, 1986), 55-73.

92. ZSA, RP 1510-13, *1512*, fol. 1.

93. Gustav Sommerfeldt, "Teufelsaberglauben im Zwickauschen 1535," *Alt-Zwickau* 4 (1922): 15.

94. ZSA, A^x AIII 26, Nr. 2, item 16.

95. ZSA, RP 1540-45, *1542*, fol. 28.

96. *The European Witch-Craze of the Sixteenth and Seventeenth Centuries and Other Essays* (New York, 1969), 100.

97. ZSA, RP 1534-36, *1535*, fol. 10.

98. Ernst Fabian, "Hexenprozesse in Zwickau und Umgegend," *MAZU* 4 (1894): 122-31. Zwickau did not take part in the witch-craze of the later sixteenth century. In the fifteenth and sixteenth centuries, only five women were found guilty of practicing witchcraft. Of those, two were burned and the others exiled.

99. Fabian, "Die handschriftlichen Chroniken," 36.

100. Ibid., 32.

101. Falk, "Zwickauer Chroniken," 10 (1925): 40.

102. Herzog, *Chronik*, 2, 252; Falk, "Zwickauer Chroniken," 10 (1923): 39.

103. *The German Legends of the Brothers Grimm*, ed. and trans., Donald Ward, 1 (Philadelphia, 1981), 344-45 (notes to legend no. 84, "The Mandrake").

104. "Das Evangelium am Tage der heiligen drei Könige Matthej ij," WA, 10, pt. 1, sec. 1, 590-91.

105. WA, 10, 2, 408-9.

106. References to these and others are simply legion in Luther's works, and although I have collected a number of citations, they are a fraction of those available; I saw no point in listing them here.

107. *The Waning of the Middle Ages: A Study of the Forms of Life, Thought and Art in France and the Netherlands in the Dawn of the Renaissance* (New York, 1954), 177.

108. *Ueber das Euangelion Johannis da Christus seyne Mutter auch seine Junger waren auff die Hochtzeyt geladen Wass mit worten vnd wercken daselbst gehandelt. Eyn Sermon dem Ehlichen standt fast freudesam vnd nutzlich. 1524.* p. Bi. RSB XVII, XII, 4 (11); Fabian, "Die Einführung," 124; Claus, *Die Zwickauer Drucke,* 96-97.

109. WSA, Reg. Ii 1360, fols. 2-10.

110. Falk, "Zwickauer Chroniken," 9 (1924): 36.

111. Ibid.

112. Otto Langer, "Der Kampf des Pfarrers Joh. Petrejus gegen den Wohlgemutischen Altar in der Marienkirche," *MAZU* 11 (1914): 31-49.

113. Otto Langer, "Ueber drei Kunstwerke der Marienkirche zu Zwickau: den Altar, die Beweinung Christi und das heilige Grab," *MAZU* 12 (1919): 77. The Reformation did not help Peter Breuer, but he did not die in poverty. In 1531 he owned a house and land near Pöhlau valued at two hundred florins.

114. Langer, "Der Kampf des Pfarrers."

115. "Predigt am Fronleichnamstage," 4 June 1523, WA 10, pt. 3, 125.

116. Falk, "Zwickauer Chroniken," 2 (1923): 6.

117. *Eyn Sermon von dem hochwirdigen Sacrament des heyligenn waren Leychnams Christi. Vnd von den Bruderschafften.* Fabian, "Die Einführung," 113, dates this in 1523, but Claus, *Die Zwickauer Drucke,* 123, list it in 1525.

118. Preller, "Nicolaus Hausmann," 363.

119. Engelhardt Forstmann, *Sammlung vermischter Nachrichten zur sächsischen Geschichte,* 4 (Chemnitz, 1770), 353-54.

120. Fröhlich, "Die Einführung der Reformation," 9.

121. Quoted by Fröhlich from Tobias Schmidt, *Chronica Cygneae* 1, 374-76.

122. ZSA, RP 1525-28, *1527,* fol. 42.

123. Reinhold Hofmann, "Das älteste Zwickauer Armbrustschiessen (1489)," *MAZU* 8 (1905): 42.

124. "Fastenpostille," Sonntag Oculi, WA 17, pt. 2, 208-9.

125. Ibid.

126. Ibid.

127. WA, *Tischreden,* 2, no. 1249, 9, before 14 December 1531.

128. Ernst Fabian, "Die Zwickauer Schulbrüderschaft," *MAZU* 3 (1891): 60–81.

129. Friedrich, *Das Armen- und Fürsorgewesen*, 95.

130. ZSA, *Kopialbuch* II, C1b/IIId, Nr. 14, fols. 9–10.

131. "Ein Sermon von dem hochwürdigen Sakrament des heiligen wahren Leichnams Christi und von den Bruderschaften. 1519," WA, 2, 754–55; see n. 119 above.

132. Karant-Nunn, "Continuity and Change," 35–36.

133. Hahn, "Paul Rebhun," 22.

134. Thomas I. Bacon, *Martin Luther and the Drama* (Amsterdam, 1976), 44.

135. Ibid., 62.

136. *Popular Culture*, 208.

137. *Lay Culture, Learned Culture: Books and Social Change in Strasbourg, 1480–1599* (New Haven, 1982), 32–34, 69–70, and fig. VIII, p. 290, "Production of Vernacular Literature Book Editions in Strasbourg, 1480–1599."

138. (New York, 1971), 77, passim.

139. *Die Reformation im Reich*, 157–60.

On the Fringe of Society

1. Friedrich, *Das Armen- und Fürsorgewesen*, 8–87.

2. See, for example, A. N. Galpern, *The Religions of the People in Sixteenth-Century Champagne* (Cambridge, Massachusetts, 1976), 20–43.

3. ZSA, A^x AI 23, Nr. 48^a, 21 May 1546. Roth directed that two florins was to be divided among the schoolboys, about one heller each. He left two florins to the community chest, a paltry sum for a statesman. He allotted each inmate of any of the city's hospitals one groschen each "in his hand," which may have come to three and a half or four florins. All his books, worth, he said, a thousand florins, went to the grammar school.

4. Scribner, "Reformation . . . in Erfurt," especially chap. 2, 53–107.

5. "Orenung eyns gemeynen kastens. Radschlag wie die geystlichen gutter zu handeln since," WA, 12, 1–30.

6. ZSA, RP 1525–28, *1527*, fol. 38; RP 1534–36, *1535*, fol. 44.

7. ZSA, RP 1536–38, *1538*, fols. 53b–56a.

8. Ibid., fols. 81, 97, 99.

9. Herzog, *Chronik*, 1, 226. Herzog may, of course, err.

10. Friedrich, *Das Armen- und Fürsorgewesen*, 6.

11. ZSA, RP 1519–22, *1521*, fol. 6, 2 November.

12. Fabian, "Die Einführung," 120; Claus, *Die Zwickauer Drucke*, 116.

13. ZSA, RP 1519–22, *1521*, fols. 7, 13, 17a.

14. Friedrich, *Das Armen- und Fürsorgewesen*, 17.

15. Ibid., 46–47.

16. ZSA, RP 1522–25, *1525*, fols. 74, 85.

17. ZSA, *Kopialbuch* VIa, C1f/IIId, Nr. 18, fols. 3–6.

18. ZSA, RP 1528–29, *1528*, fol. 14.

19. ZSA, RP 1539–40, *1540*, fol. 72.

20. ZSA, RP 1528–29, *1528*, fol. 27.

21. Langer, "Ueber Totenbestattung," 2.

22. ZSA, Aˣ AII 11, Nr. 28b, fols. 6–7.

23. ZSA, RP 1528–29, *1529*, fol. 63.

24. For the story of Mrs. Barbirer's vain attempt to divorce her husband, see Karant-Nunn, "Continuity and Change," 32–33.

25. ZSA, RP 1528–29, *1529*, fol. 86.

26. ZSA, Aˣ AII 7, Nr. 21, 26 September 1539.

27. *Chronik*, 1, 229–32.

28. ZSA, Aˣ AII 17, Nr. 6, the 1542 Türkensteuer ordinance (printed). Widows of nobles must give twenty percent of their *leipgedinge*, money allotted to them for their maintenance. Noble land and property was taxed at only one percent, while burghers and peasants paid one and one half percent.

29. *Calendarium Eberi*, Falk, "Zwickauer Chroniken," 9 (1923): 35.

30. Friedrich, *Das Armen- und Fürsorgewesen*, 41–42.

31. Falk, "Zwickauer Chroniken," 7 (1923): 27.

32. Ibid., 28.

33. ZSA, RP 1543–44, *1544*, fol. 19.

34. ZSA, RP 1540–43, *1543*, fol. 55. In 1519 a woman from Neustädtel was drowned for theft (Herzog, *Chronik*, 2, 187).

35. *Zwickauer Rechtsbuch*, ed. Hans Planitz and Günther Ullrich (Weimar, 1941), pt. 3, sec. 1, art. 31.

36. ZSA, Aˣ AIII x¹, Nr. 69, *Schultheiss Gerichtsbücher* 1486–91.

37. ZSA, RP 1536–38, *1537*, fol. 42.

38. Falk, "Zwickauer Chroniken," 8 (1923): 31.

39. ZSA, RP 1536–38, *1538*, fol. 67.

40. Falk, "Zwickauer Chroniken," 5 (1923): 20.

41. Ibid., 6 (1923): 23.

42. Ibid., 2 (1923): 8.

43. Ibid., 1 (1923): 4.

44. ZSA, RP 1539–40, *1540*, fol. 53.

45. ZSA, Aˣ AIII x¹, Nr. 69, fol. 1.

46. ZSA, RP 1540–43, *1543*, fol. 44.

47. This meant sexually receptive to all males.

48. ZSA, *Abtragbuch*, III x¹ 138, 1521–49, fol. 42.

49. ZSA, RP 1544–45, *1545*, fol. 43.

50. Two such stones still survive in the collection of the city hall of Freiberg. They were restored for the city's eight hundredth birthday in 1986 and hang in the entry hall. Depicted on one are two women hitting each other.

51. ZSA, RP 1536–38, *1537*, fol. 41.
52. Ibid., fol. 25.
53. ZSA, RP 1519–22, *1522*, fol. 44; RP 1525–28, *1526*, fol. 11; RP 1536–38, *1537*, fol. 25.
54. Falk, "Zwickauer Chroniken," 8 (1923): 32.
55. ZSA, RP 1539–40, *1539*, fols. 34, 43.
56. Falk, "Zwickauer Chroniken," 1 (1924): 3, 4.
57. ZSA, A^x AII 11, Nr. 27, fol. 6.
58. ZSA, RP 1536–38, *1537*, fol. 22.
59. ZSA, A^x AII 11, Nr. 27, fol. 6.
60. ZSA, *Amtsbuch* IIIb^1 54, 1–6, vol. 5, fol. 98.
61. Ibid., vol. 6, fol. 17.
62. ZSA, A^x AII 11, Nr. 28b, fol. 6.
63. Ibid., fol. 8.
64. ZSA, IIId 27, fol. 45.
65. ZSA, *Schultheissbuch* III x^1, 73, 1508–18: "Glimpfflich est pluris, quam tota scientia Juris. Quid milti de glimpo gewynne ich dy sake ick heb gelimps genugt."

The End of an Era

1. ZSA, A^x AIII 25, Nr. 17 contains documents from 1536, 1543, 1579, and 1590. In the first proclamation against Jews, dated 6 August 1536, Johann Friedrich says that he and his father had wanted to let a few Jews stay in their lands to teach Hebrew, "etc." Now they were all banned. They were given fourteen days to go, and after that, anyone turning in Jews would get half their goods. On 6 May 1543, the prince forbade Jews even to pass through his lands.
2. Susan C. Karant-Nunn, *Luther's Pastors: The Reformation in the Ernestine Countryside* (Philadelphia, 1979), 67–70.
3. ZSA, RP 1536–38, *1537*, fols. 13–17.
4. Ibid., fol. 14.
5. Ibid., fols. 15–16.
6. Ibid., fol. 17.
7. ZSA, RP 1536–38, *1538*, fol. 36.
8. The prince imposed a tax of three percent on property (Herzog, *Chronik*, 2, 262). Even impecunious laborers had to pay six groschen each.
9. This is stretching the truth. See pp. 30–31, above.
10. ZSA, A^x AII 7, Nr. 27, fols. 1–8.
11. Before this Pastor Beyer was earning two hundred florins a year plus housing. When in May 1546 Johann Friedrich perused the records of the community chest, he concluded that there was extra money every year and that the pastor had to be given a fifty-florin raise (ZSA, A^x AIII 2, Nr. 12). This was done. Beyer was also to have a new house (A^x AIII 2, Nr. 14).

12. ZSA, A^x AII 7, Nr. 27, fols. 11–15.

13. ZSA, *Regesten* IIId, Nr. 8I, fol. 143.

14. Ibid., fols. 154–55.

15. Ernst Fabian, "Die Stadt Zwickau unter den Einwirkungen des schmalkaldischen Kriegs," *MAZU* 1 (1887): 47–48.

16. ZSA, *Regesten* IIId, Nr. 8I, fols. 171–73.

17. Ibid., fols. 160–71.

18. ZSA, A^x AI 3, Nr. 2; also IIId, 13c.

19. ZSA, *Regesten* IIId, Nr. 8I, fols. 173–74.

20. For a complete account, see Fabian, "Die Stadt Zwickau unter den Einwirkungen," 1–93.

21. ZSA, A^x AII 16, Nr. 17.

22. ZSA, A^x AIII 1, Nr. 28.

23. ZSA, A^x AII 7, Nr. 32.

24. ZSA, A^x AIII 1, Nr. 30.

25. Ibid.

26. Ibid.

27. Fabian, "Die Stadt Zwickau unter den Einwirkungen," 75–83.

28. Reinhold Hofmann, "Zwickauer Kleinstadtleben um das Jahr 1850," *MAZU* 11 (1914): 113. At the end of the Thirty Years' War the population was 2,691 (Rudolf Kohler, "Der Einfluss des 30 jährigen Krieges auf die Bevölkerungszahl deutscher Städte [handwritten Ph.D. diss., University of Leipzig, n.d.], 93).

29. Herzog, *Chronik*, 1, 175.

The East-Elbean Reform

1. This is the standard translation of "Ein' feste Burg" by Frederick H. Hedge, found in most American hymnals.

Bibliography

The Archives

Zwickauer Stadtarchiv, Lessingstrasse 1, Zwickau, German Democratic Republic. Most of the late medieval and early modern documents pertaining to Zwickau, including the council minutes, are preserved here. This archive is under the direction of the city council of Zwickau, from which the applicant must gain permission to use the archive. At present there is no one very familiar with this phase of Zwickau's history on the staff.

Zwickauer Ratsschulbibliothek, Lessingstrasse 1, Zwickau, German Democratic Republic. This library occupies the same building as the Stadtarchiv but is under wholly separate direction. Its collections include what remains of Stephan Roth's early printed as well as books from other sources, Roth's own sizable correspondence, and such gems as the Peter Schumann annals. It is necessary to write separately for admission to this library, though the libraries are technically open to the public and permission is comparatively easy to obtain.

Weimarer Staatsarchiv, Marstallstrasse 2, Weimar, German Democratic Republic. This archive contains a rather vast remnant of the records of the Ernestine Wettins. Its holdings are indispensable to anyone studying Ernestine affairs. Unfortunately, it is difficult to gain access to this archive. One has to apply to the Zentrale Archivverwaltung in Potsdam; this is governed by the Ministry of the Interior (Ministerium des Innern), which also oversees the state intelligence and security apparatuses. The pervasive view of this branch of the bureaucracy is that it is almost always best to keep Westerners out. One must persist in one's efforts to use this archive and never believe the story that one's letters of application have never arrived. The reward of perseverance is getting to examine the relevant parts of a documentary treasure. The following registers were useful to me in varying degrees: Aa, Bb, Cc, N, O, Hh, Ii, Kk, Ll, Pp, and Qq.

Books and Articles

Zwickau having long been the object of native sons' and daughters' pride, there is considerable patriotic and antiquarian literature on the city during the Reformation era. Some of this literature is useful to the historian, and much of it is not. I hope that the list below reflects a satisfactory level of discernment.

283

Agricola, Georgius. *De re metallica*. Trans. and intro. Herbert Clark Hoover and Lou Henry Hoover. New York, 1950.

Bachmann, Richard. *Niclas Stroch, der Anfänger der Zwickauer Wiedertäufer: Ein Lebensbild*. Zwickau, 1880.

Bacon, Thomas I. *Martin Luther and the Drama*. Amsterdam, 1976.

Baier, Helga. *Der Dom St. Marien zu Zwickau*. Berlin, 1977.

Berthold, Hildegard; Hahn, Karl; and Schultze, Alfred, eds. *Die Zwickauer Stadtrechtsreformation 1539/69*. Leipzig, 1935.

Blaschke, Karlheinz. "Entwicklungstendenzen im Städtewesen Sachsens zu Beginn der Neuzeit." *Die Stadt an der Schwelle zur Neuzeit*. Ed. Wilhelm Rausch. Linz/Donau, 1980, 245–58.

————. *Wittenberg die Lutherstadt*. Berlin, 1877.

Blickle, Peter. *Die Reformation im Reich*. Stuttgart, 1982.

————. *The Revolution of 1525: The German Peasants' War from a New Perspective*. Trans. Thomas A. Brady, Jr. and H. C. Erik Midelfort. Baltimore, 1981.

Boehmer, Heinrich. "Die Waldenser von Zwickau und Umgegend." *Neues Archiv für sächsische Geschichte* 36 (1916): 1–38.

Bräuer, Helmut. "Luther und der Zwickauer Rat (1527–1531)." *Martin Luther. Studien zu Leben, Werk und Wirkung*. Ed. G. Vogler, S. Hoyer, and A. Laube. Berlin, 1983, 223–33.

————. "Der politisch-ideologische Differenzierungsprozess in der Zwickauer Bürgerschaft unter dem Einfluss des Wirkens Thomas Müntzers (1520/21)." *Der deutsche Bauernkrieg und Thomas Müntzer*. Ed. Max Steinmetz. Leipzig, 1976, 105–11.

————. *Zwickau und Martinus Luther: Die gesellschaftlichen Auseinandersetzungen um die städtische Kirchenpolitick in Zwickau (1527–1531)*. Karl-Marx-Stadt, 1983.

————. "Zwickau zur Zeit Thomas Müntzers und des Bauernkrieges." *Sächsische Heimatblätter* 20 (1974): 193–223.

Bräuer, Siegfried. "Müntzers Feuerruf in Zwickau." *Herbergen der Christenheit* (1971): 127–53.

————. "Die zeitgenössischen Dichtungen über Thomas Müntzer und den Thüringer Bauernaufstand." Doctoral dissertation, Karl Marx University, Sektion Theologie. Leipzig, 1973.

Brod, Carl. *Rat und Beamte der kurfürstlichen Stadt Zwickau 1485–1547. Ein Beitrag zur Verwaltungsgeschichte*. Zwickau, 1927.

Buchwald, Georg. *Allerlei aus drei Jahrhunderten: Beiträge zur Kirchen-, Schul- und Sittengeschichte der Ephorie Zwickau*. Zwickau, 1888.

————. "Die Protokolle der Kirchenvisitationen in den Aemtern: Zwickau Crimmitzschau und Werdau vom 12. bis zum 31. Januar 1529." *Allerlei aus drei Jahrhunderten*, 1 (1888): 1–30.

————. *Stadtschreiber M. Stephan Roth in Zwickau in seiner literarisch-*

buchhändlerischen Bedeutung für die Reformationszeit. Archiv für Geschichte des deutschen Buchhandels 16 (1893): 6–246.

————, ed. *Zur Wittenberger Stadt- und Universitäts-Geschichte in der Reformationszeit: Briefe aus Wittenberg an M. Stephan Roth in Zwickau.* Zwickau, 1893.

Camerarius, Joachim. *Vita Philippi Melanchthonis.* Leipzig, 1723.

Chidamian, Claud. "Mak and the Tossing in the Blanket." *Speculum* (April 1947): 186–90.

Claus, Helmut. *Die Zwickauer Drucke des 16. Jahrhunderts.* Gotha, 1985.

Clemen, Otto. "Eine merkwürdige Inschrift am Altar unserer Marienkirche." *Alt-Zwickau* 2 (1929): 8.

————. "Hermann Mühlpfort." *Alt-Zwickau* 6 (1922): 20; 12 (1922): 46–48.

————. "Johannes Sylvius Egranus." *Mitteilungen des Altertumsvereins für Zwickau und Umgegend* 6 (1899): 1–39; 7 (1902): 1–32.

————. "Magister Oswald Lasan, der Bekenner." *Zwickauer Tageblatt und Anzeiger. 800-Jahrfeier der Stadt Zwickau* (1–9 June 1935): 49–50.

————. "Stephan Roth." *Sächsische Lebensbilder,* vol. 2. Ed. Sächsische Kommission für Geschichte. Leipzig, 1938, 340–51.

————. "Zu Erasmus Stella." *Mitteilungen des Altertumsvereins für Zwickau und Umgegend* 8 (1905): 177–84.

————. "Zwei theologische Abhandlungen des Georg Agricola." *Neues Archiv für sächsische Geschichte* 21 (1900): 265–73.

Czok, Karl. "Revolutionäre in mitteldeutschen Städten zur Zeit von Reformation und Bauernkrieg." *450 Jahre Reformation.* Ed. L. Stern and M. Steinmetz. Berlin, 1967, 128–43.

Edward, Mark U., Jr. *Luther and the False Brethren.* Stanford, 1975.

Elliger, Walter. *Thomas Müntzer. Leben und Werk.* 2nd ed. Göttingen, 1975.

Elsas, M. J. *Umriss einer Geschichte der Preise und Löhne in Deutschland vom ausgehenden Mittelalter bis zum Beginn des neunzehnten Jahrhunderts.* 2 vols. Leiden, 1936, 1949.

Erler, Georg, ed. *Die Matrikel der Universität Leipzig (1409–1559).* 2nd main part, *Codex diplomaticus Saxoniae Regiae,* 16–18. Leipzig, 1895, 1897, 1902.

Fabian, Ernst. "Die Beziehungen Philipp Melanchthons zur Stadt Zwickau." *Neues Archiv für sächsische Geschichte und Altertumskunde* 11 (1890): 47–76.

————. "Die Einführung des Buchdrucks in Zwickau 1523." *Mitteilungen des Altertumsvereins für Zwickau und Umgegend* 6 (1899): 41–128.

————. "Fürstenbesuche und Volksbelustigungen in Zwickau im 16. Jahrhundert." *Mitteilungen des Altertumsvereins für Zwickau und Umgegend* 10 (1910): 119–28.

————. "Die handschriftlichen Chroniken der Stadt Zwickau: I, Die (Osw. Losanschen) Annalen der Stadt Schwanfeld oder Zwickau von 1231–1534."

Mitteilungen des Altertumsvereins für Zwickau und Umgegend 10 (1910):1–68.

——. "Hexenprozesse in Zwickau und Umgegend." *Mitteilungen des Altertumsvereins für Zwickau und Umgegend* 4 (1894): 122–31.

——. "Die Protokolle der zweiten Kirchenvisitation zu Zwickau vom 10. bis 28. November 1533." *Mitteilungen des Altertumsvereins für Zwickau und Umgegend* 7 (1902): 37–140.

——. "Die Stadt Zwickau unter den Einwirkungen des schmalkaldischen Kriegs." *Mitteilungen des Altertumsvereins für Zwickau und Umgegend* 1 (1887): 1–93.

——. "Der Streit Luthers mit dem Zwickauer Rate im Jahre 1531." *Mitteilungen des Altertumsvereins für Zwickau und Umgegend* 8 (1905): 75–176.

——. "Zwickauer Gelegenheitspoesie im 16. Jahrhundert." *Mitteilungen des Altertumsvereins für Zwickau und Umgegend* 10 (1910): 129–39.

——. "Die Zwickauer Schulbruderschaft." *Mitteilungen des Altertumsvereins für Zwickau und Umgegend* 3 (1891): 50–81.

Falk, Rudolf. "Zwickauer Chroniken aus dem 16. Jahrhundert" [portions of the Peter Schumann annals]. *Alt-Zwickau* 1, 2, 4–11 (1923); 1, 2, 5–10 (1924); 2, 9, 10, 12 (1925).

Foerstemann, Carolus Eduardus, ed. *Album Academiae Vitebergensis ab A. Ch. MDII usque ad A. MDLX.* Vol. 1. Leipzig, 1841.

Forstmann, Engelhardt. *Sammlung vermischter Nachrichten zur sächsischen Geschichte.* Vol. 4. Chemnitz, 1770.

Friedrich, Herbert. *Das Armen- und Fürsorgewesen in Zwickau bis zur Einführung der Reformation.* Würzburg, 1934.

Fröhlich, Anne-Rose. "Die Einführung der Reformation in Zwickau." *Mitteilungen des Altertumsvereins für Zwickau und Umgegend* 12 (1919): 1–74.

Fuchs, Walther Peter, ed. *Akten zur Geschichte des Bauernkrieges in Mitteldeutschland.* Vol. 2. Jena, 1942.

Gess, Felician, ed. *Akten und Briefe zur Kirchenpolitik Herzog Georgs von Sachsen.* Vol. 1, 1517–24. Leipzig, 1905.

Götze, Ruth. *Wie Luther Kirchenzucht übte: Eine kritische Untersuchung von Luthers Bannspruchen und ihrer exegetischen Grundlegung aus der Sicht unserer Zeit.* Berlin, 1959.

Greyerz, Kaspar von. "Stadt und Reformation: Stand und Aufgaben der Forschung." *Archive for Reformation History* 76 (1985): 6–63.

Gritsch, Eric. *Reformer Without a Church: The Life and Thought of Thomas Müntzer 1488(?)–1525.* Philadelphia, 1967.

Gross, Reiner. "Eine Denkschrift des Pfarrers Nikolaus Hausmann an den Rat zu Zwickau von Ende 1529." *Regionalgeschichtliche Beiträge aus dem Bezirk Karl-Marx-Stadt* 4 (1982): 58–67.

Hahn, Karl. "Alte Zwickauer Goldschmiede." *Alt-Zwickau* 5 (1928): 17–20.

————. "Biographisches von Peter Breuer." *Mitteilungen des Altertumsvereins für Zwickau und Umgegend* 14 (1929): 1–20.

————. "Martin Römer der Reiche." *Zwickauer Kulturbilder aus acht Jahrhunderten.* Ed. Ewald Dost. Zwickau, 1939, 48–53.

————. "Paul Rebhun." *Alt-Zwickau* 6 (1921): 21–24.

————. "Schauspielaufführungen in Zwickau bis 1625." *Neues Archiv für sächsische Geschichte und Altertumskunde* 46 (1925): 95–123.

————. "Die Zwickauer Schneiderinnung." *Alt-Zwickau* 6 (1925): 21–24.

Herzog, Emil. *Chronik der Kreisstadt Zwickau.* 2 vols. Zwickau, 1839, 1845.

————. *Geschichte des Zwickauer Gymnasiums.* Zwickau, 1869.

————. "Hanns Federangel, ein mittelalterliches Lebensbild." *Archiv für die sächsische Geschichte,* n. F. 1 (1875): 260–67.

————. "Martin Römer, ein biographischer Beitrag zur sächsischen Kulturgeschichte." *Mittheilungen des Königlichen Sächsischen Vereins für Erforschung und Erhaltung vaterländischer Geschichts- und Kunst-Denkmale* 14 (1865): 49–63.

Hildebrand, T. W. *Das Verhältniss der Stadt Zwickau zur Kirchen-Reformation.* Zwickau, 1817.

Hoffman, Reinhold. "Das älteste Zwickauer Armbrustschiessen (1489)." *Mitteilungen des Altertumsvereins für Zwickau und Umgegend* 8 (1905): 40–59.

Ilberg, Hugo. "Bemerkungen zur Schwanensage." *Alt-Zwickau* 9 (1921): 33–36.

Karant-Nunn, Susan C. "Continuity and Change: Some Effects of the Reformation on the Women of Zwickau." *The Sixteenth Century Journal* 12, 2 (1982): 17–42.

————. *Luther's Pastors: The Reformation in the Ernestine Countryside.* Philadelphia, 1979.

Keussen, Hermann, ed. *Die Matrikel der Universität Köln.* Vols. 1, 2. Bonn, 1892, 1919.

Kirchner, Hubert. *Johannes Sylvius Egranus. Ein Beitrag zum Verhältnis von Reformation und Humanismus.* Berlin, 1961.

Kius, Otto. *Das Finanzwesen des Ernestinischen Hauses Sachsen im sechszehnten Jahrhundert.* Weimar, 1863.

————. *Das Forstwesen Thüringens im sechszehnten Jahrhundert.* Jena, 1869.

Kobuch, Manfred. "Zur Frühgeschichte Zwickaus. Bemerkungen zu Stadt und Vorstadt im 12. und 13. Jahrhundert." *Regionalgeschichtliche Beiträge aus dem Bezirk Karl-Marx-Stadt* 2 (1980): 49–64.

Köhler, Rudolf. "Der Einfluss des 30-jährigen Krieges auf die Bevölkerungszahl deutscher Städte." Handwritten Ph.D. dissertation, University of Leipzig. Leipzig, n.d.

Kummer, Paul. "Gewerbe und Zunftverfassung in Zwickau bis zum Jahre 1600." Ph.D. diss., University of Leipzig. Leipzig, 1921.

Langer, Otto. "Der Kampf des Pfarrers Joh. Petrejus gegen den Wohlgemuthschen Altar in der Marienkirche." *Mitteilungen des Altertumsvereins für Zwickau und Umgegend* 11 (1914): 31–49.

————. "Ueber drei Kunstwerke der Marienkirche zu Zwickau: den Altar, die Beweinung Christi und das heilige Grab." *Mitteilungen des Altertumsvereins für Zwickau und Umgegend* 12 (1919): 75–101.

————. "Ueber Totenbestattung im sechszehnten Jahrhundert, vornehmlich in Zwickau." *Neues Archiv fü sächsische Geschichte und Altertumskunde* 28 (1907): 1–12.

————. "Zur religiösen Bewegung in Zwickau während der Reformation." *Mitteilungen des Altertumsvereins für Zwickau und Umgegend* 8 (1905): 65–70.

————. "Zwickauer Lohntaxen aus dem 16. Jahrhundert." *Mitteilungen des Altertumsvereins für Zwickau und Umgegend* 8 (1905): 22–39.

Laube, Adolf. *Studien über den erzgebirgischen Silberbergbau von 1470 bis 1546.* Berlin, 1974.

Luther, Martin, *D. Martin Luthers Werke: Kritische Gesamtausgabe.* Weimar, 1883–.

Melanchthon, Philip. *Philippi Melanchthonis opera quae supersunt omnia.* 28 vols. *Corpus Reformatorum.* Ed. Karl Gottlieb Bretschneider. Halle, 1843–60.

Moeller, Bernd. *Imperial Cities and the Reformation: Three Essays.* Ed. and trans. H. C. Erik Midelfort and Mark U. Edwards, Jr. Philadelphia, 1972.

Mühlpfordt, Günter. "Deutsche Täufer in östlichen Landen." *Die frühbürgerliche Revolution in Deutschland.* Ed. Gerhard Brendler. Berlin, 1961, 234–94.

Müller, Georg. "Mag. Stephan Roth, Schulrektor, Stadtschreiber und Ratscherr zu Zwickau im Reformationszeitalter." *Beiträge zur sächsischen Kirchengeschichte* 1 (1882): 43–98.

————. *Paul Lindenau, der erste evangelischen Hofprediger in Dresden.* Leipzig, 1880.

Müller, Max. *Das Tuchmacher-Handwerk und der Tuchhandel in Zwickau in Sachsen, ein Beitrag zur Wirtschaftsgeschichte Sachsens.* Oehlau in Schlesien, 1929.

Müller, Nikolaus, ed. *Die Wittenberger Bewegung 1521 und 1522.* 2nd ed. Leipzig, 1911.

Müntzer, Thomas. *Thomas Müntzer, Schriften und Briefe. Kritische Gesamtausgabe.* Ed. Günther Franz. Gütersloh, 1968.

————. *Thomas Müntzers Briefwechsel.* Ed. Heinrich Boehmer and Friedrich Kirn. Leipzig and Berlin, 1931.

Nickel, Holger. "Die Inkunabeln der Ratsschulbibliothek Zwickau. Entstehung, Geschichte und Bestand der Sammlung." Ph.D. dissertation, Humboldt University. Berlin, 1976.

Niemeyer, Wolfgang. "Die Zwickauer Stadtpfeifer im 16. Jahrhundert." *Mitteilungen des Altertumsvereins für Zwickau und Umgegend* 14 (1929): 41–102; 15 (1931): 34–79.

Ozment, Steven E. *Mysticism and Dissent: Religious Ideology and Social Protest in the Sixteenth Century.* New Haven, 1973.

————. *The Reformation in the Cities: The Appeal of Protestantism to Sixteenth-Century Germany and Switzerland.* New Haven, 1975.

Planitz, Hans and Ullrich, Günther, eds. *Zwickauer Rechtsbuch.* Weimar, 1941.

Preller, Ludwig. "Nicolaus Hausmann, der Reformator von Zwickau und Anhalt." *Zeitschrift für historische Theologie* 3 (1852): 352–79.

Rau, Erich Wilhelm. "Gerichtsverfassung der Stadt Zwickau im 16. Jahrhundert." Handwritten Ll.D. dissertation, University of Leipzig. Leipzig, 1923.

Rau, Max. "Ueber die Herkunft der Zwickauer Bevölkerung." *Alt-Zwickau* 3 (1925): 9–12.

————. "Zwickauer Bäckerleben im 16. Jahrhundert." *Alt-Zwickau* 9 (1924): 33–35; 10 (1924): 37–38.

Rudiger, Karl August. "Ueber die Kaland- und Schulbruderschaft zu Zwickau." *Mittheilungen des Königlich Sächsischen Vereins für Erforschung und Erhaltung vaterländischer Alterthümer* 11 (1859): 68–72.

Schaumkell, Ernst. *Der Kultus der heiligen Anna am Ausgange des Mittelalters: Ein Beitrag zur Geschichte des religiösen Lebens am Vorabend der Reformation.* Freiburg im Breisgau and Leipzig, 1893.

Schmidt, Oswald Gottlob. *Nicolaus Hausmann, der Freund Luther's.* Leipzig, 1860.

Schulzke, Regina. *Zwickauer Handwerkerordnungen aus dem 14.-17. Jahrhundert.* Vols. 96 and 99, *Beiträge zur Geschichte der deutschen Sprache und Literatur.* Halle, 1976, 1979.

Schwanfelder, Moritz. *Die Kreisstadt Zwickau und ihre Umgebung, für Fremde und Einheimische historisch-topographisch geschildert.* Hildburghausen and Amsterdam, 1847.

Scribner, Robert W. *For the Sake of Simple Folk: Popular Propaganda for the German Reformation.* Cambridge, England, 1981.

————. "Reformation, Society and Humanism in Erfurt, c. 1450–1550." Ph.D. dissertation, University of London. London, 1972.

————. and Benecke, Gerhard, eds. *The German Peasant War 1525: New Viewpoints.* London, 1979.

Seeliger, Konrad. "Zur ältesten Geschichte der Stadt Zwickau." *Mitteilungen des Altertumsvereins für Zwickau und Umgegend* 4 (1894): 1–23.

Seidemann, J. K. *Thomas Müntzer.* Dresden and Leipzig, 1842.

Sieber, Siegfried. "Geistige Beziehungen zwischen Böhmen und Sachsen zur

Zeit der Reformation." Part 1: "Pfarrer und Lehrer im 16. Jahrhundert."
Bohemia 6 (1965): 146–72.

Simon, Adolf. *Die Verkehrsstrassen in Sachsen und ihr Einfluss auf die Städteentwicklung bis zum Jahre 1500.* Stuttgart, 1892.

Smirin, M. M. *Die Volksreformation des Thomas Müntzer und der grosse Bauernkrieg.* Berlin, 1956.

Sommerfeldt, Gustav. "Teufelsaberglauben in Zwickauschen 1535." *Alt-Zwickau* 4 (1922): 15.

Steinmetz, Max. "Philipp Melanchthon über Thomas Müntzer und Nikolaus Storch." *Philipp Melanchthon, Humanist, Reformator, Praeceptor Germaniae.* Ed. Melanchthon-Komitee der Deutschen Demokratischen Republik. Berlin, 1963, 138–73.

Steinmüller, Karl. "Agricola in Zwickau." *Freiberger Forschungshefte* D18 (1957): 20–44.

————. "Zur Lage der Zwickauer Tuchmacherei zwischen 1470 und 1530." *Die frühbürgerliche Revolution in Deutschland.* Ed. Gerhard Brendler. Berlin, 1961, 220–24.

Vogel, Curt. "Ein zeitgenössisches Bildnis Martin Römers und seiner Gattin." *Mitteilungen des Altertumsvereins für Zwickau und Umgegend* 14 (1929): 103–8.

————. "Einiges zur älteren Musikgeschichte Zwickaus." *Alt-Zwickau* 8 (1922): 29–30.

————. "Zwickau im Hussitenkrieg." *Alt-Zwickau* 3 (1924): 9–12; 4 (1924): 13–16; 5 (1924): 17–19; 6 (1924): 21–23.

Wappler, Paul. "Inquisition und Ketzerprozesse in Zwickau zur Reformationszeit." *Mitteilungen des Altertumsvereins für Zwickau und Umgegend* 9 (1908): 1–219.

————. "Thomas Müntzer in Zwickau und die 'Zwickauer Propheten'." Wissenschaftliche Beilage zu dem Jahresberichte des Realgymnasiums mit Realschule zu Zwickau. Zwickau, 1908.

Weissenborn, J. D. Hermann, ed. *Acten der Erfurter Universität.* 3 vols. Halle, 1881, 1884, 1899.

Wiesner, Merry E. *Working Women in Renaissance Germany.* New Brunswick, New Jersey, 1986.

Wilhelm, Laurentius. *Descriptio, urbis Cycneae.* Zwickau, 1633.

Index